THE RHETORICAL TURN

THE RHETORICAL TURN

INVENTION AND PERSUASION IN THE CONDUCT OF INQUIRY

Edited by Herbert W. Simons

The University of Chicago Press

Chicago and London

Herbert W. Simons is professor of rhetoric and communication at Temple University. He is the author of *Persuasion: Understanding, Practice, and Analysis* and the editor of numerous books, including *Rhetoric in the Human Sciences* and *The Legacy of Kenneth Burke.*

The University of Chicago Press, Chicago 60637
The University of Chicago Press, Ltd., London
© 1990 by The University of Chicago
All rights reserved. Published 1990
Printed in the United States of America
99 98 97 96 95 94 93 92 91 90   54321

Library of Congress Cataloging-in-Publication Data

The Rhetorical turn : invention and persuasion in the conduct of
  inquiry / edited by Herbert W. Simons.
    p. cm.
  Includes bibliographical references.
  ISBN 0-226-75901-6 (cloth). — ISBN 0-226-75902-4 (paper)
    1. Invention (Rhetoric)   2. Persuasion (Rhetoric)   I. Simons,
  Herbert W., 1935–
  PH221.R48   1990   89-48007
  808—dc20   CIP

∞ The paper used in thus publication meets the minimum requirements of the American National Standard for Information Sciences—Permanence of Paper for Printed Library Materials, ANSI Z39.48-1984.

CONTENTS

v

130075

PART TWO
The Politics of Rhetoric and the Rhetoric of Politics

PART THREE
Philosophical Probes and Reflections

PREFACE

At the 1984 Iowa Symposium on The Rhetoric of the Human Sciences, Richard Rorty observed that recent movements to reconceive inquiry in the human sciences seem to have been marked by "turns." "First the 'linguistic turn,' then the 'interpretive turn,' and now the 'rhetorical turn.' " Rorty is among those whose critiques of objectivist credos have inspired the new movement. Initially conceived by the ancient Greeks as an art of persuasion by which ordinary citizens could exercise their responsibilities in civic affairs, rhetorical theory is increasingly being brought to bear upon expert and scholarly discourses. What John Nelson dubbed the *rhetoric of inquiry* provides a disciplined way to address issues within and across the disciplines, ranging in this volume from evolutionary biology to conversation analysis, and from Machiavelli to MOVE. A common denominator of these issues is that they resist resolution by formal proofs. But this does not mean that they cannot be addressed wisely and articulately.

Indeed, many contributors to this volume advance the position that the discipline of rhetoric can provide the tools, not just for deconstructions of objectivist pretensions, but also for much-needed, much sought-after reconstructions of inquiry in the wake of those debunkings. They do so, not simply by affirming in unison the wonders of rhetoric, but, rather, by getting down to cases and addressing specific issues. The 1986 Temple University conference on the rhetoric of the human sciences from which this book was derived was billed as a sequel to the Iowa Symposium but with a focus on specific cases. *The Rhetorical Turn* is the second of two edited volumes to have come out of that conference. The other collection, *Rhetoric in the Human Sciences*, was published by Sage (London) in 1989.

In the introduction to this book I attempt to place the essays that follow in the context of recent scholarship, and I also propose a reconstructive rhetoric of my own. *The Rhetorical Turn* then takes a number of turns of its own. It moves from biology to politics via brief excursions into the rhetorics of psychoanalysis, decision science, and conversation analysis. It concludes with four philosophical explorations of the problems as well as the potential of the new rhetoric.

A distinctive emphasis of the book is on the role played by rhetorical invention in the conduct of inquiry. The ancient Greeks and Romans understood that on any issue to be debated in the law tribunal or deliberative assembly, there was a finite range of possible stratagems of argument that could be called upon to support one's case. What Lyne here calls the "art of the sayable" is shown by the contributors to be very much in use by scientists and other scholars in their personal deliberations, and also in processes of communal inquiry and advocacy. Of particular interest to Lyne is the use made of inventional techniques in the construction of "bio-rhetorics," strategies for making the discourses of biology mesh with the discourses of social, political, or moral life. Inventional strategies are also at the heart of Campbell's investigation of Darwin's thinking processes, as reflected in the notebooks Darwin prepared following his expeditions on the *Beagle*. Campbell argues that Darwin's notebooks anticipate his mature rhetorical art; it was by means of his facility with imagistic language and informal logic that Darwin was able to embark so successfully on his "second voyage of discovery," the creation of a factually correct and rhetorically credible theory of evolution.

The next two essays explore relationships between rhetoric and the demarcation criteria of a science. Gross shows how rational reconstructions of evidence for the existence of new evolutionary species can be recast and reinterpreted in exclusively rhetorical terms. He resists concluding, however, that the branch of evolutionary biology aimed at discovering new species is any the less a science. Maranhão likewise asks whether, if psychoanalysis is a rhetoric, it must be a failed science. He does so in part as a way of undermining the distinction itself. By Maranhão's reading, psychoanalysis spearheads the development of science: "It dilutes the differences between invention/discovery and explanation/interpretation, making indirect persuasion the instrument of treatment, of inquiry, and of scholarly demonstration."

In his essay on rhetoric's role in the making of a science, Sanders distinguishes between weak and strong versions of a rhetoric of science. The weak version, which he endorses, is that rhetoric—here conceived of as persuasion—plays an important role in debates between rival schools about the adjudication of rival claims. The strong version, which he rejects, is that rhetorical practices can be a primary source of knowledge claims. The case that he takes up is that of conversation analysis, an area of study, suggests Sanders, that has managed to accumulate findings while remaining divided about how to make sense of them.

The question of rhetoric's relationship to science is raised yet again in Miller's essay on decision science. This she characterizes as an antirhetorical rhetoric "that ignores the best capacities of human beings—to reason with and learn from each other; it encourages our submission to technical, knowledge-based solutions for what are social, value-based problems."

What can rhetorical theory teach us about how to adjudicate among competing values, or prescriptions, or knowledge claims? This, I believe, is a pivotal question for the new rhetoric of inquiry movement, and it is probably the central question of this book. Here rhetoric's 2,500 years of experience at assisting in deliberations over civic matters may be of some help to the working scholar. In what Stanley calls the "convergence" of thinking about politics and social science, the new wave of theorizing about the rhetoric of scholarly inquiry might also suggest new ways of addressing old issues in the public sphere. The middle section of this book explores these possibilities. Garver takes counsel from Machiavelli on how to deliberate in the face of plural ultimate values. While Garver's (and Machiavelli's) focus is on politics, his treatment bears generally on the human sciences.

Susan Wells's essay is at one level a conventional rhetorical analysis of the report of an investigating committee. It seeks to discern the meanings, methods, and motives of its authors from a close reading of the report. At that level the essay has some very interesting things to say about the relationship between invention and arrangement in the construction of the report's narrative. But the report is of a series of actions and events and consequences so extraordinary as to defy conventional treatment by the authors and ultimately by Wells herself. Hence Wells is led to further consideration of the report in Habermasian terms, and also as a kind of postmodern document, a pleasurable, albeit nightmarish, fiction, best understood from a poststructuralist literary perspective.

As the utility of rhetorical perspectives and methods is demonstrated through scholarship, one begins to consider the enormous implications for pedagogical reform. Ought there to be greater attention in colleges and universities to techniques of informal argumentation, modes of expression, forms of appeal? How can scholars be trained to become more discerning critics of their own and others' rhetoric? Should ordinary citizens be energized to participate in discussions, not just of the immediate issues that

ix

concern them but of the conditions that typically render the mass of citizens apathetic and quiescent? Only the last of these questions is addressed directly in this volume, but what Manfred Stanley has to say about civic education applies to other arenas as well.

What with politics as both object and model in the middle section, it is fitting that we conclude it with Nelson's case for political foundationalism. Rather than looking to philosophical foundations for one's epistemic groundings, Nelson urges scholars "to take comparison of sciences to communities and of truth-seeking to politicking seriously enough to develop their implications." Nelson finds especially intriguing the metaphorical implications for the human sciences in the idea of a founding, as in the founding of a nation-state, and derives insights and inspiration from the work of Hannah Arendt.

The emerging consensus among contributors to this book is that, much as evolutionary biologists or others engaged in the conduct of inquiry might wish to rely exclusively on hard fact and cold logic in support of their claims, there is no escape from rhetoric: no escape from informal argument, or from figures and tropes, or from the enthymematic appeals to good sense that mark the discourse of the civic arena. Nor, many of them would argue, should there be an escape, given rhetoric's reconstructive potential.

Yet there is a real question whether a rhetoric of inquiry is not inherently self-deconstructive. In maintaining, as some do, that reason is rhetorical, or that one can never move beyond the limits of culture and linguistic convention, do rhetoricians undermine the grounds for taking their own claims seriously? To avoid having the "checkmate" *by* a deconstructive rhetoric of inquiry become a checkmate *of* rhetoric, Kenneth Gergen urges a positive program as a complement to the "rhetorical revolution's" critique of empiricist assumptions. The most pressing needs, he maintains, are for an elaborated metatheory, alternative theories of human action, new products of inquiry, and a revivified vocabulary of understanding.

Joseph Margolis poses the problem more generally as the essential post-Nietzschean dilemma: how to construct and defend an ungrounded, ineliminably partial, and historically situated realism—a realism, in other words, that is also thoroughly relativistic. Richard Brown, like Margolis, would look to rhetoric for ways of reconciling realism and relativism. "Symbolic realism" is the name he gives to a philosophy of rhetoric aimed at retaining the best of Anglo-American empiricism and Continental hermeneutics while also serving as a dialectical way out of the problems of each.

The final essay in this volume could be considered a rhetorical analysis of the rhetoric of inquiry project. Noting that the discipline of rhetoric has forever been in quest of a legitimizing history, and for affiliation with more substantive disciplines to fill out its "formal emptiness," Dilip Gaonkar asks whether the animating myth of the new rhetoric as an epistemological alternative to foundationalist philosophy is yet another vainglorious rhetoric of self-legitimation. He concludes that rhetoric is parasitic upon the various specialized disciplines but also an unavoidable component of them. Thus, while there is no exit for rhetoric over the long run from its culturally determined role as disciplinary supplement, neither is there an exit from rhetoric. "If rhetoric is an unavoidable component in discourses as diverse as theoretical physics, economics, literary criticism, and psychoanalysis, then the story of rhetoric is a tale worth telling."

The 1986 conference on Case Studies in the Rhetoric of the Human Sciences was Temple University's seventh on the general subject of discourse analysis, all of them sponsored by Temple's Department of Rhetoric and Communication. The conference was an intense affair, featuring some 60 papers and 150 participants from a dozen or more disciplines, many of whom had been symposiasts at the Iowa conference or were contributors to the University of Wisconsin Press series on the Rhetoric of the Human Sciences.

Now in their eleventh year, the Temple conferences have spawned a number of products, among them a book in the Wisconsin series, *The Legacy of Kenneth Burke*. The 1984 conference on Burke, coorganized by Trevor Melia and myself, became the organizing model for the 1986 conference. Frances Spisak and Don Stewart put in long hours helping to coordinate the 1986 conference, and Linda Tilli came to our rescue just when we needed her. The conference could not have gotten off the ground without the help of other graduate students, as well as of our office staff, led by Ronye Smaller and Diane Johnson. My wife, Gayle, and son, Michael, provided valuable assistance, as did my departmental colleagues. Richard Brown and Kathleen Jamieson served as unofficial consultants on the project, and Bruce Gronbeck, Mike Leff, John Lyne, Donald McCloskey, Allan Megill, and John Nelson gave good advice on both the conference and my book-publishing efforts. The conference was made possible by grants from the Research Board of the Speech Communication Association, and from the Faculty Senate Lectures and Forums

Committee at Temple, but it remained dependent on the generosity of the participants and of their home institutions for support.

As with other books in the conference series, this one has taken on its own separate identity. All of the essays are by conference participants, but most were newly crafted for the book or were substantially revised. Assisting in the revision process were several contributors: John Campbell, Gene Garver, John Lyne, Tullio Maranhão, Carolyn Miller, Manfred Stanley, and Sue Wells. A few of their reviews prompted discussions among us which are still reverberating. I am especially indebted to Walt Fisher and Mark Pollock for their extraordinarily thorough critiques of my chapter, and to Art Bochner, Miles Orvell, and Allen Scult for their continuing provocations.

INTRODUCTION

The Rhetoric of Inquiry
as an Intellectual Movement

Herbert W. Simons

If we would speak of things as they are, we must allow
that all the art of rhetoric, besides order and clearness;
all the artificial and figurative application of words
eloquence hath invented, are for nothing else but to
insinuate wrong ideas, move the passions, and thereby
mislead the judgment; and so indeed are perfect
cheats; and therefore, however laudable or allowable
oratory may render them in harangues and popular
addresses, they are certainly, in all discourses that
pretend to inform or instruct, wholly to be avoided;
and where truth and knowledge are concerned, cannot
but be thought a great fault, either of the language or
person that makes use of them.

>   **John Locke,** *Essay on Human Understanding,*
>   Book 3

Rhetoric in the highly expanded sense in which I
speak of it might even become the central discipline
for which we have been looking for so long—which
"science" has proven not to be—by which the others
can be defined and organized and judged.

>   **James Boyd White,** "Rhetoric and Law: The Arts
>   of Cultural and Communal Life"

The Rhetorical Turn is one among many recent works to counterpose
rhetorical perspectives on inquiry against the dominant objectivist presuppositions of our age.[1] The book arises at a time of widespread dis-
satisfaction with objectivism, and out of a conviction that the practice of

1

inquiry might more usefully be understood in rhetorical terms.[2] This chapter is designed to place the essays of this volume within the context of the larger intellectual movement of which it is a part. It seeks to explain why it is that sophisticated theorists and critics in dozens of fields have elected to rally around a term that is so often preceded by the words *mere, only,* or *just.*

That rhetoric should these days be allowed on center stage in matters "where truth and knowledge are concerned" may be a reflection of our times. Typically it has been accorded such attention only as a foil for philosophy or where philosophy was a bit down in the dumps and in need of an understudy.[3] We live in an age, however, in which the philosophical moorings of inquiry have been found none too secure. Enlightenment philosophy's proclamation of the triumph of scientific knowledge (*episteme*) over mere belief (*doxa*) now seems at least a bit premature.[4] No longer do philosophers speak with great confidence about the epistemological foundations of knowledge. Such demarcation criteria as verification and falsification, used to distinguish science from nonscience, have been called into question.[5] Nor is there as much talk these days of encompassing physics or biology or anthropology or history—let alone all of scholarly inquiry—within some grand, idealized methodological scheme. There appears to be increased recognition that the human sciences,[6] especially, need to develop on their own terms.[7]

Out of these developments have come some of the most important seeds of the rhetoric of inquiry movement. And there have been others. Indeed, it is now argued that the entire process of inquiry, far from being a fully rule-bound process as the positivists had hoped or supposed, is, at all stages, underdetermined by rules; it is dependent, therefore, on individual and communal judgments.[8] Correspondingly, it is now clearer than ever that *good* scholarship involves much more than hard fact and cold logic and, moreover, that what gets called *fact* or *logic* is symbolically mediated if not symbolically (i.e., socially) constructed.[9] In place of Method, there is talk of methods: variable, creative, nonalgorithmic.[10] In place of covering laws, there is talk of contingent, historically situated truths, reflective of values and interests, and found more or less useful by cultures and communities which are themselves symbolically constituted.[11] And there are faint suspicions that scholarly communities are no less influenced by "fuzzy" logics than by formal, deductive, "close-fisted" logics; by arguments from sign and analogy; by anecdotes and exemplars; and even by appeals to authority, tradition, convention, intuition, and aesthetic goodness-of-fit.[12]

2

The critique of objectivism has also sparked new interest in the language and style of scholarly inquiry. Relatively few scholars still assume that the language of the philosopher, historian, or scientist can be a clear windowpane upon the world, or that scientists can somehow be "saved" from rhetoric by writing in what Joseph Gusfield has called "a style of non-style."[13] Some critics have attended to the norms and conventions guiding the production of scholarly texts.[14] Others have sought to "de-center" or "de-familiarize" scholarly texts, the better to discern the rhetorical devices by which the illusion of objective representation—of science untouched by human hands—is maintained.[15]

Critics have attended as well to the influence of discursive forms on thought and expression—to the role of metaphors, for example, as ineliminable building blocks of philosophical argument and scientific theory.[16] Under the impress of Continental critical theory, the image of the autonomous language-user has given way in some circles to the image of language as autonomous agent, a return to the Coleridgean dictum that "language itself does, as it were, think for us."[17] Deconstructionists have delighted at the apparent ubiquity of metaphor and other such rhetorical figures and tropes even in the writings of philosophers, such as Locke, who so sharply condemned their use.[18]

Clifford Geertz noted in this connection an infusion of metaphors about inquiry from the humanities into the social sciences.[19] As part of this "sea-change" in "the way we think about how we think," it is now quite common to "read" behaviors, cultures, or entire historical epochs as though they were texts, or to treat scientific data as symbolic constructions, scientific research reports and theories as narratives, mathematical proofs as rhetorical tropes, the ongoing discursive activities of scholarly communities as conversations.[20]

In rhetorical analyses of scholarly writings, the critic is also apt to explore likenesses with the discourse of such prototypical persuaders as editorialists, propagandists, advertisers, political campaigners, ministers, lawyers, courtiers, and seducers.[21] Analyses of this kind are inherently ironic insofar as science, history, philosophy, and the like have traditionally enjoyed privileged positions outside the provinces of rhetoric and literature. Moreover, the critiques are liable to extend beyond the discursive practices of individual scholars to entire schools, disciplines, and professions, in some cases challenging their most vaunted self-images. For example, Thomas Gieryn and Anne Figert scrutinized not just the scandalous fabrications and misrepresentations of intelligence test findings by Sir Cyril Burt; they also examined the extensive "public relations" efforts

3

of psychologists to maintain the perceived legitimacy of their science in the wake of that scandal.[22]

One common thread in the rhetoric of inquiry movement is its rejection of the conventional split between inquiry and advocacy. That scientific inquiry is a communal enterprise, dependent on argument and counter-argument in the testing of claims, is, after Kuhn, no longer in dispute.[23] But the dominant image of the individual scholar distinguishes sharply between stages of private inquiry and public advocacy. Jaegar and Rosnow characterize the self-image of most of their colleagues as Talmudic in the conduct of inquiry ("On the one hand, on the other hand . . .") but highly positivistic at the point at which they go public with their arguments.[24] They dub the pattern "Think Yiddish, speak British!" Perelman and Olbrechts-Tyteca argue to the contrary that scholars are already anticipating objections and formulating possible responses to those objections at the very earliest stages of inquiry.[25] Campbell (this volume) offers evidence in support of this claim from his examination of Darwin's notebooks. Billig goes further than Campbell in suggesting that our internal dialogues display much the same patterns of argument and counterargument as our public discourse.[26] He goes so far as to propose that cognitive psychologists study public speeches and conversations for clues to internal patterns of thought and cognition. He notes, however, one important difference between internal dialogue and public discourse: as ideas are readied for public presentation, doubts, anxieties, shadings of opinion, and acknowledgments of the truth of opposing positions tend to be repressed or inhibited. If scholars and others were more forthcoming, he implies, they would not only think Yiddish but speak Yiddish![27]

The foregoing sketch offers some sense of the animating impulse of the rhetoric of inquiry movement and of its common assumptions, but says little about its variations in approach or points of division. The assault on objectivism has provided an opening for rhetoric "where truth and knowledge are concerned," but just how big an opening and what kind of opening are matters that continue to be debated. Among philosophers of inquiry there continue to be those who suggest new groundings for knowledge; not all have abandoned the quest for an epistemological court of last resort. Similarly, while some philosophers speak of worlds brought into being by language, others cling to theories of representation. Even those who call themselves relativists or antirealists have had to confront the paradoxical character of their own claims upon the world and their own insistence upon being taken seriously.

These differences in philosophical perspective are mirrored in conceptions of the rhetoric of inquiry. For example, William M. Keith and Richard Cherwitz propose a managerial role for rhetoric that is consistent with a commitment to objectivism, rather than endorsing the counter-objectivist position, which they identify with the "Iowa School."[28] John Locke's reduction of rhetoric to the artificial and figurative application of words and James Boyd White's expanded sense of rhetoric as master discipline are but two of a number of conceptions which have entered as contending voices in the postmodern conversation about the conduct of inquiry currently taking place within and among the various disciplines.

RHETORICS OF INQUIRY

The point is, then, that there is not one rhetoric of inquiry, there are several. The term *rhetoric* is rich in meaning and history but also, and for the same reason, rife with ambiguity. How one conceives of rhetoric necessarily influences one's attitude toward the rhetoric of inquiry as an intellectual movement. For example, Habermas apparently views rhetoric with some suspicion as an antirational aesthetics of discourse, resurrected by postmodernists to reverse the dominance of positivist science.[29] Yet, by another conception, Habermas's own project might well be viewed as a philosophy of rhetoric.

Most neutrally, perhaps, rhetoric is the study and practice of persuasion.[30] But this broad conception permits varying emphases or narrowings: thus, rhetoric as invention, as argumentation, as figuration, as stylistics, as audience and situational adaptation, and as an art of composition or arrangement. These may be viewed coequally as component parts of a comprehensive rhetorical theory of inquiry, or any one of them may be featured as the central organizing term of such a theory, the others thus relegated to a subordinate status. In contemporary rhetorical treatments one finds echoes of classical divisions. For example, Geertz and Billig display strong affinities in their writings with the playful and flexible, yet skeptical and self-questioning turns of mind of the sophists of ancient Greece and Rome. But Geertz tells us very little about the argumentative structures of the ethnographies he examines in *Works and Lives*, and a great deal about how they use language. Billig, on the other hand, would have us regard argumentation as central to rhetoric but is downright contemptuous of the tropological and stylistic strands in sophistic rhetorical theory.[31]

Paralleling these varying theoretical conceptions of rhetoric as persuasion are conceptions of rhetoric as forms, patterns, or genres of persuasive discourse, such as the rhetoric of the research report, the rhetoric of academic professions, the rhetoric of scientific sociologists, the rhetoric of sociobiology.[32] Lyne (this volume) is more precise in characterizing *a rhetoric* as "a discourse strategy spanning and organizing numerous discourses, and acting as a trajectory for discourses yet unorganized." The rhetoric of sociobiology, suggests Lyne, is an example of a *"bio-rhetoric,* a strategy for inventing and organizing discourses about biology in such a way that they mesh with the discourses of social, political, or moral life."

Then too there are the various senses of "mere" rhetoric and worse: of manner rather than matter, style rather than substance, form rather than content; of rhetoric as an art of gulling people, and of bombast, exhibitionism, ingratiation and decoration. These provide the basis for "deconstructions" of scholarly pretensions, as in Thomas Szasz's well-known critique of the mental health professions for what he described as a self-serving secular theology promoted in the guise of objectivity.[33]

At the opposite pole from these dyslogistic conceptions of rhetoric are its eulogistic senses. Much of the reconstructive work of the new rhetoric of inquiry is built around conceptions of rhetoric as the study of how one ought to argue and use language in situations and on issues for which there can be no proof in the strict sense of that term. Presupposed here is the possibility for reasoned judgment and comparison—for discovering, as Booth puts it, those "good reasons" that really warrant assent.[34] To Booth's discovery of good reasons, Margolis (this volume) adds the need to discover *forms of argument* suited to the tasks of assembling the elements of our collective history and of addressing effectively our habits of conviction.

RETHINKING RHETORICAL THEORY

Out of the rhetorical tradition, then, have come not just concepts, methods, and perspectives used in critical analyses of scholarly practices but also guidelines for communicators—on invention, argumentation, stylistic adaptation, and the like—that might be used reconstructively in the development of rhetorical alternatives to objectivism. Moreover, as the boundaries of rhetoric have been pushed outward—as rhetoricians of inquiry have evidenced its relevance to the discourse of the academy and not just to public address—rhetoricians have found it necessary to rethink rhetorical theory's intellectual history, in some cases identifying as rhetorical theorists persons who would never have labeled themselves as such. One consequence of this revisionist history has been the elevation in significance of the ancient sophists and of the doctrines and perspectives that bear their name.[35] Another consequence has been a renewed interest in the rhetoric of boundary relations among disciplines, a subject no less applicable to the history of rhetoric itself.[36] For the most part rhetoric has subsisted on the margins of other fields—as jester to philosophy the king, for example, or as tool of religion or politics or law. From the time of the seventeenth-century Enlightenment until our own, rhetoric's status was greatly diminished, its doctrines and functions having been taken over by other sciences and other formal disciplines. Still, even through the worst of times for rhetoric, an underground rhetorical tradition persisted. Gaonkar (this volume) credits Kenneth Burke with having resurrected that tradition while at the same time extending the reach of rhetorical theory by way of his own concept of identification. Among the post-Enlightenment figures whom Burke cites as having contributed to his own expanded view of rhetoric are Carlyle, Coleridge, Diderot, Freud, Nietzsche, De Gourmont, and La Rochefoucauld, as well as such ostensibly "antirhetorical" theorists as Marx and Bentham.[37]

It is within our own century that the intellectual climate for a new rhetoric of inquiry seems to have proven most hospitable. Gaonkar speaks in this connection of "implicit" rhetorical theories—not labeled as such but clearly relevant to the purposes at hand. What theories ought to qualify as implicit rhetorics of inquiry is an interesting question. Does Roland Barthes' critical stance as a structuralist qualify him? Does Levi-Strauss's more scientistic stance disqualify him? Hayden White's *Metahistory* marks him clearly as a rhetorician of inquiry,[38] but what of Foucault's archaeology of knowledge[39] in light of White's masterful reading of Foucault as having wittingly or unwittingly organized the archaeology of knowledge around the four master tropes?[40]

Surely the candidates for implicit, if not explicit, status as contemporary rhetorics of inquiry would have to include Kuhnian postpositivism,[41] social constructionism,[42] various ethnomethodological approaches to analyses of scientific texts,[43] symbolic anthropology,[44] the critical legal studies movement,[45] critical pluralism,[46] deconstructionism,[47] and a good deal of feminist, neo-Marxian and neo-Freudian criticism.[48] Even this list paints a very incomplete picture. Nelson has gone so far as to maintain that a "new sophistic" has been taking shape since at least the time of Vico and Nietzsche, and that this "counter-tradition to objectivism" includes such figures as Freud, Wittgenstein, Heidegger, Arendt, Foucault, Derrida, Hayden White, and Kenneth Burke.[49]

7

ISSUES AND PERSPECTIVES

I want now to review some of the controversies surrounding the rhetoric of inquiry movement and, in the process, attempt to place the contributions to this volume within the context of recent rhetorical scholarship. The first question that needs to be addressed is how far to go in counterposing one or another rhetorical perspective against the dominant objectivist view. It is generally acknowledged that scientific discourse is inherently rhetorical at the point of paradigm clash[50] and, furthermore, that scholars have no choice but to rely on rhetorical appeals and arguments in the forging of a discipline. What now of what Kuhn referred to as "normal" science? Is Sanders (this volume) correct in arguing that disputes between scientific theorists are useful objects of rhetorical analysis but that the research leading to the accumulation of findings is not? Are there reliable boundary markers separating rhetorical/hermeneutic disciplines from scientific/ epistemic disciplines, or is Maranhão (this volume) persuasive in pointing to Freudian psychoanalysis as both science *and* rhetoric?

How in particular should we regard evidences of rhetoric in the dyslogistic senses referred to earlier? In an early article, Weigert accused his empirically oriented colleagues in sociology of an "immoral rhetoric of identity deception."[51] They were, he said, purporting to base their knowledge claims on objective methods of proof when in fact they were relying upon persuasion to carry the day. Among the evidences of deceptive or otherwise questionable writing practices that he cited were some that readers will no doubt recognize as familiar. Assemblages of value-laden propositions are selectively evidenced and labeled for rhetorical purposes as "scientific theory." Misrepresentations of the way research actually took place are dubiously justified in the name of reconstructed logic. Questions are begged concerning what is normal and what is deviant in human existence. A vocabulary of legitimating motives is employed to cover up real motives. Magical and ritualistic procedures for data-gathering and statistical analysis are treated as scientific imperatives and clothed in the appealing jargon of "reliability" and "validity," of statistical significance" and ".01 confidence levels." Meanwhile, acceptance is granted to such violations of "the rules" as using parametric statistics on nonrandom samples, "shotgunning" questionnaires, utilizing previously discredited measuring instruments, justifying new instruments on grounds of "face validity," and selectively reporting research findings.

Some of these charges are serious indeed. But it would help to know how many of the practices referred to are inherent in scientific sociology

8

and how many are merely commonplace or even aberrant. Weigert does not make this clear. Nor is it clear which practices are endemic to the social sciences, which to the sciences as a whole, and which to scholarship generally.

We need not assume, moreover, that rhetoric functions in scholarly discourse solely for purposes of self-aggrandizement and mystification. Broadly speaking, virtually all scholarly discourse is rhetorical in the sense that issues need to be named and framed, facts interpreted and conclusions justified; furthermore, in adapting arguments to ends, audiences, and circumstances, the writer (or speaker) must adopt a persona, choose a style, and make judicious use of what Kenneth Burke has called the "resources of ambiguity" in language.[52] That the style of a scholarly article may be influential in a given case need not invalidate its logic and may even enhance it. In fact, argues Geertz, "The strange idea that reality has an idiom in which it prefers to be described, that its very nature demands we talk about it without fuss," stems from a confusion, traceable to Plato, "of the fictional with the false, making things out with making things up."[53] Once we recognize that ethnographic tests are made, "and made to persuade," says Geertz, "those who make them have rather more to answer for." Similarly, McCloskey has argued that the so-called objectivity of his own field of economics "is exaggerated, and, what is more, overrated."[54] He adds:

> A rhetorical approach to economics is machine-building, not
> machine-breaking. It is not an invitation to irrationality in
> argument. Quite the contrary, it is an invitation to leave the
> irrationality of an artificially narrowed range of argument and to
> move to the rationality of arguing like human beings. It brings out
> into the open the arguing that economists do anyway—in the dark,
> for they must do it somewhere, and the various official rhetorics
> leave them benighted.[55]

But even assuming a view of rhetoric as the promotion of false consciousness,[56] it is possible that rhetorical—i.e., extrafactual and extralogical—factors weigh more heavily in some cases than in others. Among the proposed candidates are the social sciences as contrasted with the "hard" sciences; applied mathematics as opposed to "pure" mathematics; issues of policy and application versus questions of fact; the interpretation of data as against the data themselves; and discourse addressed to granting agencies, or to the press, or to one's students, rather than to one's peers.

Among rhetoricians of inquiry, some focus exclusively on these extrafactual, extralogical factors, while others treat fact and logic themselves as rhetorical constructs, extending to the very ideas of the real and the rational. This turns out to be a pivotal distinction in approaches to the rhetoric of inquiry. For example, Lyne (this volume) maintains that "rhetoric alone . . . cannot substitute for all the methods, plodding, tools, rationales, and (let us not forget) observables that the various sciences depend on." But Gross (this volume) argues that "there is no empirical or theoretical core, no essential science that reveals itself all the more clearly after the rhetorically analyzed components have been set aside."

Illustrative of the first position is Joseph Gusfield's analysis of "drunk driver" research reports.[57] It focused upon forty-five such studies, and in particular on one by Waller entitled "Identification of Problem-Drinking among Drunken Drivers." The analysis is principally concerned with how these investigators *frame* their studies (as "doing science") and with how they *picture* the external world.[58] Through numerous examples Gusfield shows how rhetorical choices function to conceal or reveal, magnify or minimize, simplify or complicate, link or divide, elevate or degrade, sharpen images or blur them. In the Waller study, for example, drinking drivers are classified as "problem drinkers" or "social drinkers." By Waller's use of language, observes Gusfield, these two types are presented as caricatures, the former conjuring up an image of a reeling, low-status drunk, the latter depicted as a solid citizen who just happens to take a drink now and then.

Gusfield acknowledges that one effect of his analysis has been to demonstrate that social science knowledge was in a certain sense rhetorically constructed. Yet Gusfield is quick to add:

> It is not that Science is "reduced" to rhetoric and thus rendered corrupt and useless. It is rather that the rhetorical component seems to be unavoidable if the work is to have a theoretical or policy relevance. Thus an analysis of scientific work should also include its rhetorical as well as its empirical component.[59]

Contrast Gusfield's plea for "peaceful coexistence" between the rhetorical and empirical components of science with Gross's (this volume) more aggressive stance in behalf of rhetoric. For every rational reconstruction provided by evolutionary biologists in support of their claims to the discovery of new biological species, Gross counterposes a rhetorical view. His analysis calls attention to the theory-determined character of their observations and classifications, and to the way their reality claims depend for their credibility on rhetorical techniques of foregrounding and selective representation.

Whatever the merits of their respective positions, the critiques offered by Gusfield and Gross are a welcome addition to a growing discourse-analytic tradition within the rhetoric of inquiry movement. They illustrate how rhetorical theory may serve as an inventional resource, a storehouse of codified ways of thinking, seeing, and communicating that may be tested for their goodness-of-fit to the matter at hand, and which, once applied to particular cases, provide exemplars for subsequent analyses.

Closely allied to the rhetoric of inquiry movement is the doctrine of social constructionism. Against the view that reality exists independently of the language used to characterize it, the social constructionist maintains that language is in a certain sense *constitutive* of reality, rather than merely reflective of it. People and places, problems and causes are all in effect "created" by language. Part of the job of the rhetorical analyst is to determine how constructions of "the real" are made persuasive. For example, social constructionists have evidenced the influence of reformist groups in helping to transform "child abuse" into child abuse.[60] Admittedly there is another sense in which the problem of child abuse "existed" long before it was named and reified, but even that understanding of things is a product of social influence. Whether focused on the first proposals to recast some forms of punitive treatment of children as "abuse," or on the process of disquotation leading to the ontologizing of child abuse, rhetorical analysis functions to make problematic the concept of child abuse, prompting us to situate the concept historically and to ask what interests were served by its rhetorical invention and what value there is in its continued use. By the same token, one is prompted to ask what interests and values were served by the concept of "Biblical discipline," prior to the use of "child abuse."

However, it is impossible, or nearly so, to sustain the constructionist position consistently. For even as one term, such as "child abuse," is deontologized—for example by placing quotation marks around it—others must continue to be treated unproblematically, lest the constructionist's own prose become unintelligible. Thus, as Woolgar and Pawluch have argued, Pfohl rendered the term "discovery" problematic in his social constructionist analysis entitled "The 'Discovery' of Child Abuse," but Pfohl refrained from problematizing "child abuse," let alone the constructs "child" and "abuse," which were themselves rhetorical inventions earlier in our history.[61] Woolgar and Pawluch call the process of manipulating the boundary between the conceptually problematic and the conceptually unproblematic "ontological gerrymandering."

11

The foregoing considerations have led Woolgar to a distinction between "instrumental" and "dynamic" irony.[62] To "do" irony of any kind, he maintains, "is to say of something that appears one way, that it is in fact something other than what it appears." By this broad definition virtually all rhetorical analysis of scholarly discourse is ironic, including analyses of the kind provided by constructionists such as Pfohl. The general form of the ironic observation is that what appears as A_1 is in reality better accounted for as A_2.

But on what grounds do rhetorical analysts determine that their accounts are "really" superior? Typically the analyst goes no further than to defend his or her alternative hypothesis or explanation, and this Woolgar calls "instrumental" irony. By contrast, "dynamic" irony problematizes its own accounts, as well as accounts of those accounts, thus leaving nothing settled, except perhaps its own claim to the advantages of leaving nothing settled.

Some reflexively oriented sociologists of the sociology of scientific knowledge (SSK) have gone to great lengths in their efforts to destabilize meaning structures while at the same time explicating what Ashmore calls "the problem of the Problem." This includes experimentation in the scholarly adaptation of postmodern literary forms.[63] Were this essay written by Ashmore, for example, it might well be interrupted at this point by a "second voice," commenting critically and self-reflexively on the inventional strategies and stylistic practices of the first voice. Ashmore's second voice might note, as one prepublication reviewer did, that my "storehouse" metaphor of a few paragraphs back was more consonant with a managerial view of rhetoric than with a view of rhetoric as an epistemologically significant art of invention. The second voice might complain more generally that Voice 1 relies throughout on an objectivist style despite its insistence that objectivism is the enemy; witness such expressions as "these differences are mirrored . . . ," "At root, then . . . ," and "No doubt any concrete answer . . ." [Voice 1 will spare the reader a reply, except to agree with the reflexive SSKers that there is some value in this sort of bracketing. The alternative, they maintain, is an all-too-easy acceptance of the lures of realism and a blunting of the self-critical spirit. Billig puts the matter well when he insists that "a discipline, which itself has the persuasive mission of freeing rhetoric from its subordination to logic, cannot adopt literary forms which themselves rhetorically deny rhetoric or which seek to persuade the reader that no persuasion is intended."][64]

A good case can indeed be made that social critics and theorists tend to be more than a little a bit duplicitous in their rhetorical analyses of others' reality claims. Shweder has argued that there is a general tendency to ridicule the views of the Other in terms of criteria internal to our own paradigms of rationality; we fail to recognize that our conceptions of reality hinge on states of mind that are no more defensible than those of the Other. In particular, Shweder is critical of his anthropologist colleagues for dismissing tradition-based reality-posits as imaginary phantoms of mind.[65] They begin by assuming the positivist premise that "seeing is believing" (hence anything not seen is not believable). They then shift to the role of existentialist *ubermensch*, presuming to know what the others' reality-posits and states of mind "really" are.

In fairness to Shweder's colleagues I think it can be said that cultural anthropology has gone furthest of any field in the direction of correcting for its own ethnocentric biases. Its dominant tendency *had* been, it is true, to inscribe the Other as not just different but inferior. The model was that of scientific realism: to dissect the Other's culture as though it were a fetal pig; if possible to say something quite general about the nature of the species.[66] But in contemporary ethnographic writing the impulse seems to be in the reverse direction: to *evoke* another culture rather than *represent* it; to provide a sense of the discourse *its* actors use in making sense of *their* worlds; and, in the process of rendering the Other less remote, to render our own culture more strange.[67] The process, as Marcus and Fischer have described it, involves using the knowledge of other cultures to examine the unconscious assumptions of our own.[68] They propose this form of cultural criticism as a model for the human sciences.

From the realization that other cultures' systems of thought may be every bit as coherent as our own and no less functional for them, it is but a short step back to the conclusion that there are multiple rationalities. Indeed, one does not have to travel to distant lands to recognize that different fields of inquiry, such as science and theology, seem to operate from different concepts of rationality (e.g., as calculation, as interpretation of God's laws) and correspondingly different criteria of adequacy (e.g., repeatability, cogency).[69] Even within a given field, one might speak of multiple rationalities in the sense of alternative systems of thought that organize numerous discourses on a range of issues and guide the formulation of new arguments.

A good case can indeed be made that reason is inherently rhetorical. Such an analysis might begin with the observation that the very idea of "reason" is socially constructed; furthermore, as suggested above, it might argue that conceptions of reason are culturally, vocationally, and historically variable. Richard Brown makes the additional observation that

13

canons of validity and epistemologies generally are legitimations of belief. As such, they are rhetorical in nature.[70]

The general point is that no system of logic is ever self-validating; it depends, rather, on some other system for its support, and that system must be validated by another, and so on, in an infinite series. By this reasoning the very idea of a logical system—a logic of logics—is itself rhetorical, or perhaps tautological, for it requires a leap of logic, an intellectual bootstrap operation, to premises which, however appealing on extralogical grounds, can only be supported in terms of the very logics from which they were derived.[71] Kaplan observes that even so appealing a principle of scientific inquiry as "Use all the evidence available" is itself ineluctable.[72] Rather than speaking of transcendental laws of logic and of laws of thought corresponding to these external laws, rhetoricians of inquiry are thus prompted to speak of conventions of logic, with the understanding that these too are human inventions: some of them major accomplishments, to be sure, and not to be tampered with lightly, but only more or less useful, and thus subject to revision or replacement based on experience.[73] They argue further that, by this reasoning, the so-called psychologistic and sociologistic fallacies are themselves fallacies, for it is through the "is" of apparently successful logics-in-use that we get the "oughts" of reconstructed logics.[74] Even then, they remind us that scholarly reasoning seldom relies on sheer calculation; for example the choice of a statistic often involves a balancing among competing values.[75]

INVENTION, PERSUASION, AND JUDGMENT

What, then, of rhetoric's role in relation to divergent rationalities? Can training in rhetoric help scholars or other investigators choose more intelligently between rival theories, or methods of data collection, or seemingly incommensurate values, perspectives, or interpretations? Can rhetoric, properly conceived, serve as a bridge between realism and relativism, as Margolis suggests in his essay for this volume? Can it help us choose the best from among the concepts and precepts of the romantic and positivist traditions, as Brown seems to allege in his essay on symbolic realism? Or is rhetoric effectively foreclosed from playing any adjudicative role by dint of its tendency to reject any and all foundationalist presuppositions?

This general question is raised in a variety of forms in this book, both in essays on the rhetoric of scholarly inquiry and in those that bear upon issues in the civic arena. Assuming for example that Sanders is right in maintaining that conversation analysis has been able to accumulate a solid base of research findings in the absence of a paradigm, can rhetorical theory help scholars choose between competing attempts to account for the data? Are we well advised by Miller that the formulaic mechanisms of decision science should not be allowed to substitute for the ordinary give-and-take of rhetorical deliberations? Is Garver correct in suggesting that rhetoric can adjudicate between seemingly incommensurable values? If the theory and practice of psychoanalysis cannot be vouchsafed by the ordinary scientific criteria of verifiability and falsifiability (as Maranhão suggests), can its judgments nevertheless successfully be defended on rhetorical grounds? Can Stanley truly lay claim to rhetorical grounds for preferring one model of civic education to another? Is Wells on solid ground in suggesting that the arrangement of the details in an investigative report has a great deal to with what conclusions are drawn from them? If so, does rhetoric authorize one arrangement over another?

The great boast of the ancients was that knowledge of the principles of rhetoric together with experience in its craft could improve the quality of one's judgments and might even yield wisdom (*phronesis*) on those issues that did not admit of right or wrong answers. Yet is there any evidence in support of this view, or even of Wayne Booth's much more modest ambition for rhetoric as a vehicle for the "careful weighing of more-or-less good reasons" to arrive at "more-or-less probable conclusions—none too secure but better than would be arrived at by chance or unthinking impulse?"[76] One might indeed question what evidence there could possibly be, given rhetoric's own deconstructions of fact and logic, the real and the rational.

In his essay for this book, Gergen speaks of "The Checkmate of Rhetoric" in reference to rhetoric's undermining of the pretensions of objectivism. But does not that same critique undercut rhetoric's own credibility? By some (deconstructive) readings, does it not undermine the rhetorician's own agency if, for example, it is seen as entirely self-referential, or language-determined, or constituted by its readers? It could be argued that this tendency of rhetoric to shoot itself in the foot as it were—to checkmate itself—is a problem for postmodern discourse-analytic approaches generally. All are vulnerable to the criticism that they shift attention from ideas to words, and that in so doing they end up in endless quibbling, or in verbal seductions leading to false consciousness, or in aesthetic preoccupations.[77]

But rhetoric confronts the distinctive problem of being first and foremost an art of persuasion and only secondarily an instrument of discovery and sound judgment.[78] How can a science of "proving opposites" function

15

also as a science of reconciling opposites or of choosing between them? This in essence was the question that Plato had Socrates ask in his dialogues on the sophists. The problem with sophistic rhetorical theory, he argued, was not its presumption that there may be opposing opinions on a subject, but that it encouraged thinkers to go no further. Beyond the realm of everyday experience—of shifting opinions and contradictory arguments—was a realm of fixed essences, eternal verities, which it was the job of the philosopher to discover.[79] The sophists in general exhibited an apparent indifference to Truth, reflected in unabashedly contrived category schemes; in field-dependent, situation-dependent logics of justification; in their insistence on the inherent variability of human tastes and judgments; and, most lamentably, in their preoccupation with winning at all costs. As Leff maintains, the sophistic model "seems to undermine the boundary conditions of knowledge and argument that define conventional notions of intellectual inquiry. This problem weighs heavily on even the most ardent enthusiasts of rhetoric."[80]

I don't know that rhetoricians will ever be able to respond to Plato's criticisms compellingly. The new movement's rejection of foundationalism effectively denies it the grounds upon which to mount such a response.[81] Yet I am convinced that this very apparent weakness conceals reserves of considerable strength. Rhetoric's relativising impulse, its tendency to counter every argument with another, equally plausible, may be just the right ticket to what wisdom we can achieve at a time when, as Margolis (this volume) puts it, "the most comprehensive conceptual schemes we can imagine are all partial, fragmented, contingent, historically bounded, ultimately blind, and radically ungrounded . . ."

Margolis reminds us that all foundationalisms—Plato's included—are themselves rhetorically constructed. They are embedded, as he puts it, "in the shifting saliencies of our shared experience." These are the accepted truths, beliefs, practices of inquiry, hopes, fears, superstitions, and the like, "that form the core of what the apt members of an historical society are convergently inclined to view as requiring a considerable counterforce to upset or replace or dismantle."

What Margolis is here maintaining—and what other contributors here affirm—is that there is no escape from rhetoric. The most pressing need, then, is for a reconstructive rhetoric of inquiry, one which advances consideration of questions, and delineates their interconnections, even if it does not resolve them. Such a rhetoric will of necessity be unstable, self-questioning, reflexive—always in process of reconstituting itself in light of new historical saliencies and new habits of conviction. Its "truths," if there by any, will be situated, contextual, contingent—true for particular purposes; true under a given set of circumstances; true assuming the validity of taken-for-granted premises. And it will continually be engaged in a politics of competing pluralisms, a parliament of voices about which voices to privilege, and about how to construct, array, compare, and assess the objects of its scrutiny, including the multiple and competing rationalities about rationality with which it must contend.

But despite these uncertainties and circularities, and perhaps because of them, the new rhetoric of inquiry should be able to *prepare the way* for wiser, more judicious judgments by scholars and others engaged in the conduct of inquiry. However open-ended such a rhetoric may be, it need not be unreasonable or unempirical. However capable it may be of conceiving plausible arguments for opposing claims, it need not leave us in a state of indecision. If it cannot lay claim to fixed and immutable standards of judgment, or to formal devices by which to compel assent, it can nevertheless provide ways of engaging one's hearers, of clarifying ideas and also of rendering them plausible or probable.

THE ARTS OF THE SAYABLE

In comparing and assessing ideas, a reconstructive rhetoric of inquiry should aim at giving each its most coherent, most powerful expression. But this in turn requires further study of the arts of "the sayable"—of the possibilities for conceptual development and support of any given idea, of the inventional possibilities for refuting or countering it, and of the consequences of choosing one or another style, arrangement, or mode of presentation.

The study of rhetorical invention might well include formalistic theories of conceptual development, abstracted from particular controversies, as well as examination of the way particular terms or classes of terms can be named, defined, compared, contrasted, illustrated, contextualized, decontextualized, and so on. Likewise, one may follow the lead of the ancients in identifying general lines of argument, stripped as much as possible from particularizing contents and contexts, as well as possible lines of enthymematic argument appropriate to particular cultures, time periods, epistemic communities, paradigms, theories, and the like.

The play of conceptual possibilities has of course been the subject of numerous lines of investigation, including those by speech-act theorists, sociolinguists, structuralists, and poststructuralists. It is part and parcel of Burke's dramatism and his logology. As regards his own key concepts—the term *rhetoric* for example—Burke is apt to position any given term in relationship to its conceptual sisters and its brothers and its aunts; then to "desynonimize" seemingly related terms; then to recontextualize, perhaps by providing deliberately ironic, comedic, parodic, or otherwise incongruous renderings of the term; then to array multiple definitions of the term as if in an orderly conversation; then to "attitudinize"—to prepare the term for action.[82]

The most thoroughly developed of the contemporary theories of rhetorical invention is Richard McKeon's. As Douglas Mitchell describes it, it is a vehicle for discovery of the unknown.[83] Building on the systems of topics and opposed commonplaces developed by the ancients, it offers an architectonic scheme of schemes, a system of terms and coordinates by which to profile similarities and differences in philosophic schools, compare and account for variations in their textual interpretations, and provide the basis for generating new ideas and assessing old ones. The system also permits exploration of ambiguities within positions and overlaps between them. McKeon has inquired, for example, as to what the consequences would be were Aristotle read as a Platonist and Plato read as an Aristotelian.

Billig has shown how the topoi and pairs of opposed commonplaces from ancient rhetorical theory may be brought to bear upon contemporary issues in social psychology. Against the tendency among psychological theorists to characterize humans as either categorizers or particularizers, for example, Billig urges avoidance of one-sidedness. In the spirit of Protagoras he proposes as a general guideline that "if one psychological principle appears reasonable, then try reversing it, in order to see whether the contrary is just as reasonable."[84] He adds that in this dilemmatic world of ours, awards for wisdom are most likely to go to those who can move beyond either/or oppositions, often by way of reformulations of the terms themselves.

As part of a thoroughgoing theory of rhetorical invention, we need further consideration of the relationship between arguments and modes of expression. What are the consequences, asks Wells (this volume), of arraying the findings of an investigation into a single coherent narrative, compared with structuring the investigative report as a series of discrete facts and conclusions? What are the generic expectations and epistemic implications, asks Maranhão (this volume) of presenting one's work as an authoritative text rather than in the form of a narrative or dialogue?

What are the characteristics of "better" and "worse" scholarly narra-

18

tives? Is a fully coherent narrative intrinsically superior to one with numerous loose ends? Is a simple or conventional narrative preferable to a complex or unconventional one? Here are issues deserving of a good deal more attention than they have received. For example, Landau likened paleoanthropological accounts of shifts in the ape's habitat to fictive narratives—made all the more appealing because of their resemblance to children's tales.[85] She argued, however, that these structurally symmetrical tales were much too simplistic to be believed and needed to be replaced by theories with larger and more complicated plots. In the field of psychology, on the other hand, Gergen and Gergen found that the more enduring theories tended to exhibit aesthetic and structural characteristics similar to those of conventional narratives.[86]

What, finally, are the similarities and differences between civic and scholarly discourses, and between the discourses of the various disciplines and subdisciplines? How do civic and scholarly rhetors adapt to their respective audiences? How do they constitute their audiences? How are scholarly discourses modified when they must be presented outside their disciplines or origin, as well as to lay audiences?[87]

Among the rewards of studying rhetorics of inquiry is that one discovers how similar many of the problems are across disciplines. Likewise, we are accustomed to drawing sharp boundaries between town and gown rhetorics—between, say, the rhetoric of a nation's founding fathers and the rhetoric of philosophical foundationalists. Yet, as Nelson argues (this volume), the metaphors associated with political foundings may be far more appropriate as a rhetorical grounding for the human sciences than the ontological and epistemological groundings that philosophical foundationalists have supplied. Similarly, Garver (this volume) takes from Machiavelli's writings on political rhetoric some general strategies for dealing with incommensurabilities that have obvious bearing upon debates over values and over first principles in the scholarly arena. That the art of living has all but been replaced by the science of living is evidenced in Miller's account of the farflung uses of decision science. Here, too, suggests Miller, the academy might well look to rhetorical models of civic deliberation as alternatives, or at least as supplements, to a formulaic decision science. While the focus of this essay has been on the rhetoric of scholarly inquiry, the reach of the book extends well beyond the academy to include civil and expert inquiries. At root, then, it is about the rhetoric of inquiry generally, and, indeed, Stanley's essay is singularly important for its applications of general models of inquiry to civic education.

19

CONCLUDING COMMENTS

In the course of providing an introduction to the rhetoric of inquiry movement, this essay has staked out a perspective of its own. The essay has moved from deconstruction to reconstruction: from an emphasis on the dyslogistic senses of "mere" rhetoric and worse to an exploration of the possibilities for a eulogistic rhetoric of invention and sound judgment in the conduct of inquiry. Recent assaults on foundationalist presuppositions, I have argued, have provided an opening for a rhetoric of inquiry, particularly as applied to the discourse of the human sciences. That rhetorical theory offers a handy set of tools by which to pick away at objectivist pretensions was illustrated by several of the case studies briefly reviewed. But the central question raised here (and elsewhere in this book) was whether rhetoric was up to the task of adjudicating between competing rationalities.

The great irony of the rhetoric of inquiry movement is that the more trenchant and far-reaching its critique of objectivism, the more is the claim of its reconstructive potential rendered suspect. Conceived of in fairly conventional terms as the extrafactual, extralogical in discourse—the part not played by hard fact and cold reason—rhetoric's role becomes that of a Derridean supplement, a potentially important, albeit ancillary instrument for the expression of truths (or falsehoods) independently arrived at. But once you conceive of reality as rhetorically constituted, and of reason as rhetorically justified, you are left vulnerable to the charge of being unable to vouchsafe your own claims, including claims about the possibilities for a reconstructive rhetoric of inquiry.

There are no pat answers to this line of argument, and, indeed, its best refutation probably comes by pointing to acknowledged touchstones of rhetorical excellence. This is what James Boyd White does in his readings of texts ranging from the *Iliad* and Plato's *Gorgias* to Samuel Johnson's essays and the Declaration of Independence.[88] What White's readings point up again and again is the transformative potential of a dialogic rhetoric—built paradoxically on the speaker or writer's capacity to operate within the limits of his or her language and culture. Of the *Gorgias* he says, for example, that the text

> offers its readers the experience of a mind dialectically
> reconstituting the language. The language so made is powerful, in
> a sense unanswerable, in large part because it does not seek to
> eliminate but accepts and clarifies the variabilities and complexities

and inconsistencies of ordinary life and language. . . . What the text really seeks to teach its reader is not how to speak this language but how to remake a language of his own. It does not teach a particular set of questions and dialectical responses, to be repeated on other occasions, but . . . how to ask questions of one's own. To do this, the reader must be a center of independent intellectual energy, a remaker of language and a composer of texts, and it is with helping him to become these things that this text is ultimately concerned.[89]

This ideal of an emancipatory, dialogic rhetoric is one worthy of a central place in the academy. But it requires of us that we conceive of rhetoric, not simply as an art of proving opposites, but also as an art of arraying and comparing ideas after first having attempted to give each its most forceful expression.[90] And it invites us to further conceive of rhetoric, not simply as an art of expression or of reader-reception, but as one of intellectual exchange. One reason for the appeal noted earlier of the conversation metaphor in the human sciences is that it speaks to the tentativeness of our claims upon the world, to our dependence upon each other for validation of those claims, and to the inherent ongoingness of communal inquiry. It implies as well that inasmuch as we are in this together, we had better attend carefully to how we converse and to who we are, both as speakers and as audiences.

What, then, are the optimal conditions for productive intellectual exchange? What norms of discourse ought to guide processes of scholarly reporting, discussion, and debate? What institutional arrangements are most likely to facilitate adherence to those norms? Implicit in our very nature as dialogic beings, argues Gadamer, are norms of sharing, respect, mutuality, and equality. Ideally there is a risking of self and of one's prejudices through a process of joining with the other in a "giving in" to the subject matter.[91] Like Gadamer, Habermas deduces conversational norms from our nature as symbol-using, symbol-sharing, interdependent beings.[92] But to Gadamer's list he adds a critical component, the human critical faculty, and he emphasizes as well the need to transform material conditions that block and distort communication. How then to facilitate understanding while at the same time bringing critical standards to bear on the exchange of ideas?

No doubt any concrete answer to that question will have to take account of all manner of circumstances and of purposes to which the conversation is put. But the general requirement of a truly reconstitutive rhetoric is that it must be radically open to all manner of changes, including changes in the meanings ascribed to its texts, the character and identities of its participants, its language and language practices, and the community and culture out of which it is constituted. Of the process of law, which White proposes as a model for the human sciences,[93] he argues that it involves both interpretation and reconstitution of the materials with which it works. It is an art of persuasion which also creates—or at least recreates—the objects of its persuasion. Correspondingly, its language and its strategies are constantly being tested and are forever being remade. This means, he says, "that the process of law is at once creative and educative: one is perpetually learning what can and cannot be said. It also means that both the identity of the speakers and their wants are in perpetual transformation."[94]

Elsewhere I have expressed my reservations about trusting to the highly structured, impersonal, contentious discourse of the law tribunal as a model for scholarly inquiry.[95] There are surely other models of intellectual exchange that might well be preferable for certain purposes.[96] The important point for our purposes is that White is right in underscoring the systemic, process-oriented character of a reconstructive rhetoric and the potential for alteration, occasioned by the process, of the system's component parts. It need not be assumed that a reconstitutive rhetoric is defeated by challenges to its epistemic grounding. The general premise of the rhetorician must be, rather, that *even if* reality is symbolically constructed, some constructions are surely preferable to others. Similarly, *even if* reason is rhetorical, some reasons are surely superior to others. Rhetorical engagement may help us to discover the better reason and also help make the better *appear* the better reason. That is reason enough for a rhetoric of inquiry.

N O T E S

1. See for example Richard H. Brown, *Society as Text* (Chicago: University of Chicago Press, 1987); Michael Billig, *Arguing and Thinking: A Rhetorical Approach to Social Psychology* (Cambridge: Cambridge University Press, 1987); Donald N. McCloskey, *The Rhetoric of Economics* (Madison: University of Wisconsin Press, 1985); Carolyn R. Miller, "Invention in Technical and Scientific Discourse: A Prospective Survey," in *Research in Technical Communication: A Bibliographic Sourcebook* ed. Michael G. Moran and Debra Journet (Westport, Conn.: Greenwood, 1985); John Nelson, Allen Megill, and Donald N. McCloskey, *The Rhetoric of the Human Sciences* (Madison: University of Wisconsin Press, 1985); Herbert W. Simons, *Rhetoric*

in the Human Sciences (London: Sage, 1989). Subsequent references in the notes are to the last names of authors cited, and a short title.

2. Objectivism is used here synonymously with what Jerome Bruner refers to simply as "the paradigmatic mode" of scholarly thought and with what McCloskey refers to as modernism. See Bruner's Actual Minds, Possible Worlds (Cambridge: Harvard University Press, 1986). See also McCloskey, Rhetoric of Economics, 7–8 for a list of the "Ten Commandments" of modernism.

3. See for example Kenneth Burke's essay on "Traditional Principles of Rhetoric" in his Rhetoric of Motives (Berkeley: University of California Press, 1969). See also George A. Kennedy, Classical Rhetoric and Its Christian and Secular Tradition from Ancient to Modern Times (Chapel Hill: University of North Carolina Press, 1980); A. Grimaldi, Studies in the Philosophy of Aristotle's Rhetoric (Wiesbaden: Franz Steiner Verlag GMBH, 1972); and the essays by Nelson and Gaonkar in this volume.

4. For a thoroughgoing critique of foundationalist presuppositions see Richard Rorty, Philosophy and the Mirror of Nature (Princeton: Princeton University Press, 1979). See also Richard Bernstein, Beyond Objectivism and Relativism (Philadelphia, University of Pennsylvania Press, 1983); John S. Nelson, "Political Thinking and Political Rhetoric," in What Should Political Theory Be Now? ed. John S. Nelson (Albany: SUNY Press, 1983), 160–240, especially 194–204.

5. See for example Imre Lakatos and Alan Musgrave, eds., Criticism and the Growth of Knowledge (Cambridge: Cambridge University Press, 1970). See also Maranhão (this volume).

6. This term is a continental European construction, reflecting traditions of thought that brook no distinction between the humanities and social sciences. I use it as McCloskey (Rhetoric of Economics) does to encompass a wide array of disciplines, from politics to paleoanthropology, but with the sense as well that all sciences are human constructions.

7. On the uniqueness of the human sciences, see Alasdair MacIntyre, After Virtue (Notre Dame, Ind.: University of Notre Dame Press, 1981). For a useful critique of grand methodological schemes, see Abraham Kaplan, The Conduct of Inquiry (San Francisco: Chandler, 1964).

8. See for example Sigmund Koch, "Psychology and Emerging Conceptions of Science as Unitary," in Behaviorism and Phenomenology, ed. T. W. Wann (Chicago: University of Chicago Press, 1970), 21–2; Thomas S. Kuhn, The Structure of Scientific Revolutions, 2d ed. enlarged (Chicago: University of Chicago Press, 1970); Brown, Society as Text ch 3. On the theory-laden character of facts, see M. B. Turner, Psychology and the Philosophy of Science (New York: Appleton-Century-Crofts, 1967), 15; Walter

Weimer, *Notes on the Methodology of Scientific Research* (Hillsdale, N.J.: Erlbaum, 1979), 21.

9. See for example Kenneth J. Gergen, "The Social Construction of Self-Knowledge," in *The Self, Psychological and Philosophical Issues*, ed. T. Mischel (Oxford: Blackwell, 1977); "The Social Constructionist Movement in Modern Psychology," *American Psychologist* 40(1985): 266–75; John D. Peters and Eric W. Rothenbuhler, "The Reality of Construction," in *Rhetoric in the Human Sciences*, ed. H. W. Simons (London: Sage, 1989); John Shotter and Kenneth J. Gergen, *Texts of Identity* (London: Sage, 1989). Karin D. Knorr-Cetina, *The Manufacture of Knowledge: An Essay on the Constructivist and Contextual Nature of Science* (Oxford: Pergamon, 1981).

10. See McCloskey, *Rhetoric of Economics*, ch. 2

11. This argument is advanced by several contributors to this volume, including Brown, Gergen, Margolis, Miller, and Nelson. See also James Boyd White, *When Words Lose Their Meaning* (Chicago: University of Chicago Press, 1984); Murray J. Edelman, *Constructing the Political Spectacle* (Chicago: University of Chicago Press, 1988).

12. See Billig, *Arguing and Thinking*; McCloskey, *Rhetoric of Economics*, ch. 3.

13. See Joseph Gusfield, "The Literary Rhetoric of Science: Comedy and Pathos in Drinking Driver Research," *American Sociological Review* 41 (1976): 16–33.

14. See for example Bazerman's essay in Nelson, Megill, and McCloskey. He argues that as psychology became increasingly geared to experimentalism, and as the APA style manual grew from 7 pages in 1929 to 32 pages in 1944 to 61 pages in 1952 to 200-plus pages in 1974, it increasingly restricted the psychologist's inventional resources, including for example the possibility of arranging the scholarly narrative to best suit the subject matter of the report. See also Bazerman's *Shaping Written Knowledge* (Madison: University of Wisconsin Press, 1988); James Clifford and George E. Marcus, eds., *Writing Culture: The Poetics and Politics of Ethnography* (Berkeley: University of California Press, 1986); Linda Brodkey, *Academic Writing as Social Practice* (Philadelphia: Temple University Press, 1987).

15. See for example Michael J. Shapiro, *The Politics of Representation* (Madison: University of Wisconsin Press, 1988); Michel Foucault, *The Archaeology of Knowledge*, trans. A. M. Sheridan Smith (New York: Pantheon, 1972).

16. See for example Michael S. Halloran and Annette N. Bradford, "Figures of Speech in the Rhetoric of Science and Technology," in *Classical Rhetoric and Modern Discourse*, eds. R. J. Connors, L. Ed, and A. Lunsford

24

(Carbondale: Southern Illinois University Press, 1984), 179–92; Hayden White, *Tropics of Discourse* (Baltimore: The Johns Hopkins University Press, 1978); George Lakoff and Mark Johnson, *Metaphors We Live By* (Chicago: University of Chicago Press, 1980); Mark Johnson, *The Body in the Mind* (Chicago: University of Chicago Press, 1987); Paolo Valesio, *Novantiqua: Rhetorics as a Contemporary Theory* (Bloomington: Indiana University Press, 1980); Ernesto Grassi, *Rhetoric as Philosophy: The Humanist Tradition* (University Park: Pennsylvania State University Press, 1980).

17. See Cary Nelson, "Writing as the Accomplice of Language: Kenneth Burke and Poststructuralism," in *The Legacy of Kenneth Burke* ed. H. W. Simons and T. Melia (Madison: University of Wisconsin Press, 1989), 86–87.

18. See Paul de Man, "The Epistemology of Metaphor," *Critical Inquiry* 5(1978): 13–30.

19. Clifford Geertz "Blurred Genres: The Refiguration of Social Thought," *American Scholar* 49(1980): 165–79.

20. These metaphors can be spun out in a variety of ways. As regards the conversation metaphor, for example, writers are said to be in conversation with imagined readers; readers are urged to enter into imagined conversations with the texts that they read, definitions of a term are placed in conversation with other definitions. There are literal conversations within texts (the exchanges between Socrates and Callicles in the *Gorgias*, for example), and also metaphorical conversations between texts, or within our own heads. Likewise, there are conversations within disciplines and conversations between disciplines; and, as Burke suggests, there are conversations across the ages to which we attempt to contribute some small part. See Kenneth Burke, *The Philosophy of Literary Form* (Berkeley: University of California Press, 1978), 110–11. See Brown (1987) for other examples.

21. See for example Brown, *Society as Text* ch. 8; Billig, *Arguing and Thinking*, ch. 2; Shapiro, *Politics of Representation*, ch. 1.

22. See Thomas S. Gieryn and Anne E. Figert, "Scientists Protect Their Cognitive Authority: The Status Degradation Ceremony of Sir Cyril Burt," in *The Knowledge Society*, ed. G. Boehme and N. Stehr (Durdrecht, Holland: D. Reidel, 1986). See also E. E. Sampson, "Cognitive Psychology as Ideology," *American Psychologist* 36 (1981): 730–43; David Faust and Richard A. Miner, "The Empiricist and His New Clothes: DSM-III in Perspective," *American Journal of Psychology* 143 (1986): 962–67.

23. See Thomas S. Kuhn, *Scientific Revolutions*; Barry Barnes, T. R. Kuhn and Social Science (New York: Columbia University Press, 1982).

24. Maryanne E. Jaegar and Ralph L. Rosnow, "Contextualism and Its

Implications for Psychological Inquiry," *British Journal of Psychology* 79(1988): 63–75.

25. Chaim Perelman and L. Olbrechts-Tyteca, *The New Rhetoric: A Treatise on Argumentation*, trans. J. Wilkinson and P. Weaver (Notre Dame, Ind.: University of Notre Dame Press, 1969), 40–44. See also S. Michael Halloran, "The Birth of Molecular Biology: An Essay in the Rhetorical Criticism of Scientific Discourse," *Rhetoric Review* 3(1984): 70–83; Michael A. Overington, "The Scientific Community as Audience: Toward a Rhetorical Analysis of Science," *Philosophy and Rhetoric* 10 (1977): 143–64.

26. Billig, *Arguing and Thinking*, 48–50, 110–17. See also Billig et al., *Ideological Dilemmas: A Social Psychology of Everyday Thinking* (London: Sage, 1988).

27. Billig, *Arguing and Thinking*, ch. 9

28. See William M. Keith and Richard Cherwitz, "Objectivity, Disagreement, and the Rhetoric of Inquiry," in *Rhetoric in the Human Sciences*, ed. H. W. Simons (London: Sage, 1989).

29. Jürgen Habermas, *The Philosophical Discourse of Modernity* (Cambridge: The Polity Press, 1987), 183–85.

30. Among the major classical conceptions of rhetoric are those by Aristotle, Cicero, and Quintilian. See *The Rhetoric of Aristotle*, trans. Lane Cooper (Englewood Cliffs, N.J.: Prentice-Hall, 1932); Cicero's *De Oratore*, 2 vols., Latin text with English trans. by E. W. Sutton and H. Rackham (Cambridge: Harvard University Press, 1942); Quintilian's *Institutio Oratoria*, 4 vols., Latin text and English trans. by H. E. Butler (Cambridge: Harvard University Press, 1920). For a useful review of conceptions of rhetoric, see Donald Bryant, "Rhetoric: Its Functions and Its Scope," *Quarterly Journal of Speech* 39(1953): 461–24, see also Burke's "Traditional Principles" essay in *A Rhetoric of Motives* (see n. 3). Burke and others sometimes treat rhetoric as the art of symbolic inducement in all its manifestations. See for example Walter R. Fisher, *Human Communication as Narrative: Toward a Philosophy of Reason, Value, and Action* (Columbia: University of South Carolina Press, 1987); Richard Gregg, *Symbolic Inducement and Knowing* (Columbia: University of South Carolina Press, 1984).

31. See Billig, *Arguing and Thinking*, ch. 3; Clifford Geertz, *Works and Lives: The Anthropologist as Author* (Palo Alto: Stanford University Press, 1988). Billig appears to have softened his position in a recent essay, "Conservatism and the Rhetoric of Rhetoric," *Economy and Society* 18 (1989): 132–48. See also Miller's typology of conceptions of rhetoric (this volume).

32. Implicit here is the notion of rhetoric as social practice, impelled and constrained by communal norms and values. One object of rhetorical inquiry about scholarly inquiry is to discover recurrent discursive practices within the various disciplines, and to infer the implicit "rules" guiding these practices. See the introduction to H. W. Simons and Aram Aghazarian, eds. *Form, Genre, and the Study of Political Discourse* (Columbia: University of South Carolina Press, 1986). See also Steven Yearley, "Textual Persuasion: The Role of Social Accounting in the Construction of Scientific Arguments," *Philosophy of Social Science* 11(1981): 409–35.

33. See Thomas Szasz, *Ideology and Insanity* (Garden City: Anchor, 1969).

34. Wayne Booth, *Modern Dogma and the Rhetoric of Assent* (Chicago: University of Chicago Press, 1974), xiv. See also Karl R. Wallace, "The Substance of Rhetoric: Good Reasons," *Quarterly Journal of Speech* 49(1963): 239–49.

35. For an introduction to the sophistic movement, see G. P. Kerferd, *The Sophistic Movement* (Cambridge: Cambridge University Press, 1981).

36. See for example Robert Hariman, "The Rhetoric of Inquiry and the Professional Scholar," in *Rhetoric in the Human Sciences*, ed. H. W. Simons (London: Sage, 1989).

37. Burke, *Rhetoric of Motives*, 49–180.

38. Hayden White, *Metahistory: The Historical Imagination in Nineteenth Century Europe* (Baltimore: The Johns Hopkins University Press, 1973).

39. Michel Foucault, *The Order of Things: An Archaeology of the Human Sciences* (New York: Pantheon, 1970).

40. See White, *Tropics of Discourse* (see n. 16), ch. 11.

41. See for example Thomas S. Kuhn, *The Essential Tension* (Chicago: University of Chicago Press, 1977).

42. See for example Gergen, "The Social Constructionist Movement" (see n. 9).

43. G. N. Gilbert and Michael Mulkay, *Opening Pandora's Box* (Cambridge: Cambridge University Press, 1984); also Mulkay's *The Word and the World* (London: Allen & Unwin, 1985). See Jonathan Potter and Margaret Wetherill's *Discourse and Social Psychology* (London: Sage, 1987) for an introduction to these and other discourse-analytic approaches.

44. Geertz, for example (see n. 19, n. 31). Also see Richard A. Shweder and Robert A. LeVine, *Culture Theory: Essays on Mind, Self, and Emotion* (Cambridge: Cambridge University Press, 1984); Stephen A. Tyler, *The Said and the Unsaid* (New York: Academic Press, 1978).

45. See for example Roberto Unger, *The Critical Legal Studies Movement* (Cambridge: Harvard University Press, 1984).

46. For example, Wayne Booth, *Critical Understanding: The Powers and Limits of Pluralism* (Chicago: University of Chicago Press, 1979).

47. See, for example, Jonathan Culler, *On Deconstruction* (Ithaca: Cornell University Press, 1982); Christopher Norris, *The Deconstructive Turn: Essays in the Rhetoric of Philosophy* (London: Methuen, 1983).

48. For a useful review see Catherine Belsey, *Critical Practice* (New York: Methuen, 1980). Nearly neglected in this brief review of works on the boundaries of "the field" are theoretical writings about the rhetoric of inquiry that are clearly within the field. See for example Thomas B. Farrell, "Knowledge, Consensus, and Rhetorical Theory," *Quarterly Journal of Speech* 62(1976): 1–14; Robert L. Scott, "On Viewing Rhetoric as Epistemic," *Central States Speech Journal* 18(1967): 9–16. For a review of essays on rhetorical epistemology, see Michael Leff, "In Search of Ariadne's Thread: A Review of the Recent Literature on Rhetorical Theory, *Central States Speech Journal* 29(1978): 73–91. See also the succinct summaries of writings by Burke, Richards, Toulmin, Weaver, Perelman, and others by Sonja K. Foss, Karen A. Foss, and Robert Trapp, *Contemporary Perspectives on Rhetoric* (Prospect Heights, Ill.: Waveland, 1985).

49. Nelson, "Political Thinking and Political Rhetoric," 176–93.

50. Because data cannot be theory-neutral, argued Kuhn in *Scientific Revolutions*, they are rarely if ever decisive. Rather, they are among a number of considerations weighing on scientists at the point of paradigm clash, including questions of breadth and parsimony as well as judgments as to which puzzles are most worth solving. The process, said Kuhn, is one of persuasion, but it is not irrational. See also Eugene Garver, "Paradigms and Princes," *Philosophy of the Social Sciences* 17 (1987), 21–48.

51. Andrew Weigert, "The Immoral Rhetoric of Scientific Sociology," *American Sociologist* 5(1970): 111–19.

52. See *A Grammar of Motives* (Berkeley: University of California Press, 1969).

53. Geertz, *Works and Lives*, (see n. 31), 140. See also Richard Rorty, *Consequences of Pragmatism* (Minneapolis: University of Minnesota Press, 1982), especially 193.

54. McCloskey, *Rhetoric of Economics*, 36

55. Ibid.

56. Burke has characterized Marx's orientation to rhetoric as "the knack of speaking ill in civil matters." See his *Rhetoric of Motives*, p. 101.

57. Gusfield, "Literary Rhetoric" (see n. 13).

58. Ibid. See also Donald Spence for a similar distinction between the "rhetorical voice of psychoanalysis" and what he calls the "evidentiary voice."

Paper presented at the conference on Rhetoric of Social Science, University of Maryland, April 1989.

59. Gusfield, "Literary Rhetoric," p. 31.

60. See Stephen Pfohl, "The 'Discovery' of Child Abuse," *Social Problems* 24(1977): 310–24.

61. Steven Woolgar and Dorothy Pawluch, "Ontological Gerrymandering: The Anatomy of Social Problems Explanations," *Social Problems* 32(1985): 214–27.

62. See "Irony in the Social Study of Social Science," in *Science Observed: Perceptions of the Social Study of Science*, ed. K. D. Knorr-Cetina and M. Mulkay (London: Sage, 1983).

63. Malcolm Ashmore, "The Critical Problems of Writing the Problem: A Double Text," paper presented at the conference on Argument in Science, Iowa City, Ia., October 9–11, 1987. For a sense of the flavor of the reflexive SSK approach, see Steven Woolgar, ed., *Turning the Pages of Science: Knowledge and Reflexivity* (London: Sage, 1987).

64. Billig, "Rhetoric of Rhetoric," 143 (see n. 31).

65. Richard A. Shweder, "Post-Nietzschian Anthropology: The Idea of Multiple Objective Worlds," in *New Essays on Relativism*, ed. M. Krausz (Notre Dame, Ind.: University of Notre Dame Press, in press). See also Richard A. Shweder, "Divergent Rationalities," in *Metatheory in Social Science*, ed. D. W. Fiske and R. A. Shweder (Chicago: University of Chicago Press, 1986).

66. See Geertz, *Works and Lives*, 136–7 (see n. 31).

67. See for example Renato Rosaldo, "Where Objectivity Lies: The Rhetoric of Anthropology," in Nelson, Megill, and McCloskey, *Rhetoric of the Human Sciences*.

68. George E. Marcus and Michael M. J. Fischer, *Anthropology as Cultural Critique* (Chicago: University of Chicago Press, 1986).

69. See Brown, *Society as Text* ch. 3. See also Stephen Toulmin, *The Uses of Argument* (Cambridge: Cambridge University Press, 1958); Charles Willard, "Argument Fields," in *Advances in Argumentation Theory and Research*, by J. R. Cox and C. A. Willard (Carbondale: Southern Illinois University Press, 1982); Paul Diesing, *Reason in Society: Five Types of Decisions and Their Social Conditions* (Westport, Conn.: Greenwood, 1962).

70. Brown, *Society as Text*, 186.

71. See Margolis' essay in this volume for further elaboration of this point.

72. Kaplan, *Conduct of Inquiry*, 24–27 (see n. 7).

73. See for example Richard Bernstein's discussion of Habermas on reconstructive analysis, *Beyond Objectivism and Relativism* (Philadelphia:

University of Pennsylvania Press, 1983), 193.

74. See Kaplan, *Conduct of Inquiry*, 3–11. See also Thomas Kuhn, "Reflections on My Critics," in Lakatos and Musgrave, *Growth of Knowledge* (see n. 5) cf. 235–39. This point is developed at greater length in the chapter and is a central theme of the book.

75. See Donald N. McCloskey, "The Rhetoric of Statistics," paper presented at a conference on the Rhetoric of the Disciplines: The Next Steps (Iowa City, Ia, March 1988); Frank T. Denton, "The Significance of Significance: Rhetorical Aspects of Statistical Hypothesis Testing in Economics," in *The Consequences of Rhetoric in Economics: A Conference*, ed. A. Klamer, D. N. McCloskey, and R. Solow (Cambridge: Cambridge University Press, 1988).

76. Booth, *Modern Dogma*, 59 (see n. 34).

77. See Geertz, *Works and Lives*, 142–3.

78. Admittedly, one may quarrel with this view, maintaining, for example, that the tools of rhetorical invention were understood by Aristotle, Cicero, and Quintilian, and by the early Greek sophists to be instruments of inquiry and judgment and not just of advocacy. See for example Richard McKeon, *Essays in Invention and Discovery*, edited with an introduction by Mark Backman (Woodbridge, Conn.: Oxbow Press, 1987), ch. 4. Still, the dominant sense of rhetoric, as even Billig *(Rhetoric of Rhetoric)* acknowledges, has been that of an art and practice of persuasion.

79. See Billig, *Arguing and Thinking* 43. See also Susan C. Jarratt, "Toward a Sophistic Historiography," *PRE/TEXT* 8(1987): 9–28.

80. Michael C. Leff, "Modern Sophistic and the Unity of Rhetoric," in Nelson, Megill, and McCloskey, *Rhetoric of the Human Sciences*, 21. But see Richard A. Engnell, who argues that even Gorgias had a conception of sound judgment: "Implications for Communication of the Rhetorical Gorgias of Leontine, *Western Journal of Speech Communication* 37(1973): 175–84.

81. By the same token, as my colleague Mark Pollock points out, the rejection of foundationalism can also be turned back upon Plato's indictment. If Socrates "wins" in *Gorgias*, it is because Plato has Gorgias argue from his framework rather than his own.

82. See the "Traditional Principles" essay in Burke's *Rhetoric of Motives*.

83. See McKeon, *Essays in Invention*. See also Douglas Mitchell, "Richard McKeon's Conception of Rhetoric and the Philosophy of Culture," *Rhetorica* 6(1988): 395–414. See in particular Mitchell's repeated references to an as yet unpublished essay by McKeon, "Philosophical Semantics and Philosophical Inquiry."

84. Billig, *Arguing and Thinking*, 11.

85. Landau, in Nelson, Megill, and McCloskey, *Rhetoric of the Human Sciences*.

86. Kenneth J. Gergen and Mary Gergen, "Narrative Form and the Construction of Psychological Science," in *Narrative Psychology*, ed. T. R. Sarbin (New York: Praeger, 1985).

87. See for example John Lyne and Henry Howe, "Punctuated Equilibria: Rhetorical Dynamics of a Scientific Controversy," *Quarterly Journal of Speech* 72(1986): 132–47.

88. White, *When Words Lose Their Meaning* (see n. 11).

89. Ibid., 109. See also Henry W. Johnstone, Jr., *Validity and Rhetoric in Philosophical Argument* (University Park, Pa.: Dialogue Press of Man and World, 1978).

90. Indeed, Billig *(Rhetoric of Rhetoric)* argues that the rhetorical ideal of the *Gorgias* is that of *aporia*, in which nothing is settled, yet consideration of the issues is advanced.

91. Hans Georg Gadamer, *Truth and Method*, trans. Garrett Barden and John Cumming (New York: Seabury, 1975).

92. See the comparison between Gadamer and Habermas's approaches in Bernstein, *Beyond Objectivism*, 183–87.

93. White, *When Words Lose Their Meaning* (1984).

94. Ibid., 304.

95. Herbert Simons, "Chronicle and Critique of a Conference," *Quarterly Journal of Speech* 71(1985): 52–64. See also Wayne Booth, *The Company We Keep: The Ethics of Narrative* (Chicago: University of Chicago Press, 1988).

96. See for example Jeanine Czubaroff, "The Deliberative Character of Strategic Scientific Debates," in *Rhetoric in the Human Sciences*, ed. H. W. Simons (London: Sage, 1989).

PART ONE

Rhetorics of Science

1

Bio-Rhetorics:
Moralizing the Life Sciences

John Lyne

Since David Hume it has been all but axiomatic among analytic philosophers that no *ought* can be derived from an *is*. Statements vested with moral or valuative content, held to derive only from presentiment, are seen as occupying a different logical category from statements of fact. This dogma pervades much of the academic world, and one of its widespread effects is to leave much of that world mystified and powerless to connect the rhetoric of knowledge convincingly with that of judgment and action. The doctrine sets philosophy at odds with what we must do as human beings, whose need to act often does not run in sync with the knowledge at hand, but whose failure to act will have practical consequences. The official story should make us flounder at the point of "imposing" a value judgment and demur from action, should we not know what logic warrants it. We would tremble in our awareness of jumping the chasm between logical types.

The psychological brunt of this conflict is softened by accepted strategies of deferring judgment ("Hamletic" strategies, Kenneth Burke [1969] calls them), such as calling for more research. At the same time, the notion that knowledge in itself contains no moral lesson represses understanding of the ways that the discourses of knowledge harbor moral and aesthetic lessons of all sorts. Being "taken in" is only one of the costs of such repression; another is the failure to appreciate discursive resources of the sort necessary for making powerful connectives between fact and affect. These connectives are fuzzy—logically unclean—and therefore often jettisoned once noticed.

This hygenic attitude toward knowledge is an easy target for neo-Marxian social philosophies, which identify and attack the neurosis by showing its historical sources. Ideology is shown to mask an entire hierarchy of values and privileges beneath claims to objectivity. For the captives of false consciousness, there is always a hidden agenda in the very depiction of reality, and they are its victims. Their everyday reality is both structured and given the sanction of naturalness by those who would arrange the world to their own liking. The "is" is thus a routinization of someone's else's "ought." Once this false consciousness is penetrated, however, an historical objectivity becomes possible. Ironically, perhaps, thought and action become renaturalized by their relationship to history.

The interaction of these two academic attitudes seems a vital part of our current intellectual climate (Peters and Rothenbuhler 1989). They are often played out antagonistically as when critical theory makes a foil of positivism, and vice versa; but they are also "polar" accounts, neither of which can be wholly victorious. Science does in many ways accommodate to society and make society accommodate to it, but scientists also tackle unsolved puzzles and unreconciled observations. In that sense the discourse is always caught in a tension between a social pole and another pole just outside the reach of society. The quest to know is charged at the second pole, the quest for integrative understanding at the first, and the resolution of this tension determines the social import of scientific claims. The two attitudes just sketched have in common a neglect of how this polar tension is mediated, and more specifically, each in its way denigrates the *rhetorical invention* required in order to make facts support judgments and actions. The analytic approach renders is-ought connections logically indefensible and thereby closes off the space for their invention; whereas the critical approach makes the connection seem inevitable, and hence theoretically uninteresting.

As bids for complete accounts, neither meets the demands of experience. Like Zeno's paradoxes, Hume's analytic feat forces us to stop and question the routine inferences we often make without knowing precisely what warrants them. As Zeno's paradoxes never really convinced many people that motion is impossible, however, the radical separation of is's and ought's is at best sustained only as a logical point. In practical life, jumping categories (when we are willing to make the jump) is assisted by rhetoric, which functions to make is's dovetail smoothly with ought's. The rhetoric which accomplishes that smoothness of fit—or disrupts it—is something more, and more crafted, than an ideological pattern alone. It is in the nature of rhetoric that it can "prove opposites," whatever its ideological starting points. But the relationship between *is* and *ought* is complex.

An ideology can be seen as a field against which discourses are figures. Ideological critique of a specific discourse is thus a kind of field-figure analysis, that is, an attempt to account for the given discourse in terms of that broader field, and nothing else. Some ideological moorings may be so deep as to elude conscious control or notice until a later age. In their work in developing the theory of punctuated equilibrium, for instance, Niles

Eldredge and Stephen Jay Gould called attention to the possibility that the prevalent interpretation of the Darwinian theory reflects an unconscious bias toward progressivism and gradualistic change (Lyne and Howe 1986). With some historical distance, it seems rather obvious that Darwin's own language and perception were shaped in part by the cultural assumptions of his age.

It will not do to assume that all Western discourses are simply figures on the same ideological field, however, especially when one enters the domain of science. For there is an ideology of science as such, which mediates the impact of the broader social ideology. The force of scientific ideology—one exalting objectivity, instrumental rationality, and so on—might be felt whether the science is being practiced in a liberal, socialist, or fascist state, for instance, and it will have to negotiate, compete with, or even absorb aspects of those state ideologies (Lyne and Howe 1989). Such interaction requires something more than the ideologies in question: it requires being mediated by rhetoric.

Rhetoric is the counterpart of ideology. It proceeds from an understanding of broad dispositions and applies them to concrete situations, whether the ideological content is a matter of focal interest or only an undertow. When the values of scientific discourse negotiate with state ideologies, or with private interests, different rhetorical strategies bring these different vectors to bear in different ways. When there is an uncontested ideology, rhetorical mediation is required just in order to assimilate new findings to accepted principles (except in those uninteresting cases in which interpretation is a mechanical procedure). Like a constitution, which must continually be extended in light of new realities, an ideology must be laboriously stretched over any new terrain to which it would lay claim.

The task for rhetoric goes beyond interpretive understanding, or hermeneutics. In guiding the creation of discourses, and not just the interpretation of existing texts, the work of rhetoric is to invent language strategies that bring about change. To address a discourse community in the role of the inquirer is actively and selectively to extend understanding by means of persuasion—by a rhetoric that lays the path from accepted beliefs to proposed ones. Such rhetoric is not all invented *de novo* with each discourse, of course. In fact it might be relatively stable across a range of discourses; more negotiable than ideology or "culture," yet not quite so up for grabs that all possibilities are seen as competing equally. The middle ground between cultural determination and unconstrained invention, I would suggest, is occupied by a *rhetoric, a discourse strategy spanning and organizing numerous discourses, and acting as a trajectory for discourses yet unorganized.* As a way of talking, picturing, making signifying relations, and inducing inferences, a rhetoric constitutes a model for organizing and inventing discourses.

A special instance of this is what might be called a *bio-rhetoric,* a strategy for inventing and organizing discourses about biology in such a way that they mesh with the discourses of social, political, or moral life (Lyne 1987). The term is meant to call attention to the potential for borrowing rhetorical resources from one domain and using them in another. Such a strategy makes biological considerations discursively available to discussions of social, political, or moral issues, or vice versa—the flow can be in either direction. That is, social, political, or moral issues can be cast within a biological framework, or conversely, the discussion of biological issues can be influenced by ways of talking that have developed outside of biology. In either case, there is a cross-fertilization, where heuristic resources from one discursive domain enter and animate another. Furthermore, a tension is created between morally-laden social categories and the cognitive-instrumental categories of science. A bio-rhetoric is thus talk "on its way" from an "is" to an "ought," making that connection only in the play of language. Like the motion of an arrow, it will seem to dissolve under an analytic stare.

When Richard Dawkins (1976) wrote of "the selfish gene," in a book bearing that title, he had condensed into a phrase an entire bio-rhetoric based on the putative science of sociobiology. To explain why is to identify some of the characteristic features of the more general phenomenon being described here. The phrase is striking because it apparently commits what Ryle (1949) would call a *category mistake:* the quality of selfishness belongs to attitude-bearing, purposive beings, yet it is here being applied to a mechanism for biochemical replication. Selfishness is an attitude toward oneself and others, a vice or a virtue, depending upon one's ethical stance, and a variable trait of a personality. A gene by nature has no attitude toward itself or others, is not purposive according to the principles of biology (although it is called *teleonomic,* a tribute to the irradicability of purpose talk), and hence can only in a metaphorical sense be vested with such attributes as selfishness. And although Dawkins presents the phrase as a metaphor, the spirit of the metaphor suffuses the entire analysis of his book. It is the very point of the analysis, in fact, and the heart of the bio-rhetoric placing the gene in the imagination by allowing the reader to picture it.

The ascription of selfishness to the gene is only a slight rhetorical twist upon the analysis provided by sociobiology's leading popular advocate, entomologist Edward O. Wilson. Dawkins' phrase personifies the gene, but the gene had already been the focus of agency talk (e.g., "the morality of the gene") in Wilson's work (Wilson 1971, 1975). Sociobiology, as the study of the relationship between gene populations and animal societies, had some years of serious science behind it before Wilson began to posit a genetic explanation for human social behavior. Although genes were not made the sole source of social behavior, one might easily forget this in reading Wilson's later work. By steps, nature overtook culture in the rhetoric. Genetic determinism was affirmed in image and in story, even while being denied in theory. Pressed on the point in a public forum, Wilson retreated to the claim that genes might account for no more than 15 percent of the variance in human behavior (*Time* 1976); but this is scarcely the impression one gets from his prose, where terms such as *hidden masters* are used to describe genes (Wilson 1978, 4).

It is instructive to consider the trajectory that moved Wilson from ants to the human condition, and from entomologist to cultural analyst, in discourse developed over a period of some years. The final chapter of his 1971 book, *The Insect Societies*, ended with speculation that "the same principles of population biology and comparative zoology that have worked so well in explaining the rigid systems of social insects could be applied point by point to vertebrate animals." In the preface to his 1978 work, *On Human Nature*, Wilson recounted his progression in terms that explicitly suggest the power of the bio-rhetoric he had latched onto. "Unable to resist the rhetoric of my own challenge," he would write, "I set out to learn the large and excellent literature on vertebrate social behavior and wrote *Sociobiology: The New Synthesis*." This book, essentially a textbook, would gain widespread attention and stir controversy, not for the twenty-six chapters examining animal behaviors from a biological viewpoint, but for the final chapter in which Wilson extended his speculation further by envisioning a biological explanation of human behaviors.

This was followed with *On Human Nature*, which was offered as a "speculative essay" on evolutionary theory, the social sciences, and the humanities. Wilson argued here that sociobiology might be the key to closing the gap between the humanistic and scientific cultures. But in the process, he seemed simply to beg the question against those who consider human behavior from any other vantage than that of origins (perhaps giving new meaning to the term "genetic fallacy."):

> Science may soon be in a position to investigate the very origin
> and meaning of human values, from which all ethical pronounce-
> ments and much of political practice flow.

Philosophers themselves, most of whom lack an evolutionary perspective, have not devoted much time to the problem. They examine the precepts of ethical systems with reference to their consequences and not their origins (Wilson 1978, 5).

The gap, he seemed to be saying, would be eliminated simply by leaping over the "nonscientific" approaches. This manifesto had its admirers, particularly among those who felt the one-sidedness of philosophies that cut off ethics from consideration of our biological condition (Hartshorne 1983). And it was a best-selling paperback.

With *On Human Nature*, Wilson's transformation from ant specialist to cultural theorist was complete. He had chronicled it for the reader as a logical development, "a trilogy that unfolded without [his] being consciously aware of any logical sequence until it was finished" (Wilson 1978, xi). One might call this unfolding a logical development, but there is good reason to think of it as a rhetorical one, following as a matter of invention, not as a matter of necessity. Wilson had found a way of moving persuasively from facts. Wilson's program is to reduce social behavior to biology and biology to genetics, or at least to press the reduction for all it is worth. Thus genes appear to control not only individual organisms, but culture as well. Yet the force of this reduction is accomplished more by configuration than by evidence, while the causal connections are inferred abductively, but not tested. Using Wilson's metaphor, genes hold culture "on a leash" (Lumsden and Wilson 1981). On the basis of such metaphors, the reader is moved into new imagistic configurations. From the gene as regulator, for instance, it is really only a rhetorical extension to make the gene a self-directing, self-serving agent, imbued with survival "strategies" and a ruthless nature. This is presumably why altruism becomes a central theoretical problem for sociobiology.

In addressing such issues as altruism, the anthropomorphic overlay on the genetic mechanisms sometimes seems to create more tension than the metaphors can bear. For instance, Dawkins has genes recognizing their own kind in others and enacting some sort of solidarity response when their kin are threatened. Leaving aside the question of how a gene senses the endangerment of its kin, one can see, with this sudden appearance of what by a reasonable behavioral criterion might be called altruism, that the metaphor begins to deconstruct precisely in respect to the defining attribute of selfishness. The gene is utterly self-serving; and yet it sees itself in other genes and identifies so thoroughly with them that it becomes as altruistic as a church-goer for its own kind. Thus its group identification arguably becomes a better explanatory mechanism than is self-preserva-tion. Such are the complications of negotiating imagery, expecially for a bio-rhetoric that seems better suited to supplying an imagery of action than to uncovering technical mechanisms.

One can argue about the limits of the metaphor of selfishness, but it gains its rhetorical thrust from the more basic strategy that portrays genes as agents of control. For there lies the bio-rhetoric in *nuce*. Biology deals with organisms (and populations of them), genes (and populations of them), and environments; and there are specialists in each of these areas. To speak globally about biology and to feature the gene is to make a choice of emphasis with a wide range of consequences. Not the least of these consequences is the tendency to configure the gene as a unitary, seemingly isolable entity (even if it does live in populations). And if it is the under-lying shaper of observable traits, then one is led to think in terms of one-to-one correspondence to a manifest characteristic of the organism—a gene per trait—which is worse than an over-simplification. But such think-ing is fostered not so much by explicit claims about genes as by the rhetoric that is imported once one begins to picture genes as individual actors.

Darwin's account of evolution had stressed the natural selection of the environment, nature's "selective breeder." But the organism "struggled," as Social Darwinists would emphasize, to survive the pressures of the environment. Whether the environment or the organism would be the featured player in the accounts of the life drama would depend on the particular bio-rhetoric chosen. For Lamarckians, organisms were the fea-tured part of the story, with the consequence that some erroneous con-ceptions of their adaptive capabilities were posited. Giraffes stretched their necks to reach high foliage, and so their necks grew. (This is the kind of evolutionary account selected for ridicule by creationists such as Herbert W. Armstrong.) The featuring of organisms and their strivings in this bio-rhetoric made it easy to see evidence of an organism's "success" (e.g., a long neck) in its quest to survive.

Kenneth Burke (1969) has written of the irrepressibility of purpose talk in science, although this goes against the official rhetoric of the sciences. Nature cannot be said to have purposes, as teleological explanations are not considered legitimate in the natural sciences. And yet the language of purposes seems to find its way into accounts of nature nonetheless. Perhaps the human mind is incapable of genuinely understanding a nature without purpose, any more than it can really grasp notions such as determinism, which would make the routine experience of choosing into an illusion. These are terminological embarrassments of science. An official rhetoric

41

of mechanistic causation may therefore find itself subverted by "anthropomorphic" imagery and language. Such language might be described coyly as a matter of mere stylistic convenience, but that will not necessarily diminish its persuasive force in locating *telos* in nature. If Darwin located it in the selecting environment (Nature as "selective breeder") and Lamarckians located it in the purposive organism, Wilson and followers focus on the genes as the direction givers and goal seekers of nature.

A bio-rhetoric that finds in nature itself the definition of long-term, higher purposes reduces the distance between is and ought and helps us manage the tension between them. Both Wilson and Dawkins warn against conflating is's and ought's, or drawing moral or political conclusions from their scientific work. Yet by subtly authorizing "pictures" of a certain sort, such implications seem to follow irresistibly, which is why ideologically left and scientifically astute critics such as members of Science for the People immediately sounded the alarm when sociobiology emerged into discourses about human society (Caplan 1978). They feared the inevitable spinning out of ideological implications—potential naturalization of bad social policies. This recalls other battles, often drawn along ideological lines, between those who find an essentially determinate human nature and those who find it formed by culture. Nature versus nurture is a central polarity in this historical battle which erupted, for instance, in the 1970s controversy initiated by those whose research purported to show that intelligence is biologically linked to race. The aftertaste of that controversy placed certain rhetorical burdens on the sociobiologists.

In responding to the ideological critics, Wilson toned down his own bio-rhetoric in order to play the Humean strategy, that is, to carefully distinguish between technical and normative claims (Albury 1980). Whatever issues were opened at the more purely scientific level, he found the critics' complaints about possible policy implications unfounded and shrill. Wilson does not generally make the mistake of writing anything that would raise the ire of the typical liberal; and he displays a very careful and cautious attitude toward any overt prescription based on the descriptive theory. An antecedent ideology, whatever it may be, does not in itself shape his rhetoric. Its trajectory, like any other that moves from facts to values and on toward policy, is determined within particular contexts, in light of complex purposes and the challenge of opposition.

In *On Human Nature* Wilson does make some surprisingly blunt rhetorical moves against those deemed unscientific. He configures his "new rationalism" against an old way of thinking, associated with religious dogma. The doctrinal subtext is that there are scientific *refutations* for nonrationalistic beliefs (although, of course, adjudication on science's own grounds would simply beg the question), and that these naturalistic positions warrant certain social mores. While upholding his persona as an objective scientist, he cannot help but reveal the moral conclusions of his naturalistic story. The two motifs occur together in passages such as the following:

> The Church takes its authority from natural-law theory, which is based on the idea that immutable mandates are placed by God in human nature. This theory is in error. . . . All that we can surmise of humankind's genetic history argues for a more liberal sexual morality . . . (Wilson 1978, 147).

Here one sees not only genetic history "arguing" for a particular sexual morality, but two versions of the natural law played off against one another, one mediated by interpreters of the holy texts, the other by the sociobiological gene readers. Later he poses scientific materialism as a great epic myth in competition with two others. Marxism and traditional religion (p. 204 ff.). It is of course the "right" myth, steering between two rocky shoals; and the fact that it takes on acceptable targets such as racism and sexism should not obscure the presence of implied values and directionality in the bio-rhetoric.

Again, however, the rhetorical mediation does not have to flow in a predetermined direction. Suppose one were to accept the premise that genes powerfully influence human behavior. What might follow? It would depend on how one played it. The bio-rhetoric adopted by Wilson organizes social talk around the essentially self-interested gene (practicing enlightened self-interest, no less). And the strategy is to suggest complementarity at the level of fact, value, and policy—saying, in effect, that our social world needs to take better account of its natural disposition, or the direction genetic history "argues for." Wilson would have us put philosophical and political thinking on a solid biological foundation. This line of thinking can only be pushed so far before encountering the paradox inherent in suggesting, in effect, that we should strive to make things conform more to their nature (a version of the double bind familiar to all children: "Be yourself!"). How is it, after all, that a new approach to questions about human nature could be more biologically natural than the old ways? In reversing the received wisdom of a culture, might scientific rationalism not be an interference in the natural course of things?

Such paradoxes haunt general doctrines about human nature. This should tell us something about the role of rhetoric in applying these doctrines, and it may be this: universal claims about human nature always have a dialectical underside that can also serve rhetorical ends. Determinism, for instance, holds that our every thought and action is determined; yet its advocates treat it as a proposition to be freely accepted or rejected. Morale boosters are most likely to assure us that humankind is fundamentally good at just those times when the counterevidence is strongest. These and other accounts of human nature are perennially contested, because they are always partial. Consequently, the admonition to make things conform to a uniform rule of nature might prompt a search for a counter-reading and thus the possibility of an opposing rhetorical strategy.

Social theorist Rom Harré shows us a counter-strategy when he advocates putting social institutions in course of correction for the "deficiencies" of nature (Harré 1980). If humankind is by biological predisposition aggressive, selfish, territorial, or whatever, a culture regarding these as dangerous tendencies might structure its institutions to provide a constant countervailing force (playing Hobbes to Wilson's Locke?). Exercises such as this suggest that the claims of the theory of human nature can be aligned to a variety of social conclusions, depending on the path of rhetorical invention. One can "ground" human nature in biology, in society, or in the nature of souls, for instance. Making those alignments is a matter of rhetorical strategy: facts are made to summon a set of values, which are in turn made to summon a policy attitude. This is the power of rhetoric to "prove opposites." In the case at hand one can see two broadly different strategies, which I will call the strategy of complementarity and the strategy of compensation.

The strategy of complementarity is, in effect, to embrace and adopt the "spirit" of some phenomenon, and to "go with" its logic. If the world is a cold, unfeeling place, for instance, then the strategy of complementarity would be to behave in a cold unfeeling manner. One moves "with the flow" of the thing rather than against it. This strategy is often taken in response to some perceived direction of events in the world. For instance, the notion of entropy—the inevitable running down of the universe predicted by the second law of thermodynamics—has been taken by some as warrant for a pervasive fatalism in their personal lives. If the universe is running down, the reasoning goes, then there is surely no call for any heroic effort to better things, since in the end all will come to naught.

The contrasting strategy is the one of compensation, which seeks to make amends for the condition in question. If the world is a cold, unfeeling place, the strategy of compensation would seek to chase the shadows away. Thus, one would urge one's fellows to struggle against the cosmic tide of entropy—to override the deleterious tendencies in nature by continually bringing order out of chaos. What one rhetorical strategy would make a matter of futility, the other would convert to a challenge. In the way they link facts with judgments, the two strategies yield opposites. These strategies can be adapted to a variety of scientific issues in such a way that they quietly naturalize moral judgment. (So, for instance, the "let it burn" policy toward fires in the national parks is fitted to a conception of "nature's way," despite the fact that those forests remain in existence because of human social policy.) These particular strategies represent only two of no doubt many possibilities.

Both Wilson and Dawkins realize that these strategies are possibilities—in fact, Dawkins sometimes seems inclined toward the strategy of compensation (Dawkins 1979, 215). Furthermore, he scrupulously denies that his characterizations carry moral prescriptions (p. 3), although he does not refrain from citing "good genetic reasons" for certain optional human behaviors (p. 134)—quite the little arguers these genes! What he does not seem to understand is that his word choice and imagery are doing prescriptive work for him. It is unrealistic to think that one could unleash a barrage of metaphors about the "gene machine," all suggesting control (cf. Wilson's "hidden masters"), and think that explicit disclaimers of determinism are enough.

In this respect, and through other tell-tale signs, Dawkins shows a surprisingly naive view of language. He repeatedly claims that the comparisons between human behavior and genetic "selfishness" are "only" analogies, all the while building his analysis around the imagery. Language is treated as a transparent medium, only a tool, he tells us, to be used any way we like (p. 20). So what some readers will take as a rather startling revelation—that he has made the gene the fundamental unit of self-interest by definitional fiat—is for Dawkins only a strategy of presentation (p. 35). Language in his account functions only as a set of tools for his purposes, and so he takes responsibility neither for how that language has been used in the past nor for what becomes of it once it falls into someone else's hands. This is no doubt unintentional, as Dawkins otherwise accords to language great powers of social "replication." And he is not alone in failing to anticipate that different user-audiences will find their own uses of the expert's prose (Lyne and Howe 1986).

Another aspect of the unreflective attitude toward language is the failure to notice how the subtle personification of genes might not only influence the perception of human behavior but also have the reverse effect, loading anthropomorphic baggage onto the perception of lower life forms.

45

Kitcher documents blatant examples of imposing notions such as "prosti-
tution," "power," and "rape," which derive much of their meaning from
social understandings, onto flies, ducks, and so on (Kitcher 1985). This is
part of what is meant in saying that a bio-rhetoric makes the different
discursive domains available to one another, and that the flow might be in
either direction.

RHETORIC'S UBIQUITY

It is common to think of discourses in political life as being rhetorical, but
the notion that discourses on scientific matters are rhetorical is still a bit
unconventional. The ethos of modern science as a quest for objectivity has
done much to encourage this limitation of rhetoric's domain. Likewise, it
is common to think of rhetoric in terms of individual discourses rather than
as involving strategies pursued by multiple authors over time and across
contexts. That may be largely a matter of historical circumstance, or
perhaps a consequence of American pragmatic individualism. In its way,
this essay pushes back both those limitations. By positing "rhetorics" that
span and organize discourses past, present, and future, and by focusing on
the notion of a "bio-rhetoric," rooted in scientific talk, we find ourselves in
a position to rethink both of these assumptions side by side.

Some order can be brought to this further exploration by using a basic
communication triangle (writer-text-reader) as heuristic. It would suggest
that rhetoric can be examined for the relationship to its subject matter, or
to its audience(s), or to the writer who creates it; in its reflexive moments
it can be studied in relation to rhetorical practices themselves. These
various relationships can be analytically distinguished, but probably not
concretely isolated. Looking first to the relationship of a scientific rhetoric
to its subject matter, the sense of rhetoric's ubiquity grows, because it can
be seen in several dimensions and functioning over time.

Relationship to Subject Matter

The apparently simple notion of a subject matter is in reality complex and
multidimensional. A subject matter may be constituted historically, for
instance, or as an object domain, as a problem configuration, or as a
method of inquiry. Psychologists, sociologists, and economists may often
look at the same behaviors, but they will likely see them through different
lenses. Furthermore, subject matters can be thought of either *substantially*
or *factorially*. For instance, economics might be conceived either as the
study of certain forms of activity or as the economic *aspect* of all human

activities. These different ways of constituting a subject matter are used for specific purposes, such as distinguishing one intellectual interest from another; but they are not necessarily additive, one to the other, or consistent with each other. They exist relative to purposes.

This relativity in the ways a subject matter can be thought of is not *in itself* rhetorical (nor, in general, is relativity *in itself* rhetorically interesting); but a plurality of standpoints provides both space and incentive for rhetorical activity. In the case of intellectual disciplines, it permits the rhetorical shaping of turf that might with equal rationality be divided any number of different ways. Beyond that, rhetoric has field-defining roles such as configuring activity within a field (distinguishing what is relevant *activity* and what is just background), and marking as legitimate only certain kinds of inferential moves. Other rhetorical tacks toward a subject matter, such as strategies of association and inventional strategies, are not as likely to be bounded by or confined to that subject matter. Rhetoric has access to intellectual subject matters in at least all of the following ways.

1. The existing divisions of intellectual turf are historically shaped as much by rhetoric as by logic or ideology (Gieryn 1983). Sociobiology is especially interesting in this respect because of the way it took shape as a field of research. It had a track record with ants and other animal forms; but as a study of human social behavior it called itself into being by a bold rhetorical gesture. The final chapter of Wilson's *Sociobiology: The New Synthesis* (1975) marked a new constitutive moment when an interpretive logic was extended to the analysis of *homo sapiens*. Moments such as this create the space for disciplines, which then continue to reenact rhetorically the constituting gesture. A rhetoric can further shape the contours of a field through the selection of exemplars, salient issues, and distribution of attention. Sociobiology is contoured around some kernel issues, including altruism, sexual practices, and aggression, but avoids references to past controversies over genes and intelligence, which would make an easy point of entry for critics.

2. A rhetoric configures *activity* within a field so that one can picture the subject matter not just as a state of affairs but as a direction of affairs. This is a key to the moralizing effect, because it implies a hierarchy of goals. The bio-rhetoric characterizing genes as selfish or as holding us on a leash is not merely a stylistic flourish—it is in a very compressed way the picture that the entire rhetoric upholds, whereby the genes become the actors rather than the agencies of biological activity. Configuring activity around a simple image is not unusual in academic discourse, of course. Economics,

for instance, commonly calls up the picture of a commercial exchange involving a Farmer Brown or housewife Jones. Arguably, some such image or metaphor is required to anchor human understanding (Pepper 1942).

3. A rhetoric may take the form of a working logic, establishing (in a prelogical sense) what will "count" as a legitimate inference. A characteristic move in sociobiology is the abductive inference, the positing of an explanatory account from which the facts would follow as a matter of course. Observed patterns of social behavior are taken as a legitimate basis for positing a genetic strategy. Observing the virtually universal incest taboo, for instance, Wilson reasons that such cultural proscriptions would surely arise if there were the slightest genetic disadvantage to inbreeding; avoidance of incest thus becomes a genetic "strategy." Such habitual patterns of reasoning come to seem logically implicative.

Philip Kitcher (1985) has captured the general implicative form in what he calls "Wilson's ladder."

1. Evolutionary theory yields results to the effect that certain forms of behavior maximize fitness.

2. Because these forms of behavior are found in many groups of animals, we are entitled to conclude that they have been fashioned under natural selection.

3. Because natural selection acts on genes, we may conclude that there are genes for the forms of behavior in question.

4. Because there are genes for these forms of behavior, the forms of behavior cannot be altered by manipulating the environment (p. 17).

Between any two rungs on this ladder is a gulf, in which many questions might arise (Is natural selection the only determinant of evolution? Are genes the only, or even the primary, determinants of behavior?) A working logic defines the kinds of questions that can acceptably be ignored. Does the move from Premise 1 to Premise 2 pass without objection, and likewise down the line? If so, then a structure of presumption, a shared field of taken-for-granteds, is at work that is controlled by rhetorical habit, not logic.

The force of habit is important even for straightforward syllogistic reasoning, because deduction always requires additional assumptions (Goedel proved this formally for mathematical systems, and it is *a fortiori* true for ordinary reasoning.) For instance, having an ironclad principle that all sales taxes are regressive, then asserting that X is a sales tax, the logic is able to work only against the backdrop of various assumptions and interpretive

48

judgments. (Does the "all" statement apply only to the U.S. economy? Assuming more or less its current structure? Is X a sales tax in the same sense as intended in the generalization? Can its regressivity be thwarted by countermeasures?) To the skeptic, no logic is so tight as to close all space for doubt that a conclusion must invariably follow; a rhetoric creates expectations that make the room for skepticism to wax or wane.

4. A rhetoric may embed strategies, such as the strategy of association and dissociation, into a subject matter. The reality/appearance pair, for instance, provides a strategy of contrast available within any ideology (Perelman 1969). Sociobiologists use it to regulate a culture's preferred understanding of a social behavior to the status of surface appearance and to present the inferred genetic strategy as the deeper, truer explanation (reality). This ready-made and transportable technique helped sociobiological perspectives to sweep boldly across the social sciences, where the rhetoric was borrowed. Such borrowed rhetorics are bridges among different discursive domains, making it easier to cross from, say, a discourse about biology to a discourse about politics.

5. The selection of discourse strategies is the product of invention—the art of determining "sayables." Traditional rhetorical theories have generated a variety of approaches to invention, usually featuring a checklist of topics or categories to be scanned. There are some such checklists that function as "universals," in the sense that they are applicable to any given issue. In judicial or policy questions, for instance, there are standard categories of "stock issues" to be raised. Other inventional processes are specific to their subject matter and can only be mastered by learning the discursive patterns of the subject matter in question. The rhetoric of Freudianism, for instance, has its own arsenal of strategies, topics, tropes, figures, and so on. Mastering the Freudian technique is in no small part a matter of mastering these resources.

Viewing invention as a rhetorical function (after its serious neglect by the philosophy of science) expands the relevance of rhetoric to scientific reasoning across the contexts of discovery and justification. In fact, it reconstitutes the distinction between these two contexts as one dependent upon the *rhetorical* situation. From the rhetorical perspective, invention is undertaken with an eye toward ultimate justification before some real or imagined audience. There are moments of "going public" that pervade the reasoning process itself—when the reasoner tests an intuition against facts or internalized norms, thinks of a skeptical colleague, structures research with an eye toward public presentation, and so forth. There is not one moment, but rather many moments, when going public in some real or

49

imagined sense moves discourse from the context of discovery into the context of justification. And unless it goes public, it vanishes without a trace.

Rhetoric is no enemy of boundaries per se. Rhetorical processes tend to revitalize and situate boundaries rather than erase them. To think of invention in scientific discourse as rhetorical is thus to deny any fixed line of demarcation between context of discovery and context of justification, due to the flexible and provisional nature of that line. Understanding inquiry as having both public and prepublic faces, constituted in changing rhetorical situations, makes it unnecessary and unhelpful to toss out the distinction altogether, as some have attempted (Weimer 1979).

All of the preceding considerations follow from taking seriously the embeddedness of intellectual subject matters within a social matrix, and are thus far consistent with recent interest in science as a social practice. But scientific discourse is a very special kind of social practice, which more than others is doctrinally committed to discovering its own content, not recovering it from society. It would misconstrue the activity to portray it as merely a form of social recovery, as it would shrink rhetoric to limit it to that. In an important aspect of its tradition at least, rhetoric represents flexibility and possibility. A discourse theory that left no room for the unexpected finding, the unanticipated result, the stubborn resistance of phenomena to social orderings, would fail to accommodate the processes of change and discovery. Peirce calls this resistance "secondness," and it occupies an essential role in his markedly social and rhetorically conscious philosophy of inquiry (Lyne 1980, 1982). Whether conceived in a Peircean framework or not, however, a rhetoric of science must properly take account of the social and objective polarities of scientific discourse.

Just as it would be one-sided to think that inquiry can be a direct engagement with the world, devoid of social mediation, it is also one-sided to think that social mediation is a self-enclosed process unmediated by the world. (Even if one believes with Derrida that there is no "outside discourse," there is always an outside of any given discourse.) Genuine inquiry opens the door to the unforeseen as well as the already planned-for, and a rhetoric, or a rhetorical theory, that inhibits that process would indeed be an obstacle to good science. But I do not mean to give comfort to the disdainers of rhetoric. No excess in rhetorical theory is as likely to cramp insight as much as the calcified antirhetorics in the social sciences, with their almost tyrannical prestructuring of investigation (Bazerman 1987).

Relationship to audience

Even scientific discourse is not constituted just in the relationship between discourse and subject. The role and nature of the audience is an essential factor in understanding how the discourse works and what it must do to be moralized. The invention of a discourse produces an actual performance (the path chosen) which can be seen and judged against the field of possible ones (the accessible inventory). A relationship between the two arises from the mediating role of the audience, because rhetorical choices are made in consideration of an audience. To sever the processes of invention from those of persuasion would be to lose the natural force of attraction that a real or imagined audience can have over the processes of invention and understanding.

Because the moments for a theory's going public are multiple, so therefore are the opportunities for invention. Scientific theories can engage a variety of audiences, ranging from the highly specialized to the laity. What happens when they move among these different audiences is complex, and not simply a matter of "translation" into an accessible language, because these engagements have effects on both the writers and the audience. The notion that there is a simple duality between the technical "sphere" and a public one is useful for certain purposes, but it can greatly oversimplify these multiple engagements and their effects (Lyne and Howe 1986). Part of the audience of sociobiology, for instance, is academics in the social sciences who are neither biologists nor just general readers, and who sometimes adopt its modes of explanation. One of the stalwart critics of sociobiology, Richard C. Lewontin, is critical for instance of what he sees as a would-be intellectual hegemony that provides "a cheap diet of easy explanation for the starving multitudes in the social sciences" (Lewontin 1976).

A desire for naturalizing explanations not only in the social sciences but in the general public exercises a "market" demand for them, which is bound to have effects in recasting the meaning and purposes of scientific theories. The hand of the originator may or may not be conspicuous in this ongoing invention. Darwin's theory began social Darwinism only with a lot of help, but there was no lack of people willing to play midwife. However distant from his work, theories advertised in the name of Darwin carried a rhetorical advantage in the wake of the Darwinian revolution. The craving to ground social thought in the natural world of biology will predictably attach to Wilson or Dawkins, or any other scientist who can serve that purpose (usually connection with a prestigious institution is

51

necessary), and these scientists may lose control of that process to a social environment that selects what it will. Academics, like political figures, seem constantly surprised to see their words taken out of context.

Relationship to the writer

Since its introduction to a general public, sociobiology has gained advocates in a variety of social scientific disciplines, and even followers among poets and literary critics (Kaye 1986; Lewontin et al. 1984; Schwartz 1986). Can practitioners within these fields lay claim to being sociobiologists (with emphasis on the "socio" side), rather than just being influenced by it? The question is not so much one about ontology as about credibility. The "expert" is a pivot point for the intersection of discursive domains, in that he or she makes it possible for nonspecialized publics to tap knowledge they do not directly possess. Expertise is not only a matter of the relationship of a specialist to a body of knowledge; it is also a matter of the relationship to the audience. An expert is one who mediates between the knowledge frames—who can represent psychology to a jury, for instance, or space physics to a congressional committee. To the extent that expertise is played variably before its relevant audiences, it is in part a rhetorical construct. Scientific writers are in a position to "project" their personae as experts in variously useful ways (Lyne 1983).

Wilson and Dawkins show a willingness to achieve certain advantages from being perceived as scientists, but no evident willingness to acknowledge any disadvantage when venturing into moral, philosophical, cultural, or historical issues. In fact, Wilson places himself in a position of implied superiority over philosophers and social scientists who are not sociobiologists—or at least in a position to see through their problems. Perceived competence within a discipline can afford special privileges and immunities, depending on the status of the discipline; the "outsider" status brings privileges and immunities of its own. Scientists who make a literary contribution are welcomed warmly within English departments. Philosophers who leave the gates of the citadel are these days embraced enthusiastically pretty much wherever they choose to pitch camp; but only a courageous few spend time in the world of the natural sciences. One wonders what reception, say, a sociologist might get after venturing into some part of the natural sciences and pronouncing them outmoded. A few speculative exercises such as this should show that the relationships among academic fields are not perfectly symmetrical. In making sweeping claims about human societies, Wilson is rhetorically reenacting some of the asymmetries.

Relationship to rhetoric itself

It is important to be aware of the ways that discourses originating in science may dominate other discourses. When scientific expertise is projected from its home turf onto another, it may be perceived as having more authority than is in fact warranted. Rhetorical analysis has a role to play in following rhetorics within, across, and beyond scientific specialties. Furthermore, it should help us understand the ways that considerations of culture, politics, power, and ideology can influence the discourses of science. There is a two-way flow between culture and science, mediated by discourse.

Positing movement of a strategy from one discourse domain to another also opens the theoretical question of how discourse domains should be understood relative to each other and to everyday discourse. The kind of relationship posited between discourses will have an obvious bearing on how one conceives of any commerce among them. A thoroughgoing rhetorical analysis calls for a theoretical examination of the interchange between different types of discourse, and the context in which such interchange is possible—even the context of contexts, or the inclusive space of communication. Whether or not this requires positing transcendental conditions of a highly abstract sort (Habermas 1971; Apel 1980), which it may, certain rather practical questions about the inclusive space of discourse inevitably impinge on rhetorical analysis. For instance, how insular should scientific discourses be taken to be? To what extent does the language of the polity enter and influence them? To what extent do they infiltrate their surroundings?

Applying such notions as language games, fields, paradigms, and so on, one might be led to expect some self-sufficiency in the separate discourse domains, perhaps even to think of them as hermetically sealed, and this would lead to an underestimation of the ways that special discourse communities are reciprocally influenced by the broader language community. Borrowing from biology instead of physics (and arguably engaging in an incipient bio-rhetoric), it might be more promising to imagine with Levins and Lewontin (1985) any scientific enterprise as surrounded by a semipermeable membrane, able selectively to block passage of content in either direction. Theorizing of this sort, in any case, implicates broader philosophical or political commitments, but it has strong implications for a theory of rhetoric and for rhetorical analysis.

53

CONCLUSIONS

This essay began with a consideration of two different views of the relationship between knowledge and judgments, one of them finding a logical chasm between the two and the other finding them fused through ideology. What I have attempted to show in this exploration of bio-rhetoric is a third position. This position holds that there are inevitable normative lessons in the discourses of knowledge, but that they are carried by a rhetorically mediated relationship not fully controlled by ideology. In this view, ideologies act as broad vectors that meet particular historical situations and are redirected by their encounter with other ideologies, values, and interests. Scientific values, which themselves constitute a kind of ideology, negotiate with political and social agendas. The outcome and thrust of mixing all these vectors cannot be seen in advance, but it can be influenced by the adoption of a rhetoric giving arguers the capacity to direct and filter perceptions by organizing discourses. This does not sully an otherwise clean intellectual investigation. At its best it gives impulse to it by providing inventional strategies and interpretive mechanisms.

At the same time, it would be misleading to assimilate science fully to social discourse, since science is focused on phenomena that are presocial, and not yet squared with what is known and understood. The scientist is not acting just as a voice of society in advancing knowledge claims. Before making a claim, one might say, the scientist is first *staking* a claim, which if redeemed becomes society's. In that sense, science is a discourse of the frontier and a "socializing" of the unknown. It succeeds only if it is accountable to what is on both sides of that frontier—and there are various ways of accountability. The error of scientism is to think that science can meet society strictly on its own terms and rewrite society's rules; the error on the other side is to treat science as though it were not a frontier and thus already fully socialized.

These considerations scratch the surface of rhetoric's involvement with scientific discourses. They are not intended to show rhetoric as a countertheory or an alternative to traditional scientific practices, but rather as a part of those practices. Scientific discourse, at least as it shows up in academic texts, often strikes the pose of being against rhetoric, but this "antirhetoric," as McGee and I call it (McGee and Lyne 1987), is no less a part of the unavoidably rhetorical character of all discourse. One consequence of accepting the ubiquity of rhetoric is that one sees the need for better vocabularies than those that speak only of the presence or absence of rhetoric. Another is that rhetoric alone, without expanding the meaning of the term beyond the power to discriminate, cannot substitute for all the methods, plodding, tools, rationales, and (let us not forget) observables that the various sciences may depend upon. Disclosing the rhetorical elements of doing business should not shut the business down. The job of the rhetorical analyst is instead to raise consciousness of these rhetorical elements, so that intellectual investigation, irreducibly social and communicative, can be held more socially accountable and be more carefully moralized.

REFERENCES

Albury, W. R. 1980. "Politics and Rhetoric in the Sociobiology Debate." *Social Studies of Science* 10 (Nov.): 519–36.

Apel, Karl-Otto. 1980. *Towards a Transformation of Philosophy.* Boston: Routledge and Kegan Paul.

Bazerman, Charles. 1987. "Codifying the Social Scientific Style: The APA *Publication Manual* as a Behaviorist Rhetoric," in John S. Nelson, Allan Megill, and Donald N. McCloskey, eds., *The Rhetoric of the Human Sciences.* Madison: University of Wisconsin Press, 125–44.

Burke, Kenneth. 1969. *A Grammar of Motives.* 3d ed. Berkeley: University of California Press.

Caplan, Arthur L., ed. 1978. *The Sociobiology Debate.* New York: Harper & Row.

Dawkins, Richard. 1976. *The Selfish Gene.* New York: Oxford University Press (reprint 1979).

Gieryn, Thomas. 1983. "Boundary-Work and the Demarcation of Science from Non-Science: Strains and Interests in the Professional Ideologies of Scientists." *American Sociological Review* 48:781–95.

Habermas, Jurgen. 1971. *Knowledge and Human Interests,* trans. Jeremy J. Shapiro. Boston: Beacon.

Harré, Rom. 1980. *Social Being.* Totowa, N.J.: Littlefield, Adams & Co.

Hartshorne, Charles. 1983. *Insights and Oversights of Great Thinkers.* Albany, N.Y.: State University of New York Press.

Kaye, H. L. 1986. *The Social Meaning of Modern Biology.* New Haven: Yale University Press.

Kitcher, Philip. 1985. *Vaulting Ambition: Sociobiology and the Quest for Human Nature.* Cambridge: The MIT Press.

Levins, R., and R. Lewontin. 1985. *The Dialectical Biologist.* Cambridge: Harvard University Press.

Lewontin, R. C. 1976. "Sociobiology—A Caricature of Darwinism," in

Frederick Suppe and Peter D. Asquith, eds., *Proceedings of the 1976 Biennial Meeting of the Philosophy of Science Association, II.*

Lewontin, R. C.; Rose, S.; and Kamin, L. J. 1984. *Not in Our Genes.* New York: Pantheon.

Lumsden, Charles, and Edward O. Wilson. 1981. *Genes, Mind and Culture: The Evolutionary Process.* Cambridge: Harvard University Press.

Lyne, John. 1980. "Rhetoric and Semiotic in C. S. Peirce." *Quarterly Journal of Speech* 66:155–68.

———. 1982. "C. S. Peirce's Philosophy of Rhetoric," in Brian Vickers, ed., *Rhetoric Re-Valued.* Binghamton, N.Y.: Center for Medieval and Early Renaissance Studies, 267–76.

———. 1983. "Ways of Going Public: The Projection of Expertise in the Sociobiology Controversy." D. Zarefsky, M. Sillars, and J. Rhodes, eds. *Argument in Transition.* Annandale, Va.: Speech Communication Association/American Forensic Association, 400–415.

———. 1987. "Learning the Lessons of Lysenko: Biology, Politics, and Rhetoric in Historical Controversy," in Joseph P. Wenzel, ed., *Argument and Critical Practices.* Annandale, Va.: Speech Communication Association/American Forensic Association.

Lyne, John, and Henry F. Howe. 1986. "Punctuated Equilibria": Rhetorical Dynamics of a Scientific Controversy." *Quarterly Journal of Speech* 72:132–47.

———. 1990. "Scientific and Political Rhetorics: Lessons from the Lysenko Episode."

McGee, Michael Calvin, and John R. Lyne. 1987. "What Are Nice Folks Like You Doing in a Place Like This? Some Entailments of Treating Knowledge Claims Rhetorically," in John S. Nelson et al., *The Rhetoric of the Human Sciences.* Madison: University of Wisconsin Press, 381–406.

Pepper, Stephen C. 1942. *World Hypotheses.* Berkeley: University of California Press (reprint 1970).

Perelman, Chaim, and Lucie Olbrechts-Tyteca. 1969. *The New Rhetoric: A Treatise on Argumentation,* trans. John Wilkinson and Purcell Weaver. Notre Dame, Ind.: University of Notre Dame Press.

Peters, John, and Eric Rothenbuhler. 1989. "The Reality of Construction," in *Rhetoric in the Human Sciences,* ed. Herbert W. Simons. London: Sage, 11–27.

Ryle, Gilbert. 1949. *The Concept of Mind.* Totowa, N.J.: Barnes and Noble.

Sahlins, Marshall D. 1976. *The Use and Abuse of Biology.* Ann Arbor, Mich.: University of Michigan Press.

Schwartz, B. 1986. *The Battle for Human Nature.* New York: W. W. Norton.

Time. 1976. "Genes Uber Alles." Dec. 13.

Toulmin, Stephen. 1958. *The Uses of Argument.* Cambridge: Cambridge University Press.

Weimer, Walter B. 1979. *Notes on the Methodology of Scientific Research.* Hillsdale, N.J.: Erlbaum.

Wilson, Edward O. 1971. *The Insect Societies.* Cambridge, MA: Belknap Press of Harvard University Press.

———. 1975. *Sociobiology: The New Synthesis.* Cambridge: Belknap Press of Harvard University Press.

———. 1978. *On Human Nature.* New York: Bantam Books/Harvard University Press.

2

Scientific Discovery and Rhetorical Invention:
The Path to Darwin's *Origin*

John Angus Campbell

The theory of evolution put forth in Darwin's *On The Origin of Species* is justly celebrated as a triumph of scientific thought, a bold integration of biological, geological, and geographic data organized elegantly around a limited set of concepts and principles. In abbreviated terms, natural selection, the explanatory mechanism that characterizes the *Origin* may be summarized as follows: (a) If organic reproduction naturally increases geometrically, and if food supply cannot match this increase, it must be the case that organisms must compete (struggle) for existence. (b) If it is the case that some organisms inherit variations that improve their ability to compete, it will be these organisms that ultimately survive. The process by which organisms vary, compete, change, and survive is evolution. Points (a) and (b) constitute this process; (a) and (b) constitute evolution.[1]

Huxley's famous comment, "How extremely stupid not to have thought of that," illustates how one might be tempted to imagine that a theory so seemingly coherent might have popped full blown into the mind of its discoverer—at least Huxley thought it might easily have occurred to him.[2] Yet even a cursory reading of the "transmutation" notebooks that Darwin kept to record his musings and speculations, discloses a pattern of thinking that could not possibly have been reconstructed or postdicted from a reading of the *Origin*. As David Kohn has observed, a retrospective reading from the perspective of the *Origin* ignores too much of Darwin's thinking. Even when Darwin read Malthus, Kohn observes, he "was not necessarily headed toward the discovery of natural selection."[3]

Darwin's four notebooks on transmutation—labeled *B* through *E*—including the final pages of his earlier "Red" (or *RN*) notebook, in which he recorded his first evolutionary speculations following his voyage on the *Beagle*, provide a remarkably detailed record of his thought. Kept during the period between mid-March 1837 and late 1839, the notebooks record the shifts in Darwin's thinking, from his conversion to transmutation, through his various attempts to reconcile evolution with the prevailing wisdom of his day, to the culmination in his formal "Sketch" of the theory of natural selection in 1842, his longer "Essay" of 1844, his abandoned volume *Natural Selection* (1858) and ultimately the *Origin* (1859).[4]

When one realizes that Darwin's thinking neither conformed to nor was generated out of a neat hypothetico-deductive model, it is tempting to conclude that his thought was illogical. Indeed, as Kohn has argued, Darwin's blindness to the logical inadequacies of his reasoning was central to his genius.[5] An alternative view is that Darwin's notebooks follow an informal logic, a logic of rhetorical invention.[6] Seen from a rhetorical standpoint, the defining feature of Darwin's mind is not "blindness" to errors in logic but sensitivity to the opportunities for reframing the facts available to the scientific community of his day, and for exploiting its central argumentative strategies, imageries, and received wisdom. While the sequence of Darwin's theories defies reduction into any pattern of formal logic—even the specific "problems" they address change over time[7]—Darwin's thought is coherent and, from a rhetorical standpoint, logical. The most noteworthy features of Darwin's mind—his boldness in theorizing, his free use of analogy, the scope of his speculations, his *copia*—his facility at always having at his fingertips a ready a stream of suggestive ideas—testify not only to the fecundity of his genius, but to the thoroughness with which he had absorbed the inventional resources of his tradition.

The purpose of this essay is to summarize and extend earlier accounts of how Darwin came to formulate his theory of natural selection by focusing upon his inventional strategies. Thanks to his notebooks we get an unparalleled glimpse of Darwin's processes of insight and rhetorical invention—of the interrelation in his thought between the quasi-spontaneous forming of new conceptions and his painstaking reconstruction of an intelligible path to make them clear and convincing. Each successive theory gave Darwin a temporary base from which to generate additional lines of defense or rebuttal. As Darwin developed the themes of his argument, the terrain to be encompassed came more sharply into focus, which in turn suggested to him further modifications in the form and substance of his ideas.

In rhetorical terms each of Darwin's theories is grounded in a trope—a central metaphor featuring some aspect of reproduction—and explicated by topics or sequential arguments.[8] That Darwin was unaware during the most innovative period of his career of the formal inadequacy of his reasoning makes him an apt illustration of how the working logic of science is not guided by formal systems but by what Lakoff and Johnson call "partial structures."[9] The partial structures guiding Darwin's thought were the diverse facts, images, and lines of argument from the fields of geology, biology, and natural theology, which he had begun to rethink and reintegrate while aboard the Beagle. Shielded from the radical implications of his thought by his often naive acceptance of the assumptions of his scientific and religious traditions, Darwin was free to engage in an audacious program of restructuring the field-dependent logic on which these traditions were based.

The analysis that follows begins with Darwin's conversion to transmutation following his return from the *Beagle* voyage. The study then sketches pivotal moments in the strategic logic by which Darwin arranged his fund of images and arguments into distinct narratives, until at last he arrived at his mature theory of natural selection.

THE *BEAGLE* VOYAGE AND DARWIN'S CONVERSION TO EVOLUTION

Insight, whether scientific or aesthetic, always emerges from a knowing mind that struggles creatively with prior tradition.[10] The Darwin of the *Beagle* was a promising postgraduate, well grounded in microscopy, with a keen interest and some training in geology, though not a finished naturalist.[11] He was also imbued with the orthodoxy of received religious and scientific tradition. As the meticulous detective work of Sulloway has demonstrated, the assumption that species, while capable of local extremes of variation, were immutable and specially created for the geographical region in which they were found, not only informed Darwin's general view of biology but also structured his collecting procedures. References to "laws" of "creation" mark Darwin's journals and his published *Journal of Researches* contains at least one striking proof of how, despite the diversity of life, nature offers proof that it has only one divine creator.[12] So confident was Darwin that animals were created that neither in the case of the Galápagos mockingbirds—which he fleetingly thought might provide evidence for transmutation—nor of his later famous finches did Darwin note the exact island from which the animals came.[13] Rather than collecting many specimens, as would a post-Darwinian naturalist aware of the importance of variation, Darwin tended to collect only a few specimens of each type, almost as though he had been naturalist aboard Noah's ark. His locality information for the finches was almost all obtained by borrowing from the carefully labeled collections of his shipmates after their return to England.[14]

Darwin not only failed to see proof for evolution in the Galápagos birds, but his trust in conventional classifications and in the creationist assumptions on which they were based led him to overlook the dramatic evidence of the Galápagos tortoises. The tortoises had been classified, or rather misclassified, as *Testudio indicus* on the mistaken assumption that they had been transported to the Galápagos Islands from the West Indies.[15] Although the governor of the islands had told Darwin the tortoises were so distinct that he could tell from which island any particular animal came, Darwin assumed that the animals, having been created somewhere else, were of no special scientific interest. In any event, on the two islands on which Darwin personally saw tortoises—Chatham and James—the tortoises had similar dome-shaped shells. While Darwin explored James Island, Captain Fitzroy had the crew load thirty tortoises from Chatham Island aboard ship. On the voyage home Darwin and his shipmates literally ate their way through the evidence—throwing the invaluable carapaces overboard—as they sailed west across the Pacific.[16] The only carapaces—on which the determination of species is based—to make it to London were two specimens Captain Fitzroy obtained for the British Museum. The two small tortoises to survive the voyage—Darwin had kept them as pets—were worthless as evidence, because only in adulthood do the distinctive differences in the shells emerge. It took Darwin over the next ten years to reconstruct from secondary sources the first-hand evidence of species development he had let pass across his plate.[17]

What broke the hold of orthodoxy for Darwin was not the encounter with nature but conversations with his colleagues over their unexpected interpretations of his collections. John Gould's classification of many of the Galápagos birds as species rather than varieties—including two closely related ostriches from South America (the Orpheus and the smaller Petise, which was new to science)—coupled with George Waterhouse's similar classification of South American mice, shattered Darwin's belief that species were immutable.[18] Richard Owen's evidence that an extinct mammal Darwin had exhumed, the "macrauchenia," was a camel and was thus related to the living South American camel, the llama, confirmed Lyell's law of "the succession of type" and led Darwin to believe in unlimited evolution over geologic time.[19] From the moment that these two classes of data—taxonomy and biogeography—convinced Darwin that evolution was true, he assumed the burden of proof. Henceforth, his task would be "invention"—to redescribe these and all the other relevant data in a manner convincing to his colleagues.

Formidable as was the task of reconciling taxonomy and biogeography with evolution, Darwin's case for evolution was made yet more complicated by the requirement that he integrate into his argument an additional line of proof that had played no immediate role in his conversion. Darwin would have to discover—and his colleagues would demand to know—what microscopic process explained or was at least consistent with evolution.[20] Both in his early speculations and in his mature theory of natural selection, the weakness of the microscopical or hereditary foundation of evolution nearly swamped Darwin's project. When in 1868, Darwin offered his theory of "pangenesis" to counter criticism that natural selection lacked any credible genetic foundation, not even his inner circle accepted it. Not until the twentieth-century rediscovery of Mendel and the neo-Darwinian "synthesis" of the 1940s (Mendelian genetics plus the mechanism of natural selection) would there be a scientifically coherent account of the genetic foundation of evolution.[21] Finally, Darwin would have to propose a theory in keeping with the broader wisdom of his age, both aesthetic and theological.

Why the data of the *Beagle* should have suggested evolution to Darwin and to no one else will remain a mystery. What is clear is the enormity of Darwin's inventional task. When one realizes that Darwin first attempted to explain evolution by a theory of leaps—a matter of filling in the taxonomic and biogeographic gaps by imagining a series of monstrous births— one can appreciate the distance separating Darwin's intuition that somehow evolution was "true" and the arguments that he would have to invent to persuade even a sympathetic colleague that the idea was even remotely plausible.

THE INVENTIONAL STRATEGIES OF DARWIN'S NOTEBOOKS

While a detailed account of each of Darwin's theories is beyond the scope of this essay, a brief analysis of their development is necessary to trace the rhetorical logic common to them all.

Darwin's Initial Theory

Although Darwin's belief in evolution may have begun by an intuitive leap, his attempt to find an argument to support his belief started with a specific example and proceeded by a logic of implication. Darwin begins with the case of the two ostriches and imagines how the second might have emerged from the first: "Speculate on neutral ground of the two ostriches, bigger one encroached on smaller." In the absence of any intermediate forms, he draws a radical if obvious conclusion: "change not progressif‹e›: produced at one blow" (*RN*, 127).[22] Darwin's canvass of evidence to support evolution by leaps is focused equally on physical facts and the psychology of belief.

My idea of Voc: islands elevated then peculiar plants created. if from such mere points; then any mountain, one is falsely less surprised at new creation for large.—Austrailia. = if for volc. isld then for any spot of land. = Yet new creation affected by halo of neighboring continent (RN, 127).

By reasoning topically from "greater to less," or from what Perelman would call "reciprocity," Darwin seems to argue that the principle of sudden emergence ought not to be a barrier to belief in evolution, for leaps are recognized already in the sudden emergence of species on the established creationist view. Darwin's argument here is typical of many of his later appeals. His approach is not so much to oppose creationist modes of reasoning as to subsume them within an evolutionary framework.

Having shown how the principle of evolution by leaps can account for—or is at least compatible with—the known facts of the distribution of species in space, Darwin argues from a parallel case to confirm the operation of this principle over time. "The same kind of relation that the common ostrich bears to (Petisse. . . .): extinct [macrauchenia] to recent [Llama]: in former case position, in latter time" (RN, 130). Since both examples show an absence of intermediate forms, the evidence from both present and past seems to agree. "As in first cases . . . so must we believe ancient ones: not *gradual* change or degeneration. from circumstances: if one species does change into another it must be per saltum—or species may perish" (RN, 130).

With leaps established as consistent with the taxonomic and biogeographic data, Darwin shifts his argument from specific examples to the biological principle underlying them: "Propagation. whether ordinary. hermaphordite. or by cutting an animal in two. (gemmiparous. by nature or accident). we see an individual divided either at one moment or through the lapse of ages" (RN, 132). By moving from the concrete to the abstract—from his examples to "propagation," which is the biological principle that their emergence presupposes, Darwin has arrived at a *topos* that enables him to generate a new series of images through which to envision the evolutionary process as a whole. These images ("ordinary. hermaphrodite. or by cutting an animal in two.") allow Darwin to move from both large to small animals and between sudden and gradual modes of reproduction. Again, as in his survey of geographic evidence, Darwin is concerned equally with the facts and with the psychology of belief. His last line, "we see an individual divided either at one moment or through the

63

lapse of ages," indicates his desire to downplay the precise mechanism and to insist that whatever it is exactly, it is ordinary and unsurprising.

Following his generation of new images for the evolutionary process, and in parallel with his earlier defense of evolution by leaps, Darwin now instantiates his more encompassing principle of propagation in a concrete example using a microscopic animal, the zoophyte: "Therefore we are not so much surprised at seeing Zoophite producing distinct animals. still partly united. & eggs which become quite separate" (RN, 132). In this example Darwin uses fact as metaphor. The zoophyte has some of the features of a plant and some of an animal and poses the same problems as would a plant for distinguishing between the individual and the community. Because of the ambiguities surrounding just how the zoophyte reproduces (Darwin had been studying this very problem aboard the Beagle), it serves him well as a paradigm for his revised image of evolution as a whole.[23] The zoophyte paradigm allows Darwin to equalize all forms of life, animal and vegetable, all forms of reproduction, sexual and asexual, and to combine the individual and the group into a single entity which embodies life, death, division, and continuity over time. Indeed, the image has a distinctly mystical turn: "Considering all individuals of all species as [each] one individual [divided] by different methods, associated life only adds one other method where the division is not perfect" (RN, 132).

As Kohn has noted, Darwin's first theory has transient and permanent features. The mechanism of leaps is transient. As an explanation of evolution, leaps could not be sustained theoretically, for Darwin soon learned that the closest known parallel to them—what domestic breeders called "sports" or "monsters,"—were usually short-lived. Darwin's insight that the mechanism of evolution would turn out to be some aspect of reproduction is permanent and is the basis of each of his subsequent theories.[24] Both the transient and permanent features of Darwin's first theory illustrate the rhetorical character of his logic; Darwin's first theory was generated through an interplay among fact, imagination, the resources of imagery, and the constraints of audience.

Darwin's Second Theory

Darwin's second theory of evolution marks a 180° turn from his first. Whereas his first theory initially moved from taxonomic and biogeographic examples to a general biological principle, his second begins from an explicit biological principle acceptable to his colleagues. The source of the biological principle is unmistakable. In bold capital letters at the top of the

B notebook appears the word *ZOONOMIA*, which had been the title of the medical encyclopedia and evolutionary apology of Erasmus Darwin, Charles Darwin's celebrated grandfather.[25] As with his first theory, Darwin's second is also a theory of reproduction; but whereas the first theory features leaps, the new one is gradualistic and—taking a cue from his grandfather—operates through sexually generated variations. The opening observations of the notebook signal Darwin's dramatic shift in perspective.

> Two kinds of generation: the coeval kind—all individuals absolutely similar. . . .
> The ordinary kind which is a longer process, the new individual passing through several stages (?typical or shortened repetition of what the original molecule has done) (*B*, 1).

These opening sentences recapitulate Erasmus Darwin's distinction between sexual and asexual generation—two processes that Charles Darwin's first theory had conflated—and are a close paraphrase of the theory informing the *Zoonomia*. Drawing out the implications of his grandfather's distinction, Darwin poses a further question, "Why is life short, why such high object," and leaps to the conclusion—"generation." He then defends his answer by argument from analogy:

> We *know* world subject to cycle of change, temperature and all circumstances, which / influence living beings.
> We see . . . the young of living beings become permanently changed or subject to variety, according «to» circumstance,—seeds of plants sown in rich soil, many kinds are produced, though new individuals produced by buds are constant; hence we see generation here seems a means to vary or adaptation.—Again we «believe» «know» in the course of generation even mind and instinct becomes influenced. . . . therefore generation to adapted and alter the race to a changing world (*B*, 3–4).

From the standpoint of formal reasoning, the most obvious feature of this passage is its ad hoc assumption that variation is automatically adaptive. Darwin's "error" is to assume that since the earth changes, and animals vary through sexual generation, geological change produces directional change in animals and plants. Darwin has taken an analogy—both the earth and animals change—and affirmed a causal relationship—geological change brings about evolution—without offering any explanation to account for how the environment acts on the reproductive systems of plants and animals to produce variant offspring automatically adapted to their changed settings.[26]

From the standpoint of informal logic, an additional feature of Darwin's opening passage deserves notice—how he uses conventional scientific and theological argument to make transmutation potentially acceptable to his peers.

Darwin has made a significant advance in audience adaptation in his second theory by presenting evolution as the counterpart of the gradualistic explanations characteristic of uniformitarian geology. Charles Lyell, whose *Principles of Geology* Darwin had read aboard the *Beagle* (the second volume reached Darwin at Montevideo), opposed geological catastrophism—the theory of sudden changes—by a theory of uniformitarian geology asserting the uniform operation in times past of the same causes, operating at their same rates and intensities, as are observable in the present.[27] By tying his sexual-generation theory to environmental change, Darwin reasserts a fortiori that "we see the young . . . permanently changed or subject to variety, according to circumstance." In Perelman's terms, a fortiori argument constitutes a *double hierarchy*: an analogical link between two separate categories in which one feature or set of features assumed to be true in the first is predicated to be true of the second.[28] The advantage of the double hierarchy is its heuristic and suasory power. By analogically tying biology to uniformitarian geology, Darwin discovers a way of predicating of biology the same quantitative and qualitative changes already known to operate in geology.

The double hierarchy would be a natural way for Darwin to approach the task of discovery, since it embodies the *vera causa* principle that he inherited from Newtonian science via Scottish common-sense philosophy. According to this principle a "true cause" must first be known independently of the phenomenon it is supposed to explain.[29] Technically, the parallel between sexual generation and uniformitarian geology is scientifically underdeveloped, since Darwin does not explain the precise mechanism by which the earth and the organism interact. However, as a plausible "place-holding allusion"—a means to identify and reserve a place within convention where a scientifically detailed explanation could be developed—it is a significant advance.[30] Through it Darwin has cleared a semantic space within tradition where a radically naturalistic style of explanation recognized in geology and even in the prestige science, physics, could be developed and applied to biology.

Not only has Darwin's sexual-generation theory given him a stronger connection with his scientific colleagues, both in terms of evidence and philosophy, it has also given him a stronger tie with natural theology. While Darwin's theory of "leaps" might seem supernaturalistic, it marked in fact a significant rebellion against traditional natural theology. Darwin's focus on animals in his theory of leaps, which did not illustrate the fine "fit" between organic structure and environment, put him in opposition to a major theological theme common to many of his colleagues: the adaptation of animal and environment.[31] It also put him out of touch with a significant class of arguments that could be turned into proofs for evolution.

In his second theory, by stressing the reciprocal nature of biological and environmental change, Darwin positions himself to subsume traditional arguments for "design" in nature within an evolutionary framework. In affirming evolution Darwin has not radically challenged natural theology. Rather, he has shown that in biology—as in geology—the hand of God is to be seen through the operation of observable causes, not in miraculous suspensions of natural laws. Darwin would repeat this same line of argument in his citations from Butler, Bacon, and Whewell on the flyleaf of the *Origin*.[32]

Having enunciated a principle consonant with the scientific and theological perspectives of his audiences, beliefs Darwin himself shares, he then proceeds—in parallel with the pattern of his first theory—to test it against the taxonomic and biogeographic data. Consistent with a rhetorical logic, Darwin does not develop the biological details of his theory; rather he proceeds argumentatively by showing that his new strategy of explanation is capable of addressing obvious objections and of further subsuming traditional aesthetic and theological categories to evolution.

An obvious objection to Darwin's second theory is that nature does not display anything like the quantity of variation that the theory of sexual generation would lead one to anticipate. If evolution works through or upon an inexhaustible supply of sexually generated variations, why do we not find more varieties in nature than we do? Why are species so remarkably stable?[33] Darwin responds to this implied objection by extending the parallel with geology and by applying to evolution the traditional characterization of nature as a great system of harmonious providentially directed laws: "With this tendency to vary by generation, why are species all constant over whole country. Beautiful law of inter-marriages partaking of characters of both parents and then infinite in Number" (B, 5).

The image, or "scene," governing this passage, as captured by the expression "over whole country," is a continent. Darwin's argument is that while animals over this continent will vary by region—as one would expect from his sexual generation model of evolution—another law, blending inheritance, will average out these specific variations. Blending inheritance, rather than being an objection to evolution, is actually, Darwin argues, one of its agencies. Through blending, Darwin asserts, species will be adapted to long-range average geological changes, not simply to regionally particular ones. The end result will be the stable species which in fact we see.[34]

Rhetorically remarkable in this passage is Darwin's ability to prove opposites—to turn the most obvious and seemingly unchallengeable arguments for species permanence into supports for evolution. By linking two aspects of generation, the production of variation that is characteristic of the individual, and the opposite aspect, blending or averaging characteristic of the mating pair, Darwin subsumes permanence into a larger dynamic of change. Darwin identifies the mating of two individuals— which, on the blending theory of inheritance, should cancel the effect of individual variation—as the means of preserving the average variation between them! While his assertion that the preservation of variation is the function of blending does not prove that it is, his dynamic interpretation is, at the very least, consonant with the evidence. Further, by taking his point of departure from animals that are well adapted to their settings, unlike the ostrich and llama, which seemed to illustrate the independence of organic structure from environment, Darwin positions his evolutionary argument on the same ground as natural theology, which emphasized the perfect adaptations between organism and environment. The expression "beautiful law of intermarriages" subsumes to Darwin's evolutionary argument the aesthetic theme of traditional natural theology: the divine harmony manifested by nature's laws.

In addressing one objection—how an inexhaustible supply of individual variations can be consistent with species stability—Darwin's continental model has generated another. By uniting evolution to a model of uniformitarian geology in his continental model, Darwin indicates circumstances in which evolution *might* occur, but he does not offer a clear or compelling picture of speciation—how new groups of organisms systematically diverge from old ones. Lyell had attempted to rebut in advance any theory of evolution that would apply his own principles to biology. Relying on such examples as the mummified animals of Egypt, Lyell claimed that species in fact had not changed appreciably over time and that there could be no biological corollary to the incremental processes that he had established for geology.[35] In answering Lyell,

Darwin takes a page from Lyell's own book and turns his key objections against him:

> Aegyptian cats and dogs, ibis—same as formerly, but separate a
> pair and place then fresh island, it is very doubtful whether they
> would remain constant; is it not said that marrying-in deteriorates a
> race, that is alters it from some end which is good for man.—/
> Let a pair be introduced and increase slowly, from many
> enemies, so as often to intermarry—who will dare say what result.
> (B, 6–7)

By arguing that the animals of Egypt have not changed because Egypt has not changed, and by imagining a newly formed island that would favor organic change, Darwin presents a plausible argument for evolution as a corollary of uniformitarian geology. By asserting the competence of slight variations to produce directional change, he has also displaced the notion of creation as proceeding "each according to his kind," while leaving open—or rather relativizing—the notion of creation as sudden. On Darwin's island model, evolution would be directional and would take place far more rapidly than on a continent. Darwin's continental and island models of evolution taken together present two highly visual accounts of evolution, which, by using Lyell's principles to answer Lyell's objections, subsume the supposedly antievolutionary uniformitarian model of reasoning into an evolutionary frame of reference and leave Darwin free to argue—as occasion requires—that evolution is either slow or relatively rapid.[36]

In his opening case for gradual evolution by sexual generation, Darwin has done more than subsume Lyell's principles. He has also appropriated Lyell's very style of presentation. The key to Lyell's rhetorical power was his ability to depict the world (in Lyell's case the stupendous effects of unremarkable causes: wind, water, subsidence, and continental uplift) so that the reality described seemed to be unfolding before the reader's very eyes.[37] Darwin's brief sketch of the island model of evolution, followed by his invitation to the reader (at this point himself) to extend received principles to complete the narrative ("who will dare say what result") is Lyell's very technique and underscores the cognitive function of style both in discovery and in justification. Despite the vast difference in theoretic foundations separating Darwin's early notes from his mature work, compelling visual description makes the opening paragraph of notebook B ("We know . . . we see . . . again we know. . . ." [B, 1–3]) prophetic of the Origin's first chapter: "When we look . . . when we reflect . . . I think we are driven to conclude."[38] Comparable to Galileo's "common sense" examples and experiments, which established Copernicanism as compatible with observation, Darwin has shown vividly how conventional facts and lines of argument that seemed to tell exclusively for the permanence of species are compatible with—and may even demand—an evolutionary explanation.[39]

But now, one and one-half pages into his notebook, Darwin faces a new explanatory difficulty, or rather an old one in a new guise. Will his gradualist theory, which he has advanced successfully thus far, be able to give a gradualist interpretation to his initial examples: the ostriches, macrauchenia, and llama? As he surveys the biogeographic evidence, the data on the whole seem to favor his new interpretation. "As we thus believe species vary, ‹in› changing climate we ought to find representative species; this we do in South america closely approaching." But, as he returns to his initial examples, he reintroduces a telling caveat: "We must suppose the change is effected at once,—something like a variety produced—every grade in that case [it] seems is not / produced" (B, 8). Darwin's hesitation between leaps and gradualism as he returns to the ostriches, macrauchenia, and llama reveal two major problems which his second theory has yet to overcome.

First, and most obviously, Darwin faces the question of whether the biogeograpic data can be best accounted for on the basis of gradualism or leaps. Is Darwin's second theory universally generalizable, or is evolution mostly gradual with an occasional saltation? Second is the issue of extinction: Is there some biological law that regulates the duration of species as some similar law regulates the length of the life of an individual? Darwin, initially at least, thought there was, and this is why extinction is the decisive issue on which the resolution of the biological foundation for his first explanatory theory will turn. Just as Darwin relied on analogy in his attempt to reconcile biogeography with his sexual generation theory, so Darwin also relies on analogy in his quest for a model of life on which to ground that theory biologically. Once Darwin resolves how individual and species development are alike, he uses the result as his premise for arguing whether or not the absence of transitional grades between species means there really were none or whether the transitional forms have merely not been preserved (B, 37–38).

Darwin's manner of addressing both these issues, the question of leaps vs. gradualism and the question of the hereditary grounding of evolution, reveals a marked symmetry between his first and second theories and clarifies further the structure of his inventional logic.

In his first theory Darwin follows his initial survey of the biogeographc evidence, which he thought favored leaps, with an investigation of the hereditary foundation of the evolutionary process. This second phase, when Darwin used the zoophyte as the paradigm for the evolutionary process prepared the way for Darwin's sexual-generation theory by identifying "propagation" as the common principle uniting his examples (RN, 132). Despite their marked differences in content, Darwin's first and second theories of evolution follow the same two-part arrangement. In notebook B, following the formulation of his new principle of sexual generation, Darwin once again argues that his theory was supported by biogeographic evidence (B, 1–3). His return at the end of the biogeographic survey we have just reviewed to the examples from which his evolutionary speculations first began marks the approximate point where he resumes speculation on the hereditary underpinnings of the evolutionary process.

As in his first theory, where he clarified the meaning of "propagation" by surrounding the concept with a plethora of microscopic images, Darwin once again generates an inventory of images—this time interspersed with queries—to discover resources of argument that might clarify the biological foundation for evolution.

> If we suppose monads are constantly formed, would they not be pretty similar over the whole world under/similar climates and as far as world has been uniform at former epoch. How on this Ehrenberg?
>
> Every successive animal is branching upwards different types of organisation improving as Owen says simplest coming in and most perfect and others occasionally dying out; . . . .
>
> We may look at Megatherium, Armadillos and Sloths as all offsprings of some still older type. Some of the branches dying out.—
>
> With this tendency to change (and to multiplication when isolated) requires deaths of species to keep numbers/of forms equable. But is there any reason for supposing number of forms equable: This being due to subdivisions and amount of differences, so forms would be about equally numerous.—
>
> Changes not result of will of animals, but law of adaptation as much as acid and alkali.
>
> Organized beings represent a tree, *irregularly branched*; some branches far more branched, —hence genera.—As many terminal buds dying, as new ones generated./ There is nothing stranger in death of species, than individuals (B, 18–22).

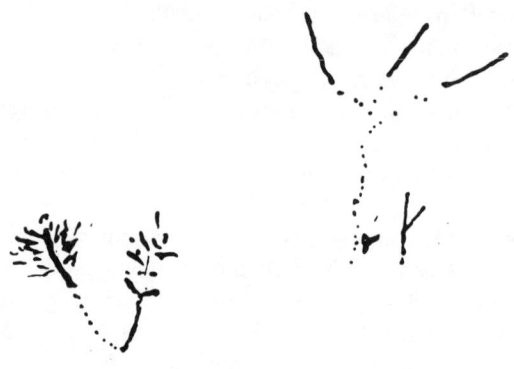

Fig. 2.1

In these passages we find Darwin attempting to identify some better-known process—in this case some process governing the development of the individual—and then arguing a fortiori that the same process will explain the development of species. The problem of extinction, as captured in his final observation about the tree, is especially illuminating. In the middle of the page containing these notes, Darwin has drawn two small models (see Fig. 2.1) of forked trees, each with straight, short, deadening branches (B, 26). Darwin clearly wants to be able to say that such and such a microscopic process allows the macrobiological tree to keep branching, but he cannot. To avoid the difficulty, Darwin considered changing the metaphor from the "tree" to the "coral" of life, but he realized that this would not solve the problem either (B, 25).

Darwin's microscopic thought is caught in a dilemma. If he acknowledges that species development cannot be modeled on individual development, then, having given up one-half of his double-hierarchy argument, he cannot ground species development in some process of growth already better known to his audience. If he persists in affirming the parallel between individual and species development, he ends up with a dead tree. Darwin's vitalism—his belief that life possesses an inherent developmental tendency—and his quest for a workable analogy between individual and species development are at cross-purposes.

The theoretical problem at the heart of Darwin's microscopical quandary has been brilliantly illuminated by the recent work of Philip Sloan.[40]

72

While the details of this issue would take us far beyond the limited purposes of this essay, a brief sketch of Darwin's manner of "resolving" this difficulty demonstrates the close relation between *invention* and *disposition* in Darwin's process of discovery.

To complement on the microbiological level the a fortiori pattern of reasoning that he established on the macrobiological level, Darwin needs to identify a process better known to his colleagues, which he can then use to ground a narrative for evolution. Darwin constructs this narrative from materials imported from Germany and relayed to him through a series of conversations with Richard Owen, whose taxonomic work was instrumental in Darwin's evolutionary conversion, as we noted earlier. During Darwin's absence on the *Beagle*, Richard Owen (along with many younger British scientists) had studied in Germany, learned the language (as Darwin was painfully to do following his voyage), and returned as a disciple of the biologist Johannes Muller. Two of Muller's ideas, as mediated by Owen, were especially central for Darwin. First, Muller's notion of "vitalist materialsm" enabled Darwin to connect matter with life and to shed his early belief that life was a property "superadded" (presumably miraculously) to matter. According to Muller, life was analogous to a chemical reaction in being a property of matter under certain modes of organization. Second was Muller's theory of the germ. Muller held that the adult organism was not—as had been held by Haller and Bonnet in the eighteenth century—"preformed" in the germ, but that the organism took its specific path of development under the force of "irritability" in interaction with its environment.[41] Muller's "irritability" theory of the germ and Darwin's environmentally centered sexual-generation theory were thus complementary.

Darwin, however, faced a major problem in using Muller's theory of individual development as a biological foundation for evolution. Muller held that the development of the germ was governed by the principle of "the conservation of force." According to this principle, the germ developed under the pressure of irritability until it achieved an equilibrium between an internal momentum sustainable by its developing parts and exernal pressures. When the germ reached the maximum of complexity, the life force (*lebenskraft*) sustained itself by giving birth to a new germ. All this was useful to Darwin—but for one snag. Muller's "conservation of force" principle affirmed an inverse relation between complexity and the amount of vital force remaining to power further development in the individual. This was the unresolved theoretical issue behind the deadening branches of Darwin's taxonomic tree. The successful completion of the second half of Darwin's double-hierarchy argument was foiled by a double bind! Converting Muller's ideas about the development of the germ into an argument for the evolution of species could be done but, a fortiori, the biologically exhausted species would promptly go extinct.[42]

After three and one-half pages of struggle, Darwin rescued Muller's germ theory from theoretical defeat as a micro model for the evolution of species by a simple *partitio*. Drawing on his own microscopical research, Darwin distinguished between the germ, which Muller took to be the ultimate biological reality, and the granules within the germ, which Darwin knew from his botany training at Cambridge and from his own observations on the *Beagle*, were nearly identical in both plants and animals. The breakthrough passage in the notebooks reads:

> If we ‹suppose› «grant» similarity of animals in one country owing to springing from one branch, & the monucle [germ] has definite life, then all die at one period, which is not case, : MONUCULE [germ] NOT DEFINITE LIFE (B, 35).

Immediately following the entry is a new taxonomic tree with ramifying branches explaining how widely separated branches, labeled A–D, could have been connected by intermediate steps that now are extinct. A note makes specific application of the diagram (fig. 2.2) to the troublesome ostriches, discussed earlier (B, 36).

Darwin's biogeographic, taxonomic, and hereditary problems were all "resolved" at the same time. Even as Darwin had earlier argued that his sexual-generation theory was consistent with a uniformitarian view of biogeography, so now he could argue that Muller's rearranged germ theory explained the biological foundation of species development. Gradualism was triumphant on both the macro and the micro levels: one double hierarchy explained sexual generation as the biological corollary of uniformitarian geology, and another explained the development of species as a corollary of the development of individuals.[43] Darwin's initial vision of evolution as somehow powered by reproduction, which was in turn somehow directed by the changing physical environment, if not proved, was now biologically intelligible and rhetorically (at least) plausible. Not direct observation of nature, but the topic "possible and impossible" (if an individual can develop, so can a species) was the pivot of Darwin's reasoning. According to Darwin's new way of reading the evidence, the granules within the germ were virtually eternal and would continually regenerate the species. Extinction was to be explained by the environment changing faster than could the animals: "Therefore that death of species is

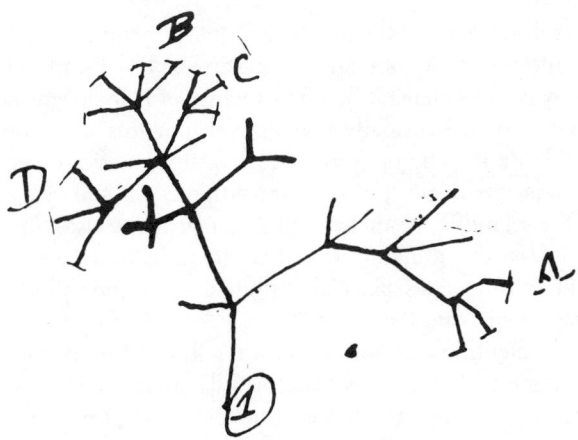

Fig. 2.2

a consequence (contrary to what would appear from America) of non adaptation of circumstances" (B, 38). The part of Muller he could not use—the "conservation of force" principle—he simply set aside. In place of it, Darwin put his own theory of eternally regenerating granules and thereby kept the developmental part of Muller's theory, which he needed if he was to complete his analogy between individual and species development.

That Darwin knew his logic was speculative, or what we have called *rhetorical*, is indicated by a note immediately following his synthesis of the micro and macro dimensions of his speculations: "Heaven knows whether any of this agrees with nature." followed by the Spanish word *Cuidado* ("caution") (B, 44). As Sloan noted, far from being essentially mechanistic in spirit or substance, the biology undergirding Darwin's initial views of evolution had deep roots in German *naturphilosophie* and was vitalistic through and through.[44] Darwin's philosophic vitalism had a rhetorical corollary: the profound empathy for nature's suffering and beauty that Darwin eloquently expressed in his notebooks and in his mature works was more than "merely" metaphoric; it was the outgrowth of an aboriginal perspective that saw each plant and animal not as shaped from without by external agency but as animated from within by laws unique to its organization.

75

Conceptual Consolidation: Lamarck, Aesthetics, and Theology

With the subsumption of the major facts of taxomomy, biogeography, and heredity into his theory of sexual generation—all within the first twenty-five or so pages of notebook B—the structure of Darwin's principal preselectionist theory is essentially complete. From this point on, Darwin's inventional task is to tie up loose ends.[45] Darwin's efforts were scientific, aesthetic, and theological. While, for purposes of analysis, we may distinguish the scientific, aesthetic, and theological aspects of the notebooks, we distort Darwin's thinking if we treat them as separate, for they were equal and simultaneous parts of a unified evolutionary vision of God, natural law, man, and the world.[46]

The key scientific addition to Darwin's thought following his biogeographic and hereditary synthesis was his subsumpton of Lamarck. Darwin was led to Lamarck by his interest in understanding the precise means by which the changing environment and the living organism interacted. His increased theoretical appreciation of the relation between reproduction and environment (which we examine more fully in the next section) in turn encouraged his reading of the literature of domestic breeders. Aside from explicit references to Lamarck, the key proof of Lamarck's influence on Darwin is the phrase "changes of habit precede changes in structure."[47] To the extent that there was any difference between Darwin and his French predecessor, it was one of emphasis. Where Lamarck stressed the conscious will of the animal, Darwin emphasized how environmental change automatically brought about changes in the "habits" of organisms. Scientifically, Darwin's incorporation of Lamarck into his own theory underscored his belief that animal psychology held the key to evolutionary change;[48] rhetorically Darwin's subsumption of Lamarck was a further instance of his search for acceptable premises that could advance the argument for evolution.

Darwin's use of Lamarck's theory is paralleled by his exploration and incorporation of aesthetic and theological arguments. While it is all but impossible for the modern reader of the notebooks not to think that he or she is following Darwin on a "path" which would inexorably "lead" to natural selection, natural selection was not the predictable outcome of Darwin's thought.[49] Throughout most of the notebooks, Darwin is convinced he has discovered the explanation of evolution already. If there was a problem with which Darwin continued to struggle, it was with the problem of meaning—to find in the new world his thought was opening a fresh anchor for traditional aesthetic, moral, and theological beliefs. Darwin's manner of addressing this problem would contribute significantly to the success of his strategies of exposition throughout the *Origin*, and to the social meaning of his metaphor, "natural selection."

In the justly celebrated final sentence of the *Origin*, Darwin affirms: "There is grandeur in this view of life with its several powers having been originally breathed into a few forms or into one and whilst this planet has gone cycling on according to the fixed law of gravity from so simple a beginning endless forms most beautiful and most wonderful have been and are being evolved."[50] The coherent aesthetic, theological, and scientific vision presented in that statement was itself one of Darwin's major discoveries, and the fruit of as much concentrated reflection as any of his scientific concepts. In the earliest prototype of what was to become the *Origin*'s conclusion, antedating the theory of natural selection by a year, Darwin placed evolution in the context of the classical theological justification of science since Galileo:[51]

> Astronomers might formerly have said that God ordered each
> planet to move in its particular destiny.—In same manner God
> orders each animal created with certain form in certain country,
> but how much more simple and sublime power let attraction act
> acording to certain law, such are inevitable consequences—let
> animal be created then by the fixed laws of generation such will be
> their successors. Let the powers of transportal be such, and so will
> be the forms of one country to another. —Let geological change go
> at such a rate, so will be the number and distribution of the
> species!! (*B*, 101–102).

The close parallel of this passage with its explicit affirmation of God as creator and its extended anaphora "let attraction act . . . let animal be created . . . let the powers of transportal be such . . . let geological changes go at such a rate. . . ." to the language of *Genesis* can hardly be accidental. In a similar passage Darwin presented evolution as "far grander" and more in keeping with the dignity of the God "who . . . said let there be light & there was light" than was the idea that the separate species of rhinoceros found on the islands of Java and Sumatra were created by individual miracles. Darwin concluded his rhinoceros entry with the curt comment "bad taste" (*D*, 36–37). In an earlier entry he observed of special creation "miserable limited view" (*B*, 216).

While most of Darwin's speculations on the grandeur of creation move within the affective spareness of Deism, the strand of vitalist materialism in his thought finds expression in a robust immanentist mysticism. In one of the most haunting and eloquent passages in the transmutation notebooks, or for that matter in any of his writings, Darwin observes:

> if we choose to let conjecture run wild, then «our» animals—our fellow bretherin in pain, disease death, suffering «& famine»; our slaves in the most laborious work, our companion in our amusements, they may partake, from our origin . . . in one common ancestor we may be all netted together (B, 232).

As this comment begins to suggest, Darwin's aesthetic and religious reflections encompassed a range of expository and suasory options; they were not merely repetitions of convention. When Darwin observes, "Once grant that «species» [and] genus may pass into each other . . . & whole fabric totters & falls. —Look abroad, study gradation, study unity of type,—Study geographical distribution. / study relation of fossil with recent. the fabric falls" (C, 76), we hear a persona whose aesthetic and theological views were far from conventional and—in Darwin's published works—carefully suppressed. This same persona reemerges when Darwin calmly speculates on the extinction of man: "But man—wonderful man . . . he is not a deity, his end under present form will come" (C, 77; also B, 252, E, 49) and anticipates his replacement by a more highly evolved intelligent being.

Darwin's aesthetic and theological speculations show his notebooks are only partially exercises in technical reason. The rhetorical legacy of Darwin's aesthetic and theological speculation is neither negligible nor incidental; it appears in the Origin's magnificent final sentence, in his numerous descriptions of animal heroism and dignity, in his celebration of nature's tragic beauty, and in the fruitful ambiguity of his trope, "natural selection."[52]

Darwin's "Path" To Natural Selection

In contrast to his earliest speculations, in which Darwin freely compared nature with domestic breeding (B, 6), his developed theory of sexual generation presented nature and domestic breeding as opposed.[53] In his mature sexual-generation theory, Darwin saw nature as producing adaptations, whereas breeding perpetuated "monstrosities" by art. Darwin's initial rereading of Malthus did not reverse this contrast. Rather than precipitating a sudden leap in his invention, Darwin's initial rereading of Malthus occasioned only a shift in his arrangement.

The transformation of Darwin's stark contrast between breeding and evolution into a comparison took place in two stages: one before Darwin read Malthus and one after. One support for Darwin's contrast between breeding and evolution was his belief that nature, in operating over eons on a species, changed the whole breed, body and psyche, whereas the breeder changed only superficial features of the animal—length of limbs, body size, thickness of fur, etc.—but not the psychology of the type. The evidence that changed Darwin's mind about the extent of the breeder's power to modify animals was the account he read of the history of a purely man-made animal—the greyhound.

Through reading and through his discussions with breeders, Darwin discovered that the precursors of the greyhound, while svelt in form, were less than ideal as runners. The problem was that they were too timid to run up hill! Only when the early greyhounds were crossbred with bulldogs did they acquire the combination of fleetness and drive found in the contemporary animal. [54] While the greyhound example modified Darwin's view of the breeders' power, it did not suggest a new analogy between breeding and nature. Only one month before reading Malthus Darwin observed: "State broadly scarcely any novelty in my theory, only slight differences, the opinion of many people in conversation. The whole object of the book is its proof" (D, 69). That Darwin's reading of Malthus did not suggest any analogy with breeding is evident by the language in which he recorded his response:

> Even the energetic language of Decandolle does not convey the warring of the species as inference from Malthus. . . . I do not doubt every one till he thinks deeply has assumed that increase of animals exactly proportionate to the number that can live. . . .
>
> Population is increase at geometrical ratio in FAR SHORTER time than 25 years—yet until the one sentence of Malthus no one clearly perceived the great check amongst men. . . . Even a *few* years plenty makes population in man increase & an *ordinary* crop causes a dearth. . . . One may say there is a force like a hundred thousand wedges trying [to] force every kind of adapted structure into the gaps in the oeconomy of nature. or rather forming gaps by thrusting out weaker ones (D, 134e–135e).

The expression *adapted structure* signals that what Darwin initially found in Malthus was not a new theory but a new argument further supporting his previous theory of automatically adaptive variations! What Darwin initially saw in Malthus was not an analogy with domestic breeding but with Lyell's *inter*specific competition, which he had incorporated already into his argument. Even as Darwin had given an evolutionary interpretation to Lyell's claim that small differences in physical environment explained the geographical distribution of species, he similarly used Malthus's *intra*specific competition to explain how automatically adapted structures would reach their proper niches. By construing inter- and intraspecific competition as analogous, Darwin could show how small differences in structure could determine the outcome of both.[55]

While Darwin has clearly gained a new idea from Malthus, intraspecific competition, and has made an analogy between it and interspecific competition, he has not yet drawn the crucial implication that species are only differentially adapted to their settings. Before as well as after reading Malthus, Darwin continued to believe that variations were automatically adaptive—that is, providentially guided. As Hodge and Kohn put it, "His talk of sorting is only to indicate the expansion and retention of the adapted and its corollary the . . . elimination of others. . . . but there is no allusion to the breeders' art."[56] Darwin's first response to Malthus was not to abandon his previous theory and formulate a new one, but to incorporate Malthus into the structure of his sexual-generation theory as a new strategy of exposition, just as he had earlier incorporated Lyell, Muller, Lamarck, and traditional aesthetic and theological arguments. Only gradually in the weeks and months that followed did Darwin realize that, given Malthus's population dynamics, variations were only differentially, not immediately adaptive, and that what he had in Malthus was not a new strategy of argument, but a radically new—and as yet unnamed—theory. As he remarks on 1 November 1839, "‹Species. are innumerable variations›. Every structure is capable of innumerable variations, as long as each shall be *perfectly* adapted to circumstances of times. . . . these variations tend to accumulate" (*E*, 57).

Having arrived in the late autumn and early winter of 1838–39 at a genuinely novel theory, Darwin now faced an equally novel problem of invention. In affirming differential adaptation, Darwin had not only arguably broken with the circular character of his earlier reasoning, but he had also broken with a significant cultural parallelism which made his sexual theory so plausible for so long—the idea of direct providential direction. For a culture accustomed to seeing everywhere in nature the marks of providential foresight, power, and goodness, differential adaptation would be very difficult to believe; indeed it would seem ridiculous. It is hardly to be wondered that Darwin, who in each of his theories was careful to present his views as implications of already accepted premises, would feel this breech in social logic acutely.

At first, following his rereading of Malthus (at the end of notebook *D*)

Darwin drew no explicit connection between Malthus's population dynamics and the practice of domestic breeding. Then, late in notebook *E*, Darwin asks, "Are the feet of water-dogs at all more webbed than those of other dogs? —if nature had had the picking she would make such a variety far more easily than man, —though *man's practiced* judgment even without time can do much" (*E*, 63). On the next page the analogy is made fully explicit. "It is a beautiful part of my theory, that domesticated races of organics are made by precisely same means as species—but latter far more perfectly & infinitely slower" (*E*, 71).

This last passage is especially important, as it illustrates the complex interplay between the order of discovery and the order of justification in structuring the exigence that gave rise to Darwin's theory of "natural selection." Contrary to the a fortiori argument Darwin would develop in his first full exposition of the theory of natural selection in his "Sketch" of 1842 and his "Essay" of 1844, in his abandoned volume *Natural Selection*, and later in the *Origin*—all of which would present first what was better known socially, the breeder, and then present what was less well known socially, evolution of organisms in nature[57]—in this passage we see a reverse argument. Here Darwin moves from what he personally knows best, that in nature species evolve, and compares that to what he knows less well—the development engineered by breeders in flocks and herds. Darwin's connection between Malthus and evolution in nature, expressed under the far different image of "a hundred thousand wedges," is not clarified in this passage; it is displaced. Darwin's "a hundred thousand wedges" or Wallace's later comparison of the Malthusian process to the "centrifugal governor on a steam engine,"[58] have far more in common with one another than with any analogy based on a goal-directed activity such as domestic breeding. In effect what Darwin has discovered in this passage is not the answer to a problem in theoretical biology but a response to a problem of persuasive exposition he deems central to the success of his latest theoretical insight.

That the problem of persuasion concerned Darwin and that he was not very successful in his early efforts to explain his Malthusian views are underscored by the following note of a conversation between his sister Elisabeth and her husband, his brother-in-law, Hensleigh Wedgwood:

Elisabeth & Hensleigh seemed to think it absurd that the presence
of the Leopard & Tiger together depended on some nice
qualifications each possess, & that tiger springing so much further
would determine preservation (*E*, 44).

Two lines later Darwin rehearses in more formal language a way of addressing this problem:

> It seems absurd proposition, that every budding tree & every buzzing insect & grazing animal owes its form, to that form being the one *alone* out of innumerable other ones, which has been preserved.—be it remembered how little part of the grand mystery is this.—the law of growth, that which changes the acorn into the oak—In short all which nutrition, growth & reproduction is common to all living beings. vide Lamarck vol. II p.115 four laws (*E*, 145).

This note marks Darwin's retreat from the breeder analogy back to his earlier preselectionist argument for the general defense of evolution. This retreat is but a temporary fallback before an all-out advance. The advance begins gradually with Darwin's choice of his key term. Darwin replaced the awkward breeder's word "picking" with the more elevated "natural selection"—an expression which first appears in a marginal note in his copy of Youatt's *Cattle*, published in 1840.[59] Darwin's realization of the persuasive power required to make differential adaptation credible to a skeptical audience may help explain the extreme exaggeration of the image of selection in his 1842 "Sketch" and his 1844 "Essay." Summarizing his comments on the "Sketch," Camille Limoges, the pioneering student of Darwin's notebooks, observes

> This short work is not a literal account of completed research; it is already a work written in which the plan, which prefigures that of the *Origin of Species*, arranges matters according to an order visibly didactic. The order of exposition does not reproduce the order of research; it envisages demonstration, persuasion.[60]

As though addressing the expository problem he faced in his earlier conversation with Elisabeth and Hensleigh, Darwin produces a virtual caricature of his theory. In the "Sketch," Darwin asks the reader to imagine "a being infinitely more sagacious than man (not an omniscient creator)" and how given "thousands and thousands of years" if this being could "select all the variations which tended toward certain ends . . . greyhound produced."[61] In a similar vein, in the 1844 "Essay," Darwin writes: "Let us now suppose a Being with penetration to perceive difference in outer and innermost organization quite imperceptible to man, and with forethought extending over future centuries . . . I can see no conceivable reason why he could not form a new race or several . . . adapted to new ends."[62] As these passages show, the Malthusian process, having rhetorically failed to supply an appropriate bridge linking nature with social knowledge, is replaced with a non-Malthusian image that occupies the same semantic space as his conceptually failed generation theory—a semantic space midway between mechanism and miracle. By linking his new theory with the images and topics of his old ones, Darwin has preserved the informal logic that gives his case for transmutation—under one explanatory mechanism or another—its social force.

From The First Sketch of Natural Selection To The Mature Theory

Darwin's discovery of the trope "natural selection" did not mark the end of his discoveries nor of his wrestling with the problem of persuasion. Indeed, so closely was Darwin's first theory of natural selection adapted to the perspectives of his peers—especially to the geology of Charles Lyell—that in important ways Darwin's first theory of natural selection was neither a consistently biological theory of evolution nor a truly radical alternative to traditional natural theology.[63]

Darwin's first theory of natural selection was not a fully biological theory of evolution because, unlike the theory of the *Origin*, it did not present natural selection as an incessantly active process, but only as an intermittent one. According to Darwin's first theory, only after geological change did natural selection come into play, for only following such environmental change was the adaptation of plants and animals to their environments sufficiently imperfect for them to be subject to population pressures. Indeed, Darwin was not even fully convinced that there was sufficient variation in nature to make his theory of the process fully credible. Further, while Darwin certainly believed progress had been the rule over biologic time, his theory of the mid-1840s does not provide a biological foundation for progress, but only an account compatible with it. Degeneration and loss of complexity would be an equally tenable result given the framework of Darwin's assumptions.[64]

Darwin's theory remained quasi-theological, not only in the benign and general sense that he believed nature's laws to be the expression of divine will, but in the scientifically less-innocent sense that perfect adaptation remained the norm until geological change upset it. Darwin's belief in the perfect adaptation of animals to their settings, like Galileo's continued use of perfect circles for astronomical computation, testifies to the power of beauty to preserve remnants of earlier systems of thought even after their premises have been destroyed. Only later did Darwin recognize perfect adaptation as a theological assumption. Neither biologically nor theolog-

83

ically does Darwin's first theory of natural selection mark the radical paradigm shift manifest in his mature theory. Distinctive as it is in its general outline, in its details it remains a sophisticated extension of conventional assumptions amplified by Darwin's special gift for reconciling innovation with the topics of argument important to his peers.[65]

Darwin's breakthrough into the mature theory of natural selection was the product of his response to yet further inventional challenges and not the result of developments internal to his theory. A new rhetorical factor now entered his thinking—timing. For nearly ten years Darwin set aside his evolutionary speculations, and from the mid-1840s until late 1854, he focused on his monumental project of describing fossil and living barnacles. While Darwin's minute and detailed work on barnacles made him more aware of the fact of variation in nature, completion of the barnacle work was not the main reason for his return to his species project nor for his ultimate shift from a theory of biological response to geological change to his mature theory of biological action and reaction. As I have argued elsewhere, Darwin returned to his species work because his friend and mentor, Charles Lyell, had seen an evolutionary essay, "On The Law Which Has Regulated The Introduction of New Species," by Alfred Russel Wallace.[66] Lyell warned Darwin that if he did not publish his views on evolution, someone else—namely Wallace—would do so first. Wallace's fateful letter to Darwin four years later in June of 1858 nearly proved Lyell right! As Darwin reassembled his notes and manuscripts in late 1854 and early 1855 and once again immersed himself in the literature of his peers, he discovered that his earlier views no longer corresponded to the latest advances in biology. In particular, the work of the French biologist, Milne-Edwards challenged Darwin's environmentally dependent views of species change. Milne-Edwards had found that (1) large genera seemed to produce the greatest amount of divergence from their parent type, and (2) there seemed to be a link between divergence and specialization.[67] The uniform character of these phenomena clearly indicated that they were rooted in a biological dynamic and were not biological responses to environmental change.

As Ospovat has shown, at first Darwin attempted to salvage his earlier theory by arguing that even a small amount of geological change could release a large stream of variation. Finally, he abandoned the geological response model entirely and thereby freed variation and selection to operate independently of geological constraints. In the summer of 1856, early in his proposed chapter on geological distribution in *Natural Selection* (the work he abandoned when he received Wallace's letter), Darwin noted that "forms of being are infinitely more related to each other" than to "physical conditions." In Darwin's new view, a "place" was now more a biological than a geological concept, and adaptation was only as complete as conditions would allow. In Darwin's new theory of selection, the Malthusian pressure of population would tend to favor divergence and at the same time encourage the emergence of what Milne Edwards had termed the "physiological division of labor."[68] Darwin completed the final segment of his path to his mature theory neither primarily by conducting fresh experiments nor by logically working through the implications of his earlier ideas, but by the inventional process of taking the facts and interpretations of his colleagues for granted and arguing that his new revised version of natural selection best explained them. In the process of adapting his ideas to the latest findings of his colleagues, his theory itself was transformed.

CONCLUSION

Five implications for our understanding of the Darwinian revolution follow from our analysis of Darwin's discovery and justification process as aspects of a rhetorical logic. First the success of Darwin's revolution owes far more than has been commonly recognized to his earlier and "discarded" theories. Darwin's earlier theories were not kicked away like scaffolding when the theory of natural selection was at last in place; their explanatory strategies were incorporated into the fabric of his completed structure.

Second, Darwin's unique discovery was peculiarly linguistic; Darwin discovered neither evolution nor natural selection, but how conventional language could be made to confess a truth it had suppressed systematically. This discovery was a work of sustained genius, and was made in the whole course of Darwin's notebooks, not just after he formulated the theory of natural selection.

Third, the topical logic that guided Darwin's path to discovery and justification and his creative use of conventional language are different sides of the same coin. Because in contingent matters opposites may always be proved, and because human perception of nature's regularities is contingent upon history, culture, tradition, and language and not just "fact," Darwin was able to reverse a previous language and logic of justification and thereby develop an informal logic of rhetorical invention. Darwin's allusive and metaphoric speech enabled him to bring to the aid of science the heuristic potential of fiction.

Fourth, the reliance of Darwin's inventional logic on the grammar of prior tradition suggests a parallel between revolutions in science and in poetry. As Harold Bloom has shown, a major new poetic talent achieves originality by subsuming classical conventions and thereby giving an entire tradition an aberrant telos.[69] The *Christian virtuosi* of the seventeenth century—Boyle, Hooke, Ray, and Newton—made perception of nature's enduring regularities seem more "natural" than the fact of change. Darwin overcame this tradition by subsuming its conventions within an evolutionary perspective.

Finally, Darwin's concern with the strategic functions of his language marks a significant continuity between his notebooks and the debate over the *Origin*. When at one point Wallace pleaded with Darwin to drop "natural selection" as fundamentally misleading to their mutual insight into Malthus, Darwin accepted most of Wallace's objections, but urged that the term was now public and must survive or perish by the "natural selection" which operated on language.[70] Peter Vorzimmer's study of the six editions of the *Origin* shows that Darwin in fact progressively moved away from natural selection and supplemented it with other preselectionist arguments in proportion as it failed to persuade. The first image Darwin jettisoned was conceptually his most accurate and chronologically the first suggested by his reading of Malthus—his image of population pressure as "a hundred thousand wedges."[71]

So far were "discovery" and "justification" from being separate processes in Darwin's thought—the one private and imaginative and the other rational and public—the notebooks and the various editions of the *Origin* reveal to the contrary an unbroken dialectical continuity between the two. From his first jotting in his first notebook through the sixth and final edition of the *Origin*, scientific discovery and rhetorical invention, technical and social reason, so effectively unite in Darwin's thought that one can only say that each is an aspect of a single logic of inquiry and presentation.

NOTES

1. Based upon Vorzimmer; see, Peter Vorzimmer, *Charles Darwin: The Years of Controversy: The Origin of Species and Its Critics 1859–1882* (Philadelphia: Temple University Press, 1970), 6–7.

2. Francis Darwin, ed., *The Life and Letters of Charles Darwin*, vol. 1 (New York: D. Appleton, 1911), 551.

3. David Kohn, "Theories To Work By: Rejected Theories, Reproduction, and Darwin's Path To Natural Selection," *Studies in the History of Biology* 4

(1980): 148; see also pp. 67–68, 152. The present study is heavily indebted to previous studies, especially to David Kohn, and to M. J. S. Hodge and David Kohn, "The Immediate Origins of Natural Selection," in David Kohn, ed., *The Darwinian Heritage* (Princeton: Princeton University Press, in Association with Nova Pacifica, 1985), 185–206; Frank Sulloway, "Darwin's Conversion and Its Aftermath," *Journal of the History of Biology* 15, (February 1982): 325–96; Philip R. Sloan, "Darwin, Vital Matter, and the Transformism of Species," *Journal of the History of Biology* 19, (Fall 1986): 369–445; John F. Cornell, "Analogy and Technology in Darwin's Vision of Nature," *Journal of the History of Biology* 17 (Fall 1984): 303–44; Dov Ospovat, *The Development of Darwin's Theory: Natural History, Natural Theology and Natural Selection* (Cambridge: Cambridge University Press, 1981).

4. Paul H. Barrett, Peter J. Gautry, Sandra Herbert, David Kohn, Sydney Smith, eds. *Charles Darwin's Notebooks, 1836–1844: Geology, Transmutation of Species, Metaphysical Enquiries* (Ithaca, N.Y.: British Museum (Natural History), Cornell University Press, 1987); Gavin DeBeer, ed., *Evolution By Natural Selection* (Cambridge: Cambridge University Press, 1958), R. C. Stauffer, *Charles Darwin's 'Natural Selection,' being the second part of his big species book written from 1856 to 1858* (London and New York: Cambridge University Press, 1975).

5. Kohn, "Theories," 152.

6. For an account of a logic of argumentation or rhetoric see Chaim Perelman and L. Olbrechts-Tyteca, *The New Rhetoric: A Treatise on Argument* (Notre Dame, Ind.: Notre Dame University Press, 1969), 11–44, 193–201; Stephen Toulmin, *Human Understanding: The Collective Use and Evolution of Concepts* (Princeton: Princeton University Press, 1972), 145–173; Dudley Shapere, "Rationalism and Empiricism: A New Perspective," *Argumentation*, (August 1988): 299–313; see also Richard McKeon, *Rhetoric: Essays in Invention and Discovery* (Chicago: University of Chicago Press, 1987), esp. 95–121.

7. Barrett et al., *Notebooks,* 19–20, 167–169, 237–330, 395–396; Sloan, "Vital Matter," 369–445.

8. Michael Leff, "Topical Invention and Metaphoric Interaction," *Southern States Communication Journal* 48 (1983): 214–28.

9. George Lakoff and Mark Johnson, *Metaphors We Live By* (Chicago: The University of Chicago Press, 1980), 52–55, 87–96, 97–105, 106–114; also, Perelman and Olbrechts-Tyteca, *New Rhetoric,* 30–133, 187–95, 234–41, 261–63, 350–56; for key issues in the debate over the logic of scientific discovery, see Nicholas Maxwell, "The Rationality of Scientific Discovery," Pt. 1: "The Traditional Rationality Problem," *Philosophy of Science* 41 (June 1974):

87

123–53; "The Rationality of Scientific Discovery," Pt. 2: "An Aim-Oriented Theory of Scientific Discovery," *Philosophy of Science* 41 (September 1974): 247–95; also Thomas Nickles, ed., *Scientific Discovery: Case Studies* (Dordrecht, Holland: D. Reidel, 1978), esp. xiii–xv.

10. Bernard J. F. Lonergan, *Insight: A Study of Human Understanding* (New York: Harper Torchbooks, 1960), 3–32.

11. Sloan, "Vital Matter," 369–397.

12. Sulloway, "Darwin's Conversion," 325–96; Charles Darwin, *Journal of Researches into the Geology and Natural History of the Various Countries Visited by H. M. S. Beagle* (New York: Hafner, 1952, facsimile reprint of the first edition), 526–27.

13. On Darwin's mockingbirds, see Sulloway, "Darwin's Conversion," 337; on the finches and mockingbirds, 345–51; see also Frank J. Sulloway, "Darwin and His Finches: The Evolution of A Legend," *Journal of The History of Biology* 15 (Spring 1982): 1–53.

14. Sulloway, "Darwin's Conversion," 346.

15. Ibid., 345.

16. Ibid., 338–44.

17. Ibid., 340–45.

18. Ibid., 344–45, 352–70.

19. Sulloway, "Darwin's Conversion," 351–56, 359, 369, 378–79; Kohn, "Theories," 73–79.

20. Sloan, "Vital Matter," 369–99.

21. Pangenesis was introduced in Darwin's *The Variation of Animals and Plants Under Domestication*, 2 vols. (London: John Murray, 1868), for the neo-Darwinian synthesis, see Ronald A. Fisher, *The Genetical Theory of Natural Selection*, 2d ed. (New York: Dover, 1958), vii–x, 1–22.

22. Barret, et al., *Notebooks*, 61. All subsequent references the notebooks will be by letter of notebook and line number and will be given in the text.

23. Sloan, "Vital Matter," 388–99.

24. Kohn, "Theories," 79–81.

25. Erasmus Darwin, *Zoonomia: or, The Laws of Life*, 2 vols. (London: J. Johnson, 1794).

26. Kohn, "Theories," 83–87.

27. Martin J. S. Rudwick, *The Meaning of Fossils: Episodes in the History of Paleontology* (Chicago: University of Chicago Press, 1976), 180–88.

28. Perelman and Olbrechts-Tyteca, *New Rhetoric*, 337–44.

29. L. L. Laudan, "Thomas Reid and the Newtonian Turn of British Methodological Thought," in R. E. Butts and J. W. Davis, eds., *The Methodological Heritage of Newton* (Toronto: University of Toronto Press,

1970), 102–131, Vincent Karl Kavaloski, *The 'Vera Causa' Principle*, (Chicago: Unpublished Ph.D. thesis, Philosophy, June 1974), Ch. 1.

30. Edward Manier, *The Young Darwin and His Cultural Circle* (Dordrecht Holland: D. Reidel, 1978), 174.

31. Kohn, "Theories," 97–99; Ospovat, *Development*, 6–38.

32. Charles Darwin, *On The Origin of Species: A facsimile of the first edition*, Ernst Mayr, introduction (New York: Atheneum, 1967).

33. Kohn, "Theories," 88–90.

34. Ibid., 87–96.

35. Ibid., 92–93; also, Rudwick, *Meaning of Fossils*, 180–188; Charles Lyell, *Principles of Geology* vol. 2, (London: John Murray, 1832), esp. chs. 1–4 and 8–11.

36. Kohn, "Theories," 92–99.

37. John Angus Campbell, "Darwin and The Origin of Species: The Rhetorical Ancestry of An Idea," *Speech Monographs* 37 (March 1970): 6–7.

38. Darwin, *Origin*, 7.

39. Maurice A. Finocchiaro, *Galileo and The Art of Reasoning* (Dordrecht, Holland: D. Reidel, 1980), 46–66.

40. Sloan, "Vital Matter," 440–43.

41. Ibid., 396–445.

42. Ibid., esp. 406–09, 432–43.

43. Ibid., 443.

44. Ibid., 415, 443.

45. Kohn, "Theories," 113–34.

46. See, for example, the notebooks: C,54, C,166, C,205e, C,210e, C,244, D,19.

47. Kohn, "Theories," 129–33; see also George Grinnell, "The Rise and Fall of Darwin's Second Theory," *Journal of the History of Biology* 18 (Spring 1985): 51–70.

48. For the relationship of Darwin's notebooks to one another, see Sandra Herbert and David Kohn, "Introduction," in Barrett, et al., *Notebooks*, 6–12.

49. Kohn, "Theories," 68.

50. Darwin, *Origin*, 490.

51. Richard S. Westfall, *Science and Religion in Seventeenth-Century England* (New Haven: Yale University Press, 1958), 26–48, 70–105.

52. John Angus Campbell, "A Reconsideration of Darwin's Affective Decline," *Victorian Studies* 18 (November 1974): 159–74.

53. Kohn, "Theories," 138; Hodge and Kohn, "Immediate Origins," 193–97.

54. Kohn, "Theories," 138; Hodge and Kohn, "Immediate Origins," 190, 195, 199–200.

55. Kohn, "Theories," 142–49; Hodge and Kohn, "Immediate Origins," 193–97; Ospovat, *Development* 56–57, 196.

56. Hodge and Kohn, "Immediate Origins," 196.

57. DeBeer, *Evolution*; F. Darwin, *The Life and Letters* (see note 2); Stauffer *Darwin's 'Natural Selection.'* For a detailed account see Cornell, "Analogy and Technology," 303–44.

58. DeBeer, *Charles Darwin*, 278.

59. Camille Limoges, *La selection naturelle: Etude sur la premiere constition d'un concept* (Paris: Presses Universitaires De France, 1970), 105.

60. Ibid.

61. DeBeer, *Charles Darwin*, 45.

62. Ibid., 114.

63. Ospovat, *Development*, 191–201.

64. Ibid., 1–5, 191–223.

65. Ibid., 210–28.

66. John Angus Campbell, "The Invisible Rhetorician," *Rhetorica* 7 (Winter 1989): 55–86. For documentation, of Lyell & Wallace, see John Langdon Brooks, *Just Before The Origin* (New York: Columbia University Press, 1984), 259–60, 272.

67. Ospovat, *Development*, 115–45, 146–69, 175–76, 181, 201.

68. Ibid., 218–23.

69. Harold Bloom, *The Anxiety of Influence* (New York: Oxford University Press, 1973), 5, 43; *A Map of Misreading* (New York: Oxford University Press, 1975), 84, 176.

70. Francis Darwin, ed., *More Letters of Charles Darwin* (London: John Murray, 1903) 2 July, 1866, 1: 267.

71. Peter Vorzimmer, *Years of Controversy*, 269–71; Morse Peckham, ed., *The Origin of Species by Charles Darwin: A Variorum Text* (Philadelphia: University of Pennsylvania Press, 1959), 150. In the notebooks, Darwin spoke of "a hundred thousand wedges" (D 135). In his sketch of 1842, he spoke of "a thousand wedges," and in his essay of 1844 and in the first edition of the *Origin*, of "ten thousand" wedges; see DeBeer, *Evolution by Natural Selection*, 47, 118.

3

The Origin of Species:
Evolutionary Taxonomy as an Example of the
Rhetoric of Science

Alan G. Gross

The rhetoric of science discipline was born late because a persistent dream of the West died hard: the dream of certain truth concerning an independent reality. Assuming its availability, philosophers from Plato to Carnap could divide science from rhetoric; suspecting its likelihood, we cannot. For us, therefore, the rhetoric of science is a branch of inquiry having as its goal "to find out in each case the existing means of persuasion" (Aristotle 1355^{b}14). Accordingly, the rhetoric of science does not look at the texts of natural science as transparent vehicles by means of which knowledge is conveyed: it looks through these texts, to persuasive structures. Since the establishment of knowledge claims in natural science is paramount, the rhetorical analysis of natural science has as its primary task the rhetorical reconstruction of the means by which scientists convince themselves and others that the assertions they make are an integral part of the privileged activity with which they are allied.

The rhetoric of science analyzes scientific texts by the same means as others analyze speeches and literature; it does not recognize that the sciences differ from the humanities in any fundamental way: it denies especially that the sciences differ in that "they do not have first to gain access to their object domain through hermeneutic means" (Habermas 1982, 274). As Latour and Woolgar (1979, 261) make explicit, "the basic prototype of scientific activity is not to be found in the realm of mathematics and logic but . . . in the work of exegesis. Exegesis and hermeneutics are the tools around which the idea of scientific production has historically been forged." Holding these views, we are obliged to see the enterprise of

The award of released time from Purdue University Calumet materially aided in the completion of this paper. I want to thank Professor David Hull of Northwestern University and Professor Herbert Simons of Temple University for their careful criticisms of earlier versions.

science hermeneutically, as a stream of texts exhibiting generally an epistemology based on prediction and control, but available nonetheless to an epistemology based on understanding. By recourse to an insight as old at least as Vico, we can view the texts of natural science as products of human interaction: phenomena to be understood in the way human beings understand each other.

From a rhetoric of science so conceived, no feature is exempt from rhetorical explanation. As we shall see, even prediction itself, as a category of judgment, is not exempt. In principle, then, the rhetoric of science discipline is as complete as the history, philosophy, or sociology of science. And as incomplete. For Gadamer's point about physics applies to any discipline that insists on ultimate coherence:

> The world of physics cannot seek to be the whole of what exists.
> For even a world formula that contained everything, so that the
> observer of the system would also be included in the latter's
> equations, would still assume the existence of a physicist who, as
> the calculator, would not be an object calculated (Gadamer 1975,
> 410).

The history, philosophy, sociology, and rhetoric of science—all must be faithful to their texts. But the rhetoric of science differs from its sibling disciplines: it must, to paraphrase Barthes, "star" its texts (1974, 13); it must use them in a special way. Only by looking at them as linguistic entities can it look through them *sub specie rhetoricae*, to their underlying persuasive structures.

RECONSTRUCTING EVOLUTIONARY TAXONOMY

A complete rhetoric of science must be able to reconstruct the natural sciences without remainder. In this paper, I want to test the hypothesis of completeness against evolutionary taxonomy, the science of classifying animals and plants as species in accordance with evolutionary theory. If a rhetoric of this science is possible, we must be able to reconstruct its central concept, the species, rhetorically without remainder. But our route to this goal must be indirect. We cannot translate the concept of species directly into rhetorical terms because we must avoid the claim that what is being translated is precisely what is *not* scientific, that after our rhetorical analysis there still remains an essential core of untranslatable scientific meaning.

To avoid this claim, we must reconstruct the species of evolutionary taxonomy rationally in the hope that the result will be recognizably a version both of this particular scientific concept and of "the methodological ideal . . . that dominates modern mathematically based natural science" (Gadamer 1975, 414); we must prepare a "schematized description of an imaginary procedure, consisting of rationally prescribed steps, which would lead to essentially the same results as the actual [historical or] psychological process" (Carnap 1963, 16). In a rational reconstruction of the species of evolutionary taxonomy, when stages are referred to—stages at which species are identified, defined, or redefined—these are not historical or psychological events, but analytical categories. It is this rational reconstruction of the species that we will translate without remainder into rhetorical terms.

I do not deny that infinitely many rational reconstructions are possible; that evolutionary taxonomists may argue with the details of my rational reconstruction; that they may even take the position that mine is the wrong rational reconstruction. But I would argue that these scientists cannot take the position that rational reconstruction is per se the wrong approach for extracting method from practice without denying that evolutionary taxonomy is a science. And that is precisely my point. To evolutionary taxonomists, ours must be a world inhabited by evolutionary species. To each of these can be applied, and from each of these can be inferred, at least in principle, a central process: the operation of natural selection on random genetic variation. Moreover, this reciprocal relationship between observation and theory presupposes objectivity: evolutionary taxonomy must describe a world whose existence is in some sense independent of its descriptions.

Our rhetorical reconstruction, on the other hand, redescribes evolutionary species by translating into rhetoric each aspect of our rational reconstruction: no aspect we have described as science remains without its rhetorical counterpart. By means of rhetorical reconstruction, evolutionary taxonomy is transformed into an interlocking set of persuasive structures. *Sub specie rhetoricae,* we do not discover, we create: plants and animals are brought to life, raised to membership in a taxonomic group, and made to illustrate and generate evolutionary theory. If a rhetorical reconstruction describes rhetorically every aspect that a rational reconstruction describes rationally, a complete rhetoric of science becomes possible.

THE RATIONAL RECONSTRUCTION OF SPECIES

In contemporary biology, species cannot be defined classically, by genus and differentia; the effort, in Wittgenstein's pungent phraseology, resembles "[trying] to find the real artichoke by stripping it of its leaves." Instead, a species must be defined by depicting and describing "family resemblances" among organisms (Wittgenstein 1965, 125).[1] Earlier, in *Origin of Species*, Darwin had placed this notion in a taxonomical context: "There are crustaceans at the opposite ends of the series, which have hardly a character in common; yet the species at both ends, from being plainly allied to others, and these to others, and so onwards, can be recognized as unequivocally belonging to this, and to no other class of the Articulata" (Darwin 1964, 419).

Identification: Family Resembances

When we define general terms like species according to family resemblances, we give up as spurious the precision of classical definition as it applies to the natural world. Nevertheless definition by family resemblance is real: it marks off a nonarbitrary class. Because I lack rules that will demarcate absolutely what I name as a new species of hummingbird, I can be puzzled about whether a particular organism belongs to the species, but I can't just drop anything in there, eagles for example. In addition, a good general term is an open class in two senses: there is always the possibility that I'll see a member I overlooked, and, anyway, at least for creatures not extinct, there is always the chance of genuinely new members. Finally, the application of a general term can be learned; that is, a learner can apply the term independently of the guidance of her teacher (Bambrough 1966).

Identification: Potential Species

In a typical paper in evolutionary taxonomy, "A New Species of Hummingbird from Peru" (Fitzpatrick, Willard, and Terborgh 1979), there is everywhere evident the extensive description and depiction that are the evidential grounding of family resemblance. These scientists, for example, record numerous qualitative visual impressions. Some are species-general, others sexually specific:

> A broad, pale buffy breast band separates the smaller throat spots
> from larger and more numerous discs on the breast and flanks. In
> a few specimens the posterior border of the breast band is entirely
> defined by a broad row of these discs. The belly is free of dark
> spots in all specimens. The downy crissum [anal region] is white as
> in males, and the undertail coverts [feathers at base] are dusky,
> edged Cinnamon. (p. 178)

In addition to qualitative visual impressions, Fitzpatrick and his co-workers define the potential species by recording its behavior. For example, we are afforded a detailed description of "male-female display":

> Initially a pair [of birds] was foraging around the walls of
> [a vine-covered sinkhole] and in the surrounding shrubs along
> the rim. Both male and female were observed perching on a
> rootlet, making frequent sallies to capture tiny flying insects.
> (p. 183)

To this abundance of qualitative information, quantitative data is added. We are given by degree, minute, and second the geographical coordinates of the area explored; to the nearest ten meters the height of the habitat above sea level; to the tenth of a millimeter the mean, range, and standard deviation of six specimen dimensions; to two decimal places the ratio of exposed culmen [upper ridge of a bird's bill] to wing chord length; to the second the length of calls.

But the most impressive attempt to establish the species is in the frontispiece, a full-color painting of two of the birds in situ: a dimorphic pair, the female perched at an angle which most clearly displays her distinctive tail and underparts. The male displays, not only his characteristic deeply cleft tail and dark coloring, but his wings extended and in rapid movement as he hovers. Moreover, the bird's feeding behavior is shown: the "deep purple petals [of its favorite flower] form a tubular corolla that hangs vertically . . . forcing the foraging [bird] to hover directly below and point its bill straight upward to retrieve the nectar" (p. 182).

The potential species is not only described and depicted in terms of family resemblances; by comparison and contrast, it is carefully differentiated from closely allied species. In this process of establishing species status, the character is the minimum unit of observation. Characters are parts of the organism or aspects of its behavior that most perspicuously establish it as a member of a genus or differentiate it as a separate species (Mayr 1982, 19–32). The harder a character works at either of these tasks, the more it is valued, the more heavily it is weighted.[2] In establishing their potential species as a member of a particular genus, Fitzpatrick and his co-workers emphasize "the relative bill length, nostril feathering, and well delineated nasal operculum [lid-like covering]" (Fitzpatrick, Willard, and Terborgh 1979, 181); in establishing the difference between the potential species and its fellows of the same genus, they give weight to the female's "elongated and deeply forked, entirely iridescent, metallic blue tail,

95

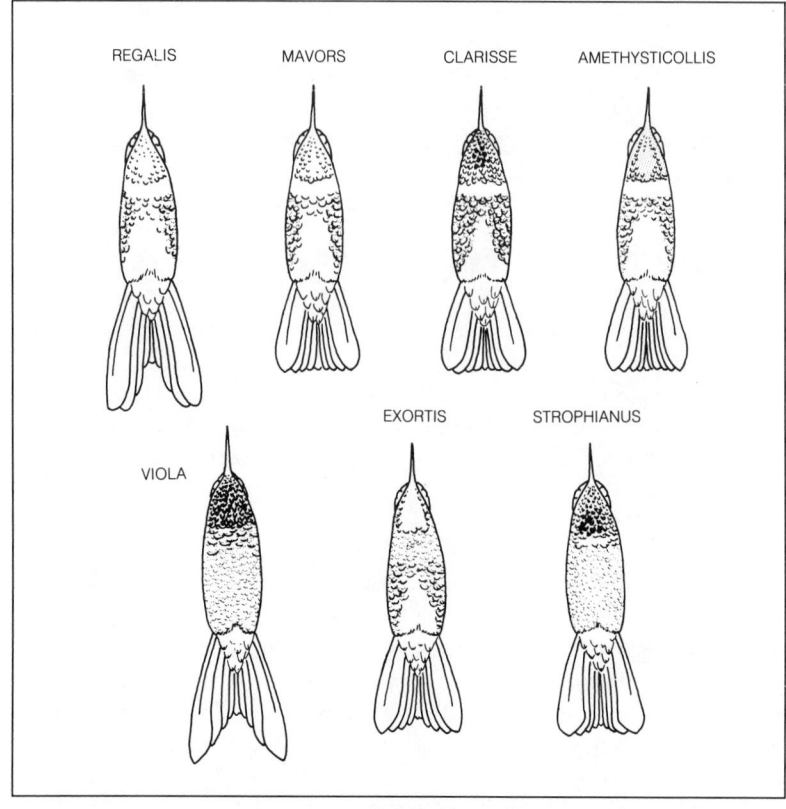

Fig. 3.1. Ventral patterns and tail forms of *Heliangelus* females, including *H. regalis*. *H. micrastur* female resembles *exortis*, and *H. spencei* resembles *amethysticollis*. Note similarity between *regalis* and *mavors*. Reprinted with permission from J.W. Fitzpatrick et al., "A New Species of Hummingbird from Peru," *Wilson Bulletin* 91 (1979): 180.

equally bright on both surfaces; combined with buffy underparts inter-rupted by a pale pectoral [breast] band" (p. 177).

Not only in the frontispiece, but throughout this paper, pictures join words in the clear display of likenesses and differences, strongly reinforcing the presence of a potential new species. In figure 3.1, for example, the seven drawings, considered in concert and without words, make equally emphatic both the family resemblances crucial for genus identity and the contrastive features essential for within-genus differentiation.

Identification: Taxonomical and Evolutionary Species

It is by means of statistical inference that this extraordinary detail is given taxonomical significance: by this means, Fitzpatrick and his co-workers definitely assert that they have a new species, a new living entity related to all such entities. Sixteen specimens have been collected:

	Adult	Subadult
Male	5	5
Female	5	1

Assuming a fair sample, the authors can describe the species by describing these specimens. Thus, when averages, ranges, and standard deviations are given (e.g., those for wing chord length), they are equally those of the specimens collected and of the species. Description, comparison and statistical inference having done their work, the species can be officially certified as new by naming: it is a hummingbird, the genus *Heliangelus*, the species *regalis*, a Royal Sunangel.

But taxonomical identification is not the final stage: taxonomic species must be redefined in evolutionary terms. A species first characterized without Darwinian assumptions is now characterized in terms of a theory concerning the origin of species: that all stem from the operation of natural selection on random variations, some of which are favored because they increase the rate of survival of those who possess them.

In taxonomic work, evolutionary theory serves at least two purposes: it explains problematic observations that arise in the process of identification, and it licenses prediction. In the process of identifying their new species of hummingbird, Fitzpatrick and his collaborators make the following problematic observation. Among the species of *Heliangelus* to which *regalis* seems most closely related, the monochromatic plumage of the male *regalis* is strikingly anomalous. To account for this irregularity, the investigators invoke the evolutionary concept of convergence (similarity in species resulting not from descent, but from environmental constraint):

> Thus, if *regalis* is indeed closest to this species as suggested by the appearance of the female, it has undergone a dramatic differentiation in which the male converged upon several more distant relatives. The elongated, narrow, metallic blue tail in both sexes of *regalis*, equally iridescent on both surfaces, is suggested only in *H. strophianus* (sexes similar) and *viola* (very large, dark green female lacks a breast band). (p. 181)

Presumably, this convergence is the direct or indirect result of as yet unidentified selection pressures.

But evolutionary theory does more than explain; it predicts. Prediction in evolutionary biology, of course, is not the same as in classical physics, where future events can often be forecast with startling quantitative accuracy. In evolutionary biology, although predictions need to be well defined and consistent with the evidence on which they are based, they can legitimately vary in precision of measurement:

> For example, population ecologists are generally satisfied to explain to one order of magnitude the increases and decreases in population size of the organisms studied, and for this purpose net fecundity and mortality are usually sufficient. Game and fish management, however, may require prediction of population changes to an accuracy of 10 to 20 percent, and for this purpose complete age-specific mortality and fecundity schedules are required. Finally, the human demographer needs to project human population sizes to better than 1 percent accuracy, and to do so needs fecundity and mortality figures by age, sex, socioeconomic class, education, geographical location, and so on (Lewontin 1984, 7–8).

Lewontin's principle is implicit in a report by Ricqlès and Bolt (1983). In this paper, these workers inquire into the origins and nature of "perhaps the most important captorhinid character," a feature whose evolutionary history they regard as a prerequisite to proper taxonomic use: jaw growth and tooth replacement, as exemplified in a prehistoric reptile, *Captorhinus aguti* (p. 7).[3] Their predictions, though far from precise, are nevertheless legitimate, since they are well defined and consistently applied: on the basis of large, clearly visible anatomical features, the scientists create a preliminary model. Later, they check the predictions of this model against effects of jaw growth and tooth replacement not visible to the naked eye. It makes sense that the dynamics of these processes should leave traces in surviving fossils, and that effects visible to the naked eye should be consistent with effects visible at between two and six magnifications.

Among the papers in evolutionary biology I have examined, falsifiability is mentioned almost as much as prediction. Falsifiability is prediction turned on its head; it asserts that a theory can be undermined by its repeated failure to predict. This notion has Sir Karl Popper (1965; 1968) as its best known exponent (see also Medawar 1984). For Popper, the possibility of falsifiability is at the root of all good science, all of which is open to being *"refuted by experience."* In other words, it is the essence of science that we can refute theory with contravening facts:

> It is possible by means of purely deductive inferences (with the help of the *modus tollens* of classical logic) to argue from the truth of singular statements to the falsity of universal statements [in the texts examined, from "observations" to "hypotheses" or "models"]. Such an argument to the falsity of universal statements is the only strictly deductive kind of inference that proceeds, as it were, in the 'inductive direction'; that is, from singular to universal statements.

Popper recognizes that theories under empirical attack can always be saved "by introducing *ad hoc* an auxiliary hypothesis, or by changing *ad hoc* a definition." His solution is "the empirical method" with "its manner of exposing to falsification, in every conceivable way, the system to be tested" (Popper 1968, 41–42).

Two papers in my sample claim an openness to falsifiability. Writing about the spread of chipmunk populations, B. D. Patterson says of an hypothesis integral to his model that it is "apparently refuted by the presence of *E. canipes*, rather than *E. quadrivittatus* [species of chipmunk], in the Gallinas mountains"; according to this model, "small mountain ranges isolated from centers of endemism [areas where species originate] should have been colonized by southwardly advancing taxa," of which *E. quadrivittatus* is one (B. D. Patterson 1982, 393–94). In their paper, Ricqlès and Bolt assert that "evidence for successive occupation by several generations of teeth at the same site would falsify [their] model" of reptilian jaw growth and tooth replacement, a model that implies "that in the MR [multiple-rowed] area a given attachment site was occupied only once" (Ricqlès and Bolt 1983, 22). Since the geography of Arizona and New Mexico allows for the apparently anomalous presence of *E. canipes* in the Gallinas mountains, Patterson's hypothesis survives; since successive same-site tooth occupation is not in evidence, the conclusion of Ricqlès and Bolt still rests on firm ground.

The rational reconstruction of the concept of species by means of an analysis of typical papers in evolutionary taxonomy supports the view that science is an inductive progress to reliable knowledge, knowledge always open to, but nevertheless so far resistant to, falsification. The induction from which this knowledge proceeds has observations as its raw material. These observations are apparently free from the evolutionary theory that explains them. For example, the collection of sixteen similar birds by Fitzpatrick and his co-workers is a task possible to earlier, evolution-free centuries. It need have been motivated by nothing more than the hunch that the birds might form a new group. Of course, once the group has actually been segregated, it can be defined taxonomically; and, once it has been so defined, it can be redefined according to evolutionary theory. Evolutionary theory can then be used to explain and predict events and entities in the natural world and to retrodict these in the fossil record.

THE RHETORICAL RECONSTRUCTION OF SPECIES

Although Perelman and Olbrechts-Tyteca's *The New Rhetoric* does not contain any extended discussion of argument in the natural sciences—no examples from these sciences appear—there is no intent to exclude the natural sciences from the sphere of rhetoric. The authors believe that scientists address their very specialized audiences, audiences that are commonly very small indeed, as a "universal audience" in the sense "that everyone with the same training, qualifications, and information would reach the same conclusions" (Perelman and Olbrechts-Tyteca 1969, 34; compare Johnstone 1978, 91). By means of the universal audience, then, the natural sciences come within the sphere of rhetoric: the purposes of a rhetorical reconstruction would be served if we were to "characterize . . . the image [the evolutionary taxonomist] holds of the universal audience he is trying to win over to his view" (Perelman and Olbrechts-Tyteca 1969, 33). To characterize this image, we must find rhetorical equivalents for the stages of the rational reconstruction we have just presented: we must show how, *sub specie rhetoricae*, scientists create an ontology that persuades their fellows, an ontology in which plants and animals have been brought to life, raised to membership in a taxonomical group, and made to illustrate and generate evolutionary theory.

Creation: Potential Species

The first stage, the creation of the potential species, is best elucidated by the New Rhetorical concept of *presence*. Through presence, writers place "certain elements" in their discourses, those on which they "[wish] to center attention," in "the foreground of the [reader's] consciousness." Initially, therefore, presence is "a psychological phenomenon"; that on which the mind and senses dwell "is, by that very circumstance, overestimated" (Perelman and Olbrechts-Tyteca, 142, 116–17; compare Gadamer 103).

This reading of presence is consistent with Gestalt principles. According to these, sensations organize themselves into wholes, or *gestalten*, certain combinations of which seem automatically foregrounded; these combinations we see as having shape and substance, outlined against a shapeless and relatively insubstantial background. Gestalten are clearly manifested to sight and hearing, less clearly to the other senses. Attributively, they can refer not only to things experienced but also to collections of thoughts and ideas (Köhler 1947). On this reading, presence becomes a special case of perception.

Presence so conceived is easily subject to manipulation. In an ordinary way, we see an object that looks like a pencil; later, we grasp it and write with it, confirming our initial impression. But this simple conformity between our perceptions and the world, a conformity that encourages a naive realism, can be dramatically realigned: optical illusions and camouflage are well-known instances. Less dramatically, it is always possible to "adopt a special attitude with regard to the field so that some of its contents are emphasized while others are more or less suppressed" (Köhler 1947, 99). In visual fields, for example, manipulation makes both normal perspective and *trompe-l'oeil* possible.

In the description and depiction of the potential species of evolutionary taxonomy, presence is created by two devices: overdescription and multiple sensory perspectives. The first, overdescription, is the characterization of sense objects in detail far beyond a reader's ordinary expectations. In science, the rhetorical effect of presence routinely generated by overdescription has been analyzed by Steven Shapin (1984); he demonstrates that Robert Boyle's resort to overdescription in his experimental papers was a deliberate attempt to create "virtual witnessing," the use of circumstantial detail as a surrogate for the actual experience of confirmation through experimentation. In evolutionary taxonomy, overdescription serves an analogous purpose: on their own, words and pictures bring potential species to life.

In pursuit of their ontological goal, evolutionary taxonomists use, not only overdescription, but also multiple sensory perspectives. Fitzpatrick and his co-workers, for example, are no purists, looking for essential differences; all descriptive features are mustered that work to increase and individuate presence. This multiplicity of perspectives combined with the extraordinary detail with which each is described creates presence so effectively because it mimics the methods by which we confirm our everyday impressions of the reality of ordinary objects. We supplement visual data with more visual data from different angles and distances; the data of one sense with the data of another; qualitative sense data with mensuration. Thus, the presence of a species increases as the paper progresses; the "whole field of consciousness" becomes filled with this creature "so as to isolate it, as it were, from the [reader's] overall mentality" (Perelman and Olbrechts-Tyteca 1969, 118).

In scientific, as distinct from literary, prose the resources of language from which presence is created are decidedly limited. Because scientific prose is designed to create the impression that its language refers unproblematically to a real world existing independently of any perceiving subject, it generally excludes the subjective dimension of description, the use of emotion-charged words or irony. For the same reason, scientific prose generally excludes any device that shifts the reader's attention from the world language creates to language itself as a resource for creating worlds. These restrictions account for the unavailability of many of the techniques of presence discussed in *The New Rhetoric*: onomatopoeia is just one example of such an exclusion.

But language so constrained is hardly free from rhetorical effect; as Barthes cogently observes: "the zero degree . . . *is a significant absence* . . . the absence of rhetorical signifiers constitutes in its turn a stylistic signifier"; "denotation is . . . the *last* of the connotations . . . the superior myth by which the text pretends to return . . . to the nature of language, to language as nature" (Barthes 1967, 77–78; 1974, 9). Since the creation of presence in science is limited to those devices by which language may be said to refer unproblematically to a real world, it seems fair to give that sort of presence a name: to call it *referential presence*.

Creation: Taxonomical Species

We can account for referential presence *sub specie rhetoricae*; but can we account for its taxonomic transformation? We can, if we can show how statistical inference, naming, and artistic rendering create the persuasive structures that transform referential presence into taxonomical species.

In evolutionary taxonomy, statistical inference is designed to convince readers that speciation partakes of the certainty generally attributed to a branch of mathematics. There is no question of the importance to evolutionary taxonomy of this frequently used, routinely foregrounded set of techniques. But it is far from clear that statistical inference is the actual basis for the establishment of new taxa. The validity of such inferences depends on the efficacy of sampling procedures: generalizations from a sample can be made only on the basis of random selection from a defined population. In practice, limitations of time and funding force reasonable compromises. But Fitzpatrick and his co-workers define *Heliangelus regalis* by means of sixteen birds! How can they assert that these are representative? This practice of unsystematic sampling, which seems the taxonomic norm (Sokal and Crovello 1984, 544, 558), provides a clue to the rhetorical nature of the taxonomic transformation.

In truth, taxonomic speciation depends less on statistical inference than on a fundamental presupposition about the existence of species in the order of nature. These species must necessarily be imagined as "discrete sets with appreciable distances between them." Taxonomic speciation absolutely "depends upon the possibility of grouping data in clusters with empty space between them" (Kuhn 1977, 312 and note). This continuity within, and discontinuity between, species is perfectly in accord with Gestalt psychology: between gestalten there is "a 'dead' interval which corresponds . . . to the mere extension or ground outside a visual shape" (Köhler 1947, 111). But this presupposition is not in accord with the conviction that species are established solely on the basis of statistically inferred regularities.[4]

A striking instance of the operation of the presupposition concerning the essential nature of species, culled from the papers I examined, concerns *Trachelyichthys decaradiatus*—a new species of a new genus of catfish identified and described on the basis of a single specimen! (Greenfield and Glodek 1977) While statistical inference is invoked, another, antithetical procedure is actually used. Greenfield and Glodek simply assume synecdoche: a single creature automatically evokes the order of nature as a taxonomic network. Forewarned by such imaginative leaps, one may question the legitimacy with which the precision demonstrated for specimens is routinely transferred to the species.

Artistic rendering also confers taxonomic identity. In Fitzpatrick, Willard, and Terborgh on hummingbirds, the full-color portrait of *regalis* in situ may strike the naive viewer as a candid glimpse. But this picture is posed: it presents these creatures in a manner designed to display, not just any characters, but only those that best distinguish them from their fellows. In the case of the line drawing reproduced in Figure 3.1, the purposes of taxonomic identification are served by another form of visual rhetoric: tendentious simplification.

Finally, naming confers taxonomic identity. As Victor Turner has demonstrated for the Ndembu (Turner 1981, 85–86, 180), and David Hull has shown for taxonomy (Hull 1984, 638), naming is a carefully guarded cultural resource whose purpose is to bestow identity: taxonomic names bestow taxonomic identity. Although taxonomic naming persuades us to credit the scientist with discovery, on the contrary,

103

wherever language and men exist, there is not only a freedom from
the pressure of the world, but this freedom from the habitat is also
freedom in relation to the names that we give things, as stated in
the profound account in Genesis, according to which Adam
received from God the authority to name creatures. (Gadamer
1975, 402)

The verbal portrait of the hummingbird consists of scattered islands of
detail. Naming alone resolves the paradox by means of which this scattered
detail becomes a new creature, but one for whom a taxonomic space
already exists (Barthes 1974, 60–63, 94–95, 209–10).

Creation: Evolutionary Species

The evolutionary species is part of at least two networks of meaning, two
versions of evolutionary theory. In the first, or strong, version, the species
is an integral part of a formulation that aspires to make quantitatively
precise forecasts of events in space-time, events directly inferred from
mathematically expressed physical laws. In the second, or weak, version,
this same concept is an integral part of a formulation that brings together
a large and otherwise disparate number of phenomena in the natural world
under a single conceptual umbrella.

Darwin himself is the source of both versions of evolutionary theory. In
The Origin, taking his cue from the explanatory model of classical physics,
he says in support of the strong version:

> Throw up a handful of feathers, and all must fall to the ground
> according to definite laws; but how simple is the problem where
> each shall fall compared to that of the action and reaction of the
> innumerable plants and animals which have determined, in the
> course of centuries, the proportional numbers and kinds of trees
> now growing on the old Indian ruins! (1962, 86)

In his letters, writing in the same vein, he compares his theory with
gravitation and with the wave theory of light (Darwin 1972, 1:150; 1959,
2:80, 83–84).

At other times, however, Darwin seems to have for evolutionary theory
explanatory goals that are far less rigorous. In his letters, he also says: "an
hypothesis is *developed* into a theory solely by explaining an ample lot of
facts"; it "[connects these facts] under an intelligible point of view." In a
letter to Lyell, though he ventures a weak prediction concerning the fossil
record, Darwin specifically abjures strong prediction, which he calls

"prophecy" (1959, 2:80, 210, 9–10). Indeed, as a whole, *The Origin of Species* exemplifies the weak version of evolutionary theory. But to adopt this version is also to abjure falsifiability as a criterion for the adequacy of theoretical formulations.

Are contemporary taxonomists strong or weak theorists? In contemporary taxonomy, as in Darwin, the weak version of evolutionary theory is predominant. In their work on a new species of hummingbird, Fitzpatrick and his collaborators are typical in their use of convergence to explain an anomalous character; in so doing, they are using evolutionary theory to connect "an ample lot of facts . . . under an intelligible point of view." In the papers examined, however, Ricqlès and Bolt, and B. D. Patterson clearly underwrite falsifiability as the chief criterion for the theoretical adequacy of their formulations. In so doing, they seem to accept the evolutionary species as part of a strong theory. But appearances are deceptive. In his analysis of falsifiability, Popper insists that the element of risk be maximized: "an attempt to solve an interesting problem by a bold conjecture, *even (and especially) if it soon turns out to be false*" (1965, 231). Although the statements of Ricqlès and Bolt look Popperian at first glance, careful scrutiny reveals the hyperbolic nature of their claims. In these papers, the theories of their authors are not seriously at risk; a fortiori evolutionary theory is never seriously at risk.

In truth, Ricqlès, Bolt, and Patterson take advantage of the impressiveness that an openness to falsification confers without taking the risks that such openness should entail. What Ricqlès and Bolt identify as falsifiable is not even central to their argument; it is only their preliminary model, a model which is no more than an artifact of their method. They elected to build this model from large, clearly visible anatomical features, and to correct it by means of anatomical features not visible to the naked eye. As they readily admit, they could have built their final model directly and entirely from submacroscopic features. If they had, potential falsifiability would have disappeared, since "[submacroscopic] evidence for successive occupation by several generations of teeth at the same site" would have been clearly absent from the beginning (Ricqlès and Bolt 1983, 22).

Patterson is no truer to Popper than are Ricqlès and Bolt. Because his model really is endangered by some awkward evidence, it is technically falsifiable. But, to save it, Patterson resorts to an ad hoc hypothesis, expressly forbidden by Sir Karl: "An elevated corridor . . . extends from the White Mountains north to the Gallinas Range. Chipmunks *evidently* [my italics] were able to move through this corridor to colonize the Gallinas

Range before it could be reached by *E. quadrivittatus"* (B. D. Patterson 1982, 395). One can only conclude that falsifiability is invoked in both these instances to give a mistaken impression of the strength of particular taxonomical claims.[5]

Despite differences, however, the weak version of evolutionary theory is importantly similar to the strong. In both, natural selection creates the phylogenies, the lines of descent, we observe in nature and in the fossil record;[6] in both also, evolution is a process theory and a theory of descent. These shared theoretical resources allow taxonomists to use either version as a completely unquestioned, utterly reliable source of intellectual underpinning, an ideational account on which they can reliably draw to explain and extend their observations. Since evolutionary theory founds evolutionary biology, by definition it has axiomatic status: in every paper, its appropriateness in species identification can be taken as settled.

In fact, it is far from settled. When Sokal and Crovello assert that taxonomy can proceed very well without the evolutionary species, "a theoretical ideal to which existing situations are forced to fit as closely as possible" (1984, 560), they are not alone, nor is their alternate approach—phenetics—without adherents. Nor is phenetics the only alternative. An advocate of "transformed cladistics" believes "that much of today's explanation of nature, in terms of neo-Darwinism or the synthetic theory, may be empty rhetoric" (C. Patterson 1982, 119).

At the heart of this problem is a paradox inherent in any taxonomic affirmation of evolutionary theory. If the theory is right, species cannot be natural kinds, entities with atemporal identities, like genes or electrons: full knowledge of intermediary varieties would demonstrate their wholly historical nature. Concerning Ernst Mayr's classic, *Systematics and the Origin of Species,* Niles Eldredge says: "His treatment of the entire problem implies a recognition that if one goes too far in embracing the principles of natural selection and adaptation as the be-all of evolution, the systematist [taxonomist] is left with nothing to explain" (1982, xix). In other words, any version of evolutionary theory eventually leads to the disappearance of the species as a legitimate natural kind. The evolutionary species is a rhetorical construct, an oxymoron created only by avoiding the full implications of the theory on which its existence apparently depends.

THE RHETORIC OF SCIENCE AS A DISCIPLINE

In their recent article on a contemporary controversy in evolutionary biology, John Lyne and Henry F. Howe (1986) demonstrate the possibility of doing first-rate rhetoric of science in the absence of explicit theory. Such a move—toward rhetorical criticism and away from theory—is understandable: one remembers how the call for a rhetoric of science decades ago ran aground when a surge of theory was unaccompanied by the outpouring of criticism that would have given that theory substance. But if the rhetoric of science is to establish itself permanently as a branch of inquiry, theory and practice must work together. By itself, rhetorical criticism can produce cogent and persuasive analyses of individual texts only by means of tacit theoretical assumptions; coupled with an adequate, coherent, and explicit theory, such criticism can establish the additional claim that the rhetoric of science is a discipline in its own right.

Joseph Gusfield makes a strong claim for the adjunct status of rhetorical analysis: "The rhetorical component *seems* to be unavoidable if the work is to have a theoretical . . . relevance. Thus an analysis of a scientific work *should* . . . include its rhetorical as well as its empirical component" (1976, 31; his italics). Gusfield's claim depends on a distinction that privileges science at the expense of rhetoric. This view has a clear and venerable source: Aristotle (trans. Ross 1971) asserts that rhetoric is not a field because it lacks a proper subject matter; furthermore, "in so far as anyone tries to construct either dialectic or rhetoric not as a knack but as a science, he will unconsciously destroy their nature, by passing over, in his attempt to reconstruct them, into sciences of definite subject-matters, and not of mere arguments" (1359b12–16). In issuing this warning, Aristotle shares with Gusfield a view of the epistemological superiority of the nomological over the hermeneutic disciplines.

When this mistaken view is set aside, the way is open to acknowledge the disciplinary status of rhetoric. As its subject matter, rhetoric has the persuasive structures of all fields, itself included. As the study of such structures in the sciences, the rhetoric of science presupposes that all components of disciplinary discourse are within its explanatory compass: there is no empirical or theoretical core, no essential science that reveals itself all the more clearly after the rhetorically analyzed components have been set aside. As a discipline, rhetoric may be expected to behave differently from classical physics: one does not expect laws of rhetoric or rhetorical predictions. But the disciplinary claim is fundamental; without disciplinary status, the rhetoric of science is not a field, but a bundle of techniques, an adjunct to fields.

When we ignore Aristotelian biases, we can easily set rhetoric beside such hermeneutical disciplines as history, Bible commentary, and literary criticism; indeed, its disciplinary status is far more ancient: the case can be made that it was the first organized body of hermeneutic study, the *ur-Geisteswissenschaft*. Throughout its long career, rhetoric has been over-shadowed first by philosophy, then by science, both of which limited its scope, and trivialized its usefulness. But such limits and such trivialization are not inherent in the nature of rhetorical theory; rather, they are the result of a continuing need in Western civilization to open up a space for the chimera of certain knowledge.

AN EPISTEMOLOGICAL PROBLEM

The disciplinary claim for rhetoric of science has as its source a funda-mental federalism about the domains of knowledge. In accord with this federalism, rhetoric is one discipline among many in a joint enterprise, a confederation of equally sovereign intellectual states. A central authority is deliberately absent; claims to such authority—the traditional claims of philosophy and theology—are wholly without merit. No discipline is, or can be, privileged over another. This paper exemplifies the absence of such privilege: it reconstructs evolutionary taxonomy in two equipollent ways.

According to its rational reconstruction, evolutionary taxonomy is a discipline at whose center lies the evolutionary species; in fact, belief in the reality of such species is the sine qua non of being an evolutionary tax-onomist. This rational reconstruction of science is both justificatory of, and coextensive with, science itself. For rhetoricians of science, on the other hand, the reality of the evolutionary species is essentially textual. Scientific texts are constituted through a symbolic interaction among scientists, an interaction constrained only by the recalcitrance of nature and by the cultural history embedded in language and lives. Rhetoricians insist that through this interaction scientists *"establish the real. The real* is as much a hypothetical construct as is the universal audience" (Karon 1976, 103).

Rational and rhetorical reconstruction differ in their fundamental mo-tivation. Rational reconstruction is clearly subsumed under "the cognitive interest in technical control over objectified processes" (Habermas 1971, 309; see also 212). Rhetorical reconstruction, on the other hand, is a manifestation of the practical interest "oriented toward mutual understand-ing in the conduct of life." This interest is "directed toward the transcen-dental structure of various actual forms of life, within each of which reality is interpreted according to a specific grammar of world-apprehension and of action." The structures of persuasion of evolutionary taxonomy are part of such a grammar (Habermas 1971, 311, 195).

108

Both reconstructions of evolutionary taxonomy are equally legitimate; each, though incomplete in the larger view, is complete in itself. But an autonomy so radical creates an epistemological problem. Each interest, the technical and the practical, has its appropriate epistemology, its bundles of pertinent analytical techniques. By way of contrast, the theoretical vantage of this paper lacks legitimation. By what right has evolutionary taxonomy been reconstructed, its reconstructions compared, and their ontological equipollence inferred?

AN EPISTEMOLOGICAL SOLUTION

Traditionally, transdisciplinary objectivity depended on our ability to "rise above" the narrow views of the "petty" kingdoms of disciplinary knowledge; to move outside their "confining" boundaries; to transcend their "parochial" concerns. Such objectivity licensed the class of statements at this paper's theoretical core. But our analysis of evolutionary taxonomy seems to confirm Wittgenstein's well-established view that objectivity consists in living by the laws of one intellectual state or another; in Wittgenstein's terminology, one form of life or another. Outside of these, there is apparently nothing, no real world we can use for our criterion.

So strict an interpretation of Wittgenstein has a certain plausibility. In particular sciences, there is the common experience that central concepts increase in ontological status, in objectivity, wholly within a single domain of interest, the technical. Did not Einstein's papers on Brownian movement put to rest any doubt about atomic reality? Did not Watson and Crick's discovery of the structure of DNA finally give the functional description of the heredity process a firm physical sense? But additional reference to the history of science reveals the incompleteness of this view. Galileo's battle against geocentricity, Young's struggle against the particle theory of light, Darwin's war against the argument from design: in each of these instances, a central concept, a scientific "fact"—geocentricity, particle theory, design—was revealed as a presupposition rooted, not only in the technical, but also in the practical interest, in tradition and in current, widespread use.

Indeed, in Habermas' view, it is in the practical interest that the true source of scientific objectivity lies. To agree with Habermas on this point is to say that science is a form of social action; that it progresses only in so far as it enhances human survival. Why does it often seem otherwise, especially to scientists?

Because science must secure the objectivity of its statements against the pressure and seduction of particular interests, it deludes itself about the fundamental interests to which it owes not only its impetus but *the conditions of possible objectivity* themselves (Habermas 1971, 311).

In this passage, Habermas explains the narrower sense of objectivity we so often meet in the sciences, and motivates a broader sense, one that encompasses both the technical and practical interest.

A strict interpretation of Wittgenstein, then, leads to a misunderstanding of science as an objective and rational pursuit. The rational and the rhetorical are far from opposites. Their alleged opposition, so deeply a part of our intellectual heritage, is nothing more than a rhetorical fiat in need of challenge. To undermine the Sophistic tenet that knowledge was rhetorically constituted, Plato and Aristotle drew a firm line where none had existed. Above *doxa*, a knowledge no more privileged than its knowers, they raised *episteme*, true knowledge: the complete and accurate depiction of an independent reality.

Without the long endorsement of this Platonic dream, an endorsement whose influence still strongly lingers in Western thought, would we not see similarity where we now see disparity? Where would definition by family resemblance be without the *topoi* of genus and difference? Need classification be independent of the *topos* of comparison? Is there an *essential* difference between scientific and rhetorical description? Between scientific and rhetorical definition? Is not the application of evolutionary theory a systematic use of the *topos* of antecedent and consequence? Is not the conflict between the rational and the rhetorical a civil war?

To negotiate a truce in this conflict, we need to draw on a sense of objectivity and rationality broader than that of any discipline. This broader sense has its source in the third and most important of Habermas's three human interests, the emancipatory, an interest one of whose purposes is to "[destroy] the illusion of objectivism [cultivated by the sciences] through demonstrating what it conceals: the connection of knowledge and interest" (Habermas 1971, 316–17). The vehicle of this emancipatory interest is critique, a discourse on discourse, dialectic in mode, ironic in manner. It is by means of critique that we reconstruct evolutionary taxonomy in two very different ways, and compare these reconstructions.

It is with critique that I would identify a broader, transdisciplinary sense of rhetoric, a sense different from that exemplified earlier by the application of the conceptual machinery of Aristotle's *Rhetoric* to the texts of evolutionary taxonomy. In this sense, rhetoric is not a discipline, but a perspective whose essential character is reflexive and ironic.[7]

In an apt political metaphor, Kenneth Burke captures this perspectival sense of rhetoric:

> Insofar as terms are thus encouraged to participate in an orderly parliamentary development, the dialectic of this participation produces (in the observer who considers the whole from the standpoint of the participation of all the terms rather than from the standpoint of any one participant) a "resultant certainty" of a different quality, necessarily ironic, since it requires that all the sub-certainties be considered as neither true nor false, but *contributory* (Burke 1962, 513).

This seems exactly right. From the point of view of rhetoric as critique, the rationality of science consists in the continuing dialectic among its legitimate reconstructions, each the surrogate for the informed assent of an interpretive community; analogously, the objectivity of science is constituted by some configuration of these reconstructions. Such configurations must be viewed ironically; only if irony is presupposed do they avoid the charge of inconsistency.

CONCLUSION

Rhetoric is both a discipline and a perspective from which disciplines can be viewed. As a discipline, it has a hermeneutic task and generates knowledge; as a perspective, it has a critical, emancipatory task and generates new points of view. The central goal of this paper is not hermeneutic, but critical and emancipatory: a new perspective is elaborated, illustrated, refined. If the job of critique has been successfully accomplished, the reader will have been persuaded of the untenability of a sharp distinction between rhetoric and rationality. She will have been convinced that such a distinction entails an unduly narrow view of both rhetoric and rationality, and a gratuitous denigration of human-centered knowledge. Finally, she will have been persuaded that evolutionary taxonomy is a species of such knowledge.

111

NOTES

1. Although scientific characterization of the species is a subject of serious controversy (Hull, 1981a, 1981b, 1983a, 1983b), I think these views are defensible.

2. This orthodox view is not held by radical pheneticists (Hull 1981a).

3. Systematists do not only use characters; they also "[inquire] into the origin and nature of the units with which [they work]" (Mayr 1982, 9).

4. According to Hull (1983a), it is a general practice in much of biology to deal with species as natural kinds: "though comparative anatomists clearly acknowledge that species evolve, they insist that they can go about their business as if they did not" (p. 76).

5. I dwell on Popper because scientists do; I am far from holding up his ideas as an accurate way to reconstruct good scientific practice. Whatever the status of evolutionary theory in relation to taxonomy, taxonomists have successfully practiced for centuries a science that is simply not about bold conjectures and crucial observations. Indeed, it is even questionable whether physics, Popper's obvious model, is such a science. Let us glance at one famous instance: the bending of light in a gravitational field, designed as a crucial test of general relativity. In this instance, the data physicists found so convincing exhibited a scatter far wider than any ordinary canons of proof would allow (Bernstein 1985, 141–46; compare Franklin 1986, 226–43). In the end, as Bernstein makes clear, physicists were persuaded as much by the elegance of the theory as by its alleged resistance to falsification, a resistance that, under different circumstances, could easily have been given the opposite interpretation. What is true in physics is true a fortiori in evolutionary taxonomy: "The reason for taxonomists paying so much attention to the works of Popper is that they think that they can use his Principle of Falsifiability to show that *their* classifications are truly scientific, while those of their opponents are not" (Hull 1981a, 142).

6. It is also possible to hold with the cladists that evolution is only a theory of descent. This narrower version of evolution does not seem pertinent to papers in my sample.

7. These two meanings of rhetoric correspond to Husserl's distinction between two sorts of reflection: the natural and the radical (Carr 1974, 16–27).

REFERENCES

Aristotle. 1982 [1926]. *The Art of Rhetoric.* Trans. J. H. Freese. Cambridge: Harvard University Press.

Bambrough, R. 1966 [1960–61]. "Universals and Family Resemblances," in G. Pitcher, ed., *Wittgenstein: the Philosophical Investigations, A Collection of Critical Essays.* Notre Dame, Ind.: University of Notre Dame Press, 186–204.

Barthes, R. 1967 [1964]. *Elements of Semiology.* Trans. A. Lavers and C. Smith. New York: Hill and Wang.

———. 1974 [1970]. *S/Z: An Essay.* Trans. R. Miller. New York: Hill and Wang.

Bernstein, Jeremy. 1985 [1973]. *Einstein.* Hammondsworth England: Penguin.

Burke, K. 1962 [1945, 1950]. "Four Master Tropes," in *A Grammar of Motives and A Rhetoric of Motives.* Cleveland: World, 503–17.

Carnap, R. 1963. "Intellectual Autobiography," in *The Philosophy of Rudolph Carnap.* Ed. P. A. Schilpp. LaSalle, Ill.: Open Court Press, 3–84.

Carr, David. 1974. *Phenomenology and the Problem of History.* Evanston, Ill.: Northwestern University Press.

Churchland, Paul M., and Clifford A. Hooker. 1985. *Images of Science: Essays on Realism and Empiricism, with a Reply from Bas C. Van Fraassen.* Chicago: University of Chicago Press.

Darwin, C. 1959. *The Life and Letters.* 2 vols. Ed. F. Darwin. New York: Basic Books.

———. 1972 [1903]. *More Letters.* 2 vols. Ed. F. Darwin. New York: Johnson Reprint.

———. 1964 [1859]. *On the Origin of Species.* 1st ed. Cambridge: Cambridge University Press.

———. 1962 [1872]. *On the Origin of Species.* 6th ed. New York: Collier.

Eldredge, Niles. 1982. "Introduction." *See* Mayr.

Fitzpatrick, J. W. 1980. "A New Race of *Atlapetes leucopterus,* with Comments on Widespread Albinism in A. *l. dresseri* (Taczanowski)." *Auk* 97:883–87.

Fitzpatrick, J. W., and O'Neill, J. P. 1979. "A New Tody-Tyrant from Northern Peru." *Auk* 96:443–47.

Fitzpatrick, J. W., Willard, D. E., and Terborgh, J. W. 1979. "A New Species of Hummingbird from Peru." *The Wilson Bulletin* 91:177–86.

Franklin, Allan. 1986. *The Neglect of Experiment.* Cambridge: Cambridge University Press.

Gadamer, H.-G. 1975 [1965]. *Truth and Method.* Trans. G. Barden and J. Cumming. New York: Crossroad.

113

Greenfield, D. W., and Glodek, G. S. 1977. "*Trachelyichthys exilis*, A New Species of Catfish (Pisces: Auchenipteridae) from Peru." *Fieldiana: Zoology* 72:47–58.

Gusfield, J. 1976. "The Literary Rhetoric of Science: Comedy and Pathos in Drinking Driver Research." *American Sociological Review* 41:16–34.

Habermas, J. 1971 [1968]. *Knowledge and Human Interests*. Trans. J. J. Shapiro. Boston: Beacon.

————. 1982. "A Reply to My Critics," in *Habermas: The Critical Debates*, ed. J. B. Thompson and D. Held. Cambridge: The MIT Press, 219–83.

Hull, D. L. 1981a. "The Principles of Biological Classification: The Use and Abuse of Philosophy." *PSA 1976* 2:130–53.

————. 1981b. "Reduction and Genetics." *The Journal of Medicine and Philosophy* 6:125–43.

————. 1983a. "Darwin and the Nature of Science," in *Evolution from Molecules to Men*, ed. D. S. Bendall. Cambridge: Cambridge University Press, 63–80.

————. 1983b. "Karl Popper and Plato's Metaphor," in *Advances in Cladistics*, vol. 2, ed. N. Platnick and V. Funk. New York: Columbia University Press, 177–89.

————. 1984 [1978]. "A Matter of Individuality," in *Conceptual Issues in Evolutionary Biology: An Anthology*, ed. E. Sober. Cambridge: The MIT Press, 623–45.

Johnstone, H. W., Jr. 1978. *Validity and Rhetoric in Philosophical Argument: An Outlook in Transition*. University Park, Pa.: The Dialogue Press of Man & World.

Karon, L. A. 1976. "Presence in *The New Rhetoric*." *Philosophy and Rhetoric* 9:96–111.

Kethley, J. 1983. "The Deutonymph of *Epiphis rarior* Berlese, 1916 (Epiphidinae n. subfam., Rhodacaridae, Rhodacaroidea)." *Canadian Journal of Zoology* 61:2598–611.

Köhler, W. 1947. *Gestalt Psychology*. New York: New American Library.

Kuhn, T. S. 1977. *The Essential Tension: Selected Studies in Scientific Tradition and Change*. Chicago: University of Chicago Press.

Latour, Bruno, and Steve Woolgar. 1979. *Laboratory Life: The Social Construction of Scientific Facts*. Beverly Hills: Sage.

Lewontin, R. C. 1984. "The Structure of Evolutionary Genetics," in *Conceptual Issues in Evolutionary Biology: An Anthology*, ed. E. Sober. Cambridge: The MIT Press, 3–13.

Lyne, J., and H. F. Howe. 1986. "'Punctuated Equilibria': The Dynamics of a Scientific Controversy." *Quarterly Journal of Speech* 72:132–47.

Mayr, Ernst. 1982 [1942]. *Systematics and the Origin of Species*. New York: Columbia University Press.

Medawar, P. 1984. *Pluto's Republic*. Oxford: Oxford University Press.

Patterson, B. D. 1982. "Pleistocene Vicariance, Montane Islands, and the Evolutionary Divergence of Some Chipmunks (Genus *Eutamias*)." *Journal of Mammology* 63:387–98.

Patterson, C. 1982. "Cladistics," in *Evolution Now: A Century After Darwin*. ed. J. M. Smith. San Francisco: W. H. Freeman, 110–20.

Perelman, C., and Olbrechts-Tyteca, L. 1969 [1958]. *The New Rhetoric: A Treatise on Argumentation*. Trans. J. Wilkinson and P. Weaver. Notre Dame, Ind.: University of Notre Dame Press.

Popper, K. R. 1965. *Conjectures and Refutations: The Growth of Scientific Knowledge*. New York: Harper & Row, 1965.

Popper, K. R. 1968 [1934]. *The Logic of Scientific Discovery*. New York: Harper & Row.

Ricqlès, A. de, and Bolt, J. R. 1983. "Jaw Growth and Tooth Replacement in *Captorhinus Aguti* (Reptilia: Captorhinomorpha): A Morphological and Histological Analysis." *Journal of Vertebrate Paleontology* 3:7–24.

Ross, D. 1971 [1949]. *Aristotle*. London: Metheun.

Shapin, S. 1984. "Pump and Circumstance: Robert Boyle's Literary Technology." *Social Studies of Science* 14:481–520.

Sokal, R. R., and Crovello, T. J. 1984. "The Biological Species Concept: A Critical Evaluation," in *Conceptual Issues in Evolutionary Biology: An Anthology*, ed. E. Sober. Cambridge: The MIT Press, 541–66.

Solem, A. 1978. "Cretaceous and Early Tertiary Camaenid Land Snails from Western North America (Mollusca: Pulmonata)." *Journal of Paleontology* 52:581–89.

Turner, V. M. 1981. *The Drums of Affliction: A Study of Religious Processes Among the Ndembu of Zambia*. Ithaca: Cornell University Press.

Wittgenstein, L. 1965 [1958]. *Preliminary Studies for the 'Philosophical Investigations.' Generally Known as the Blue and Brown Books*. New York: Harper & Row.

4

Psychoanalysis:
Science or Rhetoric?

Tullio Maranhão

In this paper it is argued that the question whether psychoanalysis is science or rhetoric is meaningless. The insistence on this dilemma stems from the assumption that science is the knowledge of essential qualities produced by invention/discovery, and rhetoric is the art of expressing knowledge by means of explanation/interpretation. The discussion begins by pointing out that the criteria of verification and falsification in the philosophy of science cannot be maintained beyond dispute. As a consequence, the kind of knowledge called scientific hardly fits the orthodox notion of science. Looking back to classical philosophy one realizes that the classification of branches of knowledge or intellectual arts was already a concern among the thinkers of ancient civilization. However, when one turns to the contemporary intellectual debates, one inevitably realizes that the distinction between discovery (or invention) and explanation (or interpretation) is not as discrete as the scientific tradition has assumed. The reason for this resides in the fact that culture has moved in the direction of restraining action at the expense of representation. This has been accomplished both in the ideology of motive, illustrated for example by the principle according to which action must be preceded by reflection, and in the evolution of the communication media (oral, visual, printed, and electronic). In this sense, psychoanalysis spearheads the development of science. It dilutes the differences between invention/discovery and explanation/interpretation, making indirect persuasion the instrument of treatment, of inquiry, and of scholarly demonstration. The essay is a critique of such developments which confine the possibility of action to the realm of simulation at the same time preserving the individual as the only source—simulacrum, I would say—of autonomous action.

The concern with rhetoric is back in the Western cultural tradition, although it seems never to have subsided entirely. But is the rhetoric of our contemporary interest the discipline resulting from the hairsplitting of Western analytics, or does it entertain some resemblance to its medieval namesake, which stood side by side with logic and grammar as a pillar of education? The Western analytic classification of spheres of discourse and knowledge started with Plato and Aristotle. The first classificatory effort applied to rhetoric opposed it to philosophy and deemed it incapable of producing knowledge. It is from this erstwhile endeavor of the ancient philosophers that we inherited our current ordinary notion of rhetoric: the art of persuasion, especially in oratory. Once separated from philosophy, from logic, from grammar, from poetics, from the emotions, from the propositional content of the statement, rhetoric was presented as insubstantial and became a supplement, that is, a collection of procedures to persuade others of anything a source of voice wishes.

But the attempt to isolate it as supplement has failed consistently, even when carried to its fullest, as by Descartes and Leibniz, by Kant, and during the heyday of logical positivism. The reason for this systematic failure resides in the fact that rhetoric, in addition to being supplement, is also complement, that is, a necessary extension of things other than rhetoric itself, an extension of the essence of language and of other systems of signs, of speech and of text, or of poetry and of drama. Insofar as it is complement, it is a part of that which it completes, and thus can metonymically refer to the whole.

The distinction between the complementary and supplementary characterizations of rhetoric will be rendered clearer by briefly looking into the etymology of the two words. They denote something which completes a whole, something unessential, incidental and additional, something which, although fitting, is not entirely necessary. Both words contain as central morpheme the Indo-European root *pelə* - or *plē-*, meaning to fill, which yielded the Latin forms *complēre*, to complete, and *supplēre*, to supply. But there is a difference in the prefixes *com-* and *sub-* (the *b* is assimilated by the *p* in *supplement*). The Indo-European prefixes are *kom-*, conveying the meaning of 'with,' 'together,' 'common,' and 'shared,' and *upo-*, 'under,' 'over,' and 'above'. Drawing on this etymological description, by *complementary* I mean a necessary extension of essence which is an identical quality of that which it extends. The *supplement* is a conjunctive quality, that is, a surplus of essence. While a complement fulfills a whole, a supplement adds to it.

No discourse has more sternly opposed rhetoric than the scientific. Descartes introduced the scientific essay as a text written in a bare, simple, and pure style which in its self-restraint would allow essence to fully express itself. In the Cartesian cosmology, we find the world divided into the divine, matter, sensation, and a complex of intellectual faculties where rhetoric would belong. The refinement of the analytic hairsplitting from Aristotle on led to a separation of the intellect, will, and emotion, which was fully realized in the Age of Enlightenment. Rhetoric became identified with each of these categories, depending on the purpose of the identification: with intellect, for example, for noble causes, or with emotion when the argument needed to be invalidated. With the triumph of science, rhetoric was swept out at the end of the analytic continuum, banned even from emotion, and reduced to the supplementary and sophistic caricature in which, as an unnecessary extension of substance, it was also considered evil and unethical.

The Freudian project for psychoanalysis was designed in the last quarter of the nineteenth century as an alternative to religious discourse in the explanation, evaluation, and correction of human conduct. The analysis of the psyche was not alone in its cultural challenging of religion. From the very moment of its creation, psychoanalysis sought a close association with medicine, an important ally in the war against religion. In the same way that the physician is the healer of the body, the psychoanalyst was cast as the healer of the psyche, and even today societies of professionals still require that their practitioners hold degrees in medicine before they undergo psychoanalytic training, despite the fact that the links between the two disciplines have faded beyond recognition, if they ever truly existed.

One hundred years after the invention of psychoanalysis, the schools of psychotherapy are counted in the hundreds, and there are many rival theories of the psyche and uncountable practices of therapy in clinical work. Psychoanalysis in its orthodox form has lost a great deal of the aplomb it enjoyed until the Second World War. From its ranks, clever practitioners have initiated processes of revision, but there have been so many that they no longer seem to be revisions of the same corpus of beliefs, and they seem even less to be complementary to one another. Moreover, the many different projects of psychotherapy do not stem from the psychoanalytic trunk alone, as we have therapies based on behaviorist theories, on theories of symbols, on literary criticism, on systems theory, game theory, cybernetics, and so on. Psychotherapeutic discourse cannot claim to be a unit as long as it is constituted by so varied a set of theories. Many psychotherapists of different persuasions cherish the hope that their particular field will stand out in the mumbo jumbo of theoretical bantering, and those harboring such hopes think that redemption shall come on the wings of scientific certification.

In the present essay I shall focus on some proposals for an updated scientific psychoanalysis as discussed in a variety of books and articles such as those by Hook (1960), Brenner (1968), Sherwood (1969), Malan (1976), Fisher and Greenberg (1977), Glymour (1980), Edelson (1984), and Grünbaum (1984). Next I shall argue that the theories in psychotherapy are rhetorical strategies—of rhetoric qua complement—and that clinical work is part of that with which we are all involved: everyday conversation, the dialogue through which we think about life as something that unfolds and goes on. Of all psychotherapies, I have chosen psychoanalysis, first because from within this field come the strongest claims for scientificity, and secondly because its theories, or rhetorical strategies, are far more developed than those of competing psychotherapies.

Let us begin with the scientific claims. Marshall Edelson candidly states some of the reasons behind his effort to prove psychoanalysis scientific by asking: "How [can we] remain mute, as policymakers in [sic] our society must decide in what way to distribute *finite available resources among competing ends, and among competing means* for *achieving the same end?* How evade, as patients must decide, among literally hundreds of treatments competing for their scarce resources, on the fastest, least costly treatment—but also on the treatment that will do the particular job the patient wants done and in the way the patient wants to do it?" (Edelson 1984, xii; emphasis added.). This can be read as a statement that the scientific foundation of psychoanalysis will help the discipline survive as commodity in a political economy in which treatment must be quick, cheap, and efficacious. However, psychoanalysis cannot compete with its rival, brief therapies, and in terms of costs, it probably is the most unaffordable therapy available. The last resort to reinstate its credibility as a competitive commodity must therefore reside in the authority of its methods. Edelson procedes: "What is at issue is whether there is a methodology that is *logically* capable of assessing the scientific credibility of psychoanalytic hypotheses, and especially whether it is in principle *logically* possible (not merely practically feasible) to use data obtained in the psychoanalytic situation to test these hypotheses" (1984, xiii).

In terms of the criteria in the philosophy of science the question is whether the data of psychoanalysis can be empirically verified, whether psychoanalytic hypotheses can be falsified, and whether the objects of psychoanalytic inquiry come from the clinical context, or whether experimental observation is possible at all in this field.

First, the question of verification. Are the psychoanalytic discoveries testable? Let us take as our example the linkage between jealousy, homosexuality, and paranoia, which I loosely paraphrase from Freud's "Certain Neurotic Mechanisms in Jealousy, Paranoia, and Homosexuality" (Freud

1953–74, 18:221–71). The extravagant jealousy of a patient leads him to suspect that his wife is cuckolding him. But as it turns out, she is absolutely faithful to him, and not the slightest evidence can be found to justify the suspicion. The case of jealousy then is explained as paranoia, as a radical departure from reality and the takeover of the faculty representing reality by the pathological intrapsychic process. The patient's jealousy is furthermore explained as a manifestation of latent homosexuality. The patient directs his intense feelings towards men, in his imagination, those represented as rivals, as threats, but indeed the objects of his affective releases. Finally, the homosexual nature of jealousy is explained as being derived from narcissistic displacement, that is, the patient is trying to construct himself as the object of his love, and the task is rendered somehow easier as long as he can project this love object onto other men. The symptom, jealousy, is explained in terms of a chain of psychological processes: narcissistic disturbance→narcissistic love→facilitating projection of self onto others of the same sex (homosexuality)→love experienced as fear, anger, threat → love experienced as jealousy (distortion of the love feelings) → arbitrarily jealous construction of reality characteristic of paranoia.

The only observable and empirically verifiable element in this chain is jealousy, the behavior to be explained and treated away, which in the psychoanalytic scientific hypothesis is converted into a symptom, a red herring. That which is claimed to be the case, that is, the sequence of narcissism-projection-homosexuality-paranoia cannot be observed. For the hard-nosed logical positivist this would be enough to impugn psychoanalysis as science, but the philosophy of science has already been forced by the natural sciences themselves to loosen up the criteria of verification, by admitting that the explanatory power of theories can only be evaluated against the backdrop of the ontological universe in which a particular theory arises (Kuhn 1969). Thus psychoanalysis overcomes the first obstacle to arriving at the pinnacle of science by falling into the loosened criteria, for its concepts do form a coherent whole describing the psyche as sets of processes which are not only meshed with one another in logical connections, but which in addition bear a strong resemblance to other processes observed in nature, such as those of body physiology or of hydraulics. The similarity of the logic of the psychoanalytic explanation to other explanatory systems would render psychoanalysis unsuspicious to science.

Now we turn to the question of falsifiability. Scientific axioms or statements such as "It is going to rain" are tested by hypotheses such as "If there

120

are clouds in the sky, it is going to rain". If the hypothesis fails, and the rain never falls, another hypothesis must be found. The more falsifiable the hypotheses stemming from an axiom are, the more rigorously proven the axiom will be when it finally finds its confirming test. For this reason, hypotheses that cannot be falsified are of no interest to science. If the hypothesis in the example above had been, "If there are clouds in the sky, it may rain or it may not rain," it would be nonfalsifiable and therefore useless for science. The condition of falsifiability was introduced by Popper (1959) in an attempt to release scientific inquiry from the straitjacket of verification. The argument against psychoanalysis on these grounds, as put forward by Popper (1974), is that its hypotheses are nonfalsifiable; in other words, they can always be proven right, and thus have no explanatory value.

In his minute answer to the Popperian indictment of psychoanalysis, Grünbaum (1984, 108–26) argues that (1) Freud did indeed submit his hypotheses to falsification, which he illustrates with "A Case of Paranoia Running Counter to the Psychoanalytic Theory of the Disease" (Freud 1953–74, 14:263–72), whose title already indicates Freud's falsifying intentions. He further shows that (2) Popper's theory of falsifiability is untenable because it depends on verification, and as we argued in the foregoing discussion, that which is scientifically valid is not only that which is empirically verifiable. Grünbaum denies that Freud wished to explain all human conduct, as in Popper's accusation. Next (3) Grünbaum reviews the argument that since there are competing psychoanalytic theories, such as Adler's and Freud's, for example, and since the differences between them cannot be decided, Freudian psychoanalysis cannot be scientific. He argues that, according to Popper himself, since these theories have no empirical basis, they cannot be objected to on verification grounds, and it is possible to decide which is the best among them only in terms of their explanatory logic. This means that the choice between two rival theories in psychoanalysis must be made on the basis of their persuasive power. We must distinguish here two facets of psychoanalytic persuasion: one directed at the general public and the other aimed at patients.

There are overlaps and discrepancies between theory and clinical work, and one of Freud's main concerns was to eliminate the gap between the theory and practice of psychoanalysis, a project which remained unfinished. Naturally, clinical success alone would be another criterion for deciding among competing approaches, but here again things are muddled because every school can present records of success, and these are difficult to compare. In addition, even if psychoanalysis were a "metaphysics"

121

Popper would not be able to know for sure whether or not it would ever become a testable theory, argues Grünbaum. Next (4), Grünbaum invokes the fact that Freud was never reluctant to change his mind, as in asserting that the psychoanalytic treatment had a prophylactic effect (Freud 1953–74, 20:20–43) and denying it later on (Freud 1953–74, 23:216–54). He then discusses the etiology of neuroses, addressing the question of whether the theory of the psyche is based on diagnoses of particular cases or on an independent formulation of the etiology. He argues (5) that Freud employed case-diagnostic and etiologic inferences as mirrors of each other, neither one being made the foundation stone of the other. This of course adds further credence to Freud's acceptance of falsifiability. Finally, he argues that (6) clinical confirmation and disconfirmation are therapeutic devices and not theoretical features; therefore they cannot be considered as creating an obdurate resistance against falsifiability. The notion of ambivalence in Freud's writings is not intended as a defense against potential falsifications, but makes an important contribution to knowledge by introducing a logic of emotions in which contradictory tendencies such as love and hate are simultaneous.

The criteria of verification and falsifiability do not have the same importance for the philosophy of science as they used to enjoy, but many advocates of psychoanalysis as science still make efforts to prove that the psychoanalytic hypotheses are both verifiable and falsifiable. Before the questions pertaining to the scientific canon can be asked about psychoanalysis, the analysts would have to show first that systematic observation can be carried out in the clinical context with predictable results, and that experimentation is possible in their field of inquiry. The clinical context is suspect to scientific observation because it is embedded in the interpersonal relationship between analyst and analysand, and because the data emanating from this context are filtered by the verbal conduct typical of conversation. The study of conversation can focus either on language per se or on the speakers' intentions lying behind the utterances, or on both. For Freud, these two emphases seemed to be mutually exclusive. In hermeneutics, or in the analytic philosophy of language, conversely, linguistic conventions and speakers' intentions are welded together; their unity is regarded as indispensible to understanding speech. However, the Freudian project for psychoanalysis did not thrust the discipline into the groove of the study of language.[1] Indeed, language was regarded as an obstacle to—although also as an instrument of—the psychoanalytic treatment, or at best a trap of which the analyst should be aware. When a suppressed motive is freed from repression and brought to the patient's consciousness, the neurotic symptom may not be removed, if the linguistico-conversational act of raising to consciousness is not accompanied by the release of the repressed affect. Language thus functions as a pilot, but the true object of psychoanalysis is the psyche.

The main reason for the psychoanalysts' wariness about regarding their discipline as a hermeneutics resides in the fact that although conversational partners use words to influence one another, in therapy the direction of persuasion cannot be determined by the meanings in language alone. The act of influencing with words in analysis is supposed to be controlled by the analyst. The patient's speech reflects the transferential bond with the therapist; it is symptomatic conduct occupying the place of a suppressed desire. A patient complains about the analyst's schedule, and this is interpreted as a fear of being controlled by the therapist, or a patient complains about her husband's bossiness, and this is interpreted as a discourse about the analyst. In the absence of the transferential bond, there can be no treatment, because the relation between therapist and client would be deprived of interest to the latter. Naturally, people who seek psychoanalytic treatment do so out of a concern with their lives, their self-images, their performances in the world, and not to exercise transference. However, in the Freudian rationale, if a person is concerned about a state of affairs, S, and if the concern is true and correct, it will bring forth a resolution, or the concern will be abandoned. Neurosis is characterized by the inappropriateness of the concern with S, by its misplacement, for the psychoanalytic hypothesis is that the presented problem is the symptom, and it only becomes so painfully outstanding because it repeats itself. On the one hand, no resolution emerges, stressing the inconvenience of the situation; on the other hand all the outcomes the symptomatic conduct can produce are frustrating for the person, because they do not address the primordial issue: a repressed desire. The patient relates to others as congeries of painful experiences, as interlocutors resulting more from his own projection than from their own real traits. The analyst is no exception in the patient's world of fantasied others. Actually, because of the intensity of the psychoanalytic relationship, the therapist becomes a privileged object of transference and fantasy.

There are no lists of symptomatic conduct and traumatic events, and whether a statement is transferential or not depends on the analyst's interpretation which, in turn, depends on the context of the analysis. Each treatment can be unique, even when several patients are treated by the same analyst, and in every treatment the patient's statements and reports are regarded as a smoke screen designed to conceal the heart of the matter.

The picture so far outlined could lead to a cynical representation of psychoanalysis with the psychoanalyst in the role of a sophist rhetor, using a confusing repertoire of rhetorical maneuvers in order to convince patients that they are wrong and that the analyst's interpretation is right. This, however, is not at all the case. The preceding description can be readily rejected on three grounds. First, psychoanalysis is not a random process of persuasion; it has a theory of the psyche, a theory of the mind, a metapsychology from which both the diagnostic description of conduct and the therapeutic techniques derive. Secondly, Freud was greatly concerned about the possibility of the influences in the therapeutic encounter failing to correspond to the affects to which they should be related. Thirdly, the state of mental health or well-being sought in analysis is not arbitrary, for it needs the seal of consensus between analyst and analysand and, furthermore, this consensus must be consilient with the cultural context within which the interaction takes place. This is not tantamount to saying that culture is the uncontroversial bottom line of psychoanalysis. Indeed, as I argue elsewhere (Maranhão n.d.), psychoanalysis is a form of cultural criticism in the face of controversial definitions of happiness and well-being. Cultural criticism, however, is not pure and simple demolition of established values; it always entails the advocacy of one form of life over another. But I do not want to discuss the theory of personality in the present essay; I shall focus instead on the issue of suggestion.[2]

What is the sign that an interpretation has worked in the sense of freeing the flow of a repressed motive to the patient's consciousness? One of Freud's main preoccupations was with the danger of the analyst's influencing the patient as far as to induce a symptom remission that does not last because it results from suggestion, not from the resolution of psychological conflicts. The psychoanalyst should beware of that ultimate threat to his success, a danger which ironically is ever more present the broader the prestige of psychoanalysis and the higher the analyst's authority. The criterion for deciding whether an interpretation had hit the right chord and whether the patient's realization constituted a turning point was problematic. It depended basically on the analysand's assent or dissent in reaction to the clinical intervention. How could the analyst tell when the assent expressed a change in the psyche and when it was to be explained as the result of the therapist's influence? In some cases the patient would be aware of his conduct as symptom as well as of the antecedent traumatic event, and yet could not help but repeat the very conduct that so distressed him.

Freud's hypothesis is that the patient does not remember what has been repressed, but acts it out. The action remains unsatisfactory because it does not meet the needs of the blocked drive or instinct. The acting out then is repeated. Transference, Freud concluded, is an instance of the repetition, an additional symptom put in the place of the forgotten past (Freud 1953–74, 12:145). Consequently, repeating or acting out is a substitute for remembering. Since these operations will come forth only through verbal actions, we can say that the psychoanalytic treatment consists in a replacement of the strategic use of language—utterances made as acting out something—with a reflexive use of language—propositions uttered for the sake of talking about something which would avoid conflict. It is interesting to observe, as we shall discuss later on, that while the patient is bonded to this principle of the reflexive use of language in the name of his mental sanity, the analyst is not. The analyst behaves as an authoritative persuader, thus resorting to a strategic use of language.

Is the moment of consciousness decisively therapeutic? If it were, the right interpretation carried out at the right time would produce the desired cure. But the experience of psychoanalysis is that after the realization, there follows the habituation. Analysts prefer to talk about this in terms of dogged resistance taking the form of rationalizations. The treatment does not end upon the first assent on the part of the patient seemingly echoing the repressed drives or instincts. One could read the program for psychoanalysis as proposing that the analyst first interrupts the belief the analysand has held. In the second stage, he replaces the old with a new belief, and meets with the patient's assent. Finally, there follows a period of apprenticeship during which the analysand acquaints himself with the new belief, learning how to reorganize his emotional life around the new worldview. Psychoanalysts naturally describe treatment differently. They say that the analyst anticipates for the patient that which may be the case, but he also needs to *treat* the patient, that is, to work the symptom through in its relation to the traumata. The corollary of this clinical insight is that the moment of the interpretation is not final and decisive, and that the release of repressed affections depends on much talking and on extensive clinical routines.

Freud never gave us a picture of the healthy person, who would not need psychoanalytic treatment. From his writings emerges a conception of the psyche according to which everyone can eventually benefit from analysis, and the termination of the treatment does not mean a passage from pathology to normality. We do not find a hierarchy of psychoneuroses in his writings in the sense, for example, of obsession-compulsion being worse than hysteria, but whatever is the nature of the affliction, what varies

125

from one treatment to the next is the ruggedness of the defense. Nevertheless, one may discover the ways to mental health in the Freudian philosophy. We have already seen that the reflexive is valued over the strategic use of language, in which the utterances are an acting out, not of that which they mean, but of something else lurking in the foldings of repression. Now we are in a position to single out a second major component of the healthy mind: the originality of its states as opposed to repetitiveness.

According to the Freudian explanation, the drives or instincts constitute the main targets of repression. But somehow, in order for the psyche to be healthy and balanced, the wishes contained in these drives must be fulfilled. Originally Freud proposed two drives: sexual and aggressive (Freud 1953–74, 7:125). The unrestrained fulfillment of these, however, would lead to the destruction of sociocultural life. As a consequence of the threat arising from the external pressures on the self, Freud felt the need to introduce a third drive, that of self-preservation, countering the tendencies of its two predecessors (Freud 1953–74, 18:3). Revising the theory in *Beyond the Pleasure Principle*, Freud changed drives from forces that move unrelentingly forward in a blind pursuit of pleasure into forces for the preservation of the self. Thus sexual restraint may be the fulfillment of a need for protection instead of the work of repression. It is on the inhibition of drives that the best of human civilization rests, Freud claimed (1953–74, 18:34–36). Nevertheless the inhibited drives press forward, and it is the differential between the satisfaction demanded and achieved which keeps the drives pressing. The theory of the drives entirely escapes the Cartesian logic, as does most of Freud's logic of emotions, in the sense that these desires harbor contradictory tendencies, sex and aggression on one hand, and sex-aggression and self-preservation on the other. The complete release of all drives is eschatological. Pushing Freud's ideas to their limit, a scenario arises in which the fulfillment of drives can only be a partial goal. This however is not something to worry about, since repression excels at its function. Indeed, it goes too far, and the role of psychoanalysis is to attenuate its effects. Psychoanalytic treatment, however, does not even come close to a complete liberation of desire, something which could be as devastating as its complete suppression.

The question comes to mind: if the outstanding characteristic of life is the state of repressed drives, is not our conduct predominantly repetitive? The quest for the originality of action in this case becomes unjustifiable. Are the psychoanalyst's interventions themselves not repetitive, the acting out of repressed drives? Repetition and originality are issues fraught with

philosophical implications and of paramount importance in the philosophies of Kant and Hegel, Nietzsche and Kierkegaard (Deleuze, 1968).
Although we do not have to go into detail in this discussion, a philosophical distinction between kinds of repetition will be helpful for an understanding of the Freudian notion. Repetition can be reproductive, that is, a
repetition of exactly the same event, and differential, that is, a repetition
which at each instance introduces a slight modification into that which is
repeated. The Freudian repetition must be regarded as differential if we
want to preserve the drive theory and account for the analyst's therapeutic
discourse as corrective, and yet part of the wide plan of repetitiveness in the
preservation of the self.

The bulk of thought then is repetitive. Moreover thinking merely
replaces that which really matters, the traumatic fears leading to repression. As a consequence, reason is of no avail to overcome distortion of
reality. The scaffolding from which one can begin to deconstruct the
rational/rationalizing whitewashing of the psychological reality, Freud
imagined, resides precisely at the antipodes of reason, that is, in dreams,
slips of the tongue and of the pen, and in the free association of ideas. The
bizarre connections established in these "faulty" expressions of meaning
catch unawares the unconscious defenses, deeply probing the forbidden
motives pent up in repression. The free association of ideas, like dreams,
breaks away from the patterns of repetition, signaling that which is not
supposed to emerge into consciousness. Free association became the
method, or rule, presiding over the patient's discourse in psychoanalytic
treatment.

The story repeats itself in every new treatment. The patient comes in
with complaints, with descriptions of how he feels and how his life is
going, and in many cases he has explanations to account for his problems,
although in spite of his understanding, he feels impotent to change things.
The explanations belong to his reasons, his rationalizations in psychoanalytic terms: defenses whose sole purpose is to prevent the resolution of the
problems. Again, in an uncharitable rendition of the Freudian project for
psychoanalysis, it could be said that whatever beliefs the patient comes in
with will eventually be dropped in the face of the analyst's interpretive
rhetoric and replaced by other beliefs. In this sense, psychoanalysis would
not change states of affairs in the psyche; it would change the explanations
of these states of affairs, thereby enabling the analysand to change things
by operating out of a new self-representation. Psychoanalysts will easily
dismiss this argument by stating that the previous beliefs brought in by the
patient were repetitions designed to conceal, while the new beliefs repre-

127

sent a liberation from the repetitive vicious circle. Nonetheless, it can be counterargued that the new beliefs, after settling within the patient's worldview, will be repetitively employed to explain life situations in the future. A few years after the changes brought about by psychoanalysis, what would be the difference between the pre- and post-analytic reasons? Undoubtedly analysis facilitates reasoning by uncluttering the way of thinking, but it is not from the point of view of reason that it raises its claims. For psychoanalysis rationality is always suspicious.

Free association is the first step towards reestablishing the primacy of memory. It is based on the assumption that there is a correct narrative. Even after Freud abandoned the assumption that the patient's narrative corresponded to actual events taking place in his life, psychoanalytic theory continued to hold fast to the supposition that there is a correct narrative which, although independent of the referents, constitutes the right account of what goes on in the psychological life. The implication of this hypothesis is that there are wrong narratives. The mind of the neurotic patient would be steeped in equivocal recountings of his life. But the congerie of misrepresentations would entertain a certain relationship with the right motives. Moreover, cracks in the narrative structure could reveal what lay underneath. A man mistakenly referring to his wife by the expression "my mother" would be letting it transpire that the feelings he was talking about, allegedly towards his wife, were indeed related to his mother. The feelings the man was talking about could be adjusted in order to fit a tale in which his mother and not his wife is the main character, without attributing to one person what he said about the other. Through free association the patient would restore the rightness of his memory with the editorial help of the therapist.

Memory and consciousness would be averse to misinterpretation. However, what would the primordial issue be: memory's aversion to misrepresentation or the unfulfillment of the desires spun by the drives? There must be a relation between the two, otherwise the psychoanalytic claim that alterations in memory can have repercussions for the flow of instincts would be unwarranted. The relations between the psychic and the somatic were left highly obscure in Freud's writings. He argued that since the instincts aimed at certain objects in the psychocultural world, they underwent a fundamentally psychic vicissitude (Freud 1953–74, 14:122). Instincts, which belong to *physis*, became transmuted into the psyche, although conserving their natural identity, for they would enter the psyche as *representatives*. The point of encounter between these two sides of the equation—the psychic and the somatic, memories and instincts, or

128

consciousness and affects—is unconscious thought, a mysterious process by definition inaccessible to reason.

The attribution of truthfulness and correctness to memory makes this function resemble text, and makes the art of recollecting true memories similar to the art of writing about that which is true because it is self-evident. Freud himself drew on the analogy in his "Note on the Mystic Writing Pad" (1953–74, 19:285). The mystic writing pad is a slab with a surface in wax, covered by a thin transparent sheet. The sheet is fastened to the slab from the top and contains two layers, the upper one of celluloid, the lower made of a thin, translucent waxed paper. One writes on it with a pointed stylus. The grooves made on the waxplate appear through the paper as dark. In order to erase the writing one raises the doublesheet from the slab. Freud uses the metaphor of the mystic writing pad to illustrate the functioning of the mind as described in *The Interpretation of Dreams* (1953–74, vols. 4–5). The mind receives stimuli through a two-tiered system. The first tier, the perceptional conscious, receives the imprints, but stores no traces. These are kept in mnemonic system, the second tier, behind the perceptional conscious. The perceptional apparatus is also divided into two layers, like the sheets in the mystic writing pad: one external, which like the celluloid paper cushions the impact of the stimuli, and a posterior system, which registers the traces. The wax slab that allows the two sheets to work together is like the mnemonic system.

Freud stopped short in his analogy by limiting himself to comparing memory to the mechanics of the mystic writing pad. Indeed the analogy is most eloquent when established not with the structure of the mind, but with the process of analysis which takes that structure for granted. The patient is invited to free associate. He talks about a variety of things, reporting what casually comes to his mind: an event which happened earlier that day, a feature of the psychoanalyst's office, and a sensation or a feeling he just had. The therapist hears these commentaries as notes towards the drafting of a composition. He has already heard many stories about the patient's life and, what is more important, has figured out the narrative mode the patient uses, his rhetorical repertoire for reporting, and has interpreted that as transferential action aimed at him; that is, he has identified the patient's narratives as an undercurrent of communicative action addressed to him.

The analyst's responses, whether directly answering those underground communicative actions or talking about them in a metacommunicative approach, are conceived with the purpose of editing the scattered notes by combining them into a coherent story, an effort closely resembling that of composing a text. The missing links, the notes that would be appropriate to fill certain lacunae, those motives which, in psychoanalytic parlance, have been repressed, are lost on a piece of paper somewhere, and looked for in efforts such as rummaging through drawers, or thinking, "I wonder whether I could remember." Eventually the lacunae are eliminated by finding the missing links, by replacing them with other notes available, or by having their need to be in the text superseded by an editorial reorganization of the composition. One may choose to call the unavailability of the notes *unconscious*. The retrieving efforts may be described in terms of *mnemonic processes*. The first exposure to the content of the notes, the act of conceiving them, may be referred to as the *perceptional conscious*. When described in terms of mnemonic processes, the picture can be as refined as when presented through the metaphor of composing a text.

Freud had an intuition of the rhetoric of the psychoanalytic project, both at the level of the therapeutic encounter between analyst and analysand and at the level of the metapsychology. His written work appeared between 1886 and 1939, the heyday of modernist thought, to which he prominently contributed. The intellectual priorities of the time can be clearly seen from today's vantage point. It was urgent to stand against religion, because in the nineteenth century the morality stemming from theology had already lost its authority. The fathers of twentieth century modernity were welcoming a new world held together not by religion but by science and politics. Because of the importance of reason as the method of science, the new disciplines should stand against romanticism and subjectivism. In this context, Freud walked on a tightrope by introducing a science of the psyche. It does not surprise us that he drew so insistently on the scientific metaphors of his day, especially those closer to him, from fields such as biology, medicine, physiology, and neurology. He rejected the romantic procedures that could bring a bad reputation to psychoanalysis, such as hypnotic suggestion, but he also rejected the realistic procedures that were incompatible with his project, such as the need of concrete referents for the patients' narratives. In so far as theory is concerned, his rhetoric was scientific, in the sense that it presented the results of the inquiry as cumulative and progressively more correct, springing from experiences of trial and error. With regard to the clinical practice of psychoanalysis, he introduced insights about interpersonal relationships with far-reaching implications for a philosophy of dialogue. It is to the latter aspect of Freud's rhetorical imagination in connection with the concern about whether or not the results of psychoanalytic treatment are induced by the analyst's suggestion that we now turn.

In 1896 Freud rejected Breuer's method of hypnotic catharsis, which suspended the repression and allowed the traumata to come to the fore of consciousness and memory. After he practised the cathartic method on his own, he realized that the therapeutic effects obtained were not lasting. Twenty-nine years later, writing about this momentous decision in the history of psychoanalysis, Freud affirmed that the interpersonal relation between doctor and patient superseded the technique of the cathartic removal of repression. He had noticed that in order for the results of analysis to settle in the patient's psyche, the therapeutic relation had to proceed steadily and undisturbed. He concluded that, "The personal emotional relation between doctor and patient was after all stronger than the whole cathartic process" (1953–74, 20:27). The cathartic removal of repression had been replaced by the analysis of transference in the interpersonal relation. The new method made the treatment longer and the obtaining of results more gradual, but it assured longer life to the results.

In his address to the Second International Psychoanalytic Congress at Nuremberg, in 1910, talking about "The Future Prospects of Psychoanalytic Therapy," Freud said that the improvement of the movement would come mainly from three sources: (1) progress in theory, (2) increased prestige of psychoanalysis, and (3) efficacy of clinical work (1953–74, 11:139). He proceeded with a brief account of how the analyst's rhetoric had evolved in the then-recent history of psychoanalysis. He said that initially, treatment was "inexorable and exhaustive"; the burden of talking was shouldered by the patient, while the analyst remained in his role as instigator. The progress he noted was that "to-day things have a more friendly air. The treatment is made up of two parts, out of what the physician infers and tells the patient, and out of the patient's work of assimilation, of 'working through' what he hears." (1953–74, 11:139–40). As a result of developments in the theory of mind, that is, with refinements in the concepts of conscious and unconscious processes, psychoanalysis could now abandon the sledgehammer of catharsis, replacing it with more sophisticated intellectual and verbal maneuvers. A broader and more minute array of concepts allowed the therapist to conduct himself in a more relaxed manner. His relaxation, in turn, was encouraging to the patient, yielding better results than the earlier prodding posture. The good results were regarded as a confirmation of the theoretical developments.

With success in the clinical work the therapist's métier became alluring, and therapeutic practices began to lend themselves to systematization and to the development of a methodology.

In his reports of clinical experiences, Freud frequently overlooked the application of theory and focused on the interpersonal aspects of the argument between his patient and him. The theory illuminated his understanding of the patient's story and provided him with guidelines on how to proceed, but the unpredictability of the verbal exchanges in the here-and-now of the session often surpassed the capacity of the theory to inform the therapist in forging the right intervention. In his analysis of the Rat Man, Freud was trying to convince the patient that although he loved his father more than anybody else in the world, he also experienced anger towards him; consequently, when the father died, he felt guilty. The patient reported cases of vindictive impulses against others during his childhood for which he felt very guilty. Freud kept trying to get back to the father, and at the same time to dispel the patient's guilt. In pursuing the latter goal he pointed out to the patient that the reprehensible impulses had arisen in his childhood and that children could not be held morally responsible. Then he added that people become morally responsible during a process of development growing out of their "infantile predispositions." The patient showed skepticism at the explanation, and Freud made the following remark in a footnote:

> "I only produced these arguments [about the nature of moral
> growth] so as once more to demonstrate to myself their inefficacy. I
> cannot understand how other psychotherapists can assert that they
> successfully combat neuroses with such weapons as these." (Freud
> 1953, 3:323, n.2)

Theory undoubtedly helped. Freud continuously tried to transform his realizations deriving from clinical practice into principles of theory, and he did the same in his self-analysis (Freud 1953–74, vols. 4–5). But what becomes clear from his case reports is that the discourse repertoires of the analyst and an eloquent patient are outstanding conditions for successful treatment. The analyst does not always know what is going to happen or when and how the patient is going to react. He probes and checks, but the very probing and checking fuel the transferential bond, introducing a channel of communication in the patient's life which, although repetitive, repeats differentially. The psychoanalytic relationship is an entirely new one for the patient. Through this channel emerges a relationship characterized by intense feelings on the part of the patient—and why not say on the part of the therapist too?—which nevertheless is constantly unmasked by the therapist. The objective of the treatment is not to find the patient a new and rewarding friend, but to help him develop a powerful understanding of himself. This understanding is present in the patient's narrative edited by the analyst. However, the staple of treatment is the quotidian dealing with the issue of transference (Gill 1982), fanning this relation which is not supposed to endure, but which, as long as treatment lasts, can neither die nor be turned into a large fire.

If the gains obtained in a psychoanalytic treatment, although credited to the analysand's "working through," are achieved with the assistance of the analyst, is it not reasonable to say that they are suggested to the patient by the therapist? Freud began his twenty-seventh lecture of the *Introductory Lectures on Psychoanalysis*, entitled "Transference," by asking his Viennese audience whether they were not eager to find out how "psychoanalytic therapy operates and what, roughly, it accomplishes" (1953–74, 16:431). At first he frustrated his listeners, for he told them that they should figure it out by themselves after having attended his long series of lectures. But the recommendation was voiced in a teasing manner, metaphorically alluding to the fact that he was bracing up to defend psychoanalysis from being just another therapy based on suggestion. Later on in the lecture he did explain how his therapy worked. But the lecture was indeed about the topic of its title, transference. The more he unraveled the mechanics of transference, the more likely it seemed that psychoanalysis made use of suggestion, even if unwittingly. He brought the suspicion to a climax and, playing devil's advocate, formulated some of the criticisms that might have been lurking in his audience. He said,

> "But here I will pause, and let you have a word; for I see an
> objection boiling up in you so fiercely that it would make you
> incapable of listening if it were not put into words: 'Ah! so you've
> admitted it at last! You work with the help of suggestion, just like
> the hypnotists! . . . Why the roundabout road by way of memories
> of the past, discovering the unconscious, interpreting and
> translating back distortions . . . when the one effective thing is
> after all only suggestion? Why do you not make direct suggestions
> against the symptoms, as the others do—the honest hypnotists?
> . . . Is it not possible that you are forcing on the patient what you
> want and what seems to you correct, in this field as well?'"
> (1953–74, 16:446–47).

After raising the level of suspense, he kept the tension high and dismissed the audience for the day, as there was no time for him to answer the question he had proposed in the name of his listeners. At the next meeting he delivered the last lecture of the series, titled "Analytic Therapy." In his answer he admitted that psychoanalysis employed suggestion, but of a different sort than in hypnotherapy. While hypnotic suggestion inhibited the symptoms, strengthening the mechanisms of repression, and leaving untouched the etiology of neurosis, the "analytic treatment makes its impact further back towards the roots, where the conflicts are which gave rise to the symptoms, and uses suggestion in order to alter the outcome of those conflicts" (1953–74, 16:450–51). The therapist anticipates to the patient what he will eventually learn about himself. He does this in an "*educative sense*". But there is nothing to be feared in terms of a domineering suggestion, argues Freud, because the patient's conflicts "will only be successfully solved and his resistances overcome if the anticipatory ideas he is given *tally with what is real in him*" (1953–74, 16:452; emphasis added). The tallying does not depend on the patient's intellectual faculties, but on the actual matching of the interpretation with the patient's own history of repression. Furthermore, this is not necessarily achieved at the level of symptoms. In the beginning of the treatment, the therapist stimulates a strong transferential bonding on the part of the patient. During this phase, "all the libido is forced from the symptoms into the transference and concentrated there" (1953–74, 16:455). Consequently, the psychoanalytic suggestion is indirect and attenuated; it is exercised through the analysis of transference, a discussion of the here-and-now of the relationship, even though it is a vicarious relationship, temporary and instrumental, with ends independent of itself.

The psychoanalytic movement evolved through a combination of assertions describing the nature of the mind and of the psyche followed by rhetorical maneuvers or therapeutical interventions designed to bring forth the content of the traumata hidden in the unconscious. The weight of analytic techniques varied from conditio sine qua non for the elimination of the symptom to the painstaking discourse freeing repressed contents in the ballet of the analysis of transference, from cure to sinecure. In the end, in the 1930s, they formed a procedure capable of helping psychoneurotics overcome their symptoms, but under no circumstances were they entitled to claim unlimited success. In "Analysis Terminable and Interminable," Freud admitted that psychoanalysis was not in a position to guarantee even that the affliction it had correctly treated according to its theories would not recur (1953–74, 13:211).

Psychoanalysis may or may not work, but its failures do not justify the outright abandonment of its techniques. This marks a sharp contrast with the ideology that animates science: where the research design breaks down, the procedures must be thought over, because the hypothesis was wrong. Fisher and Greenberg aptly sum up the Freudian quandary by writing that,

"Freud never really came to terms with the differences involved in trying to learn about people as opposed to trying to change them" (Fisher and Greenberg 1977, 363). Freud insisted on straddling both horses to the end, for although he recognized that "what is advantageous to our therapy is damaging to our researches" (1953–74, 16:452), he never allowed the psychoanalytic movement to tip to either side. Nevertheless, if his theories—for example, the explanation of conduct in everyday life in terms of sexuality—can be cast in doubt, the clinical experience he started and bequeathed to us has had a remarkable endurance in our cultural milieu. Again—it is never tiring to repeat this—clinical practice derives from theory. Thus the puzzle: how can psychoanalysis emanating from flawed theories cure people so efficaciously?

In spite of so vehemently explaining conduct as originating inside the self, in many passages of his writings Freud indicated quite clearly that mental health and sanity were not qualities attached to states of consciousness; they were inherent in the self's ability to communicate with another, to love and be loved by another. In the same way that every love story could be traced back to some internal motive in the individual, it could equally be hinged on the history of an interpersonal relation. The concern with the interpersonal dimension of the therapeutic encounter in Freud's writings has been grossly overlooked, perhaps because of the still-lingering idea that the fountainhead of human conduct is personality. Freud contributed to this impression in his writings, by emphasizing processes internal to the self rather than the history of interactions. Although talking about human conduct, at times he succeeded at making it look like an internal process, typical of the nature of the individual and not of the sociocultural context.

At the time Freud was paving the way for psychoanalytic treatment, the other two therapies available for dealing with mental problems were hypnotic suggestion and electroshock. A therapy based on talking was subversive and aroused passionate opposition. Freud was very much aware of the need to restrain the role of the analyst at the expense of the hypertrophy of the analysand's voice. The psychoanalyst was never cast in the role of an outright healer, but remained as a facilitator of processes, a triggerer and anticipator.

Indeed, the fundamental strategy of the psychoanalyst, his interactive posture as envisioned by Freud, has become enmeshed with an ideal model of conduct in Western societies. This ideal personality is subdued and collected, attentive but careful to act, giving but only when there are openings for reception, and receiving when that which is given is unambiguous. This ideal appears combined with the cultural ideology according to which the individual's autonomy is the basis for democracy, while its instrument is the dialogue between individuals. The Freudian person lives in a removed and sublimated world, a world in which actions towards others are representations, and the response to them is also representational. Practice means interpretation based on theory, and every action that is not transparent to a theoretical explanation is spurious, an acting out of something concealed.

There are two aspects of the rhetoric of psychoanalysis to be distinguished. First, there is the rhetoric of psychoanalytic discourse as a whole, that is, the rhetoric implicit in the assumption that there can be a theory of the mind and of the psyche, that the binomial mind-psyche presents problems in its ordinary functioning, and that actions conducted through talking and informed by the theory can facilitate that functioning. Secondly, there is the rhetoric of clinical practice, illustrated in the foregoing discussion by Freud's concern with suggestion on the analyst's part. The rhetoric by which the founder of psychoanalysis tries to persuade his audiences and future circles of readers of the validity of his project is an amalgamation of arguments deriving from theory and from practice, but since in psychoanalysis these two sources of rhetorical maneuvers remain far apart, Freud's discourse sounds deeply hybrid.

The psychoanalytic project is rendered clearer to us when unveiled in connection with two of its companions: politics and religion. Christian preaching is based on a prophetic narrative whose interpretive key is always in the pocket of the master. The preacher however is not supposed to appeal to personal authority, but to refer the foundation of his discourse to prophecy and to the Lord. In the Christian parable either the moral of the story is obvious or it depends on the interpretation of the preacher. In either case a question is raised, and an answer is given. In finding the answer, or in receiving it from someone else, the faithful meet with the preacher in a common belief. They accept the preacher's interpretive authority. In addition, they meet with God and achieve salvation. The politician talks about the common good and requests the support of the audience in making him their representative in the pursuit of collective well-being. Political discourse is supposed to capture the reasons of the community and express them in such a way that they can be recognized by the audience as their own reasons. What brings together politics, Christianity, and psychoanalysis is that these subcultural spheres within the Western tradition (with its Greco-Roman and Judeo-Christian roots) have established that persuasive appeals are more efficacious when they conceal the intention to persuade, that is, when they are less imperative and more representational. As Pascal tersely puts it, "People are generally better persuaded by the reasons which they have themselves discovered than by those which have come into the minds of others" (1941, 5).

The Western discourses such as politics, Christianity, or psychoanalysis have plunged ever more deeply into representation, in a history that can be traced from the oral to the written, from the written to the printed, and from the printed to the electronic reproduction of image and sound (Ong 1982). These discourse traditions have unfolded in the realm of simulation. Although keen in concealing their persuasive intents, their loquacity became hypertrophied at the expense of the discourse's essence.[3] This effect can be regarded as the transformation of discourse into either rhetoric or simulacrum (Baudrillard 1981). Thus, from the point of view of the history of representation, within a logocentric perspective (Derrida 1974), a tendency can be noticed towards a bifurcated development in which one prong identifies language with action, while the other introduces language as representation. From a logocentric point of view, language is the measure of all things, in both realms of representation and of action. As a pervasive mediator between essential meanings and intentions, language has the ability to conceal the interests inhering in every expression of meaning, making it possible for representation and action to be deceitful. Thus the simulacrum is not a social and historical product, but germinates already in language as the necessary mediator of representation and action. Perhaps it was with a good intuition of the logocentric bias that Freud tried to place his theory of the mind beyond the reaches of language, while endowing the psychoanalytic practice with the best features of simulation and deceit.

If Freud separated the discourses of patient and therapist, he kept together those of theoretician and clinician. He must be credited with furthering the Western rhetorical principle according to which, "the more dissimulated, the more persuasive". In his psychoanalytic project, while the patient's talk is a dissimulation, the analyst's is a simulation of existential possibilities. The former is cast as a defensive or distorting representation of that which is, while the latter is cast as a reality-based tentative reformulation of life representations.

In the beginning of this essay I discussed the question of rhetoric as supplement and as complement. Initially, rhetoric becomes supplementary in the face of the insufficiency of action to achieve its goals, and of reason and essence to fully express themselves. No sooner does it succeed as supplement than it is transformed into complement with the incorporation of necessity—rhetoric as a necessary condition of action and essence. Finally, it replaces action and essence altogether, not because of its imperialistic tendencies, but as a consequence of its entrapment in the folds of representation. Thus, action must be preceded by a simulation of action; knowledge must be preceded by a representation of knowledge. The complexity of representation and simulation dispenses with the contingency of knowing and acting.

The development of rhetoric as a replacement of action and of essence has the consequence of promoting self-identities, institutional identities, national, cultural, and ethnic identities, because where transformation is not possible, being becomes imperative. Being in the Western heritage is a product of language and of language use. No cultural project in the Euro-American history has understood this better than psychoanalysis. It construed a notion of self and invented a strategy for dealing with it, treating the self as a textual construct—life stories and the psychoanalytic ontogenetic history of repression—through speech in a dialogical form. Thus it guaranteed for itself the best of the two worlds, writing and representing on one hand, and speaking and acting on the other, the writing coming forth as narrated stories, and the speaking deeply resembling the art of composing a text. In the psychoanalytic treatment, analyst and analysand do not *do* things; instead they *talk about things*. Psychoanalysis realizes the Western ideal, conditioned by the history of representation, of talking about things instead of acting when the reasons for action are insufficient or equivocal. This ideal in its strongest manifestation goes further, claiming that talking about something is always preferable to acting on something. The breakdown of reason justifying action, however, is not a consequence of the deficiency of action itself, but a result of the increasing replacement of action with representation. Reasons are looked for not in the actions, but in the representation of the actions. The search for reason in representation is interpretation, and the work of interpretation is not advanced by narrowing down its goals towards a conclusion, but by opening up the universe of possibilities and multiplying the interpretations themselves (Kermode 1979), thereby creating the condition called by Paul Ricoeur (1974) "the conflict of interpretations."

The sublimation of action and its replacement with symbols is, indeed, remarkably well illustrated in psychoanalysis. The theory of drives or instincts indicates that these forces have goals, and it is the fulfillment of these objectives which so threatens the self. The drive must be repressed and its needs fulfilled by an ersatz symbol. However, the logical consequence of this theory should be that since psychoanalysis helps the patient lift repression, treatment would result in freeing the flow of repressed drives, with the fulfillment of their goals. Accordingly, cure would be reported as an increase in the patient's sexual and aggressive activities. Cure, however, is described in terms of the disappearance of the symptoms, and the outcome of treatment related to activities surfacing in the patient's narrative. This is so because the drive that gained prominence in the later development of Freudian psychoanalysis was the instinct of self-preservation, which calls for a restraint of desires in the name of protection of the self. The psychoanalytic self, therefore, is not a natural system of causes and effects, of pressure and release of pressure, but an arena for simulation where every force is prefaced by a "suppose that" and every predicate is preceded by an "as if."

We have seen that the theories of psychoanalysis can be questioned, and yet its practice thrives and presents successful results. The theory functions as a rhetorical platform, a set of principles and hypotheses coherent among themselves and extremely useful for reediting biographic narratives. The discussion of drives only appears as a justification of diagnostic. The sexual motivation of conduct is no longer as widely accepted as it used to be in the earlier part of this century. The axis of the etiology of neurosis has moved from the Oedipal conflict to narcissistic disturbances, from neurosis itself to the borderline personality that bears traits of psychosis. It does not matter; all these assumptions seem to make good in helping the analyst construe a picture of the analysand's situation and then relate to the patient in terms of that picture.

If psychoanalysts do not tell their patients how they should lead their lives, psychoanalysis contains a theory indicating what the conditions are under which people make choices. If this theory is correct, it should eventually become capable of explaining the whole gamut of life. If psychoanalysis is the science of human conduct, studying it from its roots of unconscious and id, of drives or instincts, of the growth of ego in its transactions with the superego, and so on, the knowledge it has amassed would soon explain all conduct, breaking through the boundaries of economics and the social sciences, of history, philosophy, and science. In order for this to happen, its theory and practice should evolve side by side and proportionately to one another. The results obtained in the clinic however, are not totally generalizable. What turns out to be the equation of individual problems can hardly be held accountable to ethical principles in a world context where these themselves are surrounded by skepticism. Psychoanalysis proceeds with treating individuals in the context of a world which seems to be ever more incongruous with the criteria of sanity

139

according to the theory of the psyche. One could still be assuaged by the match between theory and practice if the group constituted by analysed individuals were an outpost of enduring consciousness against the existential difficulties of mankind. However, therapeutic discourse, like every other contemporary discourse of modernist inspiration has lost sight of totality, and does not seem to aspire anymore to a mutual transparence between theory and practice. This does not mean that the theories in psychoanalysis do not reflect the practices and vice-versa, but that the practice is based on an elusive notion of cure—feeling better? acquiring happiness? developing a malaised consciousness of self?—while the theory is an ad hoc pursuit of that goal. The theory is no longer a statement of the meaning of consciousness and emotional soundness, but a rhetorical platform aiming at clinical success in whichever way this goal is defined, within certain limits.

The loss of perspective in relation to totality creates the space necessary for rhetoric to expand and replace action. Psychoanalytic treatment is not considered as dealing with human nature anymore. Psychoanalytic theories are only vaguely related to human nature, but psychoanalysts prefer to concentrate their attention on the implications of theory for clinical practice. The meaning of notions such as "cure" or "change" has been narrowed to fit particular forms of treatment in conjunction with specific diagnoses. The idea of progress in discourses undergoing such evolution is not based on the old positivist creed of accumulation, but on the removal from action based on the elliptical transformation of the "as-ifs" of representation into further "as-ifs."

The outstanding issue in this situation in which representation (the theory of personality), rhetoric (the intuition about how to convince the patient), and technology (the repertoire of clinical methods) are one is reason. The loss of perspective in relation to totality undermines the belief in the possibility of a universal reason. It does not do so in the sense of universal reason being banished from representation, but in the sense of how irrelevant the possible existence of such reason is. In everyday life it may be more justifiable to undertake something on insufficient grounds, following intuitions, than to pursue the rational (technical or scientific) procedure for doing it (Blumenberg 1987). But the baby seems to have been thrown out with the bathwater, as the concern with reason is discarded together with the concern with the representation of reason. It is as if we were being awakened from a dream and told that the critique of reason was indeed a critique of representation, and that with the unmediated critique of representation, reason had vanished. The surpassing of represented reason by the practices of quotidian life is also registered in hermeneutic philosophy, according to which the soil in which interpretation sprouts is not technical, methodological, or scientific; it is the experience with the use of language in everyday situations (Gadamer 1983). However, it must be said that everyday reasons and interpretations are always embedded in some form of particular discourse, and thus the generalized tallying of particular discourse with totality maintains its relevance.

The replacement of action with rhetoric finds its roots in the assumption shared by psychoanalysis that the individual has an interior with a dynamics of its own. Kant argued that the individual had no internal relation to himself. The interior is an exterior ("self-externality"), a representation of the interior. Inner experience, thus, must not be assigned any precedence over outer experience (cf. Blumenberg 1987). Consequently, to look at the individual as the source of meaningful action is misleading. The individual as such an autonomous agent is an invention of representation, and therefore cannot be the principal source of genuine action; it is left to be dealt with as a representation in the realm of representation.

In classical times rhetoric bore resemblance to logic as an art of thinking and to grammar as an art of using language. Plato argued that it was second to dialectic because its procedures were influenced by interests alien to the essence of truth. Aristotle put it on a par with dialectic, identifying it with oration to an audience, while dialectic was a debate between two individuals. Both were arts for making arguments, and neither replaced scientific demonstration. In Plato and in Aristotle we find the beginnings of the separation between invention and explanation, and between discovery and interpretation. Plato distinguished between knowledge and opinion. The former dispenses with the need of rhetorical persuasion. His philosophical dialogues restore the way to knowledge by combating rhetoric with dialectic, repetitive with fresh arguments, and by doing away with wrong beliefs. For Aristotle, rhetoric has a perlocutionary dimension—using Austin's (1975) terminology for speech acts—in the sense that it entreats the audience to do something, while scientific demonstration is illocutionary. The rhetorician must reason logically, understand the nature of goodness and of man's passions. This means that he must derive his art of arguing from truth, and must also know ethics and the psychology of his audiences. Plato also recognizes that it is important for the rhetorician to know the souls of his interlocutors. Clearly, these are not skills required in scientific inquiry, in which the main operations of thought are inventing and discovering, but skills necessary for teaching, preaching, or persuading, that is, the mechanics of interpretation and explanation (Plato 1961; Aristotle 1960).

Pascal writes: "Words differently arranged have a different meaning, and meanings differently arranged have different effects" (1941, 22). He invokes this realization with the purpose of justifying the originality of his texts, which in spite of using "words employed before," do it in a "different arrangement" and therefore lead him, individually, to achieve "different effects" (1941, 22). This "rearrangement of words" does not reflect a creative act of the individual, but the intervention of a subject in an already existing world of words and meanings. The history of philosophy, or of theology, can be approached as a series of attempts to understand the subject as a product of the world (the psycholinguistic individual), or vice versa, the world as a creation of the subject (voluntarism). We are perhaps in a position to set world and subject apart refilling the latter with mystery, contrary to psychoanalysis with its goal of undressing the subject and of revealing him in his most essential bareness. As it turned out, the psychoanalytic effort became lost in the arena where words and meanings are pitted against one another, losing touch with the subject which it so diligently was trying to define. Hence the suspicion that analysis may be a form of rhetoric. If psychoanalysis could say who is the subject and in addition develop ways to guide him towards changing his life, then it would have to be the work of another in relation to the subject, another looking more like God than like Freud.

N O T E S

1. Jacques Lacan has been identified as the foremost psychoanalyst attempting to rescue the linguistic dimension of analysis lost in the Freudian project.

2. For summaries of the psychoanalytic theory as proposed by Freud, cf. Rapaport 1960; Holzman 1970; Laplanche and Pontalis 1973; and Maranhão, 1986.

3. I cannot expand on this point here, but have discussed elsewhere how this rhetorical convention that "the more dissimulated, the more persuasive" entails a separation between form and content in discourse, from Plato's dialogues to contemporary psychotherapy (Maranhão 1986).

R E F E R E N C E S

Aristotle. 1960. "Rhetoric," in *The Rhetoric of Aristotle*, an expanded translation with supplementary examples for students of composition and public

speaking, trans. and ed. Lane Cooper. Englewood Cliffs, N.J.:
Prentice-Hall.

Austin, J. 1975. *How to Do Things with Words*. Cambridge: Harvard University
Press.

Baudrillard, Jean. 1981. *Simulacres et Simulation*. Paris: Galilée.

Blumenberg, H. 1987. "An Anthropological Approach to the Contemporary
Significance of Rhetoric", in *Philosophy: End or Transformation?* ed.
Kenneth Baynes, James Bohman, and Thomas McCarthy. Cambridge:
The MIT Press, 429–58.

Brenner, C. 1968. "Psychoanalysis and Science." *Journal of the American
Psychoanalytic Association* 16:675–96.

Deleuze, Gilles. 1968. *Différence et Répétition*. Paris: Presses Universitaires de
France.

Derrida, Jacques. 1974. *Of Grammatology*. Trans. Gayatri Spivak. Baltimore:
The Johns Hopkins University Press.

Edelson, Marshall. 1984. *Hypothesis and Evidence in Psychoanalysis*. Chicago:
The University of Chicago Press.

Fisher, S., and R. P. Greenberg. 1977. *The Scientific Credibility of Freud's
Theory and Therapy*. New York: Basic Books.

Freud, S. 1953–74. *Standard Edition of the Complete Psychological Works
of Sigmund Freud*. Trans. J. Strachey et al. London: Hogarth
Press.

———. 1953. *Collected Papers*. Vol. 3. Trans. Alix and J. Strachey. London:
Hogarth Press.

Gadamer, H. G. 1983. *Reason in the Age of Science*. Cambridge: The MIT
Press.

Gill, M. 1982. *Analysis of Transference*. Vol. 1. New York: International
Universities Press.

Glymour, C. 1980. *Theory and Evidence*. Princeton, N.J.: Princeton University
Press.

Grünbaum, A. 1984. *The Foundations of Psychoanalysis: A Philosophical
Critique*. Berkeley: University of California Press.

Holzman, P. 1970. *Psychoanalysis and Psychopathology*. New York:
McGraw-Hill.

Hook, S. 1960. *Psychoanalysis, Scientific Method and Philosophy*. New York:
Grove Press.

Kermode, F. 1979. *The Genesis of Secrecy*, Cambridge: Harvard University
Press.

Kuhn, T. 1969. *The Structure of Scientific Revolutions*. Chicago: The
University of Chicago Press.

Laplanche, J., and J. B. Pontalis. 1973. *The Language of Psychoanalysis.* Trans. Donald Nicholson-Smith. New York: Norton.

Malan, D. H. 1976. *Toward the Validation of Dynamic Psychotherapy.* New York: Plenum.

Maranhão, T. 1986. *Therapeutic Discourse and Socratic Dialogue: A Cultural Critique.* Madison: University of Wisconsin Press.

————. n.d. "Psychoanalysis as Cultural Criticism." Unpublished ms.

Ong, W. 1982. *Orality and Literacy: The Technologizing of the Word.* London: Methuen.

Pascal, B. 1941. *Pensées.* Trans. W. I. Trotter. New York: Modern Library.

Plato. 1961. *Collected Dialogues.* Ed. Edith Hamilton and Huntington Cairns. Bollingen Series 71. Princeton, N.J.: Princeton University Press.

Popper, K. 1959. *The Logic of Scientific Discovery.* New York: Harper & Row.

————. 1974. *The Philosophy of Karl Popper.* Ed. J. A. Schilpp. Book 2. La Salle, Ill.: Open Court.

Rapaport, D. 1960. *The Structure of Psychoanalytic Theory: A Systematizing Attempt.* Psychological Issues, Monograph 6. New York: International Universities Press.

Ricoeur, P. 1974. *The Conflict of Interpretations: Essays in Hermeneutics.* Evanston: Northwestern University Press.

————. 1981. *Hermeneutics and the Human Sciences: Essays on Language, Action and Interpretation.* Ed. and trans. J. B. Thompson. Cambridge: Cambridge University Press.

Sherwood, M. 1969. *The Logic of Explanation in Psychoanalysis.* New York: Academic Press.

5

Discursive Constraints on the Acceptance and Rejection of Knowledge Claims: The Conversation about Conversation

Robert E. Sanders

This paper has two parts. The first makes a distinction between strong and weak versions of the idea that rhetorical practices are an integral part of science, particularly the human sciences. In its strong version, this idea treats rhetorical practices as the primary source of knowledge claims, and thus undermines any view of scientific knowledge as having a privileged epistemological status. The weak version of the idea that rhetorical practices are an integral part of science supports the view that scientific knowledge is epistemologically privileged. In this version, rhetorical practices and scientific practices have a dynamic interconnection that functions over time to reveal and correct for errors in knowledge claims that result from nonscientific influences on their formulation.

The weak version of the claim is preferred here as the more productive and more descriptively accurate one. The posited interdependence between scientific and rhetorical practices is illustrated in the second part of the paper in terms of the intra- and interdisciplinary communication problems that have left studies of everyday conversation fragmented across several fields. My intent is to show that despite reasonable care in obtaining and analyzing data about conversation, there have been failures in the rhetorical practices of researchers that have prevented shared research agenda and protocols from developing, evaluative criteria from evolving, and distinct findings from being integrated into larger wholes.

ON RHETORIC IN SCIENCE

The strong version of the idea that rhetoric is an integral part of scientific practice attributes knowledge claims less to the objective data than to symbolic processes, persuasion and argument, within the scientific community. It is an easy step from there to consider any and all knowledge claims as inherently solipsistic because they are products only incidentally of the objective data available.

This resurrects a radical skepticism that dates back to some of the pre-Socratic philosophers, and it is not surprising that precisely such a radical skepticism did surface forcefully at the Iowa Conference on the Rhetoric of Inquiry (Simons 1985). Scientific generalizations end up being devalued to the status of cultural and political artifacts—the results of accidents of time and place, and especially of the rhetorical practices relied on by the scientific community. This is the kind of reassessment of our knowledge base that surfaces periodically to remind anyone who needs it that seekers after truth are only human, and therefore helpless to escape the shackles of their community's values, inviolate myths and lore, and above all, accepted methods of acquiring and substantiating knowledge.

As it happens, Nelson and Megill's (1986) overview of the topic they call the "rhetoric of inquiry" does not clearly incite radical skepticism or indicate that they would find that kind of thinking either useful or relevant. The radical skepticism engendered by the strong version of the claim that rhetoric is an integral part of scientific practice tends to obscure rather than reveal the complex process of intellectual and practical coordination that scientific communities achieve through rhetorical practices, and must achieve to make progress.

The question is not whether scientists are merely human and thus of necessity rhetorical (they are). Rather, the question is how it is possible for scientists to advance knowledge anyway—how rhetorical practices interact with scientific practices to enable diverse individuals (and teams) to arrive at *productive* agreements—not merely expedient ones—on research agenda and protocols, integration of findings, adjudication of competing interpretations, and so forth.

Of course, the focus of much of this present incarnation of radical skepticism is the "human sciences," a more apt and vulnerable target than science in general. A vulnerable target because the human sciences are generally about "institutional" rather than "brute" facts—about objects, events, situations, and relationships that do not objectively exist (despite their physical instantiations) apart from the conduct of human affairs. An apt target because, as the Critical School has insisted for some years, it is naive to think that cultural and political concerns can be prevented from directing the human examination of human ways and mores.

But the particular susceptibility of the human sciences to the subjective, the cultural, and the political—and the concomitant rhetorical practices within them—does not change the contention here that the question is how scientists manage to advance knowledge anyway. While the human sciences have a subject matter without an independent material existence and are,

146

moreover, the products of rich and varied rhetorical practices, they have succeeded nonetheless in advancing our knowledge of human ways and morés significantly in the few decades of their existence. This is something that an account of rhetoric in the human sciences has to explain, and that the strong version of the role of rhetoric in the sciences cannot.

In contrast, it is precisely the question of how knowledge is advanced even though scientific communities do engage in rhetorical practices that is addressed by the weak version of the role of rhetoric in science. The weak version distinguishes between the scientific task of developing a data base, and the rhetorical tasks of establishing shared research agenda and protocols, and integrating and generalizing from that data base across conflicting interests within the scientific community and external to it. This distinction is based on the following analysis of scientific progress as a function of self-correction over time that results from the interdependence of (a) the rhetorical task of coordinating scientific practices within a community, and (b) the scientific task of obtaining and verifying data. (It makes no difference in this analysis whether individual scientists are assumed to be objectively examining brute facts and therefore able to produce good data, or assumed to be examining institutional facts that are only visible to them in terms of their own social histories and the labels of their native languages, and thus are never able to produce good data except collectively over time.)

This distinction between rhetorical and scientific tasks lets us inspect the place of rhetoric in the "local practices" of scientists and their larger communities, without forcing us to deny the fact or the validity of the knowledge base produced through concomitant (but logically prior) asocial encounters with the objective environment. The weak version of the role of rhetoric in the human sciences thus raises questions that have more in common with the concerns of ethnomethodologists about the way the work of scientists is "accomplished," and less with the purposes of social critics to pull back the veneer of respectability from allegedly scientific undertakings that are actually driven by cultural and political agenda, and subverted by them. Garfinkel and his associates have recently been investigating precisely the local practices by which the natural sciences are "accomplished" (Garfinkel 1986, 1987).

THE INTERPLAY OF RHETORIC AND RESEARCH IN SCIENCE

In its weak version, the idea that a science depends on rhetorical practices does not rule out the possibility that there are objective data, that there are

147

systematic methods of recording and analyzing data, that the adequacy of generalizations can be evaluated, and that the claims of theories are at least falsifiable in decisive ways. The weak version just adds that whatever the characteristics of scientific practices are, rhetorical practices are as essential for making advances in knowledge—and rhetorical malpractices just as injurious—as is following or breaching the canons of scientific research.

The task now is to show how this can be, and in particular to make explicit the connection involved between rhetorical practices and scientific research. The problem is that this distinction between rhetoric and research seems at odds with the origin of the topic of rhetoric in science itself, namely, interest in the methods of argument and persuasion that are utilized to resolve controversy and unify belief in scientific communities. This interest imports into scientific contexts a sociology of argumentation, with Toulmin's (1958) and Perelman's (1958) work providing foundations and exemplars. Extending a sociology of argumentation into scientific contexts thus implies that scientific research is *not* distinct from other social endeavors in which rhetorical practices are essential (e.g., policy-making, jurisprudence).

The Aristotelian Bias Regarding Rhetoric in Science

Much of our thinking about the purpose and effect of rhetorical practices, and thus the significance of the claim that rhetoric plays an integral role in science, has an Aristotelian flavor. The Aristotelian legacy depicts argument and persuasion as institutionalized methods of advocacy that are warranted in the absence of a method of demonstration, and moreover that dictate before the fact possible issues, lines of argument, canons of evidence—in short, much of the content of statements. From this perspective, if rhetorical practices have a part in science at all, then scientific research must be subservient to them instead of being a distinct, nonrhetorical source of knowledge. It is a short step from there to radical skepticism.

The Aristotelian perspective takes as its point of departure that the warranted connections between the premises and conclusions of arguments are isomorphic with the connections warranted in *thought* between the content of various existential and experiential claims. This leads to the following line of reasoning. If scientists find themselves making and defending claims about the world in argumentative and suasory rather than demonstrative discourse, then the connections among their separate claims must be contingent and probable rather than certain and necessary. If the connections in thought among particular claims about the world are

148

only contingent and probable, those claims cannot be counted as knowledge. Ergo, by this line of reasoning, if rhetorical practices manifest themselves in science, then the product of scientific research cannot be knowledge.

Rhetoric in Science as Discourse Production

There is an alternative to the Aristotelian equation of discursive relationships with cognition that grows out of recent thinking in language pragmatics, discourse studies, and conversation analysis. Any connections within a given collection of statements, including arguments and suasory discourse, are a function of *constraints on discourse* alone, and do not have any necessary relationship to thought. Within such constraints on discourse, separate statements can be integrated in a discourse in such a way as to serve one or another among various intellectual and social purposes, of which advocacy is one. This warrants treating an argument as a special case of strategic communication, along the lines proposed by Jackson and Jacobs (1980).

In the related theoretical framework I have developed (Sanders 1987), connected discourse is a series of statements, each of which contributes to the formation of a ground of coherence that progressively narrows the range of relevant statements that subsequently can be made. Statements are made strategically insofar as their entry in the discourse is intended to narrow the range of subsequent statements that relevantly follow so as to make more probable the utterance of certain desired statements, or less probable the utterance of undesired ones. This entails that an *argument* is a series of statements calculated so that at the end of the progression of the series, only the major claim—or at least no contraries of the major claim—can be relevantly (coherently) introduced. Similarly, discourse is *persuasive* in this framework to the extent that the major claim, and only the major claim, becomes relevant in a progression of statements in such a way that uttering it (professing, endorsing, or otherwise subscribing to it) acquires a social meaning that is desirable, thus motivating its utterance (Sanders 1987, 231–39).

To avoid producing confusion by using conventional terms in a novel way, I will hereafter use *discursive construction* as an umbrella term to refer to any of the types of discourse that are produced in institutional contexts to narrow the range of statements that are subsequently coherent (relevant). Discursive constructions in scientific contexts then include certain kinds of arguments, persuasive appeals, and demonstrations, as well as research agenda, models, theories, and any other connected discourses

149

that are consequential for narrowing the range of knowledge claims and the associated research methods and paradigms that are subsequently relevant (coherent). These types of discursive constructions all rely on a single set of constraints on discourse, and differ just in terms of the strategic reasons in each case for selecting the content, style, and sequencing of their constituent statements.

Grounds of Coherence in Discursive Constructions

By definition we can say that entries in a discursive construction are relevant to each other on the basis of a common denominator among their respective meanings. Let us call the particular common denominator that coheres a collection of statements into (a segment of) a discursive construction its *ground of coherence*. We can then say that the constraints on entries in discursive constructions arise from the respective consequences of adhering to or deviating from the ground of coherence created antecedently.

Grounds of coherence are construed in a collection of statements on the expectation before the fact that a ground of coherence does exist, an expectation that generally results from the existence of some extrinsic connection among those statements (e.g., they are produced by a single source contiguously; they are arrayed on the pages of a single publication, they are visibly or audibly marked as a unit, etc.). In that case, grounds of coherence, as constructions rather than artifacts, must be considered fluid and contingent (subject to change over time). During the processing of a discursive construction, a ground of coherence construed on the basis of initial components may turn out not to apply as subsequent components are processed. In such cases, as long as the expectation persists that there is a ground of coherence, a way will be sought of revising that initial ground of coherence so that it applies both to those initial components and the subsequent ones.

Reciprocally, the construal of grounds of coherence has consequences for the interpretation of subsequent components of discursive constructions. The expressions of language we produce are inherently ambiguous—perhaps not referentially ambiguous in every case, but ambiguous in terms of whether to focus on and respond to their content, what they implicate, or their illocutionary force. The only objective index of what (type of) meaning should be focused on in any case is which among the possible meanings of a given entry is relevant to the ground of coherence among antecedent entries (as those have been interpreted and cohered). It follows that as it is warranted to revise grounds of coherence, it may be

150

necessary also to revise the interpretations of specific entries in the discursive construction.

Accordingly, an audience is more likely to focus on the meaning of an entry in a discursive construction that is relevant to its ground of coherence, regardless of whether it is the meaning that the communicator intended, even in scientific contexts. For example, even if the communicator intends the audience to focus on the propositional content of her statements (as is intended generally in scientific contexts), they may focus on the illocutionary force instead if that is the way those statements are relevant to prevailing discursive constructions. It can be argued that it was the illocutionary force (the social purpose of the statements made)—not the content—of Skinner's research agenda to which many of his critics responded (Mogdil and Mogdil 1987), particularly as Skinner extended that agenda to social issues. This is because (a) the content of Skinner's research agenda was not relevant to the grounds of coherence of the content of most contemporaneous discursive constructions about human behavior and social conduct, and (b) the specific deviations of its content from those grounds of coherence, and the revisions of those grounds of coherence that its content called for, did make Skinner's contribution relevant as an act of aggression and opposition to both the scientific and the political status quo.

Within this theoretical framework, then, statements made apart from an unfolding discursive construction, or that do not cohere in one, are not reliably interpretable. Moreover, there is also a dynamic interdependence between the way in which the separate entries in a discourse or dialogue have been interpreted and cohered, and the way new entries are interpreted. These two conditions are the basis for constraints on the production of discursive constructions that are distinct from the basis for producing the knowledge claims that engender discursive constructions in scientific contexts.

Rhetorical Practices and Scientific Progress

Given a discursive construction comprised of knowledge claims on some topic, the public utterance subsequently of a new knowledge claim on that topic will be either coherent or incoherent, depending on whether it is relevant within that discursive construction. However, this has no bearing on the truth-value of new knowledge claims, or on thoughts and beliefs about them. Accordingly, first, this makes producing and validating knowledge claims through research a separate activity from producing internally consistent discursive constructions that integrate those knowl-

151

edge claims into a coherent whole (i.e., research agenda, models, theories, and arguments or suasory discourse for or against them). Second, many of the discursive constructions in scientific contexts (e.g., interpretations, models) have as their major purpose simply to establish that all and only existing, scientifically valid knowledge claims do cohere (e.g., in theories, interpretations, models).

It is then a major test of the adequacy of the way a corpus of knowledge claims on a topic has been discursively cohered whether it succeeds in making coherent (relevant) new knowledge claims on that topic that are scientifically valid, and not making coherent (relevant) new knowledge claims that are scientifically invalid.

The foregoing describes a dynamic interdependence between (a) scientific practices in producing and testing knowledge claims, and (b) rhetorical practices in integrating them into discursive constructions. The knowledge claims on a topic produced initially, and the adequacy of the research methods and paradigms responsible for them, are tested by whether there are discursive constructions that cohere them. The adequacy of the discursive constructions that cohere knowledge claims is in turn tested by whether subsequently produced claims, valid according to prevailing scientific criteria, can be relevantly included in the given discursive construction.

This voids any warrant for radical skepticism on the grounds that research agenda, interpretations of data, and theories are products of cultural, political, or personal dispositions (albeit produced through rhetorical practices within and around the scientific community). Let us grant that there will always be such nonscientific influences on the discursive constructions of scientists, particularly in the human sciences. But as previously noted, such discursive constructions are self-correcting over time. It thus does not matter ultimately to what degree research agenda, models, and theories are buoyed up by cultural, political, and personal concerns. They will become increasingly unwieldly and tend towards collapse insofar as those discursive constructions do not make subsequent knowledge claims relevant that are scientifically valid, or do make subsequent knowledge claims relevant that are not scientifically valid (by whatever the prevailing criteria for scientific validity are at the time).

By the same token, there is no warrant for radical skepticism on the grounds that human observers are unable to escape being biased by their own histories and language, particularly in the human sciences, which are about institutional rather than brute facts. Knowledge claims—whether about institutional or brute facts—are also self-correcting along with the research methods and paradigms responsible for them, as a result of their interdependence with the discursive constructions that comprise them. A corpus of institutional facts, just as much as a corpus of brute facts, must discursively cohere insofar as it is a component of some organized process or structure. Hence, knowledge claims about either institutional or brute facts will eventually be reexamined and corrected or discarded if no internally consistent way of discursively cohering them is found, or no discursive construction results that makes relevant all and only subsequent knowledge claims that are valid according to whatever scientific criteria are in use at the time.

In practice, the self-corrections fostered by the dynamic interdependence between discursive constructions and scientific research tend to happen in fits and starts, and in principle the process could even be stalled altogether. This can happen when new knowledge claims are not forthcoming, or when inconsistency and "untidiness" are tolerated—as when a discursive construction or a set of knowledge claims becomes sacred and is protected regardless of its inconsistencies with subsequent scientific findings or attendant discursive constructions. However, so far, the suspensions of scientific development that have occurred have eventually collapsed, and the dialectical process described has resumed.

It bolsters this weak version of the claim that rhetorical practices have an integral role in science that it entails the following descriptively accurate generalizations about scientific practice. First, given the preceding analysis, it follows that knowledge is not produced in the sciences *at* a time, through flashes of insight and breakthroughs of discovery, but rather is advanced *through* time. This is because research agenda, methods, paradigms, and knowledge claims have respectively to be adjusted in the face of emergent weaknesses in the discursive constructions they engender; conversely, discursive constructions have to be adjusted against emergent knowledge claims of putative validity whose public utterance they make incoherent, or invalid knowledge claims whose public utterance they make coherent. This is unavoidably a process that takes place over time; for all practical purposes, continuously and unendingly.

Second, this analysis of the function of rhetoric in science entails that science is ultimately a communal, social activity, not an asocial, individual one. Although there have undeniably been numerous great figures whose work we consider pioneering and original, the fact is that their "breakthroughs" grew directly out of, and fed back into, the circular process their community was engaged in of testing knowledge claims against discursive constructions, and vice versa.

153

Finally, the weak version as developed here of the claim that rhetoric is an integral part of science entails that scientific progress would be impossible otherwise. The rhetorical practices of creating, revising, and challenging discursive constructions that cohere distinct knowledge claims are the only independent tests (i.e., extrascientific but not epistemologically opposed) that the scientific community has of its research agenda, methods, paradigms, interpretations, and theories. On the other hand, these discursive constructions are not considered an end product in science—they are subject in turn to being tested against new, independently valid, knowledge claims, and that is what makes science epistemologically distinct from art and theology.

STUDIES OF CONVERSATION

For the purposes of illustration, I have identified two distinct though topically related cases where scientific practices have not been joined by rhetorical practices, so that there are data in one case, and there are discursive constructions in the other, but in neither is there the kind of dialectic between the scientific and the rhetorical that results in progress. Ironically, these cases involve the study of conversation, from which some of the ideas here about discourse production were taken.

There are two distinct points from which studies of conversation have started and core disagreements within each resulting line of inquiry. In both cases there is a data base, but in one case no discursive constructions have been produced around that data base, and thus no basis for evaluating data and resolving core disagreements has developed. In the other case, several contrasting discursive constructions have been developed, but each is linked to a different scientific community with different data bases, methodologies, and evaluative criteria, so that again, no basis for evaluating data and resolving core disagreements has developed. The failure in both cases is a rhetorical and not a scientific one.

These two starting points for studying conversation are as follows. First, conversation (more broadly, dialogue and interaction) is studied from a sociological perspective as a key activity for the purpose of accomplishing social structure, and as a microcosm of a community's methods of structuration (Sacks, Schegloff, and Jefferson 1974; Atkinson and Heritage 1984). Second, conversation is viewed from a linguistic/communicative perspective as the key forum for pursuing interpersonal goals by structuring discourse so as to achieve intended understandings, and as a primary source of data about rules and constraints on language use

(Sigman 1980, 1987; Tracy 1982; Craig and Tracy 1983; Jacobs 1985; Sanders 1987).

The Sociological Perspective on Conversation

I refer here to studies that have been done under the rubric of "conversation analysis," with the account of turn-taking given by Sacks, Schegloff, and Jefferson (1974) a seminal work. This approach to the study of conversation has roots in symbolic interactionism, particularly Blumer's (1955) and Goffman's (1959) varieties, and stands as a cousin to ethnomethodology (Garfinkel, 1967). The central premise shared in all this work is that social structures only exist in and through their workings-out in the interactions of individuals.

Conversation analysis applies this premise by seeking out standardized devices and protocols of talk that are shared resources for the enactment of social structure. The notion that a great deal depends on conversants taking turns at talk has led to the discovery of discourse features that mark the boundaries of turns such as the adjacency pair, along with regularities in gaze and vocal cues that accompany turn-taking. This has led in turn to the discovery of other regularities of speech and behavior such as side-sequences, repair-sequences, procedures for topic development, techniques for the structuration of doctor-patient interviews, methods of giving and receiving compliments, the techniques of speakers for inviting laughter and, in public speeches, of inviting applause.

This work nonetheless has two problematic aspects. First, most of the data that have been produced consist of what to all outward appearances seem to be attributions, by individual observers/scientists, of the observed speakers' purposes for the inclusion in recorded conversations of particular features at particular junctures. The question that arises is how can such data be validated, or what distinguishes such data recorded by a trained observer, from the everyday attributions of intentionality that conversants routinely make in processing messages from others.

Second, this work has produced numerous descriptions of entries in conversations that form a listing of devices and protocols for accomplishing social structure, but not any theoretical formulations, models, or generalizations. However, the absence of generalizations and theoretical formulations is problematic. A progression from description to theory has become essential in this area because conversation analysis straddles competing assumptions and has produced conflicting data.

It is assumed on one hand (e.g., Sacks, Schegloff, and Jefferson 1974) that social structures exist prior to interactions and are symptomized in them, so that studies of conversation will reveal details of social structure that macrostudies in mainstream sociology will overlook. On the other hand, it is assumed that the devices and protocols utilized by conversants can alter social structures (e.g., the potential for altering social reality that motivates employing the devices inspected by Pomerantz [1978] and Brown and Levinson [1978]. Among other things, this leaves open the question of what the force is that attaches to the use of these observed devices and protocols, and what the penalties or consequences are of their misuse or disuse.

Third, there are conflicting data. For example, data that reveal turn-taking and holding or yielding the floor as orderly, highly coordinated activities (Sacks, Schegloff, and Jefferson 1974) conflict with data that reveal considerable disorder in both cases (Edelsky 1981).

By the preceding analysis of the function of rhetoric in science, the solution to these various problems depends on the production of discursive constructions against which methods, data, and assumptions can be tested at least for internal consistency. But no discursive constructions have been forthcoming because there is a core disagreement among conversation analysts about whether they would be helpful or harmful.

The issue involved surfaced forcefully at a 1986 Conference on Talk and Social Structure in Santa Barbara. Schegloff in particular took the position that the discovery of devices and protocols for enacting social structure depends on examining the transcribed interaction with no preconceptions, in particular without theoretical axes to grind, and without privileged information about the situation and participants that would engender an omniscient perspective as well as insensitivity to details of what was said and done.

Without disputing the merits of this position, it is inevitable from the analysis here that this results in a proscription on discursive constructions in conversation analysis that prevents the emergence of any shared basis for integrating data, evaluating methodologies, paradigms, and theories, and so on. This has not only resulted in having to suspend disbelief as each new study is published, but it has fostered impotence about how to resolve controversies.

An illustration of this at the Santa Barbara Conference was a dispute about Hugh Mehan's analysis of the conversational devices by which public school officials in California led parents to concur in a decision that had already been made on placing their children in special education programs, and on the specific placement. Mehan drew on background information about institutional constraints on the assignment of students to

156

special education programs, and statistics which indicated that school officials had managed to uphold those constraints even though each placement was presumably based on individual factors and consultation with parents. Working from this background knowledge, he inspected talk among school officials and parents for the devices by which parental consent must have been guided so as to uphold those constraints.

Schegloff's objection was that Mehan's use of his background knowledge in the analysis created the likelihood of reading motives and meanings into the talk that the speakers had actually not intended, and that might not have been apparent from the raw materials of the talk itself. However, Schegloff did not support this objection by citing tangible errors in Mehan's knowledge claims, nor could he have done so, because there are no discursive constructions that comprise and integrate antecedent data against which any defects in Mehan's knowledge claims would be evident.

The Linguistic/Communicative Perspective on Conversation

I refer here to studies in language pragmatics and communication that view as problematic the interpretation of uttered expressions of language, and that take as seminal Searle's (1969) analysis of speech acts and Grice's (1975) analysis of conversational implicatures. The major premise of this enterprise has been summarized by Jacobs (1985, p. 317):

> Any theory that equates message meaning with the literal meaning
> of what is said will miss how coherent and meaningful messages
> are produced and understood. . . . [Making] inferences beyond the
> information given in the text is a characteristic process invited by
> all natural language use. A basic task of any theory of linguistic
> communication is to model the different types of inferences that
> people make and to explain how people are able to systematically
> derive such information from language.

As is true in conversation analysis, a considerable amount of data has been amassed, though it has largely been obtained in other research contexts for other purposes (language pragmatics, ethnography of speaking, conversation analysis, sociolinguistics, studies of relational communication, etc.). The data in this case are sometimes observed, sometimes constructed dialogues that reveal connections among utterances in conversation that are not functions of their content alone, so that their coherence depends on further inferences (as when inferences about the utterance of "I'm bored" give it the value of a request or demand, upon which interpretation of the answer "I'm busy" is relevant).

157

In contrast to conversation analysis, however, discursive constructions have been produced to cohere and explain these data. But there are several different discursive constructions, and they have not been reconciled or tested against each other (with reference to how much of the data are relevant to each, the fruitfulness of the research protocols they engender, etc.). This again represents shortcomings in rhetorical rather than scientific practices. I will illustrate the problem in this case in terms of four contrasting discursive constructions: Jacobs and Jackson's (e.g., 1983), Tracy's (1982), Sigman's (1987) and my own (e.g., Sanders 1984, 1987).

All four of these constructions have a core theme in common—that inferences are guided and delimited by emergent "conversational demands," which set parameters on what each next utterance must contribute, relative to the utterance's content, about the speaker's intended meaning and social purpose (e.g., Grice 1975; Dascal 1977; Reichman 1978; Sanders 1980, 1984; Edmondson 1981; Atlas and Levinson 1981; Tracy 1982; Jacobs and Jackson 1983; Jacobs 1985; Sigman 1987).

Despite this common theme, Jackson and Jacobs, Tracy, Sigman, and I all differ significantly at a more detailed level because of differences in the scientific communities with which we respectively identify. These several communities each are distinguished by what they presume theoretical statements to be about, and what data they correspondingly accept as relevant. This makes a resolution of the resulting differences between Jackson and Jacobs, Tracy, Sigman and I primarily a matter of reconciling distinct universes of discourse surrounding the same phenomena—a rhetorical rather than a scientific problem.

For Jackson and Jacobs, and for Sigman, social purposes are the sources of conversational demands. However, Jackson and Jacobs are oriented more towards social psychological research traditions, which presume that theoretical generalizations are about the psychological antecedents or effects of individual behavior, and treat social purposes as originating in the history and present circumstances of individuals. In contrast, Sigman is oriented more towards symbolic interactionist and ethnomethodological traditions, which presume that theoretical generalizations are about the dynamic between individual and collective realities, and treat social purposes and related behavior of individuals as originating in and impacting on the history and present circumstances of collectives. In addition to the difference this makes in the content of theoretical statements, it makes a methodological difference. Jackson and Jacobs consider as relevant evidence the responses (or features of the responses) that individuals uniformly make under specific initial conditions (or, in the laboratory,

158

evaluative discriminations between different "stimuli" under a given condition). Sigman in contrast takes as relevant data the recurrent themes and issues in recorded talk within a particular institutional context that are uniformly relevant to that institution's traditions and maintenance.

For both Tracy and me, conversational demand does not arise from social factors but rather from discourse features, in particular, from the basis of relevance among the successive utterances in conversation. However, Tracy is oriented towards research in cognitive science on information processing, which treats the interconnections within a string of utterances as products of and as consequential for cognitive schemata. My own work, in contrast, is oriented towards studies of language pragmatics and discourse, which treat a string of utterances as interconnected by the formal relations among their pragmatic meanings. Tracy, akin in this respect to Jackson and Jacobs, considers as relevant evidence evaluative discriminations by individuals in the laboratory between different utterances in relation to a given antecedent. On the other hand, I take such empirical data as secondary and circumstantial evidence about formal relations in discourse, the primary evidence for claims about such relations being logical proofs that satisfy certain criteria (e.g., the discovery of inconsistencies or contradictions in contrary proofs, or the disproof of claims from the opposite assumption, and the satisfaction generally of such criteria as internal consistency, generality, and simplicity).

The discursive constructions that Jackson and Jacobs, Sigman, Tracy, and I have developed are thus about the same subject matter—the basis for inferences about intended meanings and social purposes that generally are required to cohere utterances in conversation—and yet each of us regards our claims to be about different topics and for that reason testable by evidence that is of uncertain or no relevance to the others. Thus, as in conversation analysis, data gathering can proceed without resulting in scientific progress—in this case because the discursive constructions that have been developed tend to cancel each other out.

REPRISE

The case studies here almost certainly involve temporary states of affairs. The scientific communities that have an interest in conversation and interaction will either develop ways of methodically overcoming the impasse they have reached, or they will arbitrarily make evaluations and choose options just to make progress, with the tacit but appropriate expectation of self-corrections over time.

The purpose of reviewing these problems was to establish the role of rhetorical practices in science in terms of cases where such practices are being avoided or prevented. The result in these cases is not an end to knowledge claims or data gathering; rather, it is an inability to progress, to evaluate, to integrate scientific findings, models, and methodologies.

REFERENCES

Atkinson, J. M., and Heritage, J., eds. 1984. *Structures of Social Action: Studies in Conversation Analysis.* Cambridge: Cambridge University Press.

Atlas, J. D., and Levinson, S. C. 1981. "It-Clefts, Informativeness, and Logical Form: Radical Pragmatics (Revised Standard Version)," *Radical pragmatics,* ed. P. Cole. New York: Academic Press, 1–61.

Blumer, H. 1955. "Attitudes and the Social Act." *Social Problems* 3:59–65.

Brown P., and Levinson, S. L. 1978. "Universals in Language Usage: Politeness Phenomena," *Questions and Politeness: Strategies in Social Interaction,* ed. E. N. Goody. Cambridge: Cambridge University Press, 56–289.

Craig, R. T., and Tracy, K., eds. 1983. *Conversation and Coherence: Form, Structure, and Strategy.* Beverly Hills: Sage.

Dascal, M. 1977. "Conversational Relevance." *Journal of Pragmatics* 1:309–328.

Edelsky, C. 1981. "Who's got the floor?" *Language in Society* 10:383–421.

Edmondson, W. 1981. *Spoken Discourse: A Model for Analysis.* London: Longman.

Garfinkel, H. 1967. *Studies in Ethnomethodology.* Englewood Cliffs, N.J.: Prentice-Hall.

———. 1986. "Respecifying the Natural Sciences as Discovering Sciences of Practical Action." Paper delivered at the International Conference on Talk and Social Structure. University of California, Santa Barbara.

———. 1987. *Ethnomethodological Studies of Work.* London: Routledge & Kegan Paul.

Goffman, E. 1959. *The Presentation of Self in Everyday Life.* Garden City, N.Y.: Doubleday.

Grice, H. P. 1975. "Logic and Conversation," in *Syntax and Semantics. Vol. 3. Speech acts,* ed. P. Cole and J. L. Morgan. New York: Academic Press, 41–58.

Jackson, S., and Jacobs, S. 1980. "Structure of Conversational Argument: Pragmatic Bases for the Enthymeme." *Quarterly Journal of Speech* 66:251–65.

Jacobs, S. 1985. "Language," in *Handbook of Interpersonal Communication,* ed. M. L. Knapp and G. R. Miller. Beverly Hills: Sage, 313–43.

Jacobs, S., and Jackson, S. 1983. "Strategy and Structure in Conversational Influence Attempts." *Communication Monographs* 50:285–304.

Mogdil, S., and Mogdil, C., eds. 1987. *B. F. Skinner: Consensus and Controversy.* New York: Falmer Press.

Nelson, J. S., and Megill, A. 1986. "Rhetoric of Inquiry: Projects and Prospects." *Quarterly Journal of Speech* 72:20–37.

Perelman, C., and Olbrechts-Tyteca, L. 1958; rept. 1969. *The New Rhetoric: A Treatise on Argumentation.* Trans. J. Wilkinson and P. Weaver. Notre Dame, Ind.: University of Notre Dame Press.

Pomerantz, A. 1978. "Compliment Responses: Notes on the Co-operation of Multiple Constraints," in *Studies in the Organization of Conversational Interaction,* ed. J. Schenkein. New York: Academic Press, 79–112.

Reichman, R. 1978. "Conversational Coherency." *Cognitive Science* 2:283–327.

Sacks, H., Schegloff, E. A., and Jefferson, G. 1974. A Simplest Systematics for the Organization of Turn-Taking for Conversation." *Language* 50:696–735.

Sanders, R. E. 1980 "Principles of Relevance: A Theory of the Relationship between Language and Communication." *Communication and Cognition* 13:77–95.

———. 1984. "Style, Meaning, and Message Effects." *Communication Monographs* 51:154–67.

———. 1987. *Cognitive Foundations of Calculated Speech: Controlling Understandings in Conversation and Persuasion.* Albany N.Y.: SUNY Press.

Searle, J. R. 1969. *Speech Acts: An Essay in the Philosophy of Language.* London: Cambridge University Press.

Sigman, S. J. 1980. "On Communication Rules from a Social Perspective." *Human Communication Research* 7:37–51.

———. 1987. *A Perspective on Social Communication.* Lexington, Mass.: Lexington Books.

Simons, H. W. 1985. "Chronicle and Critique of a Conference," *Quarterly Journal of Speech* 71:65–73.

Tracy, K. 1982. "On Getting the Point: Distinguishing "Issues" from "Events," an Aspect of Conversational Coherence," *Communication Yearbook 5,* ed. M. Burgoon. New Brunswick, N.J.: Transaction Press, 279–301.

Toulmin, S. 1958. *The Uses of Argument.* Cambridge: Cambridge University Press.

6

The Rhetoric of Decision Science, or
Herbert A. Simon Says

Carolyn R. Miller

Rhetoric, Aristotle tells us, has to do with "things about which we deliberate but for which we have no systematic rules. . . . We only deliberate about things which seem to admit of issuing in two ways; as for those things which cannot in the past, present, or future be otherwise no one deliberates about them . . . for nothing would be gained by it" (*Rhetoric*, I.2.1357a). In more contemporary language, rhetoric concerns uncertainty.

Over the centuries, we have become less certain than Aristotle was about many things, and what we call the *new rhetoric* reflects the extension of uncertainty to matters other than Athenian civic affairs—beyond ethics and politics to philosophy, science, and the academic disciplines in general; this extension represents what has been called the *rhetorical turn*. What is central to both the old, Aristotelian rhetoric and to this new, extended rhetoric is the function of deliberation, which is made possible and useful by uncertainty. Wayne Booth's definition of rhetoric highlights this central conception: "Rhetoric is the art of discovering warrantable beliefs and improving those beliefs in shared discourse" (Booth 1974, xiii). Or, as Eugene Garver (1978) has phrased it, rhetoric is concerned with the "essentially contestable." The essentially contestable cannot be decided by any procedure and can always be otherwise; it exists in the realm of the uncertain and the particular. As an art, rhetoric offers no guaranteed procedures but rather a socially grounded way of seeking adherence to particular, provisional positions. The extension of rhetoric implies that even scientific knowledge is essentially contestable; it can be no more than well-warranted belief and requires the reason-giving exchange of deliberation. The Aristotelian distinction between rhetoric as concerned with the uncertain or the probable and science as concerned with the certain or the necessary no longer seems tenable.

Rhetoric has been imperialist, laying claim to more and more territory as our understanding of the limits on epistemological certainty has grown. The extent of the territory is still the subject of exploration, of course, and

162

the subject of exchanges like that between Thomas Farrell (1976, 1978) and Walter Carleton (1978) over whether a distinction can be drawn between knowledge based on rhetorical consensus (social knowledge) and knowledge that is validated in other ways (technical knowledge).[1] But while the rhetoricians argue, the domain of uncertainty has also been staked out by the social scientists. For them, deliberation about things that "admit of issuing in two ways" is supplanted by "rational decision theory" (a phrase that Aristotle might actually have liked). What began with attempts by economists to predict economic choices through the calculation of self-interest has evolved to become "decision science," a theory of choice with an accompanying battery of "decision aids" for "modeling problems of choice" in management and public policy. The general impulse is to devise procedures that will guarantee the best—even the *correct*—decision. Because it conceives of decision making as a science rather than an art, as apodictic procedure that imports the force of necessity into the realm of the uncertain, decision science *reverses* the rhetorical turn.

In this essay, I explore the differences between these two approaches to the theory of choice, that of traditional deliberative rhetoric and that of decision science. To do so, I draw on the resources of the term *rhetoric* in several ways: first, has a term designating a particular theory of choice, one deriving from classical views and supplemented by recent epistemic theory (I refer to this as Aristotelian deliberation); second, as a term applicable to any theory of choice (thus, both Aristotelian deliberation and decision science are rhetorics); and third, as a term invoking a general critical perspective (each rhetoric, that of decision science and that of Aristotelian deliberation, has a rhetoric—a set of assumptions and implications about which it tends to persuade us). In what follows, I survey the basic methods and presuppositions of decision science, focusing on the seminal work of one man, Herbert A. Simon, who has provided the intellectual materials for the development of decision science. Simon is, in effect, a rhetorical theorist, albeit a covert one, whose rhetoric of calculation drives deliberative rhetoric out of both public and management decision contexts. My aim is to point out the nature and influence of Simon's social-scientific rhetoric and thereby to help explain the current state of decision making and the current shape of rhetorical theory and practice.

In brief, my argument is that decision science exhibits what Booth (1974) has called *motivism*, an inability to reason about values. As a body of theory predicated on the superiority of procedure, decision science abjures problems of choice about human action, the very choices that are the focus of Aristotelian deliberative rhetoric. Decision science and

163

rhetorical deliberation, I argue, differ in three major respects: their definitions of uncertainty, their need for an audience, and their understanding of human rationality.

Decision science, the social-scientific approach to decision making, aims to formalize the elements of complex decision problems so that a set of logical axioms can be used to analyze and compare alternatives, one of which will, it is presumed, emerge as an "obvious" choice. According to Ralph L. Keeney's (1982) useful overview, the axioms imply that the desirability of any alternative depends on two factors: the probability of its consequences and the preferences of decision makers for those consequences. The analysis yields a quantified "utility function," which represents the expected utility of each alternative; the quantities for a set of alternatives can be used to rank the decision maker's preferences for the alternatives. The analysis is accomplished by what seems a commonsensical procedure: (1) define the decision problem, (2) assess the possible consequences of each alternative, (3) determine the preferences of the decision makers, and (4) evaluate and compare the alternatives. Common sense also suggests, however, that if the process were as simple as it sounds, a science of decisions would be unnecessary.

But it's not that simple. Decision science must go beyond common sense, because the complex systems in which modern decision problems arise are, as Daniel Bell (1973) has put it, "counterintuitive." Arriving at calculable values for preferences and determining probabilities of consequences require more sophisticated tools. What decision science substitutes for intuition and common sense are the techniques of operations research, management science, and systems analysis, which Bell calls "intellectual technologies" (1973, 29). Techniques such as linear programming and mathematical modeling are used to establish the probabilities of consequences, and economic expected utility theory is used to establish the preferences of decision makers for those consequences.

These tools of decision science are widely used and accepted in industrial and governmental decision making. Expected utility theory, in particular, has been "the major paradigm in decision making since the Second World War" (Schoemaker 1982, 529; see also Machina 1987, 537). Operations research based on various kinds of mathematical analysis has been used in business and industrial decisions about production scheduling, inventory control, location of warehouses, and so forth (Simon 1981, 35). Other work has involved decisions on whether to seed hurricanes, how to design export controls on computer sales, where and when to build a new airport in Mexico City (Slovic, Fischhoff, and Lichtenstein 1977, 24), as well as long-range planning, resource allocation, and budgeting in corporate management (Huff et al. 1984). Most important, perhaps, was the application of systems analysis to national defense planning in the early 1960s and its subsequent permeation of governmental decision making as PPBS (Planning-Programming-Budgeting-System) and cost-benefit analysis (Keen 1977); these have, in turn, become the basis for environmental impact assessment and risk assessment. The more recent development of "multiattribute utility analysis" has been widely used in government decision making on resource allocation and program evaluation (Ulvila and Brown 1982, 139). Furthermore, most textbooks in the fields of management and administrative science treat decision making as a technical calculus that improves upon intuition and common sense. The key terms and assumptions in that pedagogy are drawn from decision science, the influence of which seems likely to persist in the next generation of managers.

THE WORK OF HERBERT A. SIMON

In the introduction to his recent book, *Reason in Human Affairs*, Simon (1983,vii) summarizes his intellectual career this way: "The nature of human reason—its mechanisms, its effects, and its consequences for the human condition—has been my central preoccupation for nearly fifty years." That's justification enough for rhetoricians to be interested in his work. A more immediate justification is Simon's influence on the developments just summarized: according to Keen and Scott Morton (1978, 11), Simon's work was a "key influence" on them in the late 1960s. As Nobel Laureate of 1978 in economics, Simon was cited for his work on decision-making processes in economic organizations. His career has been diverse and dynamic, from his 1947 book, *Administrative Behavior* (still widely cited in management textbooks), to his current work on computer simulation of human problem solving (1981). Early in my reading of Simon, I noticed that his disciplinary affiliation changed every few years— he has been identified as Professor of Political Science, Professor of Administration, Professor of Economics, Professor of Psychology; he is now Richard King Mellon Professor of Computer Science and Psychology at Carnegie-Mellon University. He is a rare generalist in the social sciences, and his contributions have influenced work in many areas (Bhaskar and Simon 1977; Bradshaw, Langley, and Simon 1983; Larkin et al. 1980). It is my contention here that he needs to be recognized as a rhetorician, too.

In a retrospective essay commemorating Simon's Nobel Prize, James

March (Simon's co-author on the 1958 *Organizations*) divides Simon's career into two major periods: the first, from 1947 to 1958, focusing on decision making in organizations (the work for which he won the Nobel Prize), and the second, after 1958, focusing on human problem solving and artificial intelligence (March 1978b). It is the work of the early period and its subsequent development by others in which I am interested, because it concerns the exercise of reason in social contexts, which I take to be the realm of rhetoric.[2]

In *Administrative Behavior* and in essays that appeared in journals of economics and business during the 1950s, Simon examined the theory of rationality underlying the traditional analysis of economic and management decisions, which has come to be known as Subjective Expected Utility (SEU) theory (see also Simon 1957, 1959). The "objective" rationality, or what he later terms "Olympian" rationality (Simon 1983, 19 ff.), of SEU theory operates like the choice process previously described: examining alternative courses of action, considering the consequences of each, and assigning a preference (or "utility") to each. In *Administrative Behavior*, Simon (1947, 81) observed that actual decision-making behavior falls short of the ideal of objective rationality in several ways. First, the alternatives for action are not "given" and often not obvious; consequently, the search for alternatives is part of the decision process and may not yield an exhaustive list. Second, the consequences of each alternative must similarly be sought and may therefore not be fully specified. Third, the preferences to be assigned to each alternative are difficult to anticipate. In a later essay, he notes two further shortcomings: first, preferences are not always commensurable (in other words, multiple criteria may be involved, in spite of the economists' assumption that there is one criterion, "utility," and that it is measurable in dollars); and second, the problem itself may be a function of selection and attention (Cyert, Simon, and Trow 1956). In spite of these difficulties, Simon believes that because SEU theory loads all preferences into a single utility function, it permits us to reason about values. He calls SEU theory "one of the impressive intellectual achievements of the first half of the twentieth century. It is an elegant machine for applying reason to problems of choice" (Simon 1983, 12).

Nevertheless, Simon proposes to substitute for this elegant but imperfect normative theory a descriptive view, based on behavior. His central insight (according to March) was to point out that "human beings and human institutions are often intelligent without being, in the usual [i.e., economic] sense, rational" (March 1978b, 858). This descriptive view of intelligent decision making has come to be called *bounded rationality*

(Simon 1957, 196–201). It replaces classical economic theory's normative model of Olympian rationality with a model that recognizes the limitations on the decision maker's knowledge and ability. The characteristics of bounded rationality are, first, that the decision maker works not with all logically possible alternatives but with a limited number, most of which are not far different from the existing situation (this feature is called *incrementalism*); second, that the decision maker is likely not to optimize (that is, to seek the single best alternative according to the utility function) but to "satisfice" (that is, to accept the first satisfactory solution that is encountered); and third, that rules of decision are likely to be influenced by past decisions and practices (Simon 1955). All these are "rational" (in the economic-scientific sense of being efficient) ways of economizing on scarce decision-making resources: attention, information, search activity, problem representation, computation. What Simon has done, then, is really not to modify but to preserve the economists' understanding of rationality by showing that behavioral rationality is exactly what Olympian rationality would predict for itself under the constraints that affect actual decision makers. Bounded rationality is not different from Olympian rationality but is simply a "rational" (that is, efficient) adaptation to a set of empirical limitations.

The crucial application of Simon's thinking about rationality has consistently been to decision making, which he sees as central to the human sciences—to administration, management, and psychology. In 1947, *Administrative Behavior* began with the claim that "decision-making is the heart of administration, and that the vocabulary of administrative theory must be derived from the logic and psychology of human choice" (p. xiv). In 1965, "The New Science of Management Decision" explicitly treated decision making as synonymous with managing (p. 53). In a 1978 essay, Simon noted that operations research "is concerned with good methods for reaching good decisions" (495).

Simon (1965) divides decisions into two types: routine (or programmed) and novel, ill-structured (or unprogrammed) decisions. He then compares the application of traditional and modern decision-making techniques to both types of decisions. Routine decisions have traditionally been handled by habit, clerical routine, and the structure of an organization (through subgoals, information channels, etc.); these methods can be successfully replaced by modern methods of operations research, including mathematical analysis, modeling, computer simulation, and data processing. Nonroutine or nonprogrammed decisions have traditionally been handled by judgment, intuition, rules of thumb, selection, and by training of the

167

executives who make the decisions (1965, 62). In 1965, Simon was optimistic about replacing these traditional methods with extensions of the mathematical methods of management science and operations research (1965, 90). But by 1981, he noted that modern methods had not been successfully applied to nonprogrammed decisions at the upper levels of management, because of the greater levels of uncertainty in such decisions, their greater computational complexity, and their incompatibility with quantitative methods (1981, 36).

These problems led to a change in the central emphasis of Simon's work, from decision making to problem solving, based in an information-processing view of human behavior (see Newell and Simon [1972] for early work, Larkin et al. [1980], Bhaskar and Simon [1977], and Bradshaw, Langley, and Simon [1983] for more recent work). Research of this sort, he claimed in his Nobel lecture of 1978, has provided "rather conclusive empirical evidence that the decision-making process in problem situations conforms closely to . . . models of bounded rationality." He presents as a conclusion implied by this evidence a theme present throughout his work, that it is the *process* of choice that should be understood, not its context or substance: "choice is not determined uniquely by the objective characteristics of the problem situation, but depends also on the particular heuristic process that is used to make the decision" (Simon 1979, 507). Because it can be managed (and the situation, being "objective," cannot), process is of central interest to him.

In the end, Simon's work all stems from his premise that "reason is wholly instrumental" (Simon 1983, 7). Reason, he says, "can't select our final goals, nor can it mediate for us in pure conflicts over what final goal to pursue—we have to settle these issues in some other way" (p. 106). Determination of goals, apparently, is not a task in which reason can be of assistance; ultimately, goals are mere "preferences"—irrational and arbitrary. I can't think of a better example than this of what Wayne Booth has called *motivism*, that dogma of modernism that insists that "there are no good reasons for changing your mind . . . Choices of ends and of world-views and of political and religious norms are value choices, and since value judgments are not about matters of fact, there can be no final superiority, in arguing about them, of one line of reasoning over another" (Booth 1974, 24). Simon's work exhibits what Booth calls *scientism*, which presupposes a dichotomy between fact and value, between procedure (which alone can be rational) and substance (which is always arbitrary), and prefers, in each case, the former. Bounded rationality, in fact, is a concept that could only have been arrived at by Booth's "scientismist." As

168

a descriptive concession to empirical limits on an Olympian ideal, it continues to postulate that ideal. Both Olympian and bounded rationality are versions of reason devoid of reason-giving.

DECISION SCIENCE AND DECISION MAKING

What hath Simon wrought? How has Simon's work been applied to actual decision making? There are several ways of addressing these questions. Because decision science is mostly a theory about how decisions *should* be made, the clearest kind of answer can be found by examining the academic literature on decision making, both the strongly normative versions in the management textbooks and the more descriptive approaches in the research literature of management and related fields. I'll begin by characterizing the norms purveyed in the textbooks, examine several empirical studies, and finally sketch some evidence about actual decision practices that show traces of the scientism of the academic literature.

The textbooks show a remarkable fidelity to the instrumental premises of Simon and to the basic model of decision making I outlined early in this essay. There is general agreement that decision-making behavior can be described on a spectrum from completely rational (the expected utility model) to completely irrational (called, variously, the social model and the cognitive model) (Keen and Scott Morton 1978, 62; Luthans 1985, 593). The weakness of "irrational" decision making is that, having no method, it must rely on judgment, intuition, inspiration: "the use of judgment and intuition is undesirable except as a last resort" (Easton 1973, 11). A scientific method for decision making is superior because it helps avoid "errors" (Janis and Mann, 1977, xvii); it helps "overcome human bias and intellectual weakness" and thus enables decision makers to decide "correctly" (Baird 1978, 4); decision making is "ideally" logical and unemotional (Hitt, Middlemist, and Mathis 1986, 74). The basic premises and explanations are persistent in these texts, both from edition to edition and from author to author. The sources authorizing the premises tend to become entrenched, remaining unexamined and unrevised. Thus, we find, for example, in a 1982 third edition a citation to a 1964 article authorizing the peremptory dismissal of "inspiration" as a method of decision making about which anything useful might be said (Hellriegel and Slocum 1982; Thompson 1964).

The empirical research, which includes both extensive case studies and laboratory experiments, repeatedly finds discrepancies between the normative version of decision making and the behavior of individuals and

169

organizations (Borstung 1982; Higgins 1982; Lock 1982; McCaskey 1979; Stagner 1969). The reactions are to show, in retrospect, how the apparently anomalous behavior can actually be explained by the theory or to reiterate the importance of applying theory to improve behavior. Perhaps the most interesting examples of this kind of literature are two mass-market books, one the best-selling *In Search of Excellence* by Peters and Waterman (1982), the other *Decision Making at the Top* by Donaldson and Lorsch (1983), which the authors describe as "clinical" research. Peters and Waterman conducted extensive field studies of fourteen exemplary companies that had excellent long-term financial performance and a record of innovation. Donaldson and Lorsch studied the decision-making of chief executive officers at twelve major industrial firms. They reach similar conclusions: that the rational model of management misses a lot (Peters and Waterman 1982, 30; Donaldson and Lorsch 1983, 8), and that something called a *belief system* is pretty important to both decision making and financial performance (Peters and Waterman 1982, 280; Donaldson and Lorsch 1983, 79).

What excites Peters and Waterman is the correlation between good financial indicators and a strongly expressed belief system: "Virtually all of the better-performing companies we looked at . . . had a well-defined set of guiding beliefs. The less well performing institutions, on the other hand, were marked by one of two characteristics. Many had no set of coherent beliefs. The others had distinctive and widely discussed objectives, but the only ones that they got animated about were the ones that could be quantified" (p. 281). Interestingly, although Peters and Waterman set much greater store on beliefs and values than most management researchers, they still show traces of scientism. Beliefs and values seem to exist only when articulated, and the greatest value they have is *in the articulation*—in the annual report, in company legends and mottos. Peters and Waterman seem able to talk about beliefs only, conceptually unrelated to action. Only thus could they recommend that "creating and instilling a value system" be understood as the most important job of company leaders (p. 291).

Donaldson and Lorsch have similar difficulties. The problem, they find, with the strong emotional commitment that CEOs have to their belief systems is that it may make them unable to "appraise their world and themselves accurately" (p. 111). They treat beliefs as evidence of "bounded rationality": since complete knowledge is not available, managers use beliefs instead: "These beliefs provide a set of concepts that enable managers to make choices in areas where hard facts are often unavailing and where the tools of management science and economics are inadequate to the job. Without these belief systems, managers would be adrift in a turbulent sea, with no charts" (p. 129). Although inferior to hard facts, beliefs are so important, Donaldson and Lorsch believe, that managers should conduct "a periodic audit of the company's belief system" (p. 172) to make beliefs explicit and to prevent them from becoming barriers to strategic change.

In spite of the academic evidence that real decision makers do not use the methods of decision science (Donaldson and Lorsch 1983, 128; Borstung 1982, 343; Lock 1982, 330; Peters and Waterman 1982, 232), I want to end this section with three brief examples suggesting that at least the scientistic attitudes of academic theory have in fact percolated into actual decision-making contexts. While I have no evidence except in the first example of any direct influence, the attitudes are so similar and the consequences so grave that the possibility of such influence should be taken seriously.

1. The top management of a government bureaucracy, having read Peters and Waterman's *In Search of Excellence*, distribute to the rest of the employees a brief memorandum identifying a set of proposed "core values": "we propose what we believe [our] core values should be . . . without any presumptions as to whether we have or have not been imbued with them up to now." Since values and beliefs are important to the performance of an organization, these managers said, in effect, let's get some. The notion that values are things that one can propose or devise, rather than inevitable, immanent aspects of what one is already doing (such as telling subordinates what their values should be), is scientistic. It assumes complete disjunction between fact and value.

2. A judge gives a sentencing jury in a capital case the following oral instructions as it prepares to decide between death and life imprisonment:

> In your deliberations it is your duty to consult with one another
> and to deliberate with a view to reaching an agreement, if it can be
> done without violence to individual judgment; to decide the case
> for yourself, but only after an impartial consideration of the
> evidence with your fellow jurors. In the course of your
> deliberations, you should not hesitate to re-examine your own
> views and change your opinion if convinced it is erroneous, but
> not to surrender your honest conviction as to the weight or effect
> of the evidence . . .

He also gives them a two-page questionnaire of yes/no questions designed to lead them through the consideration of aggravating and mitigat-

171

ing circumstances that are the legal basis for the sentencing decision. The effect of his oral instructions is to affirm the value of reasoned deliberation. The effect of the questionnaire is quite the contrary: it implies that by simply answering a series of questions yes or no ([1] Do you find from the evidence, beyond a reasonable doubt, the existence of one or more of the following aggravating circumstances? [a] Has the defendant previously been convicted of a felony involving the use of violence to the person? etc.), the jurors will *derive* a decision that, in the words of the judge, "it will be your duty to recommend." The questionnaire takes responsibility for the deciding; it turns deliberation into calculation.

3. In the absence of "conclusory" data about the probable effect of low temperatures, much lower than those previously experienced, on the performance of the O-ring seals between the segments of the booster rockets on the Challenger space shuttle, managers at Morton Thiokol, Inc., ignore the engineering "intuition" (Presidential Commission 1986, 699) of their two top experts on the seals and, reversing a prior decision, telefax to NASA their recommendation to proceed with the flight. At the Rogers Commission hearings, Chairman William P. Rogers asked the managers "why you changed your mind and how you did it so quickly" (Presidential Commission 1986, 631). The managers testified, in effect, that since the engineers couldn't provide conclusive data or calculations about the effect of temperature, it was the managers' prerogative (and theirs alone) to exercise "judgment" (Presidential Commission 1986, 773, 793). The engineers were, in their own words, arguing from "opinion and actual observation" (p. 773). In fact, according to one of the managers, the decision was based on "the only conclusive data" they had (p. 617)—the experience of prior flights, all of which had succeeded. Here, although the process of decision making is conceived as an alternative to "calculation," it does not involve reasoned deliberation between engineers and managers but requires a sharp separation of their discussions.

Recent developments within the field of decision science indicate that some researchers have noticed the limitations of scientism. A symposium in an issue of *Decision Sciences* discusses theoretical problems and research directions (Winkler 1982 and responses). In addition to many technical issues, the following problems are raised: decision theory is rarely used by real decision makers, including decision theorists themselves; the relationship between normative axioms and descriptive observations is unsettled; some preference functions may be preferable to others; criteria other than expected utility may be applicable to some problems (this issue has led to the development of a new subfield, the calculus of multicriteria decision making, MCDM, or multiattribute utility theory, MAUT); and current models do not account well for the relationship between decision analysis and the intellectual contexts of decision. Some researchers have found that technical decision methods may be rejected by decision makers who find them too difficult to explain and justify to others (Slovic et al. 1977).

Repeatedly decision scientists, economists, and policy analysts have confirmed or rediscovered the shortcomings of Olympian rationality in actual decision making, but they get no further than repostulating a version of bounded rationality. Fischhoff and co-workers (1983), for example, discuss five circumstances in which people might fail to use SEU decision rules. Keen's review of the development of the concept "optimality" in decision theory concludes that there has been a retreat from the rational ideal, a retreat characterized by several shifts—from single to multiple criteria, from absolute to situational judgments, from efficiency to effectiveness, from objectives to constraints (Keen 1977, 53). In a review of empirical studies of the generalized economic Expected Utility model (including its subjective variant, SEU theory), Schoemaker (1982) concludes that EU theory fails both as a descriptive and as a prescriptive model because it fails to take human psychology into account. He describes five strategies that humans use to achieve cognitive simplification of decision problems, strategies that constitute yet another variant of bounded rationality.

In an exploratory essay, "Bounded Rationality, Ambiguity, and the Engineering of Choice," James March (1978a) goes beyond these repetitions of Simon's descriptive version of scientistic rationality. While recognizing the contributions of Simon and others to the "technologies of reason" based on models of calculated rationality, March proposes attention to an alternate model, which he calls "systemic rationality." "Suppose we imagine," he says, "that knowledge, in the form of precepts of behavior, evolves over time within a system and accumulates across time, people, and organizations without complete current consciousness of its history. Then sensible action is taken by actors without full comprehension of its full justification" (March 1978a, 592). He goes on to declare that "decisions, like poems, are open; and good decisions are those that enrich our preferences and their meanings" (p. 601). He calls for research in decision theory that engages the issues of moral philosophy, aesthetics, and symbolism. He recognizes the superiority of learned and conventional behavior over calculated, rational behavior, because of the way conventions summarize cultural experience and learning represents personal experience. And yet, perversely, he says that what is needed to explore these issues is more engineering research.

A RHETORICAL PERSPECTIVE ON DECISION SCIENCE

The reappearance of the same problems in study after study and the repeated reinvention of bounded rationality suggest a failure of underlying theory. Although March and some other decision scientists recognize the importance of symbolic interchange in decision making, they all lack a theory that could account for that relationship. A theory of rhetoric as deliberation would do that. Such a theory makes the creation and change of belief through symbolic exchange both the goal and the means of making decisions. Some elements of the rhetorical tradition have always, like decision science, sought predictable results through persuasion, but other elements have emphasized the symbolic process of interchange and reason-giving by which we confront and accommodate the uncertain and thereby create meaning for ourselves. And this process is what decision science cannot account for.

It is suggestive that the points at which decision science breaks down (or gives up) have direct analogues in the concepts of rhetorical theory. For example, decision science has no way of treating seriously the "intuitive" or "inspirational" sources of innovation; the rhetorical tradition provides the rich concept of invention. Most decision theorists are silent on the important first stage of the decision-making process, problem formulation. Schwenk and Thomas (1983) show that it is a process that is subject to influence, but, again, they have no way to conceptualize it; the rhetorical tradition offers the concept of *stasis*. Lock (1982), as well as Donaldson and Lorsch (1983), finds that emotional commitment is an important influence on the decision process; rhetorical theory offers *pathos*. In a case account of two business decisions, Higgins (1982) finds himself at pains to account for the influence of "timing," the "organizational position" of decision makers, and "choice of language"; rhetorical theory provides the concepts of *kairos* or situation, *ethos*, and style. Lock (1982) and Judd and Weissenberger (1982) have difficulty treating what they call "participation," in the face of the assumption by decision science that there is a single, isolated decision maker; in addition to the concept of audience, rhetorical theory provides the *enthymeme*, the model of reasoning based on participation.

In what follows, I develop three major ways of characterizing the differences between the scientistic approach to decision making and the rhetorical approach. Given the parallels outlined above, one has many points of comparison from which to choose, but I will organize my discussion around their differing conceptions of uncertainty, audience, and rationality. These central concepts illustrate best the distance between rhetorical deliberation and decision making as it has been conceived by Herbert Simon and his intellectual heirs.

The first difference has to do with the way uncertainty is treated (the inverse of "uncertainty" is "probability," a concept that Conley (1984, 183) has suggested should be the subject of greater attention in rhetorical theory). Simon's definition of bounded rationality in terms of the disparity between the capacity of the human mind and the size of decision problems (Simon 1957, 198) implies that uncertainty lies in the discrepancy between information available and information needed; that is, uncertainty is wholly a problem of knowledge. Such uncertainty concerns events in the world that may have happened or may yet happen—if our information were more complete or our calculus more accurate, we could know with complete certainty whether it will rain today, whether the tossed coin will come up heads this time, whether Homer was blind, what the President knew and when he knew it. In their psychological studies of judgment under conditions of uncertainty, Kahneman and Tversky (1982) define four types of uncertainty, all as problems of knowledge. The differences are based on whether uncertainty is attributed to the event itself or to human ignorance, and on what kind of information is used to assess the problem (data about similar cases or data about the particular case).

By contrast, Aristotle observes that uncertainty concerns not knowledge but human actions: "most of the things which we judge and examine can be other than they are, human actions, which are the subject of our deliberation and examination, being all of such a character" (*Rhetoric* I.2.1357a). Our imperfect knowledge, of course, makes deliberation about our actions more difficult, but, as Aristotle says, we do not waste time deliberating about questions with only one possible answer, like whether New York is north of Rome (one of Kahneman and Tversky's examples). Problems of knowledge presuppose no real conflict—except between people and the limits of available information. Problems of action involve conflict between people; even solitary deliberators negotiate conflicts between possible versions of themselves. Problems of action are "essentially contestable"; problems of knowledge are not.

Chaim Perelman notes that in the decline of rhetoric since the sixteenth century, "problems of action [are] sometimes reduced to problems of knowledge, that is, of truth or probability, and sometimes considered as

175

completely irrelevant to reason" (Perelman 1982, 7). Thus, the decision scientists revise the problem of action—Where should we build our nuclear power plant?—to problems of knowledge, such as What will be the effect of a plant in this site on water temperature? on fish population? on operating cost? on radiation exposure? and so on (Keeney and Nair 1975). They recast the question, Should we go to court or drop the case? to What are the costs and benefits of each alternative? (Higgins 1982). They change the question, How should we revive the men's shoe line? to What is the effect, in dollars, of any given course of action? (Lock 1982).

The task in solving a problem of action is not to acquire more information or to modify a calculus; it is, rather, to exercise what Aristotle called practical reason, to adapt to a particular case general principles or values. But since scientistic reasoning does not recognize the need for deliberation about problems of action, about what we ought to do or be, it cannot accommodate values. It accepts the Cartesian dichotomy described by Perelman and Olbrechts-Tyteca (1969, 512) between "the objective and indisputably valid" and the "arbitrary and subjective," along with the resulting "unbridgeable gulf between theoretical knowledge, which alone is rational, and action, for which motivations would be wholly irrational." Simon's belief that SEU theory permits us to reason about values is mistaken; SEU theory uses a predefined value (utility) to reason *with*, but it cannot locate, create, improve, or define values. However, these are precisely the issues in decision making. Decision science thus cannot even recognize the kinds of problems decisions must ultimately address.

A second major difference between decision science and rhetorical deliberation is their treatments of audience. In decision science there is no audience. The decision problem is cast in an absolute form: a problem of knowledge measured against omniscience. The method is algorithmic, a procedure that can ideally be performed by a computer. Since the method is, by definition, rational, the adherence of an audience is irrelevant. A decision is not judged by an audience but is justified in the abstract by the rational procedure with which it complies. By contrast, deliberation about problems of action presupposes an audience—those who will take action or be changed by it, whether or not they help to make the decision directly. The standard of evaluation is neither the objective correctness of the decision as determined by an omniscient intelligence (or experimenter) nor conformity to a technical procedure, but rather the agreement of an audience that the action is relevant, beneficial, justified, inspired perhaps, and that the reasons offered are good ones, in Booth's sense—reasons that confirm or improve those who assent to them. "That which is persuasive," says Aristotle, "is persuasive in reference to some one" (*Rhetoric* I.2.1356b).

Decision science conceives of its task as the aggregation of differing individual preferences, which remain subjective, irrational, and atomistic.[3] An aggregation model erases those who hold the preferences and denies the possibility of change, consensus, or adherence. Since decision makers, as persons, naturally resist their own disappearance, they may assert their will by refusing to cooperate with formal decision procedures. We thus find frustrated observations in the literature like these: "as complex and uncertain as these decisions are, they are often made with little reference to formal studies" (Donaldson and Lorsch 1983, 128); "the decision makers were distinctly reluctant to participate in the exercises" (Lock 1982, 330); and like this one from a decision maker himself: "Many times the decision that should be made is not the answer that the analysis shows" (Borstung 1982, 343).

Decision problems arise because people have different beliefs about the uncertain future—what it will be, what it should be; these beliefs are "essentially contestable." Deliberation engages these differing beliefs in a dialectical process involving reasons, refutations, counterarguments; and it is in this process, *in the contesting*, that deliberation creates both new beliefs and the adherence of participants. Deliberation yields the synthesis of more than one imperfect point of view, whether achieved through dialogue (in a public forum, a committee, or over time in the pages of a technical journal) or represented in monologue (as in the speculative essay or the judicial opinion). Without the audience required by deliberation, decision science locates power in the decision procedure or in someone who empowers that procedure. Solutions are imposed by the authority vested in the procedure; their acceptance is not at issue.

The third area of difference between decision science and rhetorical deliberation is their conceptions of human rationality. Rationality is fundamental because it makes the difference between decision making and whimsy—or craziness. I have called "scientistic" Simon's belief that rationality is instrumental. In giving up the ideal of an absolute and omniscient rationality that yields substantive accuracy, Simon opts for a procedural rationality (Simon 1978b). But without substance, as Booth makes clear, procedure has no place to begin but the irrational, and rationality becomes, in March's (1978a) term, "calculated." Recent philosophical trends, however, have resisted the scientistic identification of rationality with procedure, the conflation of the logical and the reasonable. Perelman's work has focused on this issue. This alternative version of rationality

177

emphasizes its human source, rather than the omniscient or instrumental standpoints. In an argument similar to mine, Richard Harvey Brown characterizes the difference between instrumental-technical rationality and rhetorical rationality as primarily the difference between transcendent rules and culturally located application; thus, he says, "rationality, rather than being a guiding rule of individual or social life, turns out to be an achievement" (Brown 1987, 194)—that is, a limited, contingent, human construction. The constructive activity of rationality occurs through the discovery and articulation of good reasons for belief and action, activities that are fundamental to deliberation. Rationality concerns a process or activity (not a procedure) that guarantees criticism and change (not correctness).

Scientistic rationality emphasizes substance when it assumes that objectively correct decisions are achievable. It emphasizes procedure when, as Simon does, it assumes that they are not; what procedure can guarantee, rather than correct results, is optimal results from any given starting point. Rhetorical rationality, on the other hand, must emphasize the interdependence of substance and process. As a process, deliberation both requires and creates substance, that is, systems of meaning. The deliberative processes of reason-giving, inducement, and change can yield at least temporary agreements, the substance of which depends upon the substance of previous beliefs and the effects of rhetorical art upon them. History, convention, insight, emotion, and value all become rational, that is, possible "good reasons." And the process of deliberation, or argumentation, as Perelman and Olbrechts-Tyteca (1969, 47) note, "alone allows us to understand our decisions."; such understanding is also, surely, a prerequisite for rationality. Because both process and substance are essential, March's (1978a) term *systemic rationality* seems apt.

March concluded that Simon's "discovery of intelligence in the ordinary behavior of individuals and social institutions is an implicit pressure for reconstruction of normative theories of choice" (1978a, 593). I believe that rhetorical theory (rather than engineering research) has much to offer that reconstruction. What concerns me is not the demonstrable successes of decision science when applied to complex problems of knowledge but the invasive assumption that there are no decision problems that should not be submitted to its methods; this assumption is a form of what has been called the "technological imperative," or what we might call "technicism," the applied version of scientism. The decline of public deliberation on matters of social import has been widely noted and attributed by some to the ascendency of technical discourse (see especially Goodnight [1982]).

178

I am suggesting that this decline can be attributed at least in part to a specific form of technical discourse, that the hegemony of decision science in managerial, technical, and governmental contexts is related to the low status of the rhetorical tradition not only in those contexts but also in the public sphere.

Decision science is a rhetorical theory, that is, a theory about the exercise of reason in social action. Yet it is antithetical to the assumptions of rhetorical deliberation. As a rhetorical theory, decision science is at best too narrow to be of use in real conflicts and at worst coercive and authoritarian. It ignores the best capacities of human beings—to reason with and learn from each other; it encourages our submission to technical, knowledge-based solutions for what are social, value-based problems. The "rhetorical turn" in recent scholarship challenges the assumption that intellectual and social progress demand the certainty sought by the instrumental reason of scientism. As an art, not a science, rhetoric reaffirms the value of that which cannot be wholly systematized, that which is subject to human influence. A humane and honest theory of choice, therefore, should be based on rhetorical art, not on scientism—or technicism. Decision science, which resists the fundamental uncertainty of human life, should not replace rhetorical deliberation, which helps us to live with it.

N O T E S

1. Although the relevance of rhetorical deliberation to technical decision making might seem questionable to those who follow Farrell's distinction between technical and social knowledge, that distinction is not an issue here (Farrell claims that "actual" consensus is necessary for technical knowledge). Granting, as Farrell does, that the distinction is not absolute, what is subject to choice in the technical sphere is, by definition, the uncertain—that is, whatever is not part of an actual consensus but could become part of a social consensus. Such issues, in Farrell's terms, are therefore audience-dependent, generative of knowledge, and normative. My own position is that most of what Farrell thinks is "technical" knowledge is instead social, if only because it is a rare consensus that is actual rather than attributed. By that definition, technical knowledge would consist largely of primitive sensory observations. A technical audience to which a consensus is attributed is usually a specialized one to whom the problems and lacunae—the uncertainties—in a body of knowledge are more apparent and more significant than they are to observers (such as rhetorical theorists). The normative force of such knowledge concerns primarily the further conduct of technical inquiry, which is itself, as Farrell agrees, a social

endeavor. Much recent work in the discourse of the disciplines has emphasized the lack of actual consensus in disciplinary discourse and the consequent social work of consensus building that such discourse must do (see Bazerman's (1988) work on the agonistic nature of the experimental article in science).

2. Simon's later work, concerning the acontextual mechanisms of cognition, has served as the basis for some work in written composition studies (Flower and Hayes (1977) is an important example) and is allied to research on information-processing approaches to the psychology of judgment (see the collection in which Kahneman and Tversky's (1982) essay appears).

3. Note the following definition of a *social choice situation*: "some choosers, some choice alternatives, some information about the choosers' preferences, and an aggregation device that combines this individual preference information into a collective choice" (MacKay 1980, 13). Because it ignores the difference between consensus and aggregation, such a definition leads to the paradox known as Arrow's theorem, which is the impossibility of constructing an aggregation device that meets certain "rational" criteria.

REFERENCES

Aristotle. 1926. *"Art" of Rhetoric.* Trans J. H. Freese. Cambridge: Harvard University Press.

Baird, Bruce F. 1978. *Introduction to Decision Analysis.* Belmont, Calif: Wadsworth.

Bazerman, Charles. 1988. *Shaping Written Knowledge: The Genre and Activity of the Experimental Article in Science.* Madison: University of Wisconsin Press.

Bell, Daniel. 1973. *The Coming of Post-Industrial Society.* New York: Basic Books.

Bhaskar, R., and Herbert A. Simon. 1977. "Problem-Solving in Semantically Rich Domains: An Example from Engineering Thermodynamics." *Cognitive Science* 1: 193–215.

Booth, Wayne. 1974. *Modern Dogma and the Rhetoric of Assent.* Chicago: University of Chicago Press.

Borstung, Jack R. 1982. "Decision-Making at the Top." *Management Science* 28: 341–51.

Bradshaw, Gary F.; Patrick W. Langley; and Herbert A. Simon. 1983. "Studying Scientific Discovery by Computer Simulation." *Science* 222: 971–75.

Brown, Richard Harvey. 1987. "Reason as Rhetorical: On Relations Among Epistemology, Discourse, and Practice," in *The Rhetoric of the Human*

Sciences: Language and Argument in Scholarship and Public Affairs, ed. John S. Nelson, Allan Megill, and Donald N. McCloskey. Madison: University of Wisconsin Press, 184–97.

Carleton, Walter M. 1978. "What Is Rhetorical Knowledge? A Response to Farrell—and More." *Quarterly Journal of Speech* 64: 313–28.

Conley, Thomas M. 1984. "The Enthymeme in Perspective." *Quarterly Journal of Speech* 70: 168–87.

Cyert, Richard M.; Herbert A. Simon; and Donald Trow. 1956. "Observation of a Business Decision." *Journal of Business* 29: 237–48.

Donaldson, Gordon, and Jay W. Lorsch. 1983. *Decision Making at the Top: The Shaping of Strategic Decisions.* New York: Basic Books.

Easton, Allan. 1973. *Complex Managerial Decisions Involving Multiple Objectives.* New York: John Wiley and Sons.

Farrell, Thomas B. 1976. "Knowledge, Consensus, and Rhetorical Theory." *Quarterly Journal of Speech* 62: 1–14.

———. 1978. "Social Knowledge II." *Quarterly Journal of Speech* 64:329–34.

Fischhoff, B.; B. Goitein; and Z. Shapira. 1983. "Subjective Expected Utility: A Model of Decision Making," in *Decision Making Under Uncertainty*, ed. R. W. Scholz. Amsterdam: North-Holland, 183–206.

Flower, Linda S. and John R. Hayes. 1977. "Problem-Solving Strategies and the Writing Process." *College English* 39 (1977): 449–461.

Garver, Eugene. 1978. "Rhetoric and Essentially Contested Arguments." *Philosophy and Rhetoric* 11: 156–72.

Goodnight, G. Thomas. 1982. "The Personal, Technical, and Public Spheres of Argument: A Speculative Inquiry into the Art of Public Deliberation." *Journal of the American Forensic Association* 18: 214–27.

Hellriegel, Don, and John W. Slocum. 1982. *Management: Contingency Approaches.* 3d ed. Reading, Mass.: Addison-Wesley.

Higgins, J. C. 1982. "Decision-Making at Board Level Using Decision Analysis: Two Case Studies." *Journal of the Operational Research Society* 33: 319–26.

Hitt, Michael A., R. Dennis Middlemist, and Robert L. Mathis. 1986. *Management: Concepts and Effective Practice.* 2d ed. St. Paul, Minn.

Huff, S. L.; S. Rivard; A. Grindlay; and I. P. Suttie. 1984. "An Empirical Study of Decision Support Systems." *Infor* 22: 21–39.

Janis, Irving L., and Leon Mann. 1977. *Decision Making.* New York: Free Press.

Judd, Bruce R., and Stein Weissenberger. 1982. "A Systematic Approach to Nuclear Safeguards Decision-Making." *Management Science* 28: 289–302.

Kahneman, Daniel, and Amos Tversky. 1982. "Variants of Uncertainty," in

Judgment Under Uncertainty: Heuristics and Biases, ed. Daniel Kahneman, Paul Slovic, and Amos Tversky. Cambridge: Cambridge University Press, 509–20.

Keen, Peter G. W. 1977. "The Evolving Concept of Optimality," in *Studies in the Management Sciences,* ed. Martin K. Starr and Milan Zeleny. Amsterdam: North-Holland/TIMS, 36–40.

Keen, Peter G. W., and M. Scott Morton. 1978. *Decision Support Systems: An Organizational Perspective.* Reading, Mass.: Addison-Wesley.

Keeney, Ralph L. 1982. "Decision Analysis: An Overview." *Operations Research* 30: 803–38.

Keeney, Ralph L., and Keshavan Nair. 1975. "Decision Analysis for the Siting of Nuclear Power Plants—The Relevance of Multiattribute Utility Theory." *Proceedings of the IEEE* 63: 494–501. Reprinted in *Modern Decision Analysis.* Ed. Gordon M. Kaufman and Howard Thomas. New York: Penguin, 1977, 453–75.

Larkin, Jill; John McDermott; Dorothea P. Simon; and Herbert A. Simon. 1980. "Expert and Novice Performance in Solving Physics Problems." *Science* 208: 1335–42.

Lock, Andrew R. 1982. "A Strategic Business Decision with Multiple Criteria: The Bally Men's Shoe Problem." *Journal of the Operational Research Society* 33: 327–32.

Luthans, Fred. 1985. *Organizational Behavior.* 4th ed. New York: McGraw-Hill.

Machina, Mark J. 1987. "Decision-Making in the Presence of Risk." *Science* 236: 537–43.

MacKay, Alfred. 1980. *Arrow's Theorem: The Paradox of Social Choice.* New Haven: Yale University Press.

McCaskey, Michael B. 1979. "The Management of Ambiguity." *Organizational Dynamics* 7: 31–48.

McCloskey, Donald N. 1985. *The Rhetoric of Economics.* Madison: University of Wisconsin Press.

March, James. G. 1978a "Bounded Rationality, Ambiguity, and the Engineering of Choice." *Bell Journal of Economics* 9: 587–608.

———. 1978b "The 1978 Nobel Prize in Economics." *Science* 202: 858–61.

March, James G., and Herbert A. Simon. 1958. *Organizations.* New York: John Wiley and Sons.

Newell, Allen, and Herbert A. Simon. 1972. *Human Problem Solving.* Englewood Cliffs, N.J.: Prentice-Hall.

Perelman, Chaim. 1982. *The Realm of Rhetoric.* Trans. William Kluback. Notre Dame, Ind.: University of Notre Dame Press.

Perelman, Chaim, and L. Olbrechts-Tyteca. 1969. *The New Rhetoric: A Treatise on Argumentation*. Trans. John Wilkinson and Purcell Weaver. Notre Dame, Ind.: University of Notre Dame Press.

Peters, Thomas J., and Robert H. Waterman, Jr. 1982. *In Search of Excellence: Lessons from America's Best-Run Companies*. New York: Warner.

Presidential Commission on the Space Shuttle Challenger Accident. 1986. *Report to the President*. Vol. 4. Washignton, D.C.: U.S. Government Printing Office.

Schoemaker, Paul J. H. 1982. "The Expected Utility Model: Its Variants, Purposes, Evidence, and Limitations." *Journal of Economic Literature* 20: 529–63.

Schwenk, Charles R., and Howard Thomas. 1983. "Effects of Conflicting Analyses on Managerial Decision Making: A Laboratory Experiment." *Decision Sciences* 14: 467–82.

Simon, Herbert A. 1947. *Administrative Behavior*. New York: Macmillan.

———. 1955. "A Behavioral Model of Rational Choice." *Quarterly Journal of Economics* 69: 99–118.

———. 1957. *Models of Man, Social and Rational*. New York: John Wiley and Sons.

———. 1959. "Theories of Decision-Making in Economics and Behavioral Science." *American Economic Review* 49: 253–83.

———. 1965. "The New Science of Management Decision." *The Shape of Automation for Men and Management*. New York: Harper & Row, 53–111.

———. 1978a "On How to Decide What To Do." *Bell Journal of Economics* 9: 494–507.

———. 1978b "Rationality as Process and as Product of Thought." *American Economic Review* 68: 1–16.

———. 1979. "Rational Decision Making in Business Organizations." *American Economic Review* 69: 493–513.

———. 1981. *The Sciences of the Artificial*. 2d ed. Cambridge: Cambridge University Press.

———. 1983. *Reason in Human Affairs*. Stanford: Stanford University Press.

Slovic, Paul; Baruch Fischhoff; and Sarah Lichtenstein. 1977. "Behavioral Decision Theory." *Annual Review of Psychology* 28: 1–39.

Stagner, Ross. 1969. "Corporate Decision Making: An Empirical Study." *Journal of Applied Psychology* 53: 1–13.

Thompson, James D. 1964. "Decision-Making, the Firm, and the Market," in *New Perspectives in Organization Research*, ed. W. W. Cooper; H. J. Leavitt, and M. W. Shelly. New York: John Wiley and Sons, 334–48.

Ulvila, Jacob W., and Rex V. Brown. 1982. "Decision Analysis Comes of Age." *Harvard Business Review* 60: 130–41.

Winkler, Robert L. 1982. "Research Directions in Decision Making under Uncertainty." *Decision Sciences* 13: 517–33. Responses by David E. Bell, Peter C. Fishburn, Robin M. Hogarth, Ralph L. Keeney, and Peter A. Morris, 534–53.

PART TWO

The Politics of Rhetoric
and the Rhetoric of Politics

7

Arguing over Incommensurable Values:
The Case of Machiavelli

Eugene Garver

I

Machiavelli is an ideal case for studying the rhetoric of the human sciences. On the one hand, he exemplifies the process of making politics fully rhetorical—rhetoric is not for him as it was for Aristotle a *part* of politics but all of it—and on the other hand, paradoxically, he marks the beginning of an era in which politics begins to find rhetoric dispensable. Not every way of thinking ethically or politically requires rhetoric, but rhetoric is an indispensable means of deliberating together when faced with plural ultimate goods, and hence for engaging in and adjudicating disputes concerning incommensurable values. As the years since Machiavelli have made the *datum* of plural ultimate values more and more inescapable, they have made rhetoric less and less available as a mode of reasoning about values, as it has become more and more peripheral in both politics and education. In fact, one of the significant reasons for the recent popularity of rhetoric comes from the perception that disputes concerning conflicting ultimate values, like any disputes over first principles, cannot be approached through the more usual logical methods and require dialectical or rhetorical treatment instead. Machiavelli, in both *The Prince* and the *Discourses on Livy*, presents and teaches strategies for living in a world of plural final ends. I propose to focus on Machiavelli's strategies for forcing the reader to act in such a world, and for preventing a reader from evading the demands that multiple final goods present. I have elsewhere described those strategies in detail as they emerge from the arguments of those texts (Garver 1987a); here I want to present the strategies and explore their implications for the rhetoric of the human sciences.

Rhetorical theory and experience both show that arguments over incommensurable values are not impossible or pointless; experience also shows that they are a difficult sort of argument that most people work hard to avoid. A full use of rhetorical resources is infrequent, not because people need formal training in rhetoric, but because their avoidance is

187

often functional; if, in the time since Machiavelli, rhetoric has been increasingly marginalized, that removal of rhetoric from the center of practice must also be functional, and not blamed on a conspiracy to produce bad education. It is easier and often more pleasant to circumvent the problem of conflicting multiple ends than to face it, so Machiavelli offers arguments to forestall such avoidance behavior. The positive case that Machiavelli develops consists in confronting the problem and showing what resources exist for facing it, but he characteristically presents positive doctrine in the combative style of attacking opponents, and the lines of reasoning and action he attacks are often just those that try to find a way of avoiding the problem.[1] I am not offering Machiavelli as a model for imitation, not least because Machiavelli makes the idea of imitation so problematic, but the incentives of avoiding arguing over incommensurable values, and the ultimate rewards for finally engaging in such argument, are sufficiently independent of circumstances that his taxonomy of evasion strategies and the arguments used in opposing them can be of lasting value.

Rhetoric is not only, as Aristotle tells us, a part of politics; it is in addition, from its beginnings, an amoral skill, an ability to argue either side of any question, a knack for pleasing an audience by telling them what they want to hear. The political side of rhetoric is its ability to facilitate discourse in situations in which there are competing yet incommensurable ultimate values; the deceitful side is its ability to evade such situations by making them appear to be situations in which no such problem exists, either by making the apparently incommensurable values commensurable, or by making discourse impossible or unnecessary. The resources and methods available for treating arguments over incommensurable values and competing final goods can best be seen to emerge, as a consequence, out of opposition to the strategies people employ to evade such disputes. Machiavelli presents no theory of argument. He engages in argument. Consequently my exposition will be more systematic than his, and less dramatic. Moreover, because of the hermeneutic circle in which to read Machiavelli is to read the history of Machiavellianism, I will insert between Machiavelli's own texts and my own the argument Isaiah Berlin develops in "The Originality of Machiavelli," (1980) which offers a reading of Machiavelli that points beyond itself to a need to read more rhetorically. I will point to four primary ways of evading the problem of prudence and incommensurable values; Machiavelli has been himself accused of taking each of these positions, as people read him and make his thought more comfortable and less radical.

II

First, one can say that what people think are ends are really not ends at all, but means to the true ultimate end, or forms, species, variations, instantiations of it. Pleasure, to take the example most often encountered in ethical debates, is often held to be the one true end; apparently disinterested activities like pursuing a career of public service must be taken as sophisticated, or perverse, forms of the pursuit of pleasure alongside the enjoyment of tennis, sex, wine, and applause. When there is a conflict and a forced choice among these forms or causes of pleasure, the criterion for choice must be the role each plays in the one true end, happiness, or the amount of pleasure any given act brings.

Those who read Machiavelli as promulgating a doctrine of *raison d'etat* see him erecting the security of the state into an end of such overriding value that anything done in its name thereby becomes good.[2] Part of the Machiavellian side of Machiavelli's reputation comes from his refusal to say that an action with a good result is itself good, allowing people the comforting line of rationalization that publicly beneficial vices are really not vices at all; Machiavelli finds that the current conception of politics leads to disappointment because means and ends are not neatly arranged, but he is not promising a new world in which, once people grasp the right ultimate value, means and ends will coexist in comfortable harmony. Neither *raison d'etat* nor success more broadly conceived can serve as a more ultimate end that will subordinate and put in their proper places things that used to be taken as ultimate values.

Perhaps the most interesting, and certainly the most successful, political use of this evasion strategy occurs in the history and prehistory of capitalism. What once was called *greed* and regarded as vicious and antisocial gradually became domesticated into something with the more sanitary and scientific sounding name of the *profit motive*. What were in Mandeville private vices that had public benefits, became, by the argument that what leads to the good is itself good, a new private virtue, the virtue of making a lot of money. Along those lines, people could say that the behavior of politicians, while it looks unsavory, leads to results that we want, and therefore we want them to act that way, and therefore that way of acting is laudable. That is not a line of argument that Machiavelli himself takes.

It is no accident that money should supply the most striking example of this first evasion strategy, because money, as has been noted from Aristotle on, is a conventional means for establishing a common measure for otherwise incommensurable values. It is a nontrivial matter, and one I will pass over here, to discriminate between arguments in which money becomes a further, more ultimate value, and those in which it serves to adjudicate between competing ultimate values without making them commensurable.[3] There is, however, a second, traditionally recognized, conventional means for establishing a common measure for otherwise incommensurable values, namely discourse itself. It is a rhetorical evasion strategy often very difficult to detect to claim that making values discursively accessible, mentioning them in the same sentence, automatically makes them commensurable.[4] Such practices show that it is easy to achieve commensurability, but they also show that such easily won victories do not last very long: the true rhetorical challenge, which requires more artful uses of rhetoric, is to deliberate about incommensurable values while acknowledging their incommensurability.[5]

If ultimate values are not to be subordinated to and measured by a more ultimate value, the next obvious move is to elect a strategy of segregation, of finding proper and bounded realms governed by each end. And so people have distinguished, and found that Machiavelli distinguishes, between such pairs as the public and the private, what people say and what they do, the moral and the political, values appropriate to acquiring a state or to revolution and those relevant to holding one. Berlin (1980) rejects this comfortable interpretation of Machiavelli:

> For the defenders of the *raison d'état*, the sole justification of these
> measures is that they are exceptional—that they are needed to
> preserve a system the purpose of which is precisely to preclude the
> need for such odious measures, so that the sole justification of such
> steps is that they will end the situations that render them necessary.
> But for Machiavelli these measures are, in a sense, themselves
> quite normal (p. 65).[6]

Machiavelli does not locate his new way of acting in a domain distinct from that occupied by traditional morals and politics, because to do so would destroy his project. If the old paradigm were what people mean by politics and ethics, then a new one would not be taken as a version of ethics and politics at all, but as something else, the replacing of ethics by calculated self-interest and of politics by force and fraud, of rhetorical persuasion by propaganda, a reading that accounts for much of Machiavelli's public reputation. Machiavelli's new prince would be doomed to staying a usurper, and vulnerable to newer usurpers, instead of appearing "as old" as the traditional ruler; he could seize power only at the cost of having that

190

power cease being political. This is no idle possibility: Machiavelli recognizes that sometimes the usurpatious actions of the new prince in fact doom him to operate in such a permanently insecure world; the fact, for example, that mixed principalities are easy to acquire is exactly what makes them easy to lose. At different times in history, it may be possible to discover a new virtue (thrift is a possible example) that can manage its own domain alongside existing goods, but Machiavelli's new *virtù* cannot bear that relation to traditional virtues. (Hume's criticism of the "so-called monkish virtues" depends on the same sort of rejection of distinct domains for distinct values.) Similarly, at different times in history, it may be possible to stake out a new scientific subject-matter or new sphere of autonomous activity, as economics and aesthetics have respectively claimed to separate themselves off from politics, but Machiavelli has less modest ambitions.[7]

Machiavelli is often read as employing such a containment strategy, seeing politics as a state of nature, a war of all against all, but thereby protecting private morality, which becomes morality *simpliciter*, from contamination. One can find evidence in Machiavelli for such a containment strategy within the public world of competition for power itself: *The Prince* begins by separating the problems of acquiring a state from those of maintaining one, the distinction later thinkers will refer to as the difference between sovereignty and politics. In fact, though, he uses that distinction to demonstrate its instability. When Machiavelli strips *virtù* of its conventional associations with action in accordance with correct principles, and refuses simply to identify *virtù* with success either, he breaks down the distinction between the talents appropriate to acquiring a state and those useful for preserving one; when he reconsiders *virtù*'s contrary, *fortuna*, in chapter 25, he upsets the simple further conclusion that, if there are not two distinct abilities for these two functions, then there is some single ability, called *virtù*, useful for both acquiring and preserving states.

> Two men, acting differently, attain the same effect, and of two
> others acting in the same way, one attains his goal and not the
> other. . . . No man is found so prudent as to be able to adapt
> himself to [changing times and circumstances], either because he
> cannot deviate from that to which his nature disposes him, or else
> because having always prospered by walking in one path, he cannot
> persuade himself that it is well to leave it. . . . If one could change
> one's nature with time and circumstances, fortune would never
> change.[8]

191

That is, Machiavelli can collapse the distinction between founding and keeping, but sovereignty and politics are not thereby merged into some synthesis of a permanent revolution and the requisite talents into a new single talent; on the contrary, *fortuna* represents the extradiscursive resistance to the success of such tactics and the existence of any identifiable cause of success called *virtù*. While the unstable dances of *virtù* and *fortuna* serve to underline the way competing ultimate values inhabit a single world (although perhaps not in a state of peaceful coexistence), they raise the question, which I think goes very much to the heart of the Machiavellian enterprise, of how he can offer an ability, called *virtù*, that, because of its lack of "semantic associations" and the unpredictable interference of fortune, cannot be codified into a method. *Virtù* can neither be one method among others nor yet a single, all-encompassing method. In contemporary terms, methodological eclecticism is not the way to function rhetorically in a world of incommensurable values.

While both those evasion strategies are often successful, neither of them comes very close to the heart of Machiavelli's own enterprise. The two remaining ways of not confronting the problem have to be taken more seriously. The next alternative is a strategy of compromise: since there are many good things, and one cannot have them all, the best policy must be to forfeit some pleasure for the sake of duty, and not be an ascetic, a pharisee, but recognize that duties should be generally, although not universally, observed. It is easy to say that such a strategy is intellectually incoherent because there can be no right amount of each that is being compromised, but its intellectual emptiness does not remove its appeal—it looks like these are cases that call for intellectual emptiness—and so Machiavelli shows that it is practically unsuccessful as well: "Men generally decide upon a middle course, which is most hazardous; for they know neither to be entirely good or entirely bad.[9]

Many readers think that moderation should be the practical implication of Machiavelli's original proclamation of the existence of plural goods, but—even if he should—Machiavelli clearly does not draw that inference. It is good history, but bad reading of Machiavelli to say with Berlin (1980) that if practical reason cannot be assimilated to theoretical or technical reasoning in that way, then "the path is open to empiricism, pluralism, toleration, compromise" (p. 79). The path may be open, but it is a road obviously not taken by Machiavelli. He first rejects the fanaticism that accompanies practice directed by a single end—whether Christian virtue or success in battle (see, for example, the condemnation in chapter 13 of *The Prince* of mercenaries even when they bring victory)—and then rejects the natural inference from the absence of a single end to pluralism, toleration, and compromise. In this way he can broaden our ideas of what practical reason oriented to a plurality of ends requires, and force us to recognize that the alternative to dogmatism need not be as cheering as liberal ideas of tolerance and pluralism might suggest, as he shows that the recognition of permanently plural final ends can be reason for more combative and aggressive action. Compromise is commonly appealed to as a strategy—since we can't agree, and each of us thinks ourselves right, let's compromise and split the difference. Compromise might *sometimes* be the right response in the face of an ultimate conflict of values, but it is not always or automatically the right response. Berlin joins commentators on Machiavelli from Guicciardini and Halifax on in thinking that moderation should be the practical implication of Machiavelli's original proclamation of the existence of plural goods, but—even if he should—Machiavelli clearly does not draw that inference. Machiavelli's "intellectual consequences, wholly unintended by its originator, were, by a fortunate irony of history (which some call its dialectic), the bases of the very liberalism that Machiavelli would surely have condemned" (Berlin 1980, 79).

We will later need to show why Machiavelli does not draw the inference Berlin thinks he should, but first I want to complete the program by turning to the fourth and final evasion strategy. When attempts to construe such an "even more ultimate end", to segregate appropriate domains for different ends, and to make compromises among them are all thought to fail, the final strategy for avoiding the problem asserts that, in the absence of a single final good, the choice between plural ends must be an arbitrary and irrational one, a personal decision with which no one can disagree because no standards exist to which we can appeal in concluding that one decision is better than another. As in the third method, the recognition of plural ultimate values can here become the occasion for celebration of the irrational. As Berlin puts it: "What if [men] found that they were compelled to make a choice between two incommensurable systems, to choose as they did without the aid of an infallible measuring rod which certified one form of life as being superior to all others and could be used to demonstrate this to the satisfaction of all rational men?" (1980, 69–70).[10]

Berlin thinks that Machiavelli, in fact, takes this stand—if someone chooses Christian virtue, Machiavelli has nothing to say to him: "There was no problem and no agony for him; he shows no trace of scepticism or relativism; he chose his side, and took little interest in the values that this choice ignored or flouted" (1980).

It is not my purpose here to show where Berlin goes wrong, why

Machiavelli does not in fact see arbitrary choice as the response to incommensurable final goods, but instead to show how rhetoric offers less arbitrary and more reasoned opportunities of response. Each of these evasion strategies is defensible in some circumstances, and only objectionable insofar as it claims to be a solution to the problem of incommensurable values, a solution that can be adopted as part of a way of life. Each has an important place, as the four cohere to create a phenomenon generally called *liberalism*—an abstract *summum bonum* such as utility, money, or pleasure, spheres of autonomous values with mutual noninterference treaties, the elevation of compromise and moderation into noninstrumental goods, and taking character as a private datum beyond argument.

III

Machiavelli makes successful practical action appear more difficult than one would, perhaps, have liked to believe. The evasion strategies I enumerated are appealing not only because the prudent and rhetorical thinking that is their alternative makes heavy intellectual and moral demands but also because the evasion strategies have clear rewards. Rhetoric should allow us to do better than the abandonment of reason that Berlin thinks is the moral of *The Prince*: that a "choice" between incommensurable values must be arbitrary. Berlin is insufficiently rhetorical and does not recognize how rhetorical Machiavelli is. Machiavelli does confront the new prince with such a choice in *The Prince*, but it does not follow that he similarly confronts his *readers* with that choice. On the contrary, *The Prince* presents a dramatization of the prince's decision, so we have to ask what the reader is to make of the prince's confrontation with plural ultimate values, and ask why Machiavelli employs direct rather than indirect means of treating the problem.

That second question, at least, has an immediate answer. None of these evasion strategies will simply disappear on being refuted, because their attractions, while false, are certainly not illusory. Hence Machiavelli's strategy relies not on logical refutation but on rhetorical tactics: on dissuasion based on ridicule and on making success seem unlikely, and on persuasion based on hope and the provision of resources. And hence, Machiavelli's positive teaching will take the form of these more indirect, dramatic dealings with the reader rather than the direct choice he forces on the prince.

Each of the four evasion strategies is a commonly used response to competing ultimate values; each is a strategy that at least relies on *argu-*

ment rather than force or self-deception to impose a single value. The place of each of these evasion strategies in the description of what subsequently comes to be called *liberalism* comes from liberalism's reliance on political argument, not only argument rather than force, but also argument rather than custom and habit. The strategies fail, though, to take full advantage of the argumentative resources that rhetoric has to offer, because they leave untouched, and continue to defend, the instrumental conception of practical reason appropriate to situations in which there is a single overriding value to consider. A full appreciation of the resources of rhetoric requires some reflection on the different uses of reason in action required by an ethics grounded in a single ultimate value and one that admits plural final goods.

An ethical doctrine organized around a single ultimate value can be fully articulated, stated in a creed. If there is a single ultimate value, then practical reasoning can take the hypothetico-deductive form of a practical syllogism, and we can follow the scientific implications of that method of thinking by a righteous indifference to the particular circumstances of action, making practical action truly a matter of technique.[11] Although problems in application and in judging particulars might arise in a moral or political doctrine, the truths operative in a such a system can themselves be simply stated and understood apart from any particular act of application. Multiple final goods, however, cannot serve the same logical function as a single final good, because every application of one value to action presupposes an argument that it, and not others, is the proper value to guide this action. Because of that more complicated relation between principles and circumstances, plural ultimate values cannot be fully defined apart from their instantiations; consequently, reasoning on how to achieve such ends cannot be purely instrumental reasoning. In prudence and in rhetoric, responsiveness to circumstances is transformed from a kind of corruption into a form of merit. With more than one end, a decision must take circumstances into account, if only to choose which ultimate value is the relevant one governing a given case. (Hence the appeal of strategies for avoiding the problem of multiple final ends; each of those strategies pretends to be responsive to such a problem of judgment and application.) Appropriateness to circumstances will be a primary rhetorical virtue—*to prepon, kairos* in Greek, decorum in Latin—while adaptability to circumstances is a primary vice in a simpler ethics and politics.

Although prudence or practical reason cannot then receive full articulation in a method or technique of acting, it must be partially articulated if that responsiveness is not to turn into mere reacting, which is just what

195

happens when prudence takes on its modern meaning of amoral opportunism, and rhetoric becomes a means of manipulation, deception, and
rationalization. Machiavelli will differ from Aristotle, and from other
moral and political thinkers in judging how much articulation of practical
reason is possible. Ultimately, that decision turns on the extent to which
the principles of practical action can be abstracted from the context in
which action takes place. Figuring out a theory of practical reason means
engaging in a difficult matter of judgment, judging how much articulation
of practical reason is possible, a decision which turns on the extent to
which the principles of practical action can be abstracted from the context
in which action takes place. Different versions of practical reason locate
themselves differently on the continuum between techniques, arts, and
skills, whose rational structure can be fully articulated apart from their
circumstances of application, and passive responsiveness to circumstances,
which has no rational structure at all.

The appropriateness of prudence to shifting circumstances cannot
mean that prudence must change with *every* change in circumstances, or
it would become a completely passive mode of responding to circumstances, as in chapter 25 of *The Prince*, where Machiavelli says that someone who, *per impossibile*, could change his way of acting with every
change in fortune would never lose. If every shift in the favors of fortune
changed a person's character, she would no longer have any character; her
acts would be successful by ceasing to be acts and becoming responses.
Consequently, this adaptability to circumstances required by plural ultimate values is not identical with its near-neighbor, an amoral sort of
opportunism towards ends and clever opportunism often attributed to
Machiavelli, amoral not only because it will choose any means to attain a
desired end, but also because it corresponds to a literal dissolution of
character—not the descent into a bad character, but into no character at
all.[12] Because of the shifting relation of principles to circumstances, the
more that practical reason becomes a matter of a teachable skill, the less it
is connected to character, an inverse proportion that Machiavelli illustrates
and that partially justifies his historical reputation. From the time of the
Greek sophists, the analogous relation between rhetoric and character,
between speaking well and speaking the truth, which is focused in the issue
of whether the good rhetor must be a *vir bonus*, has been a source of both
embarrassment and opportunity for rhetorical theory. Whether decorum
and adaptability will be virtuous or vicious depends on whether the good
use of practical reason is tied to character or technique.[13]

Skills do not have to take circumstances into account and do not have to worry about competing claims of other views of the subject or other methods; Machiavelli points this out when he says that anyone can judge the beauty of ancient artistic achievements without knowing much about the context in which those artists worked, while judgments about the goodness of ancient moral and political deeds requires knowledge of their circumstances, and an awareness of our own points of view. If I am calculating, I don't have to worry about whether I'm adding cattle or coins, and if it's an addition problem, I don't have to think about the propagation of calves or the inflation of money as alternative methods of increase, either. But look at what happens to methods of moral reasoning that follow the same model. A moral system that stated its major premises has no room for prudence.

> No morality can be forcible enough to bind the enthusiastic zealot. The sacredness of the cause sanctifies every measure which can be made use of to promote it. . . . The steady attention alone to so important an interest as that of eternal salvation is apt to extinguish the benevolent affections, and beget a narrow, contracted selfishness. And when such a temper is encouraged, it easily eludes all the general precepts of charity and benevolence (Hume 1947, 90).[14]

Any moral system that does, by contrast, require prudence must permit a partial—and consequently debatable—articulation of the principles of practical reason. If there were no articulation at all, if it were just opportunism, then there would be nothing to debate; if moral principles could be fully stated apart from their application, then the debate would be closed. Consequently the role played by discourse, by political deliberation and argument, in politics as a whole is a function of where prudence is located on this continuum between a technical indifference to circumstances and an amoral passivity in the face of circumstances. I began by quoting Aristotle's dictum that rhetoric is a part of politics; how large a part (to the extent that such quantitative imagery is permissible) depends on this location along the continuum of kinds of indifference, kinds of relations of form and matter. In *The Prince*, not only is responsiveness to circumstances a fundamental theme, but Machiavelli at the same time must constantly make judgments about how much of *virtù* and practical intelligence can be made the subject of teaching and advising. Hence the fundamental puzzle of *virtù*, an ability that cannot be codified into a method. The distance between prudence and art takes a different, but no less critical, form in the *Discourses*, where it appears as a judgment of how

197

to abstract principles of success from Roman history and use them in contemporary action.

While technical and scientific reasoning should be untainted by considerations of the circumstances to which it is applied—just as the laws of addition apply to cows and ounces of gold, so all sinners are equally blessed in the eyes of God—the plurality of ultimate values demands that prudential reasoning be responsive to the circumstances in which it is applied. When prudential reasoning replaces technical calculation, and when we participate in Machiavelli's revolution and find ourselves choosing ends rather than means, then that need to take circumstances into account changes all the dimensions of choice. In particular, we have to reconceive the nature of the agent doing the choosing. Machiavelli's discussions of the prince, hero, lawmaker and other "characters" show that one cannot specify or characterize the kind of person who can choose rightly, that it is impossible to make such a characterization outside the acts of choice involved because choosing ends inevitably implies the paradoxical idea of choosing one's character.

Machiavelli thus causes discomfort in his readers by refusing to make practical achievement seem simple, refusing to see action as permitted treatment by a reliable and teachable technique. Any mode of action is more or less appropriate to different manifolds, and there are occasions when we can isolate a sufficiently self-contained manifold for which technical skill will consequently be adequate, but for the more challenging, and the most glorious, practical tasks, prudence and not technique is required.[15] The acquisition of techniques is suitable for military, but not for political, actions; practical, rather than productive, acts call for character, not technique. This is not to deny that military methods are sometimes perfectly adequate; the mistake consists in thinking that such techniques will be an adequate substitute for politics. (Again, the Aristotelian rhetorical point is that people do not dispute over what can be securely known. "There is no room for deliberation about matters fully ascertained and completely formulated as sciences; such for instance as orthography, for we have no uncertainty as to how a word ought to be spelt" (*Nichomachean Ethics* 3.3.1112b1–3).

Moreover, the material on which action and choice work changes the objects of Machiavelli's attention, and the attention of the political actors in his dramas, from things to people.[16] The correlative of technique is inert matter; the correlative of praxis is people, whether oneself or others. Just as Machiavelli refuses to allow us the easy inference from the recognition of plural ultimate values to tolerance and compromise and liberal democracy, so he prevents us from resting content with the commonplace that it is better to treat people (and to be treated) as people rather than things.[17] Just as the idea of the character doing the choosing becomes complicated as one slowly comes to acknowledge the implications of choosing ends rather than means, so this shift from a military or technical mode of action to a more practical one changes our conception of the material on which choice is exercised from inert matter to people with their own capacities for self-motion. As the argument of *The Prince* proceeds, two things happen to the life of *virtù*, of choosing ends, of prudent rather than technical reasoning. First, these things become less and less second-best methods forced upon us by circumstances; the lost world of one final end and correspondingly simple duties becomes less and less attractive. Although republics are harder to hold than traditional monarchies, and despite the fact that it is easier to operate on inert matter than on people, the more difficult prospect has its own appeals. "A republic, being able to adapt herself, by means of the diversity among her body of citizens, to a diversity of temporal conditions better than a prince can, is of greater duration than a princedom and has good fortune longer" (*Discourses on Livy* 3.9).[18] (Once again, political attitudes towards rhetoric shift correspondingly. Initially one might regret that knowledge of social facts is not yet adequate for us to be governed by science, and meanwhile we unfortunately have to rely on disputation; further reflection on such architectonic social science makes rhetoric more and more directly, not just provisionally, appealing.) And second, as the reader is thus gradually seduced into the world of multiple values, problems of action become more difficult; *virtù* is no longer one among several possibly defensible modes of action, as we learn what it is like when the man of *virtù* encounters others who operate in the same way—that is, when there are no alternatives to prudence.[19] Pocock (1975) puts the difference between a world with one virtuous prince and the republican world of nothing but *virtù* this way:

> In the final, Boethian, analysis, the price to be paid for a life of civic activity was vulnerability to fortune; and the republic, being that community in which each individual was defined by his activity, was the community committed by its political form to contend against that vulnerability. States and nations, like individuals, might rise and fall as ambition condemned them to mount upon the Wheel, but only the republic obliged the individual to pit his virtue against fortune as a condition of his political being. Virtue was the principle of republics (pp. 349–50).[20]

199

Here prudence and *virtù* are not optional, and Machiavelli does not present them, as he does in *The Prince,* as alternatives that might or might not be chosen. As we read Machiavelli's examples and precepts, we are forced to abandon the usual, technical model of choice, in which someone chooses means to a given end, chooses to mold some matter into a certain form. Instead we are invited to consider the problematic nature of each term of that definition, the character who does the choosing, the means or matter—people, not things—and the end or form: a stable yet responsible community, not a product so self-subsistent that it will no longer require connection to human action.[21]

This is not the place to work out the details of Machiavelli's rhetorical politics. I think, however, that this short tour of his deployment of rhetorical resources should be enough to show the magnitude of the demands that his version of practical reason makes, especially in comparison to the easier responses to the world of conflicting ultimate values that he rejects. Machiavelli is a case study worth returning to, not because he offers a method for applying rhetoric in extreme ethical and political situations, but because *The Prince,* especially, offers strategies for facing, and for avoiding the refusal to face, the world of plural ultimate values in which rhetoric is *the* means of using reason in action, and because the *Discourses on Livy,* especially, illustrate what it is like to live, and even to flourish, in such a world. Machiavelli's purpose is not only to show how difficult and risky it is to take seriously the problem of incommensurable values but also, through the prospect of future rewards and glory and the fear of failure and ridicule, to make us want to enter that world. It is not a world that one should enter unarmed.

NOTES

1. The idea of incommensurable values does exist in thinkers before Machiavelli, but there is no *problem* of incommensurable values that occupies the same central place that the problem has had from Machiavelli to the present. Connected to the current revival of interest in rhetoric has been a corresponding explicit attention to the more general problem of incommensurability, largely inspired by Kuhn's invention and popularization of the idea of paradigms and paradigm shifts. The connection between incommensurability as a practical problem in conflicts of values and the more general problem of incommensurability and its connection to rationality is explored in detail in my book (1987a) and in "Paradigms and Princes" (Garver 1987b).

2. Berlin (1980) rejects this reading of Machiavelli: "In killing, deceiving, betraying, Machiavelli's prince and republicans are doing evil things, not condonable in terms of common morality. It is Machiavelli's great merit that he does not deny this. Marsilio, Hobbes, Spinoza, and, in their own fashion, Hegel, and Marx, did try to deny it" (p. 63). See also Mark Hulliung (1983): "On various occasions in his political writings Machiavelli refused to abide by what many thinkers today regard as an essential term in 'the problem of dirty hands,' namely, that only success can vindicate immoral means, so that a failed Machiavellian, no matter how moral his reasons for adopting immoral techniques, can never be excused when his schemes backfire. Directly opposed to this modern version of the dilemma of means and ends is Machiavelli's habit of siding with the Machiavellian who deserved to win but lost, and of siding against the common run of men who, he suggests, only know how to judge by consequences" (p. 121).

3. Hayden White's (1973) reading of Marx's history of money in terms of the four rhetorical master tropes is most suggestive here. See also Bernard Williams (1979): "The most basic version of the idea that utility provides a universal currency is that all values are versions or applications in some way of utility; and in this sense the claim of course rejects the idea of a universal currency. Indeed, in this version, it is not clear that there is really more than one value at all, or, consequently, real conflicts between values. Some indirect forms of utilitarianism, on the other hand, will want it to be the case both that there is a universal currency of utility and at the same time that the various values indirectly validated by reference to utility are autonomous enough for there to be recognisable conflicts between them. It is not clear how stable or coherent views of this kind are" (p. 228).

While Aristotle recognizes the existence of incommensurable values, they are not an important problem for him because the commensurability established by money, or anything else, does not destroy the *functions* of the objects or activities being compared or exchanged. Once the secure knowledge of function disappears, the problem of incommensurable values emerges in its full form. See, for example *Politics* 1.9.1257a8: "Each possession may be used in two ways, both of which belong to the thing itself but not in a similar way; for one of them is but the other is not appropriate to the thing's nature. For example, a shoe may be worn or it may be exchanged for something else, and both of these are uses of the shoe; for even he who exchanges the shoe for currency or food with a man who needs it uses the shoe as a shoe, but this is not the appropriate use of the shoe, for the shoe was not made for the sake of exchange."

4. See Rorty (1979): "That all languages are translatable into one another (for the Davidsonian reasons) does not mean that such equivalences can be

found (even 'in principle'). It just means that we cannot make sense of the claim that there are more than temporary impediments to our know-how—the claim that something called a 'different conceptual scheme' prevents us from learning how to converse with another language-user. Nor does it take away the intuition behind the false romantic claim that great poems are untranslatable. They are, of course, translatable; the problem is that the translations are not themselves great poems" (p. 355, n.35).

5. For an example of such a victory too easily gained, see Goedecke (1970): "Terms which can be used in opposite ways, such as 'due process', allow dissent to occur in an open and responsible manner, and give freedom for the [Supreme] Court to move from one sort of policy to the opposite. As Justice Frankfurter indicated, the due process clause has an 'independent potency' since it is used in practice in opposite ways over a period of time by differing majorities" (p. 588). See also Aristotle's *Nicomachean Ethics* (9.6.1167b2f): "Men are not of one mind merely when each thinks the same thing (whatever this may be), but when each thinks the same thing in relation to the same person." Each may, for example, think that he should rule, and that, Aristotle points out, does not produce concord.

6. See also Pitkin (1984): "Machiavelli nowhere says that politics is or should be different from the rest of human life, or that political action is governed by different principles than personal conduct" (p. 5).

7. Thrift is often an example of the first evasion strategy too, a vice which, by being subordinated as a means to a greater good, public welfare, gradually becomes seen as a virtue. See also Bernstein (1983): "This point, so vital for Kuhn's new image of science, which stresses the element of conflict, incompatibility, and destruction of earlier paradigms, bears a very strong resemblance to one aspect of Hegel's understanding of dialectic, his concept of *Aufhebung*. For *Aufhebung* is at once negation, preservation, and overcoming or synthesis. So, in the instance of Einsteinian and Newtonian theory, we can say that Einstein's theory at once negates Newton's (shows that it is false); preserves it (can reconstruct the 'truth' implicit in Newton's theory by explaining a transformation of it); and both negates and preserves Newton's theory by offering a new, rival theory that goes beyond what Newton achieved" (p. 84).

8. See also Pocock (1975): "The only constant semantic association is now that between *virtù* and innovation, the latter being considered rather as an act than as a previously accomplished fact, and *virtù* is preeminently that by which the individual is rendered outstanding in the context of innovation and in the role of innovator" (p. 167). See also Pitkin (1984): "It will not matter, he says, 'which of these two roads [cruelty or kindness] a general travels, if only he

202

is an able (*virtuoso*) man,' for with his 'extraordinary ability' (*virtù*) he can mitigate any 'excess' produced by his mode of proceeding" (p. 160).

9. Machiavelli (1940) "*Discourses on Livy*" 1.24; Cf. also 1. 26. 30; 2. 23. "Compromise with current morality leads to bungling, which is always despicable, and when practiced by statesmen involves men in ruin" (Berlin 1980, 64).

10. Tying choice of values to personality in this way removes values from the realm of rational discussion, and thus makes them incommensurable according to the definition of commensurability offered in Rorty (1979): "By 'commensurable' I mean to be brought under a set of rules which will tell us how rational agreement can be reached on what would settle the issue on every point where statements seem to conflict. These rules tell us how to construct an ideal situation, in which all residual disagreements will be seen to be 'noncognitive' or merely verbal, or else merely temporary—capable of being resolved by doing something further. What matters is that there should be agreement about what would have to be done if a resolution *were* to be achieved" (p. 316).

Despite all the analogies between the general problem of incommensurability and Machiavelli's more specific problem of incommensurable values—analogies which permit the use of rhetorical techniques in both fields—this tie to character makes the practical problem ultimately different from the scientific one. See, for example, Williams (1985): "The scientific understanding of the world is not only entirely consistent with recognizing that we occupy no special position in it, but also incorporates, now, that recognition. The aim of ethical thought, however, is to help us to construct a world that will be our world, one in which we have a social, cultural, and personal life" (p. 111).

11. See Bernard Crick (1973): "A doctrine is doctrinaire and likely to prove impractical less by the character of its intentions, than by whether or not it claims that its set of principles or its set of intended results must entail a unique and specific set of actions-as-means. For political theory would lead us to believe, both on empirical and moral grounds, that the means must vary according to circumstances. . . . When policies cannot be changed without undermining the authority of the doctrine, then the doctrine must have been formulated in terms over-specific and insufficiently generalized" (p. 31). See also Crick (1972): "The more one is involved in relationships with others, the more conflicts of interest, or of character and circumstance, will arise. These conflicts, when personal, create the activity we call 'ethics' (or else that type of action, as arbitrary as it is irresponsible, called 'selfish'); and such conflicts, when public, create political activity (or else some type of rule in the self-interest of a single group)" (p. 25).

12. Some Renaissance advocates of heroic self-fashioning do destroy the idea of character in just this way. For example Pitkin (1984) quotes Pico's "On the Dignity of Man": "To [man] is granted to have whatever he chooses, to be whatever he wills. On man when he came to life, the Father conferred the seeds of all kinds and the germs of every way of life. . . . Who would not admire this chameleon?" (p. 12).

13. On the connection between character and knowledge in Aristotle's *Rhetoric*, see Garver (1989).

14. Bacon (1973) notes the rhetorical dimension of this adaptation of reason to circumstances in *The Advancement of Learning*: "Logic handleth reason exact and in truth, and Rhetoric handleth it as it is planted in popular opinions and manners. And therefore Aristotle doth wisely place Rhetoric as between Logic on the one side and moral or civil knowledge on the other, as participating of both: for the proofs and demonstrations of Logic are toward all men indifferent and the same; but the proofs and demonstrations of Rhetoric ought to differ according to the auditor" (p. 208).

John Rawls (1971) aptly illustrates this sense of moral principle when he invokes the criterion that "the guiding principle [is] that a rational individual is always to act so that he need never blame himself no matter how things finally transpire" (pp. 422–23). The analogy between this and the ideal of valid inference as never leading from true premises to a false conclusion is striking. This relation of principles to action can also be conceived as "politics as the application of moral principles" (Burke 1982, 46).

15. I noted above that Aristotle too develops his conception of prudence by contrasts to *techne*. One of the contrasts is that there are many arts, but only one prudence. There are many arts because each art has a single end that can be aimed at without having to worry about other ends; the single end for prudence is the good for man which, for the reasons I have suggested, lacks the sort of unity required of the ends of art.

16. See Pitkin (1984): "Furthermore, the humanists of the earlier period had largely construed human activity on the model of production—the making of objects out of physical material, *techne* rather than *praxis*. Ficino's glorification of man as potential artificer of the heavens has already been mentioned; and indeed, these humanists presented God himself as epitomizing what he gave to man: the power of creation, understood as power over objects. As long as human power and creativity were conceived in this way, the full theoretical problems of autonomy could not be confronted. They emerged only when human power was understood not as making or manipulating objects, but as arising out of relationships among *persons*, each of whom has his own needs,

204

interests, and way of seeing the world, yet all of whom must live together" (pp. 18–19).

17. Machiavelli (1940), *Discourses on Livy* 2.2. See also Pocock (1975): "To be ruled by a free people is worse than to be ruled by a prince, apparently because the prince desires your love and allegiance and so may respect your customs, whereas the free people, being morally self-sufficient, have no interest in anything other than your total subjection" (p. 216).

18. As Pitkin (1984) puts it, "Republican authority must be exercised in a way that further politicizes the people rather than rendering them quiescent. Its function is precisely to keep a political movement or action that the people have initiated . . . from disintegrating into riot, apathy, or privatization."

19. See Pitkin (1984): "Although the Citizen is, like the fox and the Founder, an image of manhood, it embodies *virtù* in a fundamentally different way. For both fox and Founder have *virtù* through their personal, individual autonomy, understood as needing no others, having ties to no others, acting without being acted upon. For the Citizen, by contrast, *virtù* is sharing in a collective autonomy, a collective freedom and glory, yet without loss of individuality. *Virtù* is systemic or relational. Thus it not merely is compatible with, but logically requires, interaction in mutuality with others like oneself. It lies not in isolation from or domination over others, but in shared taking charge of one's objective connections with them. 'Each Man by Himself is Weak,' as a chapter title in the *Discourses* announces, but 'The Populace United is Strong.' (1.57) When individuals realize this, they act together to pursue the shared public good and thereby sustain it. When they perceive as [if they were] isolated individuals, their actions become both selfish and cowardly, for 'as soon as each man gets to thinking about his personal danger, he becomes worthless and weak,' his *virtù* vanishes; his actions begin to undermine the community and produce his isolation. Citizen *virtù* is thus a matter both of objective activity and of outlook or attitude, each affecting the other. And in both respects, such individual *virtù* is available only in a republic; it presupposes an ethos and an institutional framework. Individuals can achieve only 'such excellence [*perfezione*]' as the 'way of life [*modo del vivere*]' of their community 'permits' (3.31)" (p. 81).

20. Cf. Pitkin (1984): "The point is never just getting others to do what you want, but changing them, introducing new patterns of action and of relationship. Such redirection of human affairs is the most challenging task a man can undertake, for nothing is 'more difficult to plan or more uncertain of success or more dangerous to carry out than an attempt to introduce new institutions' (*The Prince*, c. 6)" (p. 52). This parallels Aristotle's distinction

between legislation and politics (*Nichomachean Ethics* 6. 8. 1141b24–27), and Machiavelli uses it continually to distinguish short-term success from the laying of foundations.

21. See Pocock (1975): "Not only is the legislator's *virtù* related to *fortuna* in a way utterly different from that of the new prince; he is performing an innovation of a different order. He finds his *materia*—the people he is to mold—in a condition so anomic that his *virtù* needs only a sword to impose form upon it; very little is said of the previous structure of accustomed behavior which other innovators displace. Moreover, in imposing form upon matter he is the founder of a political order: Cyrus, Theseus and Romulus founded kingdoms, Lycurgus a polity and Moses a nation in covenant with God. The word *stato*—normally employed by Machiavelli and Guicciardini to mean 'rule by some other'—does not appear to denote what the legislator brings into being, a highly viable political community, stabilized by his *virtù* and (at least if it is a republic) the *virtù* of its citizens; a kingdom is stabilized by use and inheritance. By contrast, the new prince does not find matter lacking all form; he takes possession of a society already stabilized by customs of its own" (p. 175).

REFERENCES

Bacon, Francis. 1973. *The Advancement of Learning*, ed. G. W. Kitchin. Dent: London.

Berlin, Isaiah. 1980. *Against the Current: Essays in the History of Ideas*. New York: Penguin, 25–79.

Bernstein, Richard. 1983. *Beyond Objectivism and Relativism*. Philadelphia: University of Pennsylvania Press.

Burke, Richard J. 1982. "Politics as Rhetoric." *Ethics* 93: 45–55.

Crick, Bernard. 1972. *In Defence of Politics*, Chicago: The University of Chicago Press.

———. 1973. "On Theory and Practice", in *Political Theory and Practice*. New York: Basic Books.

Garver, Eugene. 1987a *Machiavelli and the History of Prudence*. Madison: University of Wisconsin Press.

———. 1987b "Paradigms and Princes." *Philosophy of the Social Sciences* 17: 21–48.

———. 1989. "Making Discourse Ethical: The Lessons of Aristotle's *Rhetoric*," *Proceedings of the Boston Area Colloquium in Ancient Philosophy*, v. 5, ed. John Cleary. Lanham, Md.: University Press of America.

Goedecke, Robert. 1970. "On the Use of Crucial Terms in Jurisprudence." *Philosophy and Phenomenological Research* 30: 576–89.

Hulliung, Mark. 1983. *Citizen Machiavelli*. Princeton: 1983.

Hume, David. 1947. *Dialogues Concerning Natural Religion*. Bobbs-Merrill.

Machiavelli, Niccolo. 1940. *The Prince and the Discourses*. Trans. Luigi Ricci and Christian E. Detmold. New York: Modern Library.

———. 1964. *The Prince*. Trans. and ed. Mark Musa. New York: St. Martin's.

Pitkin, Hanna. 1984. *Fortune as a Woman*. Berkeley and Los Angeles: University of California Press.

Pocock, J. G. A. 1975. *The Machiavellian Moment*. Princeton:

Rorty, Richard. 1979. *Philosophy and the Mirror of Nature*. Princeton:

Rawls, John. 1971. *A Theory of Justice*. Cambridge: Harvard University Press.

White, Hayden. 1973. *Metahistory: The Historical Imagination in Nineteenth-Century Europe*. Baltimore and London: Johns Hopkins University Press.

Williams, Bernard. 1979. "Conflicts of Values," in *The Idea of Freedom: Essays in Honour of Isaiah Berlin*, ed. Alan Ryan. Cambridge: Oxford University Press.

———. 1985. *Ethics and the Limits of Philosophy*. Cambridge: Harvard University Press.

8

Narrative Figures and Subtle Persuasions:
The Rhetoric of the MOVE Report

Susan Wells

The more significant the object, the more detached
the reflexion must be.

Benjamin

Rhetoricians of inquiry have two ambitious items on their agenda: producing concrete analyses of specific discursive forms, and defining a common method for carrying out such analyses (see the essays by Sanders and
Gross in this volume). Both are normal projects in the formation of a
discipline, especially one embedded in the academic professions; they are
analogous to the primitive accumulation of capital or to the first produc-
tions in a literary genre. And since rhetoricians of inquiry are aware of the
strategic value of such initiating moves, these projects are performed under
an extra burden of reflexive self-consciousness. As an interested visitor
from literary theory, I mean to add to that burden in two ways: by taking
as my case a piece of public discourse that poses questions of rationality in
intractable terms, and to approach this text using methods drawn from the
Frankfurt School and from contemporary literary theory, two disciplines
which are deeply critical of professional business as usual.

The text I have chosen is the report of the Philadelphia Special Inquiry
Commission (PSIC), also known as the MOVE Report. This document
investigates the events of 13 May 1985, when the Philadelphia Police Force
and Fire Department attacked a house occupied by members of MOVE,
a radical black organization. This document can be placed within a genre
of public documents that report on civic disasters, especially incidents of
racial violence, a genre which began with the 1922 Report of the Chicago
Commission on Race Relations, and which includes the Kerner Report
(1970) and the Attica report (1972). This official genre is difficult, marked
by conflict, fixed on the attempt to contain resistant objects. The writers
of the MOVE report also faced special problems: the violence they were to
normalize was almost entirely performed by the police; it led to serious loss

of life and property; and it occurred under the leadership of Philadelphia's first black mayor. The MOVE Commission responded to this difficulty by producing a complicated text, singular in its form and in its mode of reasoning. [1] Commission reports normally narrate a comprehensive account of events, comment on them, and then make recommendations. The MOVE report uses narrative as its sole structuring principle, disperses its commentary among the episodes of the narration, and segments the narrative into numbered, sequential, but discontinuous "findings." Thus, the MOVE Commission report does not begin with an initial episode of riot, but a description of its narrative preconditions. Further, in the MOVE report, the narration is repeatedly interrupted by subordinated analyses, reflections, and assignments of blame. If it is like other reports in that it reasons instrumentally, treating complex social issues as problems of adapting means to ends, the MOVE report is unlike others in that it cannot finally produce a coherent instrumental analysis of the events it recounts. This essay reflects upon that failure of both ideological and narrative coherence, seeing it as an expression of the commission's political and discursive situation, a situation that was difficult and contradictory. I will examine how this situation marks the element of the text, moving from relatively formal questions—How are characters named? How are episodes connected?—to a discussion of what counts as a good reason within the bounds of the text. My interest is to show how provisional are the boundaries between formal questions and political questions in this text; here, nothing is more deeply political than the text's representation of subordination.

The MOVE report's narration is built upon a simple armature (Brooks 1985). MOVE, a small group of black radicals, at once authoritarian and countercultural, has operated in Philadelphia since the early seventies, under the leadership of John Africa. A number of MOVE members have been imprisoned, most of them on charges stemming from the 1978 battle between MOVE and the police. Having exhausted legal remedies for freeing its jailed members, MOVE formally initiated a state of confrontation with the city of Philadelphia on Christmas, 1984. They signaled this state by continuous, all-day broadcasts of abusive language and threats of violence into their neighborhood, a predominantly black, middle and working class area called Osage. Eventually, on 13 May 1985, after evacuating the neighborhood, police called for the surrender of several MOVE members on criminal charges. When this call was refused, the MOVE house at 6221 Osage Avenue was fired on and gassed; eventually a bomb was dropped onto its roof, igniting a cache of gasoline. This fire was allowed to burn out of control. Eleven occupants of the house, including six children, died, and the city block on which it stood was destroyed.

Days after this catastrophe, the Mayor appointed eleven citizens to the Philadelphia Special Investigation Commission, and empowered them to tell the story of 13 May 1985. Their report was issued unanimously, with only two reservations on specific findings. Although it included a disproportionate number of clergy and lawyers, the commission was a relatively diverse group, both racially and politically. The full impact of this document has not yet been felt; although none of the grand juries indicted an elected official, and Mayor Goode narrowly won re-election, public protest continues to raise the issues posed by the PSIC report. We can know, however, that the report has changed the generally accepted account of 13 May 1985. No longer is it seen, as in Mayor Goode's initial version, as a series of tragic accidents provoked by MOVE's intransigence.

The MOVE report does not tell the story I summarized above in any straightforward way. It is not composed as a discursive narrative: at its heart, it is a series of thirty-one separate "findings," each with its own apparatus of "dot points," some of which are further supported by "check points." The conventions of administrative report writing have established these devices as common means of segmenting documents. In fact, the Commissioners adopted a well-known report format, the Minto (1980) pyramidal report, in order to avoid the problems of presenting a continuous narrative (Moran 1986). The pyramidal format allowed the commissioners, after many false starts, to focus their debates, to divide the task of writing, and to produce their report in less than a year. However, the commission made one crucial change in the pyramid format. As the name implies, the pyramidal report enforces a relentless focus on a central idea, supported by subpoints; each point is then developed hierarchically. But the MOVE report works against this centralized form: it is not unitary in its focus, but presents material in discrete segments, treating each finding as a self-contained unit. Such a segmentation of the events it narrates is one of the MOVE report's most important deviations from the normal format of commission reports, which rely heavily upon continuous narrative. These segments, suggestive of the most alienating structures of official discourse, are an innovation in the genre: most commission reports are structured quite differently. Those collected in Anthony Platt's *The Politics of Riot Commissions, 1917–1970* are commonly organized in three parts: a narrative of the riot, a commentary on its causes, and a series of recommendations. Or, as the Kerner Commission put it:

What happened?
Why did it happen?
What can be done to prevent it from happening again?
(Kerner, quoted in Platt 1971, 174)

Whether an investigative commission writes an enlightened document that exposes the cost of racism, like the 1935 Harlem report, or a silly and punitive one that blames violence on the black press, like the 1943 Detroit report, the document it produces is tripartite in structure. It opens with a narrative reconstruction of the event and then discusses, more or less convincingly, the causes of violence:

> What, then, was the deeper significance of the events of March nineteenth? (Harlem report, in Platt [1971, 174]
>
> Frequent reference has been made in Part I of this report to the racial tension prevalent in certain Negro and white groups prior to the outbreak of June 20 and 21. This report would be incomplete without some reference to factors which have created and inflamed that tension. (Detroit report, quoted in Platt [1971, 210–211])

Finally, the report makes both social and tactical recommendations for racial justice and riot control. Although those recommendations are presented as the serious business of the report, the basic political assumptions of the text are also—even, especially—communicated in its tripartite structure, which assumes a knowable current history open to administrative intervention. Whatever their attitudes toward the events they describe, the commission reports express a faith in narrative, a belief that political stories can be told, preferably with a great deal of specificity and density. Consider the opening sentences of the Detroit report, brandishing dates, times, and places: "In the early evening of June 20, 1943, there began in Detroit's Belle Isle Park a series of incidents between whites and Negroes which finally culminated in a serious riot. Acts riotous in character continued from that time until approximately 11 P.M., June 21, 1943." (Platt 1971, 201). Such stories assume that the violent disorders they describe, which may involve hundreds of people, can be understood within the categories of instrumental reason.[2] Limited, knowable causes produce discrete effects; means are well or poorly adapted to ends. Such a structure contains conflicts, manages struggle—the need for public order rationalizes any measure that might be proposed to preserve it, from the end of unemployment to the regulation of minority newspapers. These documents escape politics by evoking a public interest, and escape history by

211

assuring their readers that the transgression they represent is over, part of the past, never to be repeated.

The MOVE report would like to believe all of these comforting truths. But it cannot. The MOVE report does not purport to be a comprehensive narrative; it never addresses the significance of the facts it presents, it discusses racism as a cause of the disaster only in an embarrassed addition comment. And the commission's recommendations, found in a separate document, are deliberately secondary, technical tips for crisis management. It is as if the commission attempted to write a continuous narrative, from a standpoint of unitary common sense, in a situation which would permit neither continuity nor common sense. While the same gestures that introduced other reports, then, open the MOVE Commission's text— the description of the laborious production of the text, the hope that the report will heal the wounds of the city—here, they frame quite a different action, an action that is marked by gaps and discontinuity, an action that resists normalization. The report reproduces the resistance of the MOVE catastrophe to being known, normalized, or reduced to an official story. Paradoxically, it is the gaps and inconsistencies that make the document both unsatisfying and powerful, since it is the very resistance to being normalized that is important in the story of MOVE.

That story is deeply scandalous. It is the story of the disruption of a neighborhood, of an escalating exchange of threats and sanctions, of the violent destruction of both MOVE and the neighborhood—a story that cannot be told badly, and cannot be told correctly. The pleasures of hearing such a story are very strong, since its lines of opposition are simple, and the arc of its action is irrevocable. But these events also derail the ideologies available for making sense of it: many of the major conflicts are black on black; MOVE's transgressions are at once intolerable and maddeningly minor; there is a scandalous disparity between those transgressions and the police violence that followed, and the police violence itself often seemed to be marked by mistakes, bungling, and misunderstood commands. These events fit neither the politics of interest groups nor those of the bureaucracies that would broker among them; they cannot be interpreted from the point of view of the neighbors, of MOVE, or of the police. No instrumental maxims are compelling enough to rationalize events so deeply transgressive. Since the story cannot be told without violating some norms, since no available civic ideologies explain the catastrophe, it is not surprising that the document that recounts it is singular. Rather, the report's gaps in both narrative structure and in mode of reasoning allow it to contain and limit its own transgressions of narrative coherence.

Repeatedly, the reader is brought to the edge of absurdity: we see the mayor blandly accepting that people will die if the Osage house is assaulted, or police colluding with the illegal transfer of powerful explosives, or the medical examiner's careless destruction of the corpses of MOVE members. Each of these junctures is contained within a single numbered point that assigns a discrete share of the blame to an unnamed but precisely designated individual: the mayor, the bomb disposal unit, the medical examiner. And, after this pause, the narrative resumes, introducing a new absurdity, making a new assignment of blame. Each narrative segment operates, as it were, within its own explanatory envelope; the positions they advance need not be consistent. The report can describe the impossibility of dealing with MOVE in one finding and the irresponsible passivity of city officials in the next: the relentless cohesion of a numbered series seals over these narrative breaks.

One of the most striking ways that the MOVE report diverges from its genre is in its focus on designated characters, a focus that emerges in spite of the commission's decision to focus on offices rather than individuals: there was, for example, a decision to use titles, rather than proper names, as the normal way of referring to people. Only two individuals are prominently named in the report. One, John Africa, is invoked in the first finding:

1. BY THE EARLY 1980s MOVE HAD EVOLVED INTO
AN AUTHORITARIAN, VIOLENCE-THREATENING CULT.
- John Africa and his followers in the 1980s came to reject and
  to place themselves above the laws, customs, and social
  contracts of society. They threatened violence to anyone who
  would attempt to enforce normal societal rules. They
  believed that only the laws of John Africa need be obeyed.
- The members of MOVE saw themselves as the targets of
  persistent harassment by regulatory agencies, unjust treatment
  by the courts, and periodic violent attempts to be suppressed
  by the police.
- John Africa and his followers believed that a catastrophic
  confrontation with "the system" was necessary, if not
  inevitable, because of the campaign by "the system" to force
  MOVE to conform to society's rules.
- MOVE's last campaign for confrontation began in the Fall of
  1983, and was predicated on (1) the unconditional demand

213

that all imprisoned MOVE members be released; and (2) that harassment of MOVE by city officials cease. The stridency and extremism of individual MOVE members escalated during the first years of the Goode administrations. (PSIC 1986, 1)

Individuals are commonly named in commission reports, but usually as characters in episodes: this policeman was distinguished for bravery; that youth was unjustly beaten. In this report, only one proper name is as prominent as John Africa's: that of Mayor Wilson Goode. These two characters do not simply figure in episodes; they organize the connections of the narrative. Goode is constituted as protagonist and Africa as antagonist: the report's line of action simplifies into a combat between two individuals, whom we can identify as sites, named but unstable sites, upon which the theses of the report are ranged. The MOVE report's focus on these two individuals, moreover, is quite closely connected to its segmented structure. Character, organized by a proper name, can be moved intact from segment to segment. No theme or concept could bear these contradictory ideological pressures.

With John Africa, the narrative is initiated, and with him it closes. He is invoked in the first finding as the initiator of MOVE's lawlessness: "They believed that only the laws of John Africa need be obeyed," and as the prophetic instigator of the "catastrophic confrontation" between MOVE and the city that he believed to be inevitable. We should note that, while there are any number of violent and disturbing actions that could be assigned to John Africa, the report reprehends him first of all as a producer of unauthorized discourse. Without holding office, he made laws; without authority, he taught an ideology that presented a distinct vision of the future. In his discourse, which speaks over the instrumental rationality of the report, John Africa created a scandal. His offense, then, was ideological; he usurped the power to make laws and imagine history.

But while John Africa is named, even singled out, as a source of discourse, he is not individualized. In this report, he has no more personal specificity than the "sergeant from the pistol range" mentioned in passing elsewhere in the report. He functions as a place from which the narrative can begin, and on which it can close. The creation of such a site is itself an ideological act; it reverses John Africa's initial discursive transgression, and this reversal is both dreamlike and instrumental. The final pages of the report account for the victims of 13 May. Among them is "Vincent Leapheart (a/k/a John Africa)." The proper name is here rendered in the style

214

of an arrest warrant, even though this person has been counted, in the segmented form of the report, among those dead who were adults not under warrant. The choice of a primary name is taken from John Africa and returned to official discourse. If the disaster of 13 May took the life of a person named John Africa, the MOVE report, un-naming him and renaming him, erases John Africa as a character who originates discourse, and substitutes a character who is a victim, an object of violence. The report succeeds in deleting a contending discourse that the practice of instrumental reason had failed to silence.

It is helpful, I think, to notice that such a construction of character is not simply a move to dehumanize John Africa: we are dealing with discursive imperatives, as well as with the ritual need for a scapegoat or the ethical need for a villain. One of the problems posed by the structure of the report was that of establishing the document's coherence, of preserving its narrative momentum, while allowing each of the findings to remain self-sufficient. This problem of organizing data, of course, is related to a problem of explanation: the commission translates the impossible task it has been given—to rationalize and make sense of the MOVE catastrophe—into a more manageable program—to show how the MOVE catastrophe can be recuperated as a crime, a moral failure, or as a mistake, a maladaptation of means and ends. However, both the organizational segmentation of information and, as we shall see, the narrative presentation of the event as a violation of instrumental reason make it very difficult to connect elements of the text; the MOVE report's structure makes the normal stylistic devices that connect narratives problematic. The numbered findings cannot connect with normal repetitive anaphoric ties: each finding must subsist by itself; each had to survive an individual review by a critical commission. The fragmentation of the report into separate findings also makes it quite difficult to sustain chronological connections through collocating adverbial expressions (*then, later, at the same time*). Virtually the only adverbial devices that the segmented report form permits are specific indicators of time ("by the early 1980s," "on May 13"), so that the reader must assemble the narrative within his or her own sense of the chronology of events, rather than locating the events of the report within an emerging connected schema. Within this very attenuated set of connectives, then, the characters of the narrative, which tie its episodes together, assume an unusually prominent role.

It had been traditional to assert, in the analysis of literature, that characters properly emerge as convincingly "round" when they respond flexibly to the unfolding of events (Forster 1927). But in the MOVE report, the narration of events is so fragmented that the story emerges as a series of transactions among and connections between stably designated characters. In order to sustain such a connection, characters can be formed only as minimally specified locations in the text onto which meanings, themes, and patterns of action can be summoned. John Africa reads as transgression answered by expulsion, but if we were to consider how the report presents the character of Mayor Goode, we would find a similar attenuation. Goode is constructed from two minimal traits, passivity and caution. At one point, however, the narrative is inflected to blame him for failing to be sufficiently cautious; the commission does not motivate any departure from the passivity they have so carefully established. Goode's caution is not explained or motivated by any of the conventions of realism; when this caution is reversed, and Goode deviates into activity, initiative is simply assigned to other characters in the text: the Osage neighbors, the police commissioner.

At this point, the MOVE commission report might begin to seem like a postmodern novel, or like Balzac read by Barthes. Such a defamiliarization, I think, is all to the good: it suggests that the devices associated with postmodern literary criticism can have many functions, can occupy many political and ideological positions, can emerge in all kinds of discourse and in all kinds of analysis. In the remainder of this paper, I would like to suggest some other ways, besides the construction of character, in which the MOVE Commission report uses devices that we normally associate with literary discourse. These devices permit the report to keep its power and momentum, to travel lightly over its own gaps and inconsistencies.

First, normal temporal connections among events are disturbed, so that events are organized under topics that direct a reader's interpretation of them. Literary criticism analyzes such disturbances as reorderings of narrative time (Genette 1980). Further, instrumental discussions of means and ends are used to create a writing subject who, like the characters in the report, is inconsistent, even contradictory. Such a writing subject taxes our notions of narrative voice. Finally, the report deploys these devices—construction of character and temporal reordering—to generate a document in which narrative functions as evidence. If, as Fredric Jameson (1981) says, narrative is the political unconscious, a document like the MOVE report provides us with a political dream text; its segmented and disjoined elements trace out a royal road for analysis, even though our path will travel through the uninviting terrain of conventions and formats for administrative reports.

216

In all of these devices, the segmented report presents itself as a discourse about order, as a piece of administrative writing. But the pleasures it provides the reader are of a different, more imaginatively charged, kind. Let me begin with disturbances of normal temporal order (Genette 1980). Contemporary narrative theory takes as one of its central notions the necessary disturbance of time that allows stories to be told. Ever since *Tristram Shandy*, it has been apparent that the only impossible narrative would be one that told everything, in the order in which it happened, taking the same amount of time in the telling as the events themselves. Compression, elision, and the reordering of events are the necessary conditions of any story being told at all. The MOVE report presents itself, generally, as a document that reduces the events of 13 May, but maintains their order: it begins with the background of the early 1980s, and ends with the disposition of corpses. Within the text of the report, however, there are disparities between the order in which events transpired and the order in which they are told. Only when the bomb has been introduced into the text, for example, do we learn that the explosives had been obtained months before. Within the various episodes of the text, these reorderings can have explanatory and persuasive power. A particularly important reordering occurs in the sequence that reports the events leading to the police opening fire on 6221 Osage Avenue, findings 11–19 (see Appendix 1, following References). The major episode narrated in these findings are as follows. I have numbered them according to the order in which they are presented; the number of the finding is given parenthetically.

1. The commissioner chooses planners (11).
    1a. Exclusion of command structure, experts, and city agencies (11).
2. The planners work in haste (12).
    2a. The mayor and other officials receive no plan (12).
    2b. Other sources of information are not consulted (12).
3. The planners make mistakes (12).
4. City officials agree to use low-grade explosives and tear gas to evacuate the house (13).
5. Previously existing conditions, unknown to the planners, make this plan unworkable (13).
6. The children remain in the house (14).
7. The mayor allows the plan to proceed, knowing that the children are in the house (15).

8. The managing director and police commissioner also allow the plan to proceed (16).
9. The mayor did not take active part in the planning (17).
10. Ten thousand rounds of ammunition were fired into 6221 Osage Avenue (18).

These episodes elide an event that is mentioned in the introductory chronology: police claim to have heard gunshots from 6221 Osage Avenue. We could call this Episode 0, since it only figures outside the bounds of the narrative. Besides eliding a significant event, the text also has reordered the events it narrates. If the events had been presented in the order in which they occurred, we would read a text structured like this:

9, 1, 1a, 2, 2b, 3, 5, 2a, 4, 6, 7, 8, 0, 10

We could summarize such a version of events: the mayor was not involved in a confused and disorganized process of planning. However, the mayor agreed to use explosives and tear gas to evacuate the house. During this operation, the police claim to have heard gunshots; they fired ten thousand rounds of ammunition into the house. Here, the mayor's inactivity appears as part of the general context of the action, and the police fire appears as a reaction, probably as an overreaction, to the reported gunshot. Such a sequence would assign responsibility for the gunfire to MOVE, the agent contiguous to the police assault. Instead, the events are organized as failures of planning by city government, failures of oversight by the officials on the spot, and, in a doubling of counterfactuals, as a failure by the Mayor to halt the operation when it had become clear that there were children in the house. It is the unprotected children, rather than the desperate gunfire of the MOVE members, who appear in the report next to the police decision to open fire on 6221 Osage Avenue.[3] A circuit of agency has been established: the Mayor delegates planning to the Managing Director; the Managing Director hands off to the Police Chief; the Police Chief bypasses his own command structure. That circuit surrounds the children, who speak to no one; only the discourse of the report gives them a voice. Precisely because they had been ignored and were silent, the report can promote the children to a powerful discursive position: they are the objects of the police attack, and so they define the agency of the police, of the city officials, and of the mayor. It is in this repositioning of the children that the MOVE report undertakes its most audacious act of discursive rectification. The children who had been ignored are here taken up and protected, and this passionately desired narrative sheltering substitutes

218

for a normal articulation of episodes, turning the document aside from the rational economy of retribution that would inform the sequence, "MOVE shot at the police; the police returned fire." And that attack on children is defined most especially as the result of the mayor's disengagement; his failure to act is juxtaposed directly against the reckless gunfire of the police.

Rather than presenting this act as disproportionate retribution, the commission establishes, in its staging of the opening of the confrontation, alternate topics: civic responsibility, the right to protection, a horror of official recklessness. The report disengages the disaster of MOVE from any craziness or irresponsibility imputed to the cult, from any ideological transgressions assigned to them, and more importantly, from any understanding of MOVE as an inassimilable challenge to the norms of urban life. Instead, the commission found a common topic that, even within the dispersed and contested discourse of contemporary urban politics, can be expected to win unanimous assent: acts of violence should not be done to children by armed policemen. The police operation against MOVE is syntagmatically defined as such an act, and therefore, as wrong. The commission can derive from this originary act of violence a narrative rhetoric that ideologically categorizes all the tragedies of 13 May as extensions and elaborations of an attack on children.

That rhetoric is put to use in the rest of the document. In the final findings of the report, the deaths at 6221 Osage will be divided into groups: deaths of children and deaths of adults; deaths of adults under warrant and deaths of adults not charged with a crime. The original division between children and adults extends the topic "innocent death," which was mobilized with the account of the first police shots. While many witnesses testified, during the commission's hearings, that they considered the children to be combatants or hostages, the commission's report redefines them as victims, victims whose innocence establishes the guilt of the police beyond—and without—argument.

Such dislocations of time, such contradictory characters, transform the MOVE disaster from a catastrophe into a crime. And it is named as a crime in the text, which speaks of "gross negligence," of "unconscionable" force, of "unjustifiable homicide." This language is addressed—consciously addressed—to the District Attorney, and to possible grand juries (Moran 1986). But the writers of the report, who wished to address one audience, the grand jury, in their own terms of art, also wished to speak to another, broader audience about matters of guilt and responsibility. For that audience, the message is more diffuse, and more reassuring. MOVE was a mistake, a terrible mistake, but a mistake that could have been avoided.

The MOVE report creates a world of policy for which the occupants of 6221 Osage are a problem, but a problem which is in principle soluble. One of the functions of this report is to indicate those junctures in the action—and they are many—which could have generated a solution, focusing, as mandated, on city officials and city government. Paradoxically, however, the repeated solutions and re-solutions of the MOVE dilemma proposed by the report constitute the commission as a special sort of writing subject, a subject who repeatedly unties the knots that baffled a phalanx of elected officials. In the report, the MOVE disaster is averted and effaced, not once, but many times: it is resolved both by negotiations and also by energetic enforcement of regulations. It is resolved piecemeal, by episodes: not so many rounds of ammunition are authorized; the bomb is not dropped on the roof; the fire that followed is extinguished in good time. Having segmented the events of the MOVE disaster into thirty-one separate findings, the commission is free to establish a new position in each of them. The speaker of the report can be both a hard-headed law enforcer and a suave, supple negotiator, a bemused technician who could have told them that this sort of bomb wouldn't work, and a concerned humanitarian who would never use any kind of bomb around children, ever. And each of these locations is entirely legitimate: once we have made the rhetorical choice that constitutes MOVE as a problem, then each solution to that problem is independent of the others. After all, very many errors had to have been made to kill eleven people.

The creation of such a subject, the repeated proffering of multiple solutions, and the definition of the discursive situation as a problem are not accidents of production. The system of reason articulated within the report is neither universal nor transcendent; this piece of administrative writing articulates the maxims and rules of evidence of instrumental reason, the form of thought that Horkheimer and Adorno analyzed forty years ago in *The Dialectic of Enlightenment,* tracing the contours of another holocaust. A compressed explanation of instrumental reason will do for now; later I will deal more explicitly with how rhetoricians of inquiry can use Horkheimer and Adorno's theory. Instrumental reason is a calculation of means and ends, which establishes the world as an object of control, thus circumscribing it, excluding from thought both mythical and mysterious discourses, the traditional discourses of religion. Instrumental reason, however, also excluded from public speech and writing the discourse of self-reflection; critique becomes an unacceptable risk. "Thinking objectifies itself to become an automatic, self-activating process; an impersonation of the machine that produces itself, so that ultimately the machine can replace it" (Horkheimer and Adorno 1969, 25). The machine that reproduces itself in this text operates through the agency of the document's format, which establishes what counts as a good reason in the text.

Earlier in this essay, I referred to the Commissioners' changes in the Minto pyramidal format, so that a centralized form was used to organize a discontinuous, contradictory document. Within the individual findings, however, the commissioners use the conventional hierarchical format recommended by Minto:

> Making a statement to a reader that tells him something he does not know will automatically raise a logical question in his mind—for example, Why? or How? or Why do you say that? The writer is now obliged to answer that question horizontally on the line below. In his answer, however, he will still be telling the reader things he does not know, so he will raise further questions that must again be answered on the line below.
>
> The writer will continue to write, raising and answering questions until he reaches a point at which he judges the reader will have no more logical questions.

But the "logical question" that the narrative scheme of the MOVE report suggests to a reader is not "Why?" or "Why do you say that?" but "What next?" And it is that question that the supporting materials for the findings are most likely to answer. Within the structures of the report, issues of responsibility and guilt are first segmented instrumentally and then resolved with minimal narrative ties: the person who is mentioned next to an action is responsible for it. Finding 9 provides a convenient example (see Appendix 2.)

The claim of the ninth finding is supported by five dot points, establishing what the Osage residents did, describing the Mayor's new strategy, and specifying its anticipated consequences. These points are cogent and powerful in advancing the narrative and deepening its thematics, but they are quite weak in demonstrating the finding they support: they do not "prove" that the Mayor was incited to action by a specific tactic of the Osage neighbors; such a proof might be established by showing that the Mayor saw the Osage neighbors as a threat, or by drawing a causal connection between the Mayor's perception and his course of action. Instead, the report simply states the elements of the neighbors' frustration, and

221

metonymically associates the Mayor's response to their reaction. All the elements of the Mayor's strategy are subordinated to the topic "response to neighborhood pressure," rather than emerging as a narrative episode in their own terms. Such a choice of the initial themes might seem to be simply a formal matter, a question of arrangement. But, like the decision to juxtapose the police assault on 6221 Osage to the mayor's inaction, the decision to open a description of planning with the introduction of the angry neighbors has persuasive force. Since the mayor has been defined as passive and cautious, he can be excluded from initating action; the formulation of a plan can be derived from neighborhood pressure rather than the mayor's decision. Indeed, the mayor is presented as a drain on the energy of the narrative, as a retarding device: he "responded to pressure;" he "held little hope." Activity, energy, and initiative are predicated elsewhere—to the neighbors, to the "strategy," or to those discussions that acknowledged the likelihood of death. All the devices of a narrative of character are deployed to explain an instrumental connection.

We cannot, of course, rectify the MOVE Commission's report by comparing it to some "real" or "objective" account of the MOVE disaster. But in other narratives of these events, the episode of the mayor's planning for the confrontation is prominent, and displays him favorably. In Commissioner Charles Bowser's independent report, a document that is generally critical of the Mayor, we read: Mayor Goode did an adequate job in developing the policy which he enunciated to govern the May 13th operation. (Bowser 1986, 57) Although Bowser faults the Mayor for not using resources outside city government, he concludes that the Mayor's policy "provided clear guidelines, which could have avoided much of the disaster which occurred on May 13th" (Bowser 1986, 58). We do not know that Bowser's account was being fair to the Mayor, or that the Commission was not. The Commission made certain discursive choices, especially their choice of the Minto pyramidal format, that permitted them to array the facts at hand differently than Bowser did in a conventional narrative. The Commission's report darts in and out among events, arranging them at different levels of its hierarchy as assertions and support. Having established a strong cohesive chain associating Mayor Goode with inaction, the Commission was able to preserve that association even at a moment when other writers, in other documents, show the Mayor as active and powerful. The hierarchical structure of the pyramid, usually a device for stabilizing and managing a document's domain of signification, becomes, within this finding, a scheme that allows the boundaries of that domain to shift continually. The pyramid form did not simply provide the commission with a way of sorting out findings and support; it provided them with a device for inflecting events in the narrative by directing them into the categories of fact and evidence, and so prompting how they should be read. What counts as a good reason is whatever happened next.

The conventional report format, then, is subverted to the demands of narrative. The formula of segmentation, which could have fragmented the audience, here allows the document to recreate a new audience at each finding. A hierarchical report organization allows the Commission to present narrative movement as logical support, to lend the force of events moving through time to the movement of its own argument.

What are we to think of such a document? Answering this question requires us to recognize, I think, the inadequacy of traditional evaluative language for coming to terms with documents like the MOVE commission report. To speak at all of the success or failure of the document that rationalizes eleven deaths would be callous; such an event can be decently approached, perhaps, only with the deepest critical irony, or with all the resources and resonances of literary language. And if success means anything more serious than the deft preservation of official skins, it could only be achieved by placing the events of the MOVE catastrophe within some context of political understanding that could explain them, differentiating the plot strands of crime, error, and guilt that are tangled in the present report, arraying them in an order that could allow them to be seen, to be taken in. But the document that we have testifies to the absence of such an explanatory framework; its multiplied voices and dispersed locations represent the silence and absence of that civic common sense which, after all, would have prevented the MOVE disaster. We might even, in a compassionate reading, see it as a way of keeping faith with the impossible resistance of the event it recounts.

But there are a number of evaluative actions I can properly perform in this essay: evaluations of the limits, contradictions, and possibilities of our own critical discourse. Our analysis of the MOVE report shows us, most of all, something about the limits of rhetorical analysis. The rhetorician does not arrive at the scene of the public document with any rectifying discourse ready to hand. Nor does the rhetorician succeed in office the foundationalist philosopher, charged with stamping the safe conduct of each idea as it enters the borders of discourse. In fact, the rhetorician's warrant is in some ways more limited than that of, say, a journalist. If I hear a story in the course of my research—the story, perhaps, of the police and fire commissioners sitting across the street from 6221 Osage and deciding to "let the motherfucker burn," I cannot decide to verify the story without opening to reinvestigation the whole array of evidence that the MOVE commission assembled in its hearings. Since I am not the eight professional investigators that the MOVE commission hired, but a lone academic, I decide to leave those investigations closed. The practice of rhetorical analysis is a material practice, with its own material limits.

But, unlike the journalist, rhetoricians are permitted to bring certain theoretical tools to bear on an event and a text; we are also invited to reflect on our use of those tools. Let me take up that invitation here. A classically trained rhetorician might see my essay as a discussion of the relation between arrangement and invention. Such a reading could be supported: researchers of student writing processes have, for a long time, spoken of arrangement schemes as heuristics (Winterowd 1970; D'Angelo 1975). But this classically well-formed reading solves several major problems all too easily. What does it mean, for example, to speak of invention in a document that has been produced by a committee, written by a paid staff member, and edited by a group? Embedded within such a use of *invention* is an assumption of an individual writer who makes things up, or who surveys a finite body of facts looking for the "available means of persuasion." Even those who disagree with the postmodern critique of the centered subject might wonder, in purely empirical terms, who the writer of the MOVE report is, and how this writer can be said, in any sensible way, to discover discourse. Further, the writers of the MOVE report accepted certain serious constraints: to appear objective, to let the facts speak for themselves. Those constraints barred the writers from deploying many of the normal devices for establishing ethos or for appealing to the reader's emotions: they could not appear to be grinding an axe, and they renounced any overt stylistic appeal. The writers' project of persuasion had to be implicit. Arrangement, then, was the most salient variable that the writers of the report could manipulate rhetorically; they made full use of their limited opportunity. When we notice that invention has been conflated with arrangement, this easy triumph simply reproduces in words that Aristotle would have recognized the situational constraints that the PSIC experienced as a series of practical limits.

We need an analytic framework that permits us to say something new about such texts, and also about other administrative documents, about scholarly articles, about short stories. There are two locations in contemporary culture that can generate such a framework: critical theroy, as developed by the Frankfurt School and practiced by Jurgen Habermas, and the poststructuralist literary criticism associated with Jacques Derrida, Paul

224

de Man, and Michel Foucault. Obviously, both these enterprises and the thinkers they comprise differ seriously. My purpose here is to indicate, however crudely and schematically, how they might be used by rhetoricians of inquiry, and to use them to reflect on my practice in this essay.

Two central themes of the Frankfurt School's work—the problematizing of instrumental reason and the development of ideology critique—are, I think especially useful to rhetoricians of inquiry. For Max Horkheimer and Theodor Adorno, reason was not an undifferentiated whole, the logos of traditional rhetoric that is approximated, more or less, by arguments at differing levels of probability. Reason, for these writers, is discontinuous and contradictory, a social practice rather than a set of universal relations. Therefore, Odysseus' cunning is inherited both by the scientist who investigates nature in order to extend the domain of human control and by the bureaucrat who articulates social life in a network of rules (Horkheimer and Adorno 1969, 43–80). Instrumental reason itself, then, has many guises. It evokes its opposite—reflection, critique, or emancipatory reason. But, for Horkheimer and Adorno, emancipatory reason is not necessarily consoling, does not necessarily offer solutions to problems or a clear line of action. Emancipatory or critical reason is negative, disruptive, and sometimes useless. When we apply such a perspective to a document like the MOVE report, our impulse will be to look suspiciously on the document's most innocent and obvious assertions of connection, upon its blandest offerings of civic service; here, one might feel, the document is most deeply implicated in the structures of instrumental reason. Our response to this perception need not be to rectify the text, to offer a more accurate story of the MOVE catastrophe, or more humane suggestions for police intervention. Rather, we should inquire about the silence that such a text presents; in that silence, we can carry out quite a different kind of reflection.

The second notion that we can draw from Frankfurt methods is the critique of ideology. I use this term in a more restricted and less derogatory sense than it sometimes carries. The Frankfurt school generally defined ideology as a justificatory discourse, not in itself false, but falsely presented. (Insofar as ideas of freedom, humanity, and justice, for example, are presented to excuse or explain institutions—as strategies for justification—they are ideological. They are not for that reason false.) Horkheimer and Adorno differentiate such ideological justifications, which they connect with a bourgeoise market economy, from a simple analysis of false consciousness, a notion under which illusion is seen as a "fundamental property of human beings or . . . their sociation as such" (Frankfurt Institute

1972, 184). To read ideology as false consciousness is to establish a global notion of ideology, which might include such fundamental operations as name-giving. This concept is too broad to generate critique; nothing specifically distorted or justificatory, nothing distinctive of a social system or a historical juncture, is invoked by this sense of ideology. And, since the categories revealed by this broad notion of ideology can never be dissolved, but only replaced by others, the reading of ideology as false consciousness generates only parasitic critiques that assume and demand the continuation of those global and necessary illusions they expose. Finally, for Horkheimer and Adorno, the purely delusive discourses characteristic of totalitarian states—Nazi racial science, Soviet psychiatry—are simply false, simply imposed ideas; they speak of such systems as "what was once ideology."

In the case of the MOVE Commission report, my critique of ideology addresses the commission's topics of praise and blame, not as illusions, but as socially located markers of ideas that we wish were as actual as they are true: ideas of protection, of responsibility, of civic restraint and tolerance, of skillful planning as a device for controlling contingency. These ideas are ideological: in this report, as in much civic discourse, they explain the uncertain operations of instrumental reason as if it were still endowed with Odysseus' cunning. But such a justification is not illusory; the MOVE catastrophe could have been prevented by an authoritative discourse that deployed such topics, probably in more sober and ironic tones. It can never be explained or justified by them.

The specific inflection of Frankfurt School methods developed by Jurgen Habermas provides us with two additional useful notions: his definition of formal criteria for truth claims, and the idea of differentiated reason. Habermas (1981, 1:71) holds that propositions can be judged, not by their correspondence to some externally given state of affairs, nor by their internal coherence, but by their formal properties: the claims that they implicitly make in specific communicative situations, claims which can only be formally redeemed. Habermas distinguishes three claims: a claim to truth, to rightness, and to truthfulness (1982, 271). Truth, the claim that a proposition adequately represents the world, is not seen as a state of correspondence, but as a communicative act, a condition of conversation continuing. Truth claims, therefore, are judged counterfactually: we do not continue to respond to discourse that we do not see as representing the "reality" of a given situation, no matter how exactly that discourse corresponds to some other available context. If we come upon such a proposition, we reframe it by shifting to a context within which it seems representative. We hear it expressively rather than empirically, or as stating community norms rather than individual values. Or we see such discourse as disruptive: a lie, a mystification, or narrow ideology. Or an error. But we do not take it up constatively unless we recognize it formally as making an acceptable claim to truth. Habermas's other formal claims can be read in the same way: the claim to rightness means that an utterance asks to be taken as a continuation or development of the conversation in progress; the claim to truthfulness, that it is an expression of the speaker's subjectivity. Violations of these constraints are normalized, or provoke a transposition of the talk that allows them to be explained.

Such a formal understanding of truth claims implicit in speech acts suggests that the persuasive intent of a text is not a strategic addition to its logical force. And such a formal method is congruent with the basic axioms of the rhetoric of inquiry, a discipline that refuses to be embarrassed by its discovery that ostensibly neutral texts are persuasive. Such a formal definition of truth claims allows us to continue the fruitful argument over what counts as a good reason, since a rhetorical truth claim, like any other statement about probable matters, can be argued. We need not simply accept the relative norms of each conversation.

Those axioms are developed in Habermas's notion of differentiated reason. Each implicit truth claim is seen as generating a different kind of discourse, responsive most especially to one of the claims. But all claims operate, on some level, in all discourses. Habermas speaks, therefore, of cognitive, interactive, and expressive language. Each implicit claim, clearly, operates with different force in each of these kinds of texts. Claims to represent the objective world, therefore, can be identified as different speech acts in each of these differentiated language worlds. The notion of differentiated reason allows us to identify what counts as a good reason in various social settings; it grounds the agenda of the rhetoric of inquiry in a formal understanding of the implications of speech acts, so that we need not simply accumulate descriptions of an infinite number of possible social settings.

In analyzing the MOVE report, my intent has been to recover the criteria for truth under which the PSIC operated: what became clear was that, for the commission, truth meant narrative coherence and instrumental specificity. It seems sensible, faced with this document, to confront the limits of such a definition of truth, not with more pressing demands for correspondence ("What really happened?"), but by identifying the discursive setting in which such a definition of truth does indeed obtain: the situation of telling and hearing stories, of formulating and testing solutions. Once we have questioned the explanatory limits of narrative cohesion and instrumental specificity—and they do not hide their limits—it becomes useful to place our reading in the activity of hearing and understanding the specific story that the PSIC was constrained to tell. Such a location keeps faith with our material situation, which is not a dialogue with the writers of the document, but the presentation of a written analysis to readers. We are not about rectifying or improving the text, but understanding why it moves, convinces, or fails to satisfy us.

It is at this point that I wish to move beyond the themes of the Frankfurt School. To Horkheimer and Adorno, narration always seemed a cheap substitute for reflection and critique; Habermas, especially, inherits their distrust of rhetoric. I want to annex other methods, then, for analyzing discursive situations shaped by the demands of narrative. And here, of course, contemporary literary reflections about narrative become useful.[4] Reduced to axioms, they operate as two scandalous pieces of advice: Narrative, first, is neither a trick nor a figure, but a fundamental method of organizing experience in societies such as ours. It is as close as we are likely to get to a "fundamental property of human beings in their sociation." It is not, however, either true or false; it is not propositional. Since narrative establishes connections, we may begin by asking whether a particular story brings into being the right connections. But we must also ask the more difficult, more textual question: how do the connections in this story suggest or invoke other stories? How do they invite us to write the story of our sociation? Given all the possible arrangements and presentations of these events, what is gained and what is lost by the arrangement that this text undertakes?

Second, contemporary narrative theory raises the issue of pleasure, which is perhaps the most valuable prize that the rhetoric of inquiry could take in a raid on the arsenal of theory. Taking pleasure in a text is not the same as liking it, or identifying with it, or thinking that it is correct. It is an act of the reader, and a rhetorician who raises the question of pleasure has left his privileged spot at the speaker's elbow and taken an anonymous place among the audience. There, relying only on the intensity of his impolite whisper, the rhetorician addresses to whomever stands nearby an urgent and inconvenient question. "Why do you want this to go on? Why do you want it to end?" In the case of the MOVE report, the pleasures of continuing and ending are local pleasures of containment and explanation. They are ways of placing a disturbing event securely in the past, and of guaranteeing that it will not be repeated.

But what would we say if the bystander turned to us and asked, "Why all these questions? What's your game?" The practice of rhetorical analysis is not without its own investments. One of the few pleasures available to the rhetorician is the pleasure of identifying with what is insurgent, and of unmasking what is repressive, a pleasure that is only enhanced when insurgency and repression appear in the very organization of the text. The critic can bid for this pleasure through an affiliation with postmodern culture, a culture marked by deliberate discontinuity, by its exploitation of those gaps and inconsistencies that are seen as the necessary self-negations of any text. This essay, which discovers similar structures in a document with no insurgent ambitions, calls into question such an identification of politically or culturally radical projects with discontinuous narrative forms. But to raise such a question, to interrupt our pleasures of identification, is not to invite readers to a feast of judgment. If the MOVE report neither succeeds nor satisfies us, it also does not fail. The report's incoherence can be read as failure only if the writers refused a coherent alternative; no such choice was available to them.

But what can we say about the choices available to us? The rhetorician stands against the writer not as judge, but as witness. We can trace out, through the most detached of reflections, the cunning of discourse, the devious and difficult path taken by this group of writers over impossible terrain. Such a journey, which has required that the text meet the iron demands of cohesion without any of the critical resources of understanding, has not been without its sacrifices. Witnessing those sacrifices, we might remember Horkheimer and Adorno's remarks on Odysseus' cunning and sacrifice: "Every sacrifice is a restoration belied by the actual historical situation in which it occurs. The venerable belief in sacrifice, however, is probably already an impressed pattern according to which the subjected repeat upon themselves the injustice that was done them, enacting it again in order to endure it" (Horkheimer and Adorno 1969, 51). We cannot, in this or any other analysis, reverse the tragedy that provoked this text, or the discursive constraints which repeat that tragedy within the bounds of the report. But by keeping alive a sense of the significance of our object, we can perhaps choose to avoid a second, analytic, repetition of injustice.

N O T E S

1. Frank Burton and Pat Carlen's *Official Discourse* (1979) describes the structure of official administrative documents. Although their Althusserian method is at odds with my own approach, which is informed by the Frankfurt School, I have learned a great deal from their writing.

2. The central statement on instrumental reason is Horkheimer and Adorno's *Dialectic of Enlightenment* (1969); the most influential contemporary version of the theory can be read in Habermas (1971). For a comprehensive account of the theory, see Held (1980).

3. The work of Robin Wagner Pacifici of the Sociology Department at Swarthmore College has been very helpful to me, especially in clarifying the central role of the children in the report. Her analysis of the first findings is forthcoming.

4. A summary of contemporary narrative theory, with helpful bibliography, can be found in Rimmon-Kenan (1983).

REFERENCES

Barthes, Roland. 1974. *S/Z*. Trans. Richard Miller. New York: Hill and Wang.

Brooks, Peter. 1985. *Reading for the Plot: Design and Intention in Narrative.* New York: Vintage.

Burton, Frank, and Pat Carlen. 1979. *Official Discourse: On Discourse Analysis, Government Publications, Ideology and the State.* London: Routledge & Kegan Paul.

Bowser, Charles. 1986. *The Philadelphia Special Investigation Commission: Report and Opinion.* Philadelphia: 1986.

D'Angelo, Frank. 1975. *A Conceptual Theory of Rhetoric.* Cambridge, Mass.: Winthrop.

Forster, E. M. 1927. *Aspects of the Novel.* London: Arnold.

Frankfurt Institute for Social Research. 1972. *Aspects of Sociology.* Boston: Beacon.

Genette, Gerard. 1980. *Narrative Discourse: An Essay on Method.* Ithaca N.Y.: Cornell University Press.

Habermas, Jurgen. 1971. *Knowledge and Human Interests.* Boston: Beacon.

———. 1981. *Theory of Communicative Action.* Vol. 1. Trans. T. McCarthy. Boston: Beacon.

———. 1982. "A Reply to My Critics," in *Habermas: Critical Debates*, ed. John Thompson and David Held. Cambridge: The MIT Press.

Held, David. 1980. *Introduction to Critical Theory: Horkheimer to Habermas.* Berkeley: University of California Press.

Horkheimer, Max, and Theodor Adorno. 1969. *The Dialectic of Enlightenment.* Trans. J. Cummings. New York: Seabury.

Jameson, Fredric. 1981. *The Political Unconscious.* Ithaca: Cornell University Press.

Moran, Emerson. 1988. (Staff Writer for PSIC). Personal Interview.

Minto, Barbara. 1980. *The Pyramid Principle*. London: Minto.

Rimmon-Kenan, Shlomith. 1983. *Narrative Fiction: Contemporary Poetics*. London: Methuen.

Platt, Anthony, comp. 1971. *The Politics of Riot Commissions, 1917–1970*. New York: Macmillan.

PSIC (Philadelphia Special Investigations Commission). 1986. *Report*. Philadelphia.

Winterowd, H. Ross. 1970. "The Grammar of Coherence." *College English* 31: 828–35.

A P P E N D I X   1
Findings 11–18

11. THE POLICE COMMISSIONER CHOSE AS HIS PLANNERS THE HEAD OF THE BOMB DISPOSAL UNIT, A SERGEANT FROM THE PISTOL RANGE AND A UNIFORM PATROLMAN. IN DOING SO, HE EXCLUDED FROM THE FORMULATION OF THE PLAN THE ENTIRE POLICE DEPARTMENT COMMAND STRUCTURE AND OTHER AVAILABLE EXPERTISE.

• The decision to entrust an undertaking of this magnitude and delicacy to first-line operation supervisors and uniform patrolmen was irresponsible. As a result, the operation was deprived of a breadth of practical knowledge and technical expertise at a critical stage of the planning process.

• The planners designated by the Police Commissioner lacked sufficient knowledge and technical background to evaluate properly various alternatives to the operation. The central role played by the head of the bomb squad invited the operation's reliance on explosives.

• No serious effort was made by the Police Commissioner or his planners to explore alternative solutions or tactics with outside agencies or experts. Contacts with the FBI and the U.S. Treasury Department were cursory; no official attempt was made to draw on the resources of these agencies.

• Other city agencies possessing specialized knowledge of MOVE and 6221 Osage Ave. were not consulted by the planners, nor were their views sought.

12. AS A RESULT OF THE POLICE COMMISSIONER'S ORDERS, THE THREE OFFICERS RESPONSIBLE FOR DEVELOPING THE TACTICAL PLAN DID SO HASTILY AND WITHOUT SUFFICIENT INFORMATION OR ADEQUATE INTELLIGENCE. THE MAYOR, THE MANAGING DIRECTOR, AND THE POLICE COMMISSIONER NEITHER SOUGHT NOR RECEIVED FROM THESE MEN A WRITTEN TACTICAL PLAN.

• A critique of the 1978 confrontation, which had been prepared by the Police Department's highest-ranking officers, was never reviewed by the 1985 planners.

• Despite the city's experience with MOVE in 1978, and despite the resurgence of MOVE on Osage Avenue in the early 1980s, the police did nothing to establish the means for the systematic collection, analysis, and dissemination of intelligence information regarding MOVE and its members.

- Much of the intelligence which was acted upon by the planners was insufficient, inaccurate, or misleading. For example:
  - The extent of the house's interior fortification was underestimated.
  - Police believed MOVE was prepared to escape through tunnels carved out under the neighborhood. None existed.
  - Gasoline was known to the Mayor and some officers to be stored on the roof of 6221 Osage Ave. The planners did not know this.
- Though a 24-hour surveillance on the MOVE house was warranted by April 30, 1985, none began until late on the afternoon of May 9th.
- The Police Commissioner never passed on to the planners the Mayor's direction to him to "take his time" in devising the tactical plan. Instead, the planners operated on a crash basis.
- Months after the assault, the pistol-range sergeant produced a two-page undated document he claimed was the written tactical plan. He said it was available to his superiors prior to May 13th. The police commanders, up to and including the Commissioner, as well as the Mayor and the Managing Director, said they never received such a written plan, nor did they ask for one. There is no evidence to corroborate the sergeant's statement that a written plan existed before May 13th.

13. THE MAYOR, THE MANAGING DIRECTOR, AND THE POLICE COMMISSIONER SPECIFICALLY APPROVED THE USE OF EXPLOSIVES TO BLOW 3-INCH HOLES IN THE PARTY WALLS OF 6221 OSAGE AVE. TO ALLOW THE INSERTION OF TEAR GAS TO INDUCE THE EVACUATION OF THE HOUSE. THIS PLAN WAS INADEQUATE BECAUSE OF THE FLAWED INTELLIGENCE ON WHICH IT WAS BASED AND THE HASTE WITH WHICH IT WAS DESIGNED.

- The Mayor was told in advance by the Managing Director and by the Police Commissioner that the walls would be breached by explosives.
- The unanticipated fortification inside the first floor of 6221 Osage Ave. gave the house's occupants a protected firebase. Fire from this position forced "B" Team to concentrate on neutralizing the interior bunker instead of forcing tear gas into the house. This diversion in itself made the police plan inoperative.
- The plan also relied on water from the Fire Department's "Squirt guns" to dislodge the rooftop bunker, despite warnings by fire officials that the "Squirts" were incapable of performing that task.
- No alternative method of removing the bunker was seriously considered

by the planners. The use of a crane was dismissed by the head of the bomb squad, whose decision was accepted without question by the Police Commissioner.

• Police and fire mobile communication systems were incompatible, yet no consideration was given to coordinating the communication between police and firefighters during this complicated and life-threatening operation.

• The plan failed to utilize the police department's professional negotiating expertise available and trained for barricaded persons and hostage situations.

• There was no back-up plan if the explosives and tear gas failed to drive the occupants from the house. The police planned no alternative to the assault's failure.

14. DIRECTIVES TO REMOVE THE CHILDREN FROM 6221 OSAGE AVE. WERE UNCLEAR, POORLY COMMUNICATED, AND WERE NOT CARRIED OUT.

• The Mayor should not have permitted the planning to go forward when, on May 9th, he knew that the Managing Director was out of town.

• The Managing Director was instructed by the Mayor on May 7, 1985, to coordinate the efforts of the Police Department, the Department of Human Services and the Law Department to ensure that the children were removed from the house prior to the implementation of the plan. He took no action whatsoever toward achieving this, and left town the next day without even advising his staff on how to proceed.

• The Human Services Commissioner first learned of the city's interest in protecting the children four days prior to the confrontation. She responded with little interest or vigor and did not demand any information from the police regarding the protection of the children.

• On the evening of May 9th, the City Solicitor's office gave the Police Commissioner specific instructions to take the children from 6221 Osage Ave. into protective custody at the first opportunity. Nevertheless, the City Solicitor's office did not attempt to secure the legal authority to remove and detain the children until the morning of the confrontation, when it was too late.

• Police personnel responsible for carrying out the directive had conflicting impressions about when they were to detain the children, where the children could safely be retrieved, and which children were subject to the directive.

15. THE MAYOR'S FAILURE TO CALL A HALT TO THE OPERATION ON MAY 12TH, WHEN HE KNEW THAT CHILDREN WERE IN THE HOUSE, WAS GROSSLY NEGLIGENT, AND CLEARLY RISKED THE LIVES OF THOSE CHILDREN.

• On Saturday, May 11, and Sunday, May 12, the Mayor was briefed on the plan by the Police Commissioner and was aware that children were known to be inside the MOVE residence. Nonetheless, he authorized the commencement of the operation.

• No children were taken into protective custody. At least two children, who were passengers in a car, were allowed to pass through a police barricade on the day before the evacuation of the neighborhood, with no attempt made to detain them.

16. THE MANAGING DIRECTOR AND THE POLICE COMMISSIONER WERE GROSSLY NEGLIGENT AND CLEARLY RISKED THE LIVES OF THE CHILDREN BY FAILING TO TAKE EFFECTIVE STEPS TO DETAIN THEM AND BY NOT FORCEFULLY RECOMMENDING TO THE MAYOR THAT THE OPERATION BE HALTED WHEN THEY KNEW, THE EVENING OF MAY 12TH, THAT THE CHILDREN WERE IN RESIDENCE.

• The Managing Director and Police Commissioner knew, the evening of May 12th, that the Mayor's order to secure the safety of the children had not and could not be accomplished before the start of the operation. These men were obligated either to tell the Mayor that the plan should not proceed, or to order a halt to the operation themselves.

17. THE MAYOR FAILED TO PERFORM HIS RESPONSIBILITY AS THE CITY'S CHIEF EXECUTIVE BY NOT ACTIVELY PARTICIPATING IN THE PREPARATION, REVIEW, AND OVERSIGHT OF THE PLAN.

• At a meeting on May 7th, the Mayor rebuffed a suggestion that he be fully briefed on the plan, preferring instead to isolate himself by leaving that level of detail to his experts.

• The Mayor's statement that he was reluctant to "meddle" in the affairs of his subordinates in this instance represents a striking departure from his self-proclaimed hands-on method of city management.

18. THE FIRING OF OVER 10,000 ROUNDS OF AMMUNITION IN UNDER 90 MINUTES AT A ROW HOUSE CONTAINING CHILDREN WAS CLEARLY EXCESSIVE AND UNREASONABLE. THE FAILURE OF

THOSE RESPONSIBLE FOR THE FIRING TO CONTROL OR STOP
SUCH AN EXCESSIVE AMOUNT OF FORCE WAS
UNCONSCIONABLE.*

• So great was the latitude given the police planners that they were
allowed to augment the department's arsenal with military weapons and
explosives not normally available to municipal police departments.

• In a period of about 90 minutes during the morning hours, the police
fired at least 10,000 rounds at 6221 Osage Ave.

• Thirty-two police officers admitted to firing their weapons. One shooter
acknowledged that, from his post, within 50 feet of the house, he fired 1,000
rounds from his M-16 semi-automatic rifle.

• Other weapons fired included M-16's, a Browning Automatic Rifle, a
Thompson submachine gun, 30.06 and .22-250 sharpshooter rifles, two M-60
machine guns, Uzis, shotguns and a silenced .22 caliber rifle.

• Found in the ruins of the MOVE house were two pistols, a shotgun
and a .22 caliber rifle.

• The excessive gunfire was inappropriate to the force generated by
MOVE, and needlessly jeopardized the lives of the children in the house. It
also placed in serious danger the lives of police officers in Posts 1, 2, 3 and 4,
and Insertion Teams "A" and "B" immediately adjacent to the MOVE
residence, as well as the several hundred police and civilians who were on the
Osage perimeter.

*Commissioner Kauffman dissents from this finding.

Appendix 2
Finding 9

9. MORE THAN ANY OTHER FACTOR, INTENSIFIED PRESSURE FROM THE RESIDENTS OF OSAGE AVENUE FORCED THE MAYOR TO ABANDON HIS POLICY OF NONCONFRONTATION AND AVOIDANCE, AND TO DEVISE A STRATEGY FOR RESOLVING THE PROBELM QUICKLY

- By the end of April, 1985, the Osage Avenue neighbors were so intimidated by MOVE's increasing belligerence and so frustrated by the city's inaction that they sought help from outside, appealing to the Governor and expressing their grievances to the media.
- The Mayor and the police responded to this new pressure, and, in the first week of May, began to design a strategy of action. This strategy relied upon the same legal basis that existed in June, 1984, but which had not been acted upon.
- This strategy, formulated by the Mayor, had three components:
  a) To arrest as many MOVE members as possible on minor criminal charges, some pre-existing, some new.
  b) To remove, during the arrest process, all the inhabitants from 6221 Osage, including non-criminal violators and children.
  c) To prevent MOVE members from reoccupying the house.
- The City Solicitor and her Deputy suspected that outright seizure of the MOVE House after the arrests were made would be illegal. As a result, the City Solicitor was prepared for the city to be sued if this action was carried out.
- The Mayor held little hope that MOVE would vacate the house voluntarily or even permit a court-ordered search of the premises. The Mayor's strategy, accordingly, presupposed the use of police force. During the week preceding the confrontation, the Mayor, in meetings with top officials, discussed the fact that bloodshed, even death, were likely.

9

The Rhetoric of the Commons:
Forum Discourse in Politics and Society

Manfred Stanley

What is the significance of speech in a democracy? Is it primarily a medium of information necessary for rational decisions? Is it an age-old mode of representation whose fate is replacement by first the written and now the electronic "word"? Or is it somehow constitutive of the political world itself—the ultimate form of action? Particularly since World War II, disputes over the significance of speech in a democracy have affected the contours of the social sciences. Within the discipline of history, the rise of social history to virtual predominance reflects in part the critique of elitism in disciplinary perceptions of how human history is made. Social historiography embodies the desire to recover for the record the creative voices and labors of common folk. In sociology, the rise of microsociologies and methods of field research has explicitly reflected the so-called linguistic turn in philosophy stimulated by the later Wittgenstein and by movements in literary criticism. (Cicourel 1964; Brown 1977; Knorr-Cetina and Cicourel 1981) The microsociology movement has likewise been accompanied by an anti-elitist critique. In a nutshell, the argument is that

This essay is partly an outgrowth of a three year research project I direct through the Center for the Study of Citizenship at the Maxwell School of Citizenship and Public Affairs, Syracuse University. This research, focused on a medium-sized city in central New York State, is concerned with the study of indigenous political conversation as evidenced in civic associations. The purpose of the project is to search for the conditions conducive to what is here depicted as the democratic forum model, thereby contributing to the evolution of the National Issues Forum movement inspired by the Public Agenda Foundation and the Charles F. Kettering Foundation. I acknowledge with pleasure the valuable contributions made to the refinement of these ideas by my graduate student researchers on the project: Louis Aiello, John Fiset, Mary-Ann Lapinski, John Major, Ollie Owen, and Brent Snow. I owe a special word of thanks to my wife, Mary Stanley, also a participant on the research team. Major aspects of this paper were inspired by conversations growing out of her work on the evolution of American citizenship.

macrosociological models (such as structural functionalism), imposed upon the popular imagination as the "expert" view of how the world works, really reflect an elitist politics of administrative management in an increasingly corporatist civilization. (Habermas 1973; Ellul 1967; Gouldner 1970) Microsociology, it is argued, can serve politically to restore the world-making voices of ordinary people, which have been rendered mute by the abstractions of macrosociology.

In this paper my concern is with the topic of political conversation, more specifically, the idea of the forum. An aura of nostalgia beclouds this topic. With visions of Athens and New England in mind, even advocates of direct democracy unwittingly can serve reactionary sensibilities when they advocate uncritically a return to the linguistic rigors of face-to-face assemblies. Scholars are in the process of telling us that the past contained no golden age of democracy, at least as far as our present notion of democracy is concerned, affected as it is by liberalized Christianity, science, economic liberalism, and the celebration of social pluralism. (Zuckerman 1978; Daniels 1979; Wood and Wood 1978; Holmes 1979) Political conversation in contemporary democracy needs to be thought about in light of modern developments in rhetoric, philosophy of language, and social science. The forum adequate to capture the educational demands of democracy in a sophisticated secular age remains to be invented. Such a forum must find its way not only into the community lives of ordinary citizens, but also into the great cities of science and the professions. An adequate critique of elitism does not deny the existence of expertise; rather it builds bridges of demystification between worlds of discourse by revealing the ways in which the politics of discourse implicates us all in the dynamics of world-making (Stanley 1981).

In that cause, this paper seeks to elaborate the concept of the forum. I shall proceed in two steps. First I relate American political conversation to the regime that provides the context for defining such conversation. Ours is a regime commonly called liberal-democracy. What must be noted is its dual nature: liberalism, based on the concept of the market economy, and democracy, based on the principle of popular sovereignty. These two regimes coexist in some degree of tension since they imply two rather different conceptions of citizenship and politics. After noting what they are, I proceed to the second step: applying the dual regime argument to the concept of political forum conversation.

239

THE DUAL REGIME ARGUMENT AND
AMERICAN CITIZENSHIP

Recent American political science has begun to feature discussions of American political culture as affected by a mixed or dual regime. One notes this trend in various dichotomies that appear in the literature: liberalism vs. pluralism (Riker 1982), adversary vs. unitary democracy (Mansbridge 1980), procedural liberalism vs. substantive standards liberalism (Greenstone 1982), commercial liberalism vs. civic humanism (Pocock 1975), and liberalism vs. democracy (Barber 1984; Pateman, 1977. See also Lindblom 1977 and Lane 1986). Despite important differences in letter and nuance, they form a family of dichotomies revolving around an overarching division between two broad views of our present political culture and its history. Their source is the fact that our political culture is the product of two separate but now intertwining histories: the history of civic humanism or republicanism stemming from Athens and Rome through Italy and England, and the history of capitalism with its emphasis on market forces, commercial logics of exchange, and individualistic civil liberties based on an economically functional right of access to a free labor market.

Understood this way, the liberalism vs. democarcy distinction implies differences for what citizenship means in general, and political conversation in particular. Briefly, in the liberal regime citizenship is more peripheral in people's lives than it is supposed to be in a fully democratic one. Advocates of both claim the centrality of "participation," but the accents are different. Liberal politics emphasizes as its constitutive act not civically pedagogical talk but rational adaptation to the logic of market forces, including acquiescence to policies and administrative practices justified in its name. This may or may not require conversation. Indeed, mainstream social science sometimes celebrates silence, or what others might call apathy, on the ground that extreme participation is chaotic. The assumption here is that both economy and government generate objective requirements for optimal functioning, and that policy elites, informed by social science (especially by economics), are prone to more rational expert deliberations than other citizens who are laypersons in these regards (Trilateral Report 1975; Huntington 1981).

Advocates of participatory democracy, on the other hand, regard these views as "mystifications" used to cognitively disenfranchise the people of faith in their common sense and concrete knowledge. For such advocates, talk becomes less of a means and more of an end. This emphasis on talk

reinforces the urgency of questions regarding "communicative competence" (Habermas 1981) and the action status of conversation itself (Taylor
1971), restoring these age-old issues to the center of modern political
philosophy. Participatory democrats point out that making the forum central to our notion of democracy implies a pedagogical theory of institutional arrangements. The social world should be so arranged that its workings are reasonably transparent, so to speak; capable of being rationally
discussed, revealing of causal chains between acts and consequences, and
innocent of systematic communicative distortions due to radical social
inequalities of power.

This essay has been designed so as to allow for a focus upon one concept
with respect to "talk," different approaches to which distinguish what I
mean by liberal and democratic forum standards. That concept is "naturalization." In brief, I will argue that participatory democratic theory implies a more explicit awareness of this phenomenon and deliberate efforts
to control it than does the liberal standard of political conversation. On this
topic the disciplinary connections between literary theory, political philosophy and the social sciences become crucial. Scholars interested in
structuralist literary analysis have shown us how our normal usage of texts,
whether written or spoken or physicalized (e.g., fashion), predisposes us
toward stabilizing the signs and symbols amidst which we live as the
taken-for-granted world of "common sense." Social scientists have increasingly turned their attention toward the microprocesses of intersubjective,
linguistic negotiation and cooperation that sustain institutions. In the literary structuralist version of naturalization, the medium is not consciousness (intentions, intellectual projects, accepted assumptions, psychological
states, etc.) but language itself in the form of texts and their relationships
(Culler 1975 and, of course, the many works of Foucault on "discourses").
The structuralist thinkers direct our attention to the ways in which the very
process of speaking at a forum (grammar, phrasing, leaving unsaid, si-
lences, etc.) creates—not merely reflects—a structured world of social
objects, background theories, foreground claims, explicit and implicit audiences, hierarchies of value, and so forth.

The main distinction between the liberal and the democratic forum
models implicit in the subsequent discussion is the attention given to
processes of naturalization and the need—understood as part of the meaning of democratization—partially to denaturalize the social world so as to
bring it generally, and language in particular, within a common standard
of intersubjective accountability. Our focus in this paper is not on a specific formal type of forum, like a League of Women Voters debate format,

241

or a council hearing. Rather it is on what may be called forum conditions for deliberative political conversation intended as a constitutive act of political world-making on the part of people who come together as citizens (not as experts, interest group members, victims, or even as elected representatives) for this purpose. I intend to argue that liberal democracy, viewed as a dual regime, implies two ideal models of civic forum which will be called the *liberal forum* and the *democratic forum*. It is necessary to warn that these are not forum types easily observed empirically; they are theorizations of conversational practice based on philosophical assumptions associated with each regime model. The purpose of the exercise is not to describe current realities but to contribute to an evolving moral and scholarly debate about what it means to think of democratic citizenship in all areas of endeavor as political communicative competence. My purpose is to utilize a simplified dual regime argument to clarify the complexities of the debate by capturing it within two alternative, ideal typical, notions of political conversation. Our two forum models will be contrasted in terms of four criteria: 1) the type of *education* to be achieved, 2) the type of *consensus* aimed at, 3) the *experiential analogy* that provides the main metaphoric image for describing the forum as a social psychological process, and 4) the conception of the *forum participants*.

THE LIBERAL FORUM

1. The liberal forum is based largely on a *policy education* perspective. The background social theory is that of liberal market society, which assumes the causal significance of economic forces for all institutions. The problem underlying the need for the forum is a potential legitimacy crisis of distributive justice generated by newly perceived and naturally generated scarcities of public goods (resources, skills, money, etc.). The forum exists to educate people in the range of alternative policies of the sort debated by thoughtful policy elites, and to enlist the citizenry in these deliberations. The range of policies is constrained by the imperatives of the market economy, including the morale of the business classes. For instance, Daniel Yankelovich (1985), a leading American social commentator, expert on public opinion and advocate of civic forums, says:

> There is in the United States an invisible university. It is
> enormous. The faculty of that invisible university consists of
> consultants, institutes of various sorts, and foundations. They hold
> innumerable meetings, and discussion is going on all the

242

time. . . . Part of what is missing in all our institutions is that we don't have a good mechanism for translating what goes on in the invisible university for the general public. What I try to emphasize is that in the "working through" process we need choices. Alternatives have to be spelled out.

Referring illustratively to the debate on industrial policy between "thought leaders," and without questioning the terms of the debate among such persons (e.g., what issues are actually on the table) or the social range of the "thought leader" community engaged in it (thus naturalizing the implicit social hierarchy behind the term "thought leaders"), Yankelovich says that below the level of media rhetoric, "one can detect a core of agreement emerging because the different parties are influencing one another. Now the interesting question is: How do you take that debate, which is very important to the general public, and move it on to the public's agenda?"

2. In order to accomplish this educational purpose, the forum participants must be induced into disciplined habits of creating *consensus based on evaluating policy decisions*. That is to say, issues must be phrased so as to illuminate relative trade-offs between morally plausible and politically practicable policy orientations. The emphasis on trade-offs between painful alteratives seems congenial with the logic of the trilateralist view of political system overload (Trilateral Report 1975; Huntington 1981). According to this view, what ails modern democracies (the U.S., Japan, and France are represented in the report) is inflated demand, both for scarce goods and unreasonable degrees of popular participation in the governance process of all institutions. Such inflated demand makes for a condition of ungovernability. The trilateralist approach seeks ways of discouraging excessive popular participation. One way to do this is to conceive of civic education as socializing the citizenry into the system perspectives of its most responsible governors. Political participation is to take the form of values clarification by means of analyzing trade-offs between alternative policy perspectives. Such values clarification is the intended object of "choice work." Hence the consensus sought for consists in policy commitments based on consciously articulated values or master preferences. It should be added, however, that some major advocates of what I term the liberal model disclaim any connection between this Hamiltonian tradition and their own views because of the elitist managerial stance of trilateralist writings. Nonetheless, I find a complementarity of reasoning on the notion of consensus that makes the liberal forum model a more democratized

243

(i.e., population inclusive) version of trilaterism. (For a more generally articulated theory of liberal civic education in this vein, see Janowitz 1978, 1983.)

3. "Choice work" (to continue with Yankelovich's term) focuses on relative deprivations of goods or conditions that people desire. The experience most cited as an *analogy to help people understand the forum process is grief.* The plausibility of this analogy rests on the notion that because policy choice work results in the pain of being deprived of something, the "working through" process has some of the characteristics of coping with grief. Indeed, "working through" to value consensus is largely conceived in terms of this analogy and its presumed stages. A population schooled in such a process of "hard choices" can be expected to resist the temptation of wanting it all in an age of scarcity. Absent such discipline, the market-generated affluence that underwrites democracy will be sabotaged by economic or political irrationality. The delicate alliance that is liberal democracy will come asunder.

The naturalistic quality of the scarcity concept at stake here is illustrated again by Yankelovich (1985): "the classic example is 'working through' death. The information content is quickly imparted; a loved one is going to die. But it may take years to work through the cycles of grief, anger, depression, and lack of realism before we can put our lives back together (p. 27). Yankelovich's forum model, as is his general social theory on which it seems based (1980), is dominated by a naturalized economic scarcity perspective. There has been a grand debate for some generations about the exact status of the concept of "scarcity" in Western civilization (Stanley 1981, 83–135). Those who are suspicious of the rhetoric of scarcity do not deny its relevance to life. Rather, they do something most people who use the rhetoric do not do: they warn of the possibility of rhetorically naturalizing "false scarcities." False scarcities are lacks in life that people are *uncritically* persuaded to believe are inevitable. They are thus persuaded not only by elites with interests at stake, but also by the way in which society happens contingently to be organized at a given moment in its history. Without a sense of historicity, the 'way things are' gets to be naturalized. The source of persuasion may also simply be the vocabulary of distribution as construed by those who do so uncritically. For an example, consider the difficulty everyone currently has diagnosing the sources of health care costs, including medical liability insurance rates. Many uncritically believe it is rooted in too many people claiming health care as a right, or too many people living too long. They are uncritical because they fail to explore as a condition for their judgment the dynamics of the insurance industry, the legal profession, the role of the market principle in the health "industry," and the differential agenda-setting power of those with access to the federal budget.

4. Forum participants are conceived in a manner appropriate to liberal economic theory: *aggregates of individuals who bring potentially infinite wants to the political marketplace* (or interest groups made up of individuals allied in pursuit of a category of wants). The purpose of the forum, then, is—by means of value clarification—to reduce the randomness of preference orderings and to set limits to potentially unlimited wants among individuals capable by nature of infinite desire.

I think this model of the liberal forum is what most middle class people regard as the most rationally ideal form for the many concrete forums that take place in our society.

THE DEMOCRATIC FORUM

In Western culture there are rhetorical themes that support a different conception of the forum. One does not find these themes elaborated into a forum model equal in detail to the liberal one. Efforts to do so sound more "academic" partially because they carry with them severe methodological problems of translation into practice, which make the democratic forum sound abstract compared with the pragmatism of the liberal one. It is worth noting that part of what makes the rhetoric of pragmatism so congenial is that it accepts the naturalization of the social world without much question and defines what is "practical" as that which can be accomplished within its reified interstices. What usually happens in our society is that people pay lip service to the ideals of the democratic model while allowing their practices to collapse into some version of the achievable pragmatism of the liberal model. This should not be read as a denigration. It is the consequence of practical people trying to be practical and idealistic at the same time. The intimations of an alternative forum model remain largely at the level of rhetorical implication. Nonetheless they must be pursued, because embedded in them are the directions for progress in democratic political education.

I draw one such example from a speech delivered to the American public administration community by a federal ex-cabinet officer, David Mathews (1984, 123–124), now President of the Kettering Foundation:

> There can be no vital political life, no viable institutions of
> government, no sense of mastery over our shared fate, no effective

common endeavors of any kind without there being a foundation
of public awareness and spirit. . . . Certainly if there were a public
sphere, we would have more choices in solving our problems. Now
we are limited to two options in making corrections. We can
increase the responsibilities of the private (i.e., business) sector, or
we can improve the performance of government. But if the public
sphere were once again real and available, we might not only have
a third set of options, but we might also have options that would
get us closer to the problems behind the problems. If the idea of
the public were available to us, the question of who is attending to
giving us the healthiest, the richest and the best public life possible
would become important. . . . Civic literacy, the capacity of
people to think about the whole of things, of consequences and
potential, becomes education of the most crucial kind.

Rooted in classical and congregational imagery, this passage carries both
emotional and cognitive implications beyond the liberal model. To see
why, let us construct this second forum model using the same four criteria
as before: education, consensus, analogy and participants.

1. The type of education associated with this model is *civic education*
in a fairly classical though democratically updated sense. What is to be
learned are the constitutive facts, myths and categories of the political
order itself. The background social theory is the tradition of institutional
analysis that focuses on the interdependence of social practices, traditions,
and functional virtues (MacIntyre 1981). In this tradition of thought, the
self and its consciousness is a social product, continuous with its history of
group memberships and its locus in communities of collective memory
(Halbwachs 1980). Individuation is not a naturally given fact but a prescriptive norm growing out of a culturally prized dramaturgy of "person-
hood" (Nelson 1965). According to this understanding, the forum exists for
its own sake as the place where citizens meet to make justice. It also is
expected to prevent legitimacy crises, not of scarcity but of incompetent
(some would say unvirtuous) cognitive and performance standards for political conduct. Such crises can ensue from ignorance, corruption, or—as
today—from complexities of social organization producing hyperspecial-
ized factions and identities that overwhelm the "commons." The necessity
for the forum is the need to rediscover the civic commons and its associated
identity of citizenship amidst the varied settings of modern life (Stanley
1983).

Civic education does not preclude policy deliberation. But the educational function of policy deliberation is different from the liberal version of policy education. Rather than accepting policy options as described by thoughtful elites, policy issues are treated as civic pedagogical devices with which people themselves can interrogatively and cooperatively trace out the constitutive workings of their own society. In other words, democratic forum pedagogy would reveal to citizens the ways in which they not only influence policy makers but *are* policy makers, consciously or not, through means that range from how they use their language to the institutional practices in which they daily engage. This implies a notion of political education whose consequences cannot be separated from the idea of policy-making. Such an abstract idea demands an example.

Consider the policy topic of "air pollution." The liberal approach to policy education in terms of "hard choices" would encourage discussions of the pros and cons of antiindustrial zoning, pollution taxes levied on firms, community taxes to sponsor filtration technology, antipollution legislation by government, and the like. The civic education perspective would focus first of all upon how air pollution can be used to reveal the constitutive order of society as a set of practices. For example: how do firms come to make decisions whose outcome is pollution? Why do populations indulge in behavior (physical mobility, transportation modes, suburbanization, entrepreneurship) that have this outcome? How do government policies (land use, regional support, selective subsidy patterns) relate to this outcome? Any particular policy problem such as pollution becomes a starting point for talk about a mosaic of phenomena that people normally don't think about. How, for instance, do protean myths (economic growth) and classification systems (private rights vs. public goods, polity vs. economy) create the linguistic spaces within which we come to think about social problems as "natural" outgrowths of daily life? With such a background, the democratic forum participant should come to conceive of policy remedies along a wider spectrum of possibilities than will his or her liberal forum counterpart.

This may sound forbiddingly academic. Inherently it is not so. People inductively and individually ask such questions often, if sufficiently interested or angry. Normally there is no forum within which to pursue them cumulative to some purpose. Beyond that, whether the process is too academic may depend on one's conception of what sort of consensus is desirable as a forum outcome.

2. The democratic forum addresses a concept of *consensus that is much more complex than one based on a conceptually crude notion of "values."* The reason deserves a moment of attention.

The concept of "values" suffers both from moral abstruseness and false concreteness. Abstruseness because values seem like things people can agree upon with ease (compassion, dignity, equal opportunity); false concreteness because, in American social thinking, *values* tends to be a synonym for stable and measurable attitudes or preferences. Yet, so understood, values can turn out to be quite unstable, varying with circumstances such as perceived challenges from "real world" phenomena, against which values-talk can appear flaccid or open to "corruptions" of endless reinterpretation. Even when perceived as stable over time, value remains a concept of superficial reference. (For instance, suppose a person values table manners so much that he is always nauseated when forced to observe their absence. Is "table manners" the object in question here? What can one understand about someone's valuation of "table manners" without further reference to a larger symbolic order, a "world" within which the coded meanings of decorous table customs are intelligible?) In the liberal forum there seems little methodological concern for how people can come to understand what values are as ways of thinking and feeling, how these ways are learned through differential social experience, and how they are objectively encoded in social and linguistic intersubjective practices (not just carried about as "subjective" attitudes or preferences). The liberal model, like economic thought from which it largely derives, assumes that one can't get much further than this subjectivist approach, that is, that values are revealed by preferences on the market and that what can be hoped for in public opinion is the achievement of consensus by coincidence of values or by social controls designed to encourage value convergence. (For an attack on this sort of subjectivism in favor of an intersubjective approach, see Taylor 1971. For a critique of the superficiality of the American usage of "value" as contrasted with its European origin, see Bloom 1987, 194–216). If values, then, are not preferences or attitudes that people just naturally have, then one task of the democratic forum must be to develop a critical pedagogy of such naturalized abstractions; a pedagogy that unravels the implicit theories hidden within the concrete practices of everyday life, thereby helping people gain some understanding of how ideas, behavior, and emotions interact in their experience.

Consider, for example, the possibilities of collective rhetorical inquiry into a problem of thwarted value consensus seemingly as mundane as traffic congestion in a town (Greer 1961). First, one considers why it exists at all when "everyone" regards it as undesirable. Then one discovers that not everyone does, because many merchants depend for their livelihood upon the customers who park their cars downtown and help to create the congestion. That is to say, the forum participants discover that the "traffic" concept fits into at least two discourses: transportation technology and commerce. Next, it occurs to someone that the dependence of the American population on automobiles is an interesting fact in itself. Why are there so few of the other means of conveyance that modern technology permit? Is this a genuine collective preference rationally arrived at, or has the automobile somehow entered American consciousness as the only naturally desirable mode of transportation? How have we come rhetorically to associate "public" transportation with dirt and discomfort? Why is there not available an array of conveyances varied for length, distance, and complexity of trips? Why is everyone out on the road at the same time instead of there being staggered work hours? Why does the "journey to work" exist, with its road-clogging consequences, when much of existing work can be done at home or other decentralized locations? Why have some people made lucrative careers as certified experts on traffic dynamics without being required to ask such relevant questions? Along such routes of inquiry one eventually discovers something of the concrete significance of property rules, origins of land zoning, history of the fuel industry, interests affecting taxation, relationships between industry and government, and the dynamics of advertising. In time, one begins to understand what it means for someone not to have a car, to lose one's job because a traffic-dependent merchant moves from town, or to be trapped by the ontology of zoning on the "wrong side of the tracks." In short, the social "stranger" is assimilated into a broadening horizon of political understanding. The point, then, is not to "solve" the traffic problem through hard choices. That will come in time. The point is first to understand it, and by means of such examples to learn the art of cumulatively decoding society so as to make oneself civically at home within it. Such civic education is not academic learning; it is experiential inquiry.

The democratic forum, then, does have a principle of consensus. It does not imply, as it does in the liberal model, surface-structure agreement on specific value or policy directions. Rather it has to do with negotiating a shared, cumulative and ever more inclusive deep-structure narrative, as it were, regarding "our" collective story and where "we" want to take it from here. It is from within this ongoing narrative that specific problematic features of collective life are examined. Any particular policy commitment is justified in terms of its benefits as a possible contribution to the furtherance of a common aspiration for community progress. But what sort of experience is it that can mold the bonds for such an aspiration?

3. This last question brings us to the third criterion of a democratic

forum: the experiential analogy on which one's metaphoric sense of the process depends. Unlike the liberal model's dependence on grief, the democratic model is better off stressing *the experiential analogy of immigration.* To understand the benefits of the immigration analogy, one must remind oneself that the phenomenology of immigration transcends the experience of physical migration from one country to another. Immigration is really about movement between different social worlds and the consequent demands upon the self for moral reintegration (not just adaptation). There are several large-scale sociological phenomena in modern America that precipitate the problems associated with immigration. These include the following:

- Loss of local community autonomy to the external and distant political and corporate worlds that rule one's local destiny
- Physical mobility from region to region, farm to city, workplace to workplace
- Social mobility between classes
- De-skilling (i.e., loss of relatedness to one's world through the obsolescence of one's craft)
- Unemployment (i.e., transition from a public world of producers to the ranks of those socially defined as unproductive)
- Passage of one's children into the alien country of higher education if they are the first generation bound for college

All these examples involve crossing borders between worlds. Together they make immigrants or emigrants of most of us at one time or another. All place great strain on existing standards of justice and empathy. There is indeed a "working through" process required, but one of greater complexity than is posed in the liberal model. Let us pause to consider what this process ideally requires, given the democratic forum's standard of civic education. For the sake of linear order one may speak of stages of working through, although the realities of speech do not, of course, conform to such an ideal approach.

The first stage of working through the immigration analogy we may call *crystallization.* Crystallization means articulating an experience in ways presentable to others for thoughtful consideration. Narrative is an important rhetorical feature of this process (often frowned on within the liberal model because of its "anecdotal" digressions from rational argument). Given the themes of voyaging, old and new world contrasts, loss, exploration, and reconstruction, immigration imagery lends itself to dramatic story form as well as to emotional biography. The resources of local history are potentially invaluable here for translating individual narrative into community contexts. (Because of this, the democratic forum could revitalize a community's use of its Local Historical Society in very innovative ways.)

The second stage of working through the immigration analogy is, indeed, "griefwork" (another of Yankelovich's terms). Here griefwork is associated with coming to terms with the general emotional costs of social change in one's life. Among these costs is a certain primordial loss of innocence: the innocence of thinking that life is always going to continue in the manner to which one is adapted, the innocence of assuming that people's actions are always controlled by their intentions, the innocence of assuming one's identity and sense of worth can be taken for granted. Social change, "history," threatens all these. If it is not to overwhelm the psyche, the grief associated with these losses must be articulated in socially sharable ways and must not be associated with zero-sum games between things people find of primordial value.

From the perspective of history, there are indeed moments of "hard choices" when the liberal trade-off metaphor seems germane. Yet the hard zero-sum edges of this image can be somewhat illusory. Perhaps what we think we trade off (e.g., loss of community for the sake of mobility) is not what it seems. The community of nostalgia is often different from the community of direct experience. Even the sense that social change threatens all innocence can be empowering if the lesson learned is that, if nothing is eternal, things can improve as well as decline. Finally, discovering that intersubjective consciousness transcends the illusory limits of atomistic subjectivity can lead to a sense of new possibilities for compassion and for cooperative transcendence of what must appear to the isolated ego only as tragedy or pathos.

The third stage of working through the immigration analogy is the critique of one's naturalized stereotypes. Roland Barthes (quoted in Culler 1975, 140) provides a perspective on what this means in a few words: "The "I" which approaches the text is itself already a plurality of other texts, of infinite, or more precisely, lost codes (whose origins are lost). . . . Subjectivity is generally thought of as a plentitude with which I encumber the text, but in fact this faked plenitude is only the wash of all the codes which make up the "I", so that finally, my subjectivity has the generality of stereotypes." This orientation toward the self is, of course, quite congenial with social science perspectives on how stereotypes are exacerbated by the organizational features of society. It is relevant to recall, for example, that the concept of stereotype was introduced into social science thinking earlier in this century by Walter Lippman (1922) in what remains a classic

251

critique of the quality of modern public opinion. In such a critique it becomes appropriate to examine, especially, negative stereotypes of the sort often called prejudices. The issue is the generic one of "boundaries." What is the lexicon of the "ins" and the "outs," the "stranger," the threatening "others," the "sick" and the "sinful." Critically inquiring into the sources of such boundary lexicons encourages asking how a social problem arises, what political achievements result in making perceived policy alternatives seem "practical," how still other alternatives get to appear impractical or visionary, and how the history of one's community reveals one's ancestors as people who constructed, reformed or reconstituted their world as their legacy to the present.

This reference to the intersection of community and history suggests the importance of the fourth and last stage of working through the immigration analogy. Activities such as crystallizing experiences, coping with grief, and denaturalizing stereotypes are hard work and not likely to seem worth it without hope. To put it somewhat grandly, "eschatological hope" is an important stage of working through the immigration analogy. In place of fixation on the griefwork of hard choices, the democratic model stresses the importance of a type of hope rooted in the progress myth of the Enlightenment and brought to life, with the resources of local history archives, through narratives of citizens of the past who participated in social movements that reinvented America. Many elements of the progress myth have fallen on hard times. One aspect that remains important to Americans, however, is the reconstruction of institutions according to ideals of a better and more just public life. Unlike many countries whose communities resonate to themes of ancient wrongs and unfulfilled vendettas, American communities widely recognize ancestors who contributed to social betterment and political reform. American social history celebrates turning masses into persons, and persons into citizens. The point of being a citizen in America has always been hope: hope for enhanced personal dignity, hope for one's children, and hope for one's country as the most worthy among nations. The democratic forum ideal transcends adaptation and exists to help citizens work through the possibilities for a better homeland.

4. The fourth and last criterion to be considered here as defining types of forums is how the participants are conceived. In the democratic model the participants are not individual supplicants who come to the forum bearing wants. Rather they are *complex social beings whose consciousness is partly prestructured by group and institutional memberships, collective memories, mythic themes, and naturalized ideologies.* One of the tasks for

forum conversation is to understand consciousness in this manner; that is to say, to discover the presence of society within the psyche.

To take the one instance of unemployment, the problem for democratic civic literacy is not just to make hard choices between free market and government solutions. It is for all to understand that the suicidal sense of worthlessness that may afflict an unemployed person is not natural but socially induced. An unemployed person is not necessarily unproductive. Like the "housewife" or the "good cause volunteer," such people may be endlessly productive in their lives, a boon to those whose needs they serve. Not all good works appear as jobs in the marketplace. But when one's economic survival, or one's sense of worldly group identity, is based on a position in the labor market, that market becomes the determinant of what being "productive" means. To understand this is the first step toward a type of policy imagination capable of asking why the labor market is organized to be so unrewarding to the many activities that everybody knows to be productive.

The immigration analogy encourages us to think of our country not only as states and regions and communities but as multiple social worlds that reach widely across our society: corporations, professions, science, universities, armies, voluntary associations, labor unions, agencies of government. Increasingly, these structures of membership are as important to people's lives as ethnic, racial, and religious identifications. As the latter have done for so long, the newer kinds of membership also now influence what people mean by adulthood, responsibility, honor, deviance, anxiety, practicality and decadence. What is autonomy in one world may be insubordination in another; honor in one is betrayal in a second; some worlds are hierarchies, others anarchies; one world organizes time, another leaves it alone. Even as the progress of law and tolerance reconciles former antagonists into a commonwealth of civil rights, these social worlds divide them anew into polities of specialized conduct. Corporate people, market people, academic people, voluntary people, laboring people, administrative people, are not merely divided by interests in a context of competition for resources, nor by variations of ethnicity and creed. They are men and women called upon to enter the career of adulthood in fundamentally different ways, to persist in it with fidelity to ends they may not freely choose or understand, and to enact it with a strength born of seeing other social worlds as the abodes of strangers.

In response to such nation- and even globe-spanning identities, communities of more primordial loyalty often contract into a desperate localism whose gates close against the cosmopolite of any sort. As distances of land and water cease to matter, as the children depart across boundaries too subtle to define, as places rise and fall according to forces as alien as the stars, and as people confront the immigration police of a thousand borders, citizenship gives way to the specter of universal strangerhood. The democratic forum model addresses participants caught in this shifting web of membership and loneliness that forms the context of political conversation in modern America.

CONCLUDING THOUGHTS

It has not been possible in this space to move much beyond a focus on the political forum. It should be evident, however, that what has been said has significant implications for science, professions, industry, and government understood as prospective forums. All social practices are subject to uncritical naturalization. Science, for example, can be seen as a mechanism for generating objective truth (or lawlike regularities) discoverable through the rigorous cumulative application of canonical methods of inquiry. Or science can be regarded as comprised of speech communities that are always linguistically adjudicating, among other things, what will count as a fact. The same is true of the professions and all other social practices.

The literatures of history and sociology in recent years have supported the latter view of things on all fronts. Among scholars, at least, technicism as a genre of consciousness has been superceded by a new historical, sociological, and linguistic sophistication. If this critique of technicism were mounted in the name of democratic speech standards either in the university-based disciplines or in the open forums of civic politics, there would soon be reciprocal effects. It is hard to imagine politics unaffected by such a transformation of self-consciousness in the bastions of expertise. It is likewise difficult to imagine the accountability of experts unaffected by more sophisticated standards of speech competence among the civic "laity."

There is a more ambiguous theme for us with which to end, however. The myth of Enlightenment has wound its way through my own rhetoric and certainly my aspirations for the democratic forum. The forum experience, presumably, is worth pursuing for its cumulative and educative effects upon the communicative competence of the citizenry. However rich in connation, democratic consensus is not supposed to be based on arbitrary grounds, a mere outcome of contingent rhetorical seduction or conversational exhaustion.

Yet the so-called antifoundational trend of modern deconstructive

254

thought threatens with a kind of primordial skepticism all notions of competence except criticism itself. Is my own rhetoric, then, exemplary of the conceit of humanism as deconstructed by Foucault? Or does it serve to enclose us in the nostalgic hologram of a ghostly "metaphysics of presence," which Derrida says prevents us from recognizing texts as "a structure of repetition, a structure cut off from any absolute responsibility or from consciousness as absolute authority, orphaned and separated since birth from the support of the father . . ."? (quoted in Culler 1975, 132) Or perhaps we are on the terminal edge of the myth of linguistic evolution, poised to discover that

> The words of their own accord become exalted jewels, their many
> facets recognized as of infinite rarity and value to the mind, that
> centre where they hesitate and vibrate. The mind sees the words
> not in their usual order but projected around it, like the walls of a
> grotto, for so long as their mobility, that principle which makes
> them exceed whatever is said in discourse, is not exhausted. All are
> quick, before they fade away, to glitter, reflecting against one
> another, with distant, oblique and contingent flashes (Mallarme, in
> Culler 1975, 246).

In the face of such possibilities, one can only refer to the world one knows as an engaged person: a habitus of sufferings and remissions, victories and defeats, chapters open and closed, ambiguities unending, and intimacies achieved. With Aristotle, we can only hope to match our methods with the tasks at hand.

REFERENCES

Barber, Benjamin. 1984. *Strong Democracy.* Berkeley: University of California Press.

Bloom, Allan. 1987. *The Closing of the American Mind.* New York: Simon and Schuster.

Brown, Richard. 1977. *A Poetic of Sociology.* Cambridge: Cambridge University Press.

Cicourel, Aaron. 1964. *Method and Measurement in Sociology.* Glencoe, Ill.: Free Press of Glencoe.

Culler, Jonathan. 1975. *Structuralist Poetics.* Ithaca, N.Y.: Cornell University Press.

Daniels, Bruce C. 1979. *The Connecticut Town: Growth and Development, 1635–1790.* Middletown Conn.: Wesleyan University Press.

Ellul, Jacques. 1967. *The Political Illusion*. New York: Random House.

Gouldner, Alvin. 1970. *The Coming Crisis of Western Sociology*. New York: Basic Books.

Greenstone, J. David. 1982. "The Transient and the Permanent in American Politics: Standards, Interests and the Concept of Public," in *Public Values and Private Power in American Politics*, ed. J. David Greenstone. Chicago: University of Chicago Press.

Greer, Scott. 1961. "Traffic, Transportation and Problems of the Metropolis," in *Contemporary Social Problems*, ed. Robert K. Merton and Robert A. Nisbet. New York: Harcourt, Brace and World.

Habermas, Jurgen. 1973. *Legitimacy Crisis*. Trans. Thomas McCarthy. Boston: Beacon.

———. 1981. *The Theory of Communicative Action*. Vol. 1. *Reason and the Rationalization of Society*. Trans. Thomas McCarthy. Boston: Beacon.

Halbwachs, Maurice. [1950] 1980. *The Collective Memory*. New York: Harper.

Holmes, Stephen T. 1979 (March). "Aristippus in and out of Athens." *American Political Science Review*, 73.

Huntington, Samuel. 1981. *American Politics: the Promise of Disharmony*. Cambridge: Harvard University Press.

Janowitz, Morris. 1978. *The Last Half-Century*. Chicago: University of Chicago Press.

———. 1983. *The Reconstruction of Patriotism*. Chicago: University of Chicago Press.

Knorr-Cetina, K. and Cicourel, A., eds. 1981. *Advances in Social Theory and Methodology: Toward an Integration of Micro- and Macro-Sociologies*. Boston: Routledge and Kegan Paul.

Lane, Robert E. 1986 (June). "Market Justice, Political Justice." *American Political Science Review*, 80.

Lindblom, Charles E. 1977. *Politics and Markets*. New York: Basic Books.

Lippman, Walter. [1922] 1965. *Public Opinion*. New York: Free Press.

MacIntyre, Alasdair. 1981. *After Virtue*. Notre Dame, Ind.: Notre Dame University Press.

Mansbridge, Jane. 1980. *Beyond Adversary Democracy*. New York: Basic Books.

Mathews, David. 1984. "The Public in Practice and Theory." *Public Administration Review* (March): 120–25.

Nelson, Benjamin. 1965. "Self Images and Systems of Spiritual Direction in History of European Civilization," in *The Quest for Self Control*, ed. Samuel Z. Klausner. New York: Free Press.

Pateman, Carol. 1977. *Participation and Democratic Theory*. Cambridge: Cambridge University Press.

Pocock, J. G. A. 1975. *The Machievellian Moment*. Princeton, N.J.: Princeton University Press.

Riker, William. 1982. *Liberalism against Pluralism*. San Francisco: W. H. Freeman.

Stanley, Manfred. 1981. The Technological Conscience. Chicago: University of Chicago Press.

————. 1983 (Winter). "The Mystery of the Commons." *Social Research*, 50.

Taylor, Charles. 1971 (September). "Interpretation and the Sciences of Man." *Review of Metaphysics*, 25.

Trilateral Report. 1975. *The Crisis of Democracy: Report on the Governability of Democracies to the Trilateral Commission*. New York: New York University Press.

Wood, Ellen, and Wood, Neal. 1978. *Class Ideology and Ancient Political Theory*. New York: Oxford University Press.

Yankelovich, Daniel. 1980. *New Rules*. New York: Random House.

————. 1985 (Winter). "How the Public Learns the Public's Business." *Kettering Review*.

Zuckerman, Michael. 1978 (May). "The Social Context of Democracy in Massachusetts." *William and Mary Quarterly*.

10

Political Foundations for the Rhetoric of Inquiry

John S. Nelson

The rhetoric of inquiry is one of several recent movements to reject objectivism and the other forms of foundationalism central to modern philosophy.[1] Rhetoricians of inquiry argue that transcendental grounds for judgment can neither be found nor made, and that attempts to secure them typically prove violent or otherwise coercive.[2] Thus rhetoricians typically appreciate how knowledge, truth, beauty, goodness, justice, and the like must remain communal. But their special advantage is to comprehend how such communal matters depend on language and politics— that is, on rhetoric.[3] In deference to the ancient sophists, I construe *rhetoric* as the study and practice of persuasion: the who, what, when, where, and why of communication about commitments. In league with other rhetoricians of inquiry, I emphasize epistemic commitments. These arise in all communities and tie importantly to all issues of community; but they feature concerns of evidence, knowledge, inference, and truth. For rhetoricians, though, such matters of epistemology are not issues of principle apart from the conduct of particular investigations; they are specific challenges that could or do arise within actual investigations.

Thus the rhetoric of inquiry shares much with recent turns in critical theory, deconstruction, hermeneutics, pragmatism, semiotics, and the sociology of science.[4] Like various of them, it highlights contexts, conventions, figures, and perspectives in the social construction of reality—especially within the communities of scholarship that we call sciences. Like virtually all these movements, therefore, it attracts accusations of relativism and nihilism.

The charge is that, if rhetoric of inquiry will not acknowledge universal foundations of rationality or truth, then it must confess ultimate bankruptcy—intellectually, morally, and politically. No matter that, largely unlike the other movements, it subordinates epistemology to specific improvements in inquiry and understanding. No matter that it emphasizes the substance of actual studies. To accept that logic depends on rhetoric is still to invite condemnation for casting all reason, all criteria, to the wind. To deny that standards need, or can arise from, some universal ground is to weaken the walls of civilization, letting the barbarians trash all decent forms and folks.

Proponents of one or another foundationalism have yet to propose a candidate that is not bound by context. Moreover there are strong, general arguments that such transcendental foundations are not possible. But this has not stopped foundationalists from insisting that universal standards are essential. Even many who insist on human finitude feel all the more deeply a need for transcendental grounds of inquiry and action.[5] These responses must worry rhetoricians of inquiry. But they must be troubled most by people who *accept* arguments that standards, reasons, grounds, foundations, criteria and the like themselves provide contextual limitations, yet who still crave certainty or generality enough to urge that the rhetoric of inquiry resist relativism and nihilism.

The point is not to lambast this craving for foundations as some unaccountable but benighted reluctance to face unpleasant facts.[6] An advantage of emphasizing rhetoric is its capacity for realism about particular situations of persuasion. When so many different parties desire foundations for judgment, rhetoricians of inquiry cannot rest content merely to demonstrate anew that transcendental criteria do not exist and cannot be created.[7] Their distinctive impulse must instead be to explore the various rhetorics of foundations. Whereas philosophical foundationalists stipulate the features and functions of criteria for judgment by deducing them from impossible ideals of action or inquiry, rhetoricians seek to discover the character and sources of such criteria by assessing them in action and argument.[8] Likewise they need to consider how actual foundations prove valuable or perverse in practice. Therefore they must strive to comprehend foundations of judgment as aspects of rhetoric.

In fact, this need not be hard for rhetoricians of inquiry to do. Already they distrust the naïveté or authoritarianism beneath blithe talk that "anything goes" in "the human conversation," so long as the conversation is kept going. Accordingly they can sympathize with continuing quests for foundations by scholars who maintain that civilization is order, that good order is supported by reasons, and that good reasons rely on standards not only defensible but—when need be—defended. Rhetoricians of inquiry must want "circling" and "muddling through" to lead somewhere worth going, and they must learn to compare any destination with its actual alternatives. Every good rhetorician knows that contexts are crucial *because* they can be compared and communicated across.[9] The need now is to take comparisons of sciences to communities and of truth-seeking to politicking seriously enough to develop their implications. Done with political sophistication, this should be playful enough to challenge present arrangements with experiments. And it should be critical enough to know that some will prove better than others—at least for a time.

Such experiments are easy to imagine, and some are underway on a modest scale. New serials proliferate as many fields complement the bureaucratic politics of refereed publication in mainstream journals by the entrepreneurial politics of quarterlies that cross disciplines.[10] Likewise we might try to acknowledge how invitations to contribute to scholarly collections form a kind of peer evaluation attuned to the alternately creative and conservative politics of invisible colleges.[11] Given the structural upheaval in biology and the internal fragmentation in sociology, old peer-review rationales for departmental employment and evaluation might yield in some parts of multiversities to fluid working groups, with budgeting by the scholar rather than the program.[12] Some disciplinary associations might put less resources into cattle-call conventions and more into intimate gatherings designed for intensive argument or collaboration among scholars.[13] Many ventures in political restructuring stand to improve our various communities of scholarship.

To make better sense of such needs and experiments, I recommend that the rhetoric of inquiry contribute to postmodern epistemology a pointedly rhetorical conception of *political foundations*. This should lead to a specifically *political epistemology*, as an alternative to philosophical foundationalisms. Here I cannot develop this alternative at great length, but I can hope to render it plausible enough to invite further investigation. Thus I suggest how a political account of foundations can provide a better basis for critical judgments than can transcendental grounds from philosophy.

There are many ways to develop political epistemology. This essay features one inspired by Hannah Arendt. To illustrate its potential, I later join two colleagues in a dialogue about its relevance to my home discipline of political science. But first we need to examine the political interests and strategies of foundationalism in philosophy.

PHILOSOPHICAL FOUNDATIONALISM AND ITS CRITICS

Fear is the foundation of most governments.
John Adams

Three features distinguish modern philosophical foundations for existence and judgment. They respond to perceptions of pervasive decay, disintegration, or jeopardy to a community. They respond from platforms of pure thought, protected from the threat but therefore little able to engage it directly in action. And they respond with rhetorics of transcendental, incontestable criteria—seeking to generate by force of formal logic or brute fact what they lack in other practical resources. Almost of rhetorical necessity in such situations, philosophers invoke foundations utterly removed from the fray, in order to counter it decisively. Almost of equal necessity, however, this removal can have little hope of success unless it makes the foundations invulnerable. For related reasons, philosophers who invoke principles so distant from the scene can hope to carry the day only if they render the foundations virtually omniscient, omnipotent, and omnicompetent—in order to insure that they are all-controlling.

The trouble, of course, is that humans are finite, incapable of divine certainty or perfect transcendence of circumstance. Opponents of all foundations reject them as a failure to face this unsettling fact. A longer essay would trace the complicated emergence of several kinds of antifoundationalism that have evolved over the past century or more. The tale includes relativism, pragmatism, perspectivism, hermeneutics, conventionalism, contextualism, epistemological anarchism, some semiotics, and what I have elsewhere termed *postmodern sophism*.[14] Each runs into trouble when it continues to share the modern assumption that foundations are forever, for then it must contest every attempted foundation as an act of bad faith. By contrast, rhetoricians of inquiry should emphasize the reasons to recognize that *needed and effective foundations for judgment are political rather than transcendental*—whether in action or in theory, whether inside or outside the academy.

Accordingly I suggest that philosophical foundationalism may be regarded principally as a set of political rhetorics. Often it reflects public affairs such as civil war, propaganda, and governmental scandal. Even when it comes from more narrowly academic concerns of science, however, it represents communal turmoil over the standards, procedures, and institutions of scholarship. And even when such contests are kept to the academy and conducted with the greatest regard for truth, they can and should be recognized as important kinds of epistemic politics.[15] For rhetoricians of inquiry, these constitute two key bodies of argument that actual foundations—even epistemic ones—are political.

Major criticisms of foundationalism provide a third impetus toward legitimating political epistemology in general and political foundations in particular. In repudiating transcendental criteria to regulate (and thereby guarantee) knowledge or conduct, the criticisms typically appeal to concepts and arguments from politics. Time and again, the critics contrast the false simplicities of other-worldly foundations with the communal complications and accommodations that comprise this-worldly existence. The critics repeatedly favor alternatives to foundationalism that would substitute appreciation of the complexities of natural language and actual discourse for primary reliance on the clarities of formal logic. These moves mark what we acknowledge in other contexts as politics. Thus it is no surprise that the critics insistently explain how we should replace the comparisons to mathematics now dominant in the philosophical rhetoric of foundationalists with the analogies to politics already implicit in the daily conversation of scientists.[16]

I suggest that the critics are more right than they know. Two of my favorite examples are Thomas Kuhn and Richard Rorty, partly because I have so much respect for their work. Let me emphasize, though, that few critics of foundationalism forego the political option altogether. At least implicitly, most critics exploit the continuing opportunity to invoke terms and images from politics—especially when they want to show how various sciences actually pursue arguments, both good and bad.

As virtually everybody recognizes, *The Structure of Scientific Revolutions* pivots on Kuhn's analogy between scientific and political communities. Indeed the title concept depends directly on an analogy to political features of revolution.[17] The most remarkable thing about his argument, of course, is its brilliant leap to a serious comparison between national and scientific communities as settings for revolution. Before Kuhn, "scientific revolution" was a phrase used too casually to generate specific insights. Kuhn changed that for good. As I explain elsewhere, however, the second most remarkable aspect of Kuhn's argument is its simplistic conception of political revolutions and other changes in political communities.[18] As I know from a decade of discussions in the classroom, Kuhn fails to notice in science most of the complexities of revolution in nations *and* sciences readily seen by college students.

Rorty's *Philosophy and the Mirror of Nature* calls for replacing epistemology with hermeneutics.[19] In much the same way as Kuhn, Rorty opposes foundationalism in philosophy of science by promoting a loose set of analogies to politics. He argues specifically for treating sciences as communities, with importantly political institutions and practices. But Rorty fails to take the comparison seriously enough to treat the communal or political affairs of scientific disciplines in a detailed, knowledgeable way. Even more than Kuhn, Rorty leaves himself and readers with the impression that foundations must be transcendental, that such transcendence is impossible, and that scientists—like citizens? like all of us?—must learn to live without foundations.

Both Kuhn and Rorty remain resolutely modern philosophers in this respect. Neither pushes his work toward a sophisticated understanding of the substance of communal politics. This despite the many ways in which their own arguments maintain it to be crucial for comprehending inquiry, especially in the sciences. The omission is not theirs alone. Many other epistemologists who attack philosophical foundationalism in one or another form make the same mistake. Examples include Michael Polanyi, Karl Popper, Hilary Putnam, Paul Feyerabend, Wilfrid Sellars, Hans-Georg Gadamer, Calvin Schrag, Jürgen Habermas, Richard Bernstein, and some other excellent philosophers.[20] In fact, only two partial exceptions come immediately to mind among the many distinguished philosophers lately to tackle foundationalism: Stanley Cavell and Stanley Rosen.[21] Chaim Perelman is perhaps the best exception, but he began as a lawyer and became more a rhetorician than a philosopher in any disciplinary sense.[22]

I am a political theorist by trade, and this persistent mistake naturally pains me for the missed opportunities thus far to put these talented people to work at improving our understanding simultaneously of inquiry and politics. Nonetheless political theorists are themselves often something like philosophers of politics, so I must confess that the mistake also excites me for the opportunities remaining. The call to political epistemology is a call to take up the challenge implicit in this insistent turn toward politics—as we attempt to generate good foundations for judgment without projecting transcendental criteria.

THE RHETORIC OF INQUIRY

[G]reat scientists typically are great propagandists too.
The popular archetype of the great scientist as an
other-worldly recluse is kept alive by only the rarest of
instances. . . . But counterinstances abound.

Horace Freeland Judson

This is the time for the rhetoric of inquiry to enter the drama, not to displace philosophy in general or epistemology in particular so much as to improve them. The rhetoric of inquiry arises alongside other attacks on foundationalism in metaphysics, epistemology, metaethics, aesthetics, and

263

other domains of philosophy. It helps to reject the insistence on absolute, certain, noumenal, or otherwise transcendental foundations for judgment, and it curtails the impulse to search for them. It excoriates the naïve treatment of objects as simple givens of unmediated action or experience: what Wilfrid Sellars eschews as "the myth of immaculate perception." But it also criticizes the sophisticated conception of objects as transcendental givens of distorted performance or experience, susceptible to correction in light of universal criteria.[23]

Thus philosophical critics of foundationalism contribute at least indirectly to the rhetoric of inquiry. They deconstruct transcendental foundations, they celebrate the significance of language or style, and they emphasize the importance of argumentation or conversation. One advantage of the new movement is that rhetoric as an interdisciplinary field coordinates these other projects especially well, lending them unaccustomed coherence and useful substance.[24]

A second benefit is that the new movement emphasizes rhetoric as the study of arguments, tropes, images, stories, and other neglected aspects of inquiry. Though such elements of persuasion permeate all investigations, these seldom receive careful attention from scholars and scientists. Instead they often pretend to commune directly with some transcendent reality, merely reporting it through fully literalized propositions. Since the least reflection on experiences or philosophies of research is now sufficient to disclose the crucial mediation of many persuasive constructs, our inquiries need greater knowledge of rhetoric as the discipline that studies the means and ends of persuasion.[25]

A third gain is that rhetoric as a body of general theory shows in detail how immanent grounds of criticism can in principle and do in practice combine with comparisons across inquiries to respect contexts without idolizing them. I take *The Rhetoric of the Human Sciences* (see note 2) as a whole to be a strong argument for this general proposition.[26] Among my favorite examples of the rhetorical practice of immanent comparison are Brian Barry's many excellent review essays, surely among the major achievements of the social sciences.[27] In this connection, it is revealing that Barry's early work scrutinized political arguments.[28]

A fourth achievement is that rhetoric as a discipline develops consciousness of itself and its limits.[29] This can aid us immensely in learning how to improve persuasion throughout various inquiries. Thus the rhetoric of inquiry cultivates such reflexive projects as the sociology of sociology and the history of history, to help disciplines heed the implications of their own findings when assessing their own conduct.[30]

A fifth advantage is that traditions of rhetoric provoke hosts of specific principles for the conduct of daily research.[31] Many concern neglected logics of discovery, since a major project of rhetoric is the study of invention.[32] Others address how to deploy statistics,[33] when to think counterfactually,[34] and where to favor one strategy of argument over another.[35] Some even guide the visual presentation of research.[36] For these and many other issues, the rhetoric of inquiry provides practical guidance for better research.[37]

Yet there are at least two further benefits of special importance for political foundations. A sixth is that rhetoric derives its definitions of key terms from examining their meanings in actual usage. Rhetorical analysis of the meanings of *foundations* in the social sciences can help mightily to clarify the needs and kinds of epistemic foundations at issue. For example, a cursory inventory reveals at least seven different usages of *fundamental* in treatises on economics and political science: (1) *elemental*, the main parts of a subject or those suitable for beginners; (2) *original*, the earliest parts of a subject or the initial contributions to it; (3) *influential*, the inquiry most noted or imitated; (4) *theoretical*, the definitions, axioms, theorems, principles, or explanations of a subject; (5) *novel and exciting*, on the frontiers of research, a hot topic now; (6) *methodological*, the strategies, tactics, and techniques of inquiry; and (7) *criterial*, the directions or standards for research judgments.[38] Though *fundamental* seems synonymous with *foundational*, only a partial aspect of the last usage listed surfaces in most philosophical debates about foundationalism. Yet substantive troubles about foundations in actual inquiries involve various of these meanings, entangled in diverse ways. Rhetoricians of inquiry must turn attention to these troubles.

A seventh advantage is that rhetoric relates closely to politics, including the politics of inquiry.[39] Since the ancient Sophists created rhetoric as the first science of politics, rhetoricians of inquiry can promise to develop well the connections among communication, inquiry, community, and politics. Implicit in the turn against foundationalism is a continuing capacity of philosophy to restore a substantive respect for epistemic politics. Notwithstanding its hostility to rhetoricians, philosophy remains sensitive to the intertwining of rhetoric, politics, and good argumentation. After denouncing rhetoric, Plato, Aristotle, and even a few later philosophers scrambled to resurrect it in the service of good inquiry, as well as good action.[40] Now the evident need for a better sense of epistemic politics leads not only philosophy but especially other, more substantive fields toward the rhetoric of inquiry.

At the same time, rhetoricians of inquiry should become still more sensitive to the ways in which foes of philosophical foundationalism often invite (and too often deserve) charges that their radical antifoundational-isms *foster* skepticism, relativism, or even nihilism. This stems from their inclination to emphasize the incommensurability of standards, to deny the possibility of ultimate appeals, and to dismiss the generality of criteria in favor of the specificity of contexts. Against the terror of total incoherence, how can any recourse except to transcendental grounds or foundations suffice? To be sure, rhetoricians of inquiry understand the dangers of foundationalism and sympathize with its critics. But rhetoricians remain reluctant nonetheless to accept a world without some commensurations for their contexts, grounds for their conventions, and criteria for their judgments. When Feyerabend proclaims himself an anarchist and Rorty acknowledges his own relativism, then some of the modern fear about learning and life without foundations seems confirmed, if not aggravated.

A few philosophers such as Feyerabend infer from the drive to abandon foundations that we should embrace a radicalism at once epistemic and political. Their anarchism epitomizes the chaotic state of nature that Hobbes would avoid through founding the absolute and total sovereign. Most who oppose all foundations do not find themselves able to justify such general convictions, however, so that Rorty and others slide toward epistemic and political conservatism. Without foundations, such critics incline toward a pluralism without priorities, other than de facto support for the status quo. They find no ends to be both desirable and available, save continuing openness to all ends.[41]

Philosophical critics of foundationalism might seem to exempt communities or conversations from the proscription of ends, but they tend to celebrate unbounded communities and conversations without end. By contrast, rhetoricians must recognize that human finitude enjoins choices because it precludes omnicompetent attention and participation. Without substantive ends, we achieve only vague cases for "the open society" and "continuing the conversation." As a first science of politics, rhetoric appreciates that the practical challenge to attention and participation is usually to achieve reasonable priorities among competing goals in the face of various constraints.

POLITICAL EPISTEMOLOGY

Knowledge is little; to know the right context is much, to know the right spot is everything.

Hugo von Hofmannsthal

This is the point where the rhetoric of inquiry turns into rhetorical epistemology: theories of how and what we know that begin with the contextual inquiries of rhetoric rather than abstract stipulations of logic. Such rhetorical epistemology is familiar to rhetoricians, at least, from debates over "rhetoric as epistemic."[42] But this is also the point where we encounter specifically political epistemology, so let me emphasize here the political concerns and resources desirable for the rhetoric of inquiry. It should explore how the standards, procedures, and institutions of every inquiry are political. It should extend this to sciences, arts, humanities, professions, and all other studies. As Max Weber might say, every science is political precisely because it is institutional. As Kuhn shows, however, even in the quasi-charismatic times of paradigmatic revolution, the standards and procedures of all sciences involve crucial dimensions of politics.

Many critics of foundationalism in epistemology imply a virulent relativism, which takes any element of politics as proof that no criteria can coexist for justifying and criticizing our beliefs or actions. By contrast, rhetoricians of inquiry are demonstrating in diverse domains how the political aspects of every practice make criteria for knowledge possible, useful, and defensible. Thus these rhetoricians are tracing the place of politics in epistemology. Insofar as inquiry is communal, it is political. And for these reasons, inquiry is likewise rhetorical.

The close relationship between rhetoric and political epistemology is especially plain in conventions for conducting arguments about issues that are manifestly political. Consider arguments over abortion, rights to water, nuclear weapons, or homelands in the Middle East. Who are our main audiences, authorities, and arenas? What kinds of questions do we recognize? What evidence is apt for them? What reasons do we respect, where, and when? Rhetorical analysis of these issues can and must tell us about conditions of learning and knowing. It must specify criteria of knowledge in terms of their proper uses in particular contexts. Also it can instruct by stressing structures of argument: the conventions of language and living that make action and conversation meaningful. Thus principles of rhetoric can express how practices of politics and inquiry establish what counts as knowledge, how to gain or use it, and why.

In general terms, however, rhetoric can be said to do the same for any field of endeavor. As a continuing concern across fields, rhetoric enables us to judge standards of inquiry, communication, and action. Rhetoric comprehends not only grammar and syntax but also semantics and pragmatics. Therefore it permits us to create, comprehend, conserve, and criticize our worlds and our selves.[43] Yet rhetoric accomplishes this through special attention to the situations, priorities, and strategies of actual conduct. Since these *are* politics, in a perfectly straightforward sense, such epistemological concern with the conventions and conduct of arguments in any field is thoroughly political. Through appreciating these politics of research, the rhetoric of inquiry is properly a politics of inquiry. *Epistemics are rhetorics are politics.*

POLITICAL FOUNDATIONS

> The search for groundings that are sufficient but
> relative to a spirit, a society, or a particular discipline
> becomes philosophically essential for all those who,
> while refusing to consider self-evidence an absolute
> criterion, nevertheless cannot be satisfied with a
> negative and sterile skepticism.
>
> **Chaim Perelman**

That epistemology is importantly political suggests that we assess foundations of knowledge in specifically political terms. After all, the impetus to speak of epistemic foundations surely stems from useful political talk about American Founding Fathers, foundations of Anglo-American jurisprudence, the founding of Rome, and the like. Foundations of judgment present an excellent target for rhetoricians of inquiry. They should seek to turn loose, vague analogies between inquiry and politics into persuasive, useful details of political epistemology.

Generally rhetorical and specifically political foundations for judgment would avoid transcendentalism, because politics is the art of the possible, as Aristotle remarked, not the transcendental. Thus political foundations would provide sufficient rather than necessary support for addressing specific disputes or doubts at particular times in concrete contexts. In the words of Perelman, "The search for a foundation (or a proof that guarantees it) presupposes a doubt, a disagreement, or an argument, sometimes as to the existence, the truth, or the necessary character of a reality, proposition, or norm; sometimes as to the nature of that which exists, the meaning of the proposition, or the range of the norm. Everyone admits that doubts, disagreements, and disputes can arise regarding one or another of these points, and that it is then necessary to clear them up or sidestep them."[44]

Limited, political foundations address such doubts by providing practical directions for achieving assurance adequate to the situation. "In refuting an objection, justifying a rule, or defining its range, one may eliminate a doubt, reduce a disagreement, or avoid a dispute that has actually presented itself," writes Perelman, "and this procedure may furnish a *sufficient* basis for a given situation."[45] Yet the measure of political foundations is not limited to the present. Usually by design, but occasionally by fortune, political foundations must address current doubts in ways consistent with meeting the further, future needs capable of recognition by participants at the time—whatever time is at issue. Thus foundations provide principles for judgment; and they do so pragmatically, by forming persons and persuasions rather than by certifying or enforcing rules.[46] By extension, political foundations must sustain connections with our past acts and settings, reconstructing them as traditions of occurrence and judgment. Accordingly foundations afford contexts for judgment; and they do this narratively, through characters and stories that enable us to identify and distinguish ourselves in action.[47] Evoking fields of past and future to direct the present, limited foundations or grounds become our contexts—giving us continuing, specific guidance in which we can have confidence.

Political foundations cannot, however, conquer all human limits. Nor can they yield complete guarantees against error or change. As Perelman observes, "it is always possible that a dispute, temporarily avoided, may emerge later for some new reasons. A sufficient grounding at a given moment may not have the characteristics of an absolute grounding that can permanently forestall disputes concerning this matter."[48] A likely implication of political epistemology, therefore, is that the continuing desire for foundations expresses a recurrent set of needs. How are these needs actually met in various polities?

My answer here is suggestive rather than conclusive: *Political foundations are constitutive conventions and narratives for political communities.* We create them as political *myths* sufficient unto the moment, and we augment them as *traditions* amended through later politics. As myths, political foundations are principled stories that form us as we reform them. We change them, and they change us. They lead us to change our circumstances; but they eventually give way to other myths, presumably more adequate to altered circumstances.[49] As traditions, political foundations are exemplars and custodians of judgment that transmit us from one circumstance to another as they transmit themselves to us. We augment them, and they augment us. They guide our agreements with them; but

269

they also pattern our differences from them, often turning departures into corrections or extensions.[50]

To be sure, political foundations have not always been intended or construed in this way. Plato and Hobbes both projected polities founded on transcendental acts or principles, and they have not been alone in the history of the West.[51] But attempts at transcendental foundations pale in number and significance beside the rhetorical, political, and mythical founding practiced in the West as well as elsewhere. This is especially evident in parts of *The New Science* by Giambattista Vico, an early account of the functions and logics of foundational mythmaking.[52] It is also apparent in Henry Tudor's introduction to *Political Myth*—especially the rhetoric of Roman founding—and in the manifold studies of myth by Joseph Campbell, Mircea Eliade, and Claude Lévi-Strauss.[53]

Despite obvious ties to the much-studied politics of revolution, however, political founding has yet to receive the attention that it deserves. Controversy over legal interpretation of the United States Constitution often carries implications for understanding the political foundations of America, but they seldom receive direct and specific attention.[54] The same goes for work on constitutionalism.[55]

Perhaps the greatest theorist of political founding thus far is Hannah Arendt. A student of Martin Heidegger, Arendt moved beyond his philosophical critique of foundationalism to explore its political replacements. She treated revolution and the inauguration of polities as a challenge to myth and rhetoric more than transcendental philosophy. As she noted, "The very fact that the men of the American Revolution thought of themselves as 'founders' indicates the extent to which they must have known that it would be the act of foundation itself, rather than an Immortal Legislator or self-evident truth or any other transcendent, transmundane source, which eventually would become the fountain of authority in the new body political."[56] The political and philosophical impossibility of transcendental grounds was then (as now) due principally to the rhetorical implausibility of any appeal to them.

As Arendt discerned, the paradox of every legitimate foundation is that it must be given to the founders but that it also must be provided by them. Foundations are "founds" (discoveries), yet they are equally "foundings" (creations). If we—like the American Founders—cannot plausibly claim to discover foundations in God, History, Law, Nature, Self, or some other Absolute Beginning, then we—like the American Founders—must turn to our experience, our history.[57] Were it able to supply foundations, however, we would already have them. Then our situation would escape the disorder that makes a foundation—and therefore a founding—needed. But if experience does not supply good foundations, then we or other people must invent them. Yet why should *any* such invention by humans, fallible and limited as they are, bind us as humans? And why should any such invention *now by us in particular,* as humans deeply disordered by twentieth-century troubles, bind even us—let alone anyone else?[58] This is the perplexity, the vicious circle, of political foundation. Now bereft of authority, how can we produce an authoritative beginning, to beget the authority for beginning anew?

The traditionalist response is that long ago, if not far away, was a founding by some figure of humanity now largely obscured by the mists of history. Individual or group, the figure is our great giver of laws. If we suffer terrible troubles, surely we have strayed from the laws or their true meanings. To overcome our troubles, we must revive the old constitution by recovering it as our foundation. The legislator and the laws spring from better times; and they can perpetuate or recreate those times, dispelling our troubles, if only we live well by them. These laws are still our constitutive conventions: they define us, therefore they are fundamental. They are also our regulative principles: they direct us, therefore they are fundamental. We must recall, recommit, rededicate ourselves to these first principles: our foundations.[59] And as Arendt observed, "Whatever we may find out about the factual truth of such legends, their historical significance lies in how the human mind attempted to solve the problem of the beginning, of an unconnected, new event breaking into the continuous sequence of historical time."[60]

For us, however, as for the American Founders described by Arendt, the terrible troubles include our self-awareness as mythmakers.[61] *How can we make foundations or any other myths intentionally and critically?* Our perplexities of foundation seem especially acute because we know our complexities of belief and criteria as myths, we recall their origins in our own acts or needs, and we realize our continuing capacity to accept and to criticize them at the same time. How can we live responsibly in self-conscious myths or build securely on qualified foundations? How in reason do we change foundations of judgment, when we know them as our conceptions and practices of reason? How should we justify new myths of justification? As students of culture and mythmaking encourage us to recognize, these are political more than philosophical challenges.

Arendt found political inspiration in the Roman response to the perplexity of first things. Roman foundations are recollections and resumptions of former commitments, lately forgotten or betrayed but still binding.

271

Yet we find this wanting, because we conceive the human capacity for acting and learning as a facility for continual change. We see little reason to be bound by the earlier commitments of others, so we hear Roman tales of founding and virtue as manipulative fictions rather than accurate histories. May we not, however, conceive each new beginning as a recommitment to responsible change? Arendt argued that

> there exists a solution for the perplexities of beginning which needs
> no absolute to break the vicious circle in which all first things seem
> to be caught. What saves the act of beginning from its own
> arbitrariness is that it carries its own principle within itself, or, to
> be more precise, that beginning and principle, *principium* and
> principle, are not only related to each other, but are coeval. The
> absolute from which the beginning is to derive its own validity and
> which must save it, as it were, from its inherent arbitrariness is the
> principle which, together with it, makes its appearance in the
> world. The way the beginner starts whatever he intends to do lays
> down the law of action for those who have joined him in order to
> partake in the enterprise and to bring about its accomplishment. As
> such, the principle inspires the deeds that are to follow and
> remains apparent as long as the action lasts.[62]

In this respect, foundations are constellations of *principles*. Each differs in substance, but each reaffirms and reconstitutes our capacity for free and informed judgment. Principles are not ends to be pursued by whatever means seem most efficient, because they project the early choice of specific paths, and because they resist the early choice of particular results. For the same reason, principles are not motives that propel us toward preset consequences. Principles are not rules that strictly determine choice but guidelines that partially inform it.

To recognize political foundations for inquiry is to turn from philosophical criteria of knowledge or method to rhetorical principles of learning and truth. Some stem from disciplines as persuasions of scholarship, others from individuals as innovators in research, still others from rhetoricians as analysts of inquiry. In the wake of modern philosophy, we have just begun to comprehend principles within actual projects of research; but already we can appreciate their existence and their difference from transcendental rules, foundations, and criteria for science.[63] To pursue political foundations for the rhetoric of inquiry is in part to stress the roles of rhetorical principles in research.

In other words, foundations establish myths. These myths are the

272

realities of their societies. They change with the societies— telling who the societies are, how they develop, what they know, and why. This holds as much for professional societies as for others, encompassing sciences as societies of inquiry. From founding exemplars or theories to continuing tests, adjustments, and criticisms, these epistemic projects are mythic. Every foundation also projects standards and procedures for changing the community from inside—motivating critics and helping to distinguish good modifications from bad. Thus the notion of political foundations for inquiry ties directly to the epistemic creation, articulation, criticism, and demise of research projects.[64] Historical accounts of changes in particular sciences bear comparison with the alterations of meaning, method, and principle in political accounts of traditions. Consequently we should inquire rhetorically into the modes of authority and criticality in academic communities.

The perplexity and challenge of beginning anew—of constitutions as reconstitutions but not really—led Arendt to a notion of tradition as the *augmentation* of foundations, respecting and using their authority while criticizing and enriching it.[65] Such authority is rhetorical and political, not philosophical and transcendental. Arendt noted that it has disappeared in modern politics because it fails to meet the criteria for modern science; it can neither survive the modern radicalism of doubt nor satisfy the modern craving for certainty.[66] Yet we now know the folly of such transcendental criteria. Moreover critics of modern foundationalism already demonstrate that modern sciences include various exemplars and custodians of judgment that resemble the elements of other traditions. In ironical counterpoint to Arendt, perhaps we may discern in academic disciplines some updated versions of the very augmentation of authority that she believed to have been banished by modern science.

POLITICAL SCIENCES

Doctrines must take their beginning from that of the matters of which they treat.[67]

Giambattista Vico

Epistemic foundations are political and rhetorical foundations. To make this fully persuasive, of course, rhetoricians of inquiry need to discuss cases and answer objections in detail. Here I can manage only a single instance, and that in the most sketchy of terms. Mindful that foundations give

273

beginnings as well as ends, let me end this beginning with a brief example. But let it address a difficult case: a discipline that keeps alive no memory of its founders.[68] Let this be less an argument than a dialogue, to demonstrate disciplinary rhetoric, not just describe it. And let the dialogue be actual—rather than fictional—though no less relevant and scarcely less economical. An earlier version of this argument generated the following discussion.[69]

LANE DAVIS: Could you give me an example that is nonpolitical? You were talking originally about foundations and revolutions that are not political, and I am not sure what you have in mind.

JOHN NELSON: Sure, political science as a discipline could be such a community. It is basically an American community: that is an important fact about it. It was founded in America.

DAVIS: How and when and by whom?

NELSON: It was founded in the 1890s.[70] It has to do with Woodrow Wilson and others at that time. It involves the generation right before George Sabine. It does not get founded, as it were, all at once—but then most foundings do not happen that way. Still myths of founding insistently imply that it is a once-and-for-all activity, do they not? And the notion of revolution connected with foundational republicanism of this kind likewise implies that the basic changes are revolutions, breaking radically with the past foundation and revolving toward its restoration, reconstruction, or reconstitution. What then should we do with the scientific equivalent of later heroes such as Abraham Lincoln? In peculiar ways, we assimilate them to the founders. We imply an almost timeless realm of politics or truth—a time apart from mundane historical or scientific time—where such heroes are contemporaries: giants who made and strode the ground we now walk. Thus there is a series of books that say: we want a real science of politics; we want to focus on behavior! "The Behavioral Revolution" has in a sense been happening over and over in political science—compare Jefferson's generational revolutions—for the past hundred years.

DAVIS: Would the establishment of the American Political Science Association be part of founding political science as a discipline?

NELSON: Yes, George Catlin has a book of this kind about how we need to study behavior. Then someone else comes along, dismissing that as unscientific and calling for new attention to behavior. In a limited way, the discipline just is a series of these, through Charles Merriam up to David Easton. Easton, Robert Dahl, and company again proclaim the behavioral revolution.[71] As far as I know, it has not been done again successfully since. But it is being attempted again by John Wahlke and others.[72] They criticize "behavioralists" as not really behavioral for focusing on public opinion, political ideas, political attitudes, and other mental constructs. Instead the discipline should now stress biological, biochemical, and ethological phenomena, these critics argue. For political science, these are the acts of founding: they establish and extend a mythos of behavioral standards and procedures for research.

DAVIS: What about the big sixties argument in political science?

NELSON: The one involving the Caucus for a New Political Science?

DAVIS: Yes, is that an attempt again at renewing or refounding or amending the founding? And has it also failed?

NELSON: Yes.

DAVIS: So you are saying that this founding occurs over an extended time. But what about the later people of whom you are speaking? Are they redoing it, continuing it, amending it, or what?

NELSON: As Arendt tries to portray foundations, at least two things would be occurring. In Kuhn's terms, there is a lot of "normal science." In Arendt's terms, that is "augmentation of the tradition." There is a community or a tradition, and people work within it to make routine contributions. Each is an innovation, an original contribution in some sense; but all such innovations transpire within the larger framework. Second, there are repeated attempts at further revolution. An interesting point is that political science was founded so that its beginning myths of politics and science were somewhat incompatible with one another: politics is action that encompasses inner and outer, mind and body, but science studies only outer behavior. This generates a continuing sense within the discipline that it is not being scientific.

This can also create a sense that it is not being political. That is how to explain the recurrent revolutions for policy science. We have had three or more of those, too, with people proclaiming that we are at last going to have a policy science. Those revolutions are about being more political, so it is not just the Caucus for a New Political Science that has called for the discipline to become more adequately political. The discipline insistently sees itself as improving American politics.[73]

DAVIS: Is it significant that neither side of the last behavioral revolution was able to articulate clearly what it wanted to do?

NELSON: Yes, that is consistent with the incoherence of founding myths in our community. We in political science never figure them out.

STEPHEN BORELLI: It sounds as though a scientific community isn't the best analogy. "Fool" isn't the best word, but in some sense it is easier to fool scientists into saying that this is the new way of doing things. These

275

are the new myths, our assumptions for proceeding, and they are better than the old ones: so we had better go ahead. But in founding political communities, people are not so easily fooled. You can establish the Constitution and claim a new order, but people have experienced life under the old order. Therefore they know that some things have changed, but many haven't. Thus Arendt noted that France suffered so many foundings that the very act (or would-be act) of founding lost its meaning. People weren't going to be fooled any more. They realized that founding per se had spent its value. That leads me to wonder whether the analogy of science to politics works well.

NELSON: You make an interesting comparison. I had forgotten what Arendt said about France. It did have republics founded rapidly one after another. Nonetheless I would make two arguments in reply.

First, political scientists do have something like the realm of everyday experience, letting them assess how to regard any claim about a new founding. More importantly, it figures in what they want to do daily in their work, as in what they say about the work of others. In the last successful behavioral revolution, for example, few political scientists were doing "behavioral" research in any approved sense. For the first fifteen or so years after that revolution, in fact, political scientists mostly kept doing legal, constitutional, and institutional research. Only later did survey research take over, and never was there a total change. Enough people eventually learned enough about the technology, the statistics, and so on that many political scientists became "behavioral." Then others come into the picture, saying anew that they want to become scientific by becoming truly behavioral. But so far that has not happened, because too many scholars have too much investment in election and opinion data: they do not know other modes. Still the discipline might get another generation learning to do other things. Rational-choice work is one obvious possibility. The key point, though, is that scholars do use their ordinary, daily experience in producing and assessing such challenges to their normal science.

The second point concerns "fooling" the participants. Among other things, founding myths identify authorities. American founding myths identify particular republican principles and writers as authoritative. They also mark specific experiences as authoritative, paradigmatic. In the community of political scientists, whom do the myths identify as the key authorities? Oddly they do not sanctify some political scientists as the crucial authorities. Instead they favor a set of philosophers, who gave a "reconstructed" view of good scientific method. In Kuhnian terms, these

276

myths also make authorities out of a few pieces of work as "exemplars" to emulate. But only by implication do they identify a few political scientists—who created those exemplars—as authorities.

DAVIS: Even the exemplars are usually outside political science!

NELSON: That's right. Philip Converse has been an authority within and for political science, because his work on belief systems has become an exemplar. But most authorities are outsiders. The standards and concepts also come from outside political science: from philosophy, sociology, psychology, and economics. This is immensely important for what practitioners are willing to throw out, with what ease and speed.

All this coheres with Arendt's account: it highlights such issues about authorities and their influence. What it does not encompass is the issue about Jefferson and a revolution each generation. Arendt acknowledged this to be important, because she tended to favor it, yet she merely noted that it drops out of American politics. But *why* did it drop out? What changed?

DAVIS: Where do you find in political science anything like the principle of common promise and deliberation—the mutual pledging of lives, honor, and estate that makes the American founding so important?

NELSON: From the stories told to me, I infer that the things which created a sense of generational identity would count. I think of scholars who had to "retool." The retooling experience involved people pledging to one another that they would take the risks and—in the short run—make the sacrifices required for becoming truly scientific. This occurred throughout the discipline, department by department.

DAVIS: What bothers me is how the discipline consistently turns to something outside itself, something it doesn't understand well, to define what it is supposed to do. That is very different from a group of people who band themselves together to do something in politics.

NELSON: Look at the Russian Revolution. Lenin and others took Marxism from outside Russian experience. Marxism did not fit Russian circumstances, but it became the authoritative position, providing the master texts and principles. Thus it resembles reliance on philosophers and their texts to tell us what to do as political scientists. It looks like the ways in which psychological principles based on experiments become authoritative for us, though we scarcely do any experimentation. It resembles how economic theorems about individual choice become authoritative for us, though we emphasize groups and institutions. The complexities and perplexities of the Russian Revolution seem highly comparable to those of founding political science. The analogy is helpful.

DAVIS: True, the Russian Revolution looked to a set of documents outside Russian experience, but it did not produce politics in Arendt's sense. She turned instead to the American Revolution precisely because its founding was more political.

NELSON: Arendt's classical sense of politics is restrictive, of course, but even so what do we say: that there was an unsuccessful revolution, as a specifically political revolution?

DAVIS: I would say that it had a poor founding.

NELSON: What you say about the Soviet Union, I would say about political science.

DAVIS: That's what I am talking about: political science. One of the puzzles is that political scientists have gone to philosophers of science, who have been primarily concerned with talking about physics and psychology, to find out how to study politics. Or they turn to sociologists and to market researchers. The Erie County study that inaugurates one of these behavioral revolutions was done by a market researcher, who was not a political scientist and did not regard himself as doing political science. Now political scientists turn to economics, primarily to econometricians and theorists of rational choice. Once again, political scientists do not look within political science much for models of what to do in research: a most peculiar condition! If that's like the Soviet Union, I still can't think of anything even loosely analogous in the development of political science to the purges.

NELSON: I knew that you would get to the purges. But the analogy holds: political science has suffered purges of a sort.

DAVIS: No, that is a romantic exaggeration. The situation has prevented a purge: there was always someplace else to go. The most dramatic failure was the Caucus for a New Political Science. Those guys were really hated. I was on the other side and talked to people active on it. The Caucus people were not just disliked; they were hated. Yet they weren't driven out of the profession. Some left good schools for less-good schools to survive. But many have survived and done rather well. They should have, because they are good people who do good work.

NELSON: But the main equivalent of a purge was that people seriously interested in other kinds of political science somehow did not perform well enough in graduate school to keep going. The ones who made assistant professor somehow did not perform well enough to get tenure. And the ones who got tenure, somehow got quarantined: stuck in a far corner of the discipline, deprived of resources or banned as irrelevant.

DAVIS: All right, but only by exaggeration does that qualify as a purge.

Many who did not make it failed because they did not have it, not because they were persecuted. And every one of your categories would suffer its numbers reduced significantly were that noted. This is not serious enough to compare to Stalin's purges. If we are trying to find an analogy in the political realm to political science as a failed scientific revolution, then the Russian Revolution is a poor analogy.

NELSON: But there is another part of the analogy. Admitting that threats to a scientific survival are less draconian than Stalin's threats to biological survival, still I would note that the Soviet Union gets its shape from the exemplars of Lenin and Stalin, far more than Marxism or other ideals of the Soviet Revolution. Thus Soviet reality grows up gradually through specific practices and local conditions. This looks more than a little like the foundational pattern for the development of political science. Beyond the practical impact of external authorities and internal exemplars, the two share a sense of being beleaguered and under siege. Foundation- ally, political science—like the Soviet Union—combines imperial claims with a lack of self-confidence that it is a modern power deserving respect. Thus we worry that we are not a real science and that politics is not a set of real phenomena. We fear matters of polity—unlike matters of econ- omy, society, or psychology—to be mere leftovers: subjects of a grab-bag science. Parallels with the conflictual founding of the Soviet Union as a new Russian Empire are pretty plain, aren't they? What develops then is a set of practices concerning what it is to be a member of this community, living within it. In both cases, these gradually become routinized *as* the revolution.

DAVIS: Aren't the resulting practices anticommunal? It seems to me that the interesting thing about what Arendt was saying is her stress on the importance of a particular kind of beginning. That is crucial for providing a foundation for the conditions of genuine community.

NELSON: Yes, neither is effectively a community in Arendt's sense. Yet in both cases, the reasons concern their grossly defective foundings. Moreover their departures from Arendt's strictures can help to explain the strengths and weaknesses of both would-be communities.

DAVIS: Then can we think of a scientific community that did have the kind of revolutionary founding consistent with Arendt?

NELSON: For Arendt, a successful founding provides a decent basis for action. Arguing that good revolutions do not come out of nothing, she encountered the perplexity that the new order was already there in one way though not in another. It is new yet well-established. The onset of relativity physics was experienced by most physicists as the creation of a new

279

astrophysical fabric and scientific community, but there was a previous discipline dominated by Newton. Or take biology: it grows from many naturalistic investigations, though it has only recently become a single community of scientists. Is that due to studies of DNA and the like, or does it go back to Charles Darwin? The many arguments about the character of "the Darwinian Revolution" suggest the elements were mostly available for a single science of evolution, but they become fundamentally new with Darwin's coordinating arguments. These established a distinct community of discourse. That revolution has spurred much historical research into the rhetorical and political "turning operations" that Arendt argued to characterize the problem of founding: having to take the old terms, turn them against themselves in criticism, and make them into a new language for new institutions. [74]

DAVIS: One of the things that I find very impressive is to listen to very able, very serious men in the legal profession who try to tie their positions on current problems of real importance back to an interpretation of the Constitution as it was originally drafted. These are not idiots or dumb people going back, and they are going back with dead-serious purposes. They do not even think that it is funny when you try to make a little joke about it. There you begin to appreciate the mythical side of basic standards; this is where it really shows up. Yet I worry about comparing legal and political foundations to scientific ones. I remain skeptical whether there is as much reference back to the founders as we find in our political community in America, where to question the Founding Fathers gets members really hot under the collar.

NELSON: Maybe a difference between academic communities and more specifically political communities is that the latter personalize authority as you describe, but the former talk more about impersonal standards or criteria. Political scientists still get very upset if you question that there is behavior just sitting out there to be observed.

BORELLI: Another difference is that many livelihoods depend on there being behavior awaiting observation. In our political community, by contrast, most people have less at stake, making it all the more impressive that foundational issues could mean so much to so many.

DAVIS: But people do sense an immense amount at stake. If we do not stay within the bounds established by the founders, the alternative is anarchy. Anarchy means no order; it is not anarchy in the good sense. People seem to think of themselves as standing like Horatio at the bridge. Someone might try to sneak in something to undermine the polity, and then everything would fall apart.

NELSON: People sense that "The American Way of Life" is at stake. It is not a matter of jobs, let alone stereos; it is a matter of basic moral standing. Who they are as Americans is at stake. Much the same goes for disciplinary foundations and who we are as scholars. Almost any suggestion that scientific foundations or criteria are rhetorical elicits charges of selling out civilization. Barbarians are at the gates, while rhetoricians would undermine the walls and the gateposts. There are important differences between countries and disciplines, but they separate kinds of political foundations and rhetorical practices—not certain, neutral criteria of science and powerplays of politics.

The rhetoric of inquiry suggests that to take epistemic foundations seriously is to take them politically. Let us take the foundationalists seriously enough to appreciate—but not exaggerate—the importance of foundations in our immanent approaches to reality. And let us take the recent critics of foundationalism seriously enough to produce and recognize truly political foundations for human affairs. Much remains to be learned and done before such a rhetorical and mythical sense of foundations could receive an adequate articulation for our politics or our inquiry. Still the last two centuries include many provocative mandates to pattern our politics on our sciences. Perhaps the time has come to learn also from careful comparisons in the reverse direction.

N O T E S

1. See Richard J. Bernstein, *Beyond Objectivism and Relativism* (Philadelphia: University of Pennsylvania Press, 1983); *Philosophical Profiles* (Philadelphia: University of Pennsylvania Press, 1986).

2. To characterize the rhetoric of inquiry and its proponents, whom I term *rhetoricians of inquiry*, I rely throughout on conversations begun with scholars at Temple University's Seventh Annual Conference on Discourse Analysis and on others associated with the University of Iowa Project on Rhetoric of Inquiry (POROI). I take these characterizations to be supported by papers from the 1984 POROI Symposium: John S. Nelson, Allan Megill, and Donald N. McCloskey, eds., *The Rhetoric of the Human Sciences* (Madison: University of Wisconsin Press, 1987). I thank Bruce Gronbeck and Michael McGee of POROI, Robert Craig and Herbert Simons of Temple, and Stephen Borelli and Lane Davis of the Iowa Department of Political Science for comments helpful in completing this essay. Please excuse the ample citations of my own work. They note where you can find arguments for those claims preliminary to the main argument at hand. Thus they let me build

economically toward the vision of better foundations for reasoning that this essay most wants to project.

3. John S. Nelson, "Political Theory as Political Rhetoric," in *What Should Political Theory Be Now?* Ed. J. Nelson (Albany: State University of New York Press, 1983), 169–240, especially 171–76.

4. See John S. Nelson and Allan Megill, "Rhetoric of Inquiry: Projects and Prospects," *Quarterly Journal of Speech* 72 (February 1986): 20–37. Also see Quentin Skinner, ed., *The Return of Grand Theory in the Human Sciences* (New York: Cambridge University Press, 1985); Donald W. Fiske and Richard A. Shweder, eds., *Metatheory in Social Science* (Chicago: University of Chicago Press, 1986).

5. See Glenn Tinder, *Community* (Baton Rouge: Louisiana State University Press, 1980); *Against Fate* (Notre Dame, Ind.: University of Notre Dame Press, 1981).

6. Prominent among the many who make this move are Paul K. Feyerabend, *Against Method* (Atlantic Highlands, N.J.: Humanities Press, 1975); Richard Rorty, *Philosophy and the Mirror of Nature* (Princeton, N.J.: Princeton University Press, 1979); Calvin O. Schrag, *Radical Reflection and the Origin of the Human Sciences* (Purdue, Ind.: Purdue University Press, 1980) and *Communicative Praxis and the Space of Subjectivity* (Bloomington, Ind.: Indiana University Press, 1986).

7. Perhaps the best rhetorical criticism of notions that criteria can transcend contextual limitations is in Stanley Cavell, *The Claim of Reason* (New York: Oxford University Press, 1979), especially 1–243.

8. See Ira L. Strauber, "Transforming Legal Rights into Political Ones," *Polity* 16(Fall 1983): 72–95; "Political Philosophy and Political Action," *What Should Political Theory Be Now?* (see note 3), 55–74; "The Rhetoric of an Ordinary Political Argument: Liberalism and Zionism," *Western Political Quarterly* 39(December 1986): 603–22; "The Rhetorical Structure of Freedom of Speech," *Polity* 19(Summer, 1987): 507–28.

9. See Herbert W. Simons, "Chronicle and Critique of a Conference," *Quarterly Journal of Speech* 71(February 1985): 52–64; John Lyne, "Rhetorics of Inquiry," *Quarterly Journal of Speech* 71(February 1985): 65–73.

10. Recent examples include *Critical Inquiry; Cultural Critique; Economics and Philosophy; Raritan; Representations; Theory, Culture, and Society*.

11. See Diana Crane, *Invisible Colleges* (Chicago, University of Chicago Press, 1972).

12. This idea inspired the "committee" structure of the University of Chicago, but Evergreen College approximates it more completely.

13. The biennial Conferences on Argumentation cosponsored by the Speech Communication Association and the American Forensic Association would be good models for many such meetings.

14. See Nelson, "Political Theory," especially 176–193; Michael C. Leff, "Modern Sophistic and the Unity of Rhetoric," in *The Rhetoric of the Human Sciences* (see note 2), 19–37.

15. See John S. Nelson, "Stories of Science and Politics: Some Rhetorics of Political Research," in *The Rhetoric of the Human Sciences* (see note 2), 198–220, especially 198–208.

16. See Peter Winch, *The Idea of a Social Science* (New York: Humanities Press, 1958); Michael Polanyi, *Personal Knowledge*, 2d ed. (New York: Harper & Row, 1964); Hans-Georg Gadamer, *Truth and Method*, 3d ed., ed. Garrett Barden and John Cumming (New York: Seabury Press, 1975; Wilfrid Sellars, *Science, Perception, and Reality* (New York: Humanities Press, 1963); Jürgen Habermas, *Knowledge and Human Interests*, trans. Jeremy J. Shapiro (Boston: Beacon Press, [1968]1971); Karl Popper, *Objective Knowledge*, 2d ed. (Oxford: Oxford University Press, 1979); Stephen Toulmin, *Human Understanding* (Princeton, N.J., Princeton University Press, 1972); Thomas S. Kuhn, *The Essential Tension* (Chicago, University of Chicago Press, 1977); Paul K. Feyerabend, *Science in a Free Society* (London: New Left Books, 1978); Hilary Putnam, *Reason, Truth and History* (New York: Cambridge University Press, 1981); Richard Rorty, *Consequences of Pragmatism* (Minneapolis: University of Minnesota Press, 1982).

17. Thomas S. Kuhn, *The Structure of Scientific Revolutions*, 2d ed. (Chicago, University of Chicago Press, 1970).

18. See John S. Nelson, "Once More on Kuhn," *Political Methodology* 1(Spring 1974): 73–104.

19. See Rorty, *Mirror of Nature* (see note 6), especially 313–94.

20. Especially see the works cited in notes 1, 6, and 18.

21. See Cavell, *The Claim of Reason* (see note 7), especially 245–496; Stanley Rosen, *Nihilism* (New Haven: Yale University Press, 1969), and *The Limits of Analysis* (New York: Basic Books, 1980).

22. See Chaim Perelman and Lucie Olbrechts-Tyteca, *The New Rhetoric*, trans. John Wilkinson and Purcell Weaver (Notre Dame, Ind.: University of Notre Dame Press, [1958], 1969); Perelman, *The Realm of Rhetoric*, trans. William Kluback (Notre Dame, Ind.: University of Notre Dame Press, 1982).

23. Rhetoricians surely must welcome the increasing interest of philosophers in procedures of communication and standards of rhetoric. Yet rhetoricians must worry about the continued inclination toward universal ideals of speech in such philosophical work. An example is volume 1 of *The Theory of*

Communicative Action by Jürgen Habermas, trans. Thomas McCarthy (Boston: Beacon Press, [1981] 1984).

24. See John S. Nelson, Allan Megill, and Donald N. McCloskey, "Rhetoric of Inquiry," in *The Rhetoric of the Human Sciences* (see note 2), 3–18.

25. See John S. Nelson, "Models, Statistics, and Other Tropes of Politics," in *Argument in Transition*, ed. David Zarefsky, Malcolm O. Sillars, and Jack Rhodes (Annandale, Va.: Speech Communication Association, 1983), 213–29, and "Seven Rhetorics of Inquiry," in *The Rhetoric of the Human Sciences* (see note 2), 407–34.

26. Specifically rhetorical examples of immanent comparison include Donald N. McCloskey, *The Rhetoric of Economics* (Madison: University of Wisconsin Press, 1985); John S. Nelson, "Education for Politics," in *What Should Political Theory Be Now?* (see note 3), 413–78 and Nelson, "Economical Rhetoric: An Outsider Listens to Talk among the Econ" (Paper for the Wellesley College Conference on the Rhetoric of Economics, 17–19 April 1986).

27. For example, see Brian Barry, "'Exit, Voice, and Loyalty'," *British Journal of Political Science* 4(January 1974): 79–107; "'Crisis, Choice, and Change', Parts I–II," *British Journal of Political Science* 7(January–April 1977): 99–113 and 217–53.

28. Brian Barry, *Political Argument* (New York: Humanities Press, 1965).

29. As the science of persuasion of self, as well as others, rhetoric comprehends the boundaries and uses of self-awareness in ways that merge with psychology: see Donal E. Carlston, "Turning Psychology on Itself: The Rhetoric of Psychology and the Psychology of Rhetoric," in *The Rhetoric of the Human Sciences* (see note 2), 146–63.

30. On how rhetorical reflexivity helps to avoid "the fallacy of self-exception," see Nelson, "Stories of Science and Politics" and "Economical Rhetoric" (see notes 15 and 26).

31. See Nelson, "Seven Rhetorics of Inquiry" and "Economical Rhetoric" (see notes 25 and 26).

32. See Norwood Russell Hanson, *Patterns of Discovery* (New York: Cambridge University Press, 1965); Michael C. Leff, "Topical Invention and Metaphoric Interaction," *Southern Speech Communication Journal* 48(Spring 1983): 214–29.

33. See Donald N. McCloskey, "Why Economic Historians Should Stop Relying on Statistical Tests of Significance, and Lead Economists and Historians into the Promised Land," *Newsletter of the Cliometrics Society* 2(December 1986): 5–7; and "Rhetoric within the Citadel: Statistics," in

Argument and Critical Practices, ed. Joseph W. Wenzel (Annandale, Va.: Speech Communication Association, 1987), 485–90; Frank Denton, "The Significance of Significance: Rhetorical Aspects of Statistical Hypothesis Testing in Economics," *Consequences of Economic Rhetoric*, ed. Arjo Klamer, Donald N. McCloskey, and Robert Solow (New York: Cambridge University Press, forthcoming).

34. See John S. Nelson, "Accidents, Laws, and Philosophic Flaws: Behavioral Explanation in Dahl and Dahrendorf," *Comparative Politics* 7(April 1975): 435–57; Charles Arthur Willard, "Arguing from Counterfactuals," in *Argument and Critical Practices* (see note 33), 199–206.

35. This is a good use of the theory of topics, central to Aristotelian traditions of rhetoric. See Michael C. Leff, "The Topics of Argumentative Invention in Latin Rhetorical Theory from Cicero to Boethius," *Rhetorica* 1(Spring 1983): 23–44.

36. In general, see *The Journal of Visual/Verbal Languaging*; in particular, see Edward R. Tufte, *The Visual Display of Quantitative Information* (Chesire, Conn.: Graphics Press, 1983).

37. For political examples, see John S. Nelson, "Approaches, Opportunities, and Priorities in the Rhetoric of Political Inquiry: A Critical Synthesis," *Social Epistemology* 2(January–March 1988): 21–42.

38. The clear resemblance between these and other senses of *fundamental* or *foundational* add to the diverse meanings of Kuhn's *paradigm* to testify anew to his pursuit of rhetorical analysis, however incompletely or unselfconsciously: see Margaret Masterman, "The Nature of a Paradigm," in *Criticism and the Growth of Knowledge*, ed. Imre Lakatos and Alan Musgrave (Cambridge: Cambridge University Press, 1970), 59–89; Kuhn, *The Structure of Scientific Revolutions* (see note 17), 174–210.

39. See Nelson, "Stories of Science and Politics," especially 208–14.

40. See Plato, *Gorgias*, trans. W. C. Helmbold (Indianapolis: Bobbs-Merrill, 1952), and *Protagoras*, ed. Gregory Vlastos, trans. Benjamin Jowett and Martin Ostwald (Indianapolis: Bobbs-Merrill, 1956); Aristotle, *Rhetoric and Poetics*, ed. Friedrich Solmsen, trans. W. Rhys Roberts and Ingram Bywater (New York: Random House, 1954); Paul Ricoeur, *The Rule of Metaphor*, trans. Robert Czerny (Toronto: University of Toronto Press, [1975]1977).

41. See Richard Rorty, "Postmodernist Bourgeois Liberalism," *Journal of Philosophy* 80(October 1983): 583–89; William E. Connolly, "Mirror of America," *Raritan* 3(Summer 1983): 124–35.

42. See Robert L. Scott, "On Viewing Rhetoric as Epistemic," *Central States Speech Journal* 18(February 1967): 9–16, and "On Viewing Rhetoric as

Epistemic: Ten Years Later," *Central States Speech Journal* 27(Winter 1976): 258–66; Michael C. Leff, "In Search of Ariadne's Thread: A Review of the Recent Literature on Rhetorical Theory," *Central States Speech Journal* 29(Summer 1978): 73–91; Richard A. Cherwitz and James W. Hikins, *Communication and Knowledge* (Columbia: University of South Carolina Press, 1986).

43. See John S. Nelson, "Natures and Futures for Political Theory," in *What Should Political Theory Be Now?* (see note 3), 3–24, on 17–19.

44. Perelman, "Can the Rights of Man Be Founded?" in *The Philosophy of Human Rights*, ed. Alan S. Rosenbaum (Westport, Conn.: Greenwood Press, 1980), 45–51, on pp. 45–46.

45. Ibid., 45–46.

46. See Hannah Arendt, *On Revolution* (New York: Viking Press, 1963), 83–94, and "What Is Freedom?" in *Between Past and Future*, 2d ed. (New York: Viking Press, 1968), 143–71, especially 152–53.

47. See Alasdair MacIntyre, *After Virtue*, 2d ed. (Notre Dame, Ind.: University of Notre Dame Press, 1984), 60–75 and 190–209.

48. Perelman, "Can the Rights of Man Be Founded?" 46.

49. See John S. Nelson, "Orwell's Political Myths and Ours," in *The Orwellian Moment*, ed. Robert L. Savage, James E. Combs, and Dan D. Nimmo (Fayetteville, Ark.: University of Arkansas Press, 1989); Nelson, "Destroying Political Theory in Order to Save It," in *Tradition, Interpretation, and Science*, ed. J. Nelson (Albany: State University of New York Press, 1986), 281–318, on 295–307.

50. See Edward Shils, *Tradition* (Chicago, University of Chicago Press, 1981), 12–33; Arendt, *On Revolution*, 201–4.

51. See John G. Gunnell, *Political Philosophy and Time* (Middletown, Conn.: Wesleyan University Press, 1968), especially 225–59.

52. See Giambattista Vico, *The New Science*, trans. Thomas Goddard Bergin and Max Harold Fisch (Ithaca, N.Y.: Cornell University Press, enlarged, revised, unabridged edition, 1976).

53. See Henry Tudor, *Political Myth* (New York: Praeger, 1972); Joseph Campbell, *The Hero with a Thousand Faces* (New York: World, 1949), and *Myths to Live By* (New York: Viking Press, 1972); Mircea Eliade, *Cosmos and History* (New York: Harper & Row, 1954), and *The Two and the One*, trans. J. M. Cohen (New York: Harper & Row, 1965); Claude Lévi-Strauss, *Introduction to a Science of Mythology*, vols. 1–3, trans. John and Doreen Weightman (New York: Harper & Row, 1969, 1973, 1978). Also see James Oliver Robertson, *American Myth, American Reality* (New York: Hill and Wang, 1980).

54. See Ronald Dworkin, A *Matter of Principle* (Cambridge: Harvard University Press, 1985).

55. See Harvey Wheeler, "Constitutionalism," in *Handbook of Political Science*, vol. 5, ed. Fred I. Greenstein and Nelson W. Polsby (Reading, Mass.: Addison-Wesley, 1975), 1–91.

56. Arendt, *On Revolution* (see note 46), 205.

57. Ibid. "it is futile to search for an absolute to break the vicious circle in which all beginning is inevitably caught, because this 'absolute' lies in the very act of beginning itself. In a way, this has always been known, though it was never fully articulated in conceptual thought for the simple reason that the beginning itself, prior to the era of revolution, has always been shrouded in mystery and remained an object of speculation."

58. See Robert L. Heilbroner, *An Inquiry into the Human Prospect* (New York: Norton, enlarged edition, 1975).

59. See Arendt, *On Revolution* (see note 46), 209: "Inherent in the Roman concept of foundation we find, strangely enough, the notion that not only all decisive political changes in the course of Roman history were reconstitutions, namely, reforms of the old institutions and the retrievance of the original act of foundation, but that even this first act had been already a re-establishment, as it were, a regeneration and a restoration. In the language of Virgil the foundation of Rome was the re-establishment of Troy; Rome actually was a second Troy. Even Machiavelli, partly because he was an Italian and partly because he was still close to Roman history, could believe that the new foundation of a purely secular realm of politics which he had in mind actually was nothing but the radical reform of 'the old institutions,' and even Milton, many years later, could still dream not of founding a new Rome, but of building 'Rome anew.'"

60. Ibid., 206.

61. Ibid., 205–6: "The foundation which now, for the first time, had occurred in broad daylight to be witnessed by all who were present had been, for thousands of years, the object of foundation legends in which imagination tried to reach out into a past and to an event which memory could not reach." Also see David Brin, *The Postman* (New York: Bantam Books, 1985); Barbara J. Hill and John S. Nelson, "Facing the Holocaust," in *Human Rights / Human Wrongs*, ed. Robert Hobbs and Fredrick Woodard (Seattle: University of Washington Press, 1986), 189–209, especially 204–7.

62. Arendt, *On Revolution*, 214.

63. See G. R. Boynton, "On Getting from Here to There," in *Strategies of Political Inquiry*, ed. Elinor Ostrom (Beverly Hills: Sage, 1982), 29–68 and

"Linking Problem Definition and Research Activities," in Missing Elements in Political Inquiry, ed. Judith A. Gillespie and Dina A. Zinnes (Beverly Hills: Sage, 1982), 43–60; William Panning, "What Does It Take to Have a Theory? Principles in Political Science," in *What Should Political Theory Be Now?* (see note 3), 479–511.

64. See John S. Nelson, "The Life Cycle of Paradigms," in *Tropes of Political Inquiry* (Madison: University of Wisconsin Press, forthcoming).

65. Arendt, *On Revolution*, 202–3.

66. Arendt, "What Is Authority?" in *Between Past and Future* (see note 46), 91–141.

67. Vico, *The New Science* (see note 52), 92. See Edward W. Said, *Beginnings* (New York: Basic Books, 1975).

68. See Charles J. Helm, "The Undisciplined 'Discipline': Searching for the Founders of Political Science," *Social Science Quarterly* 65(December 1984): 1112–18; John S. Nelson, "Discipline and Present: Argument and History in Academic Fields," in *Argument and Critical Practices* (see note 33), 549–55.

69. Here I transcribe and condense talk from a graduate seminar in 1987. This artful version appears with the permission of the participants.

70. See Raymond Seidelman and Edward J. Harpham, *Disenchanted Realists* (Albany: State University of New York Press, 1985), viii: "The APSA was founded toward the end of a decade of national interest group formation in the United States. It was the decade when all of the modern social science associations were formed. . . . [T]he organizing took place toward the end of the nineteenth century along with hosts of other newly organized groups in the ordinary sense of the term. Academic and otherwise, all this organizing activity was to a large extent a response to the nationalization of politics . . ."

71. Compare the accounts of John G. Gunnell, *Political Theory* (Chicago: University of Chicago Press, [1979] 1987; David M. Ricci, *The Tragedy of Political Science* (New Haven: Yale University Press, 1984).

72. See John C. Wahlke, "Pre-Behavioralism in Political Science," *American Political Science Review* 73(March 1979): 9–31.

73. See Seidelman and Harpham, *Disenchanted Realists* (see note 70), 7–8: "The conflicts of institutionalists and democrats have formed the fundamental contours of American political debate and the extent of its future flexibility. . . . The consistent claims and most persistent definitions of a new science of politics in America rest heavily on replacing these two traditions with a new public philosophy. Not just a method and organization of political studies, the American science of politics is also a kind of preventive medicine concocted for a sick polity. In place of the creaky and impersonal edifice of the

nineteenth-century State, political scientists have sought a national State manned by trained experts and supported by responsible and virtuous popular democratic majorities."

74. See John Angus Campbell, "Charles Darwin: Rhetorician of Science," in *The Rhetoric of the Human Sciences* (see note 2), 69–86; "Scientific Revolution and the Grammar of Culture: The Case of Darwin's *Origin*," Quarterly Journal of Speech 72(November 1986): 351–76.

PART THREE

Philosophical Probes and Reflections

11

The Checkmate of Rhetoric
(But Can Our Reasons Become Causes?)

Kenneth J. Gergen

Many share the belief that there is an intellectual revolution taking place in Western culture of broad and significant scope. Further, the present volume may properly be viewed as but a single manifestation of this revolution. For over a century the intellectual world (along with its many associated institutions) has been governed by a particular view of knowledge—its means of discovery and justification. It is also a view of knowledge with broad-ranging implications for the structure of society. Because knowledge is believed to be a chief source of survival, those who produce and possess it are furnished with positions of power and authority. At heart, the view of knowledge is empiricist. As it is held, there is a world independent of the observer; through systematic observation the observer may develop ideas (or propositions) about this world, and through subsequent deduction and observation, test these ideas against reality. With assiduous application of appropriate method, those propositions (or theories) most adequately serving to predict real-world events will survive. Those propositions come to constitute the body of knowledge. This form of knowledge production is often called *science*, and it is thus the scientist to whom authority in matters of knowledge is typically assigned. However, by applying proper rules of procedure, other disciplines as well can generate theoretical propositions that can accurately reflect or map the world, and thereby improve the quality and quantity of life.

Yet, within recent decades this view of knowledge has been steadily eroded. Voices from many disparate domains have begun to sound a strikingly similar chord. In one way or another they have begun to question the causal sequence at the heart of the empiricist account: that is, theory driven or determined by real-world properties. It is precisely this causal sequence that permits the conclusion that theories can accurately map reality and be used for purposes of prediction and control. However, as the irreverent chorus has begun to assemble, the causal sequence has been reversed: it is the process of theorizing that engenders what we take to be properties of the real world. Theories do not mirror reality; they are

293

products of human artifice which themselves generate a sense of the real and the unreal.

Early signals of the revolution appeared in the writings of Wittgenstein and others in the ordinary language tradition. All that may be said of the mental world, proposed Wittgenstein (1963), is already locked into the linguistic conventions of the culture. It is not reality that constrains our theories of the mental world, but linguistic convention. And, as philosophers from Austin (1962a, 1962b) and Ryle (1949) to Rorty (1979) have demonstrated, such language conventions lead us into asking misleading and ultimately fruitless questions concerning, for example, how reality comes to be represented in the mind. The revolutionary shift was also evident in writings on the history of science, where theorists such as Thomas Kuhn (1970) argued that revolutions in scientific theory are not driven by accretion in fact. Rather, they are fostered by Gestalt-like shifts in the perception of relevant facts. It is not the facts that drive theorists, but the perspectives of scientists that determine what counts as fact. Although Kuhn failed to make good on the radical implications of this early view (cf. Kuhn 1977), these implications have since been amplified in the work of Feyerabend and others on scientific revolution.

In the field of sociology, the emergence of labeling theory, ethnomethodology, and the sociology of knowledge have also played out the same theme. From the standpoint of labeling theory (Becker 1963) and ethnomethodology (Garfinkel 1967), what we take to be the facts of social deviance, suicide, and the like are not the results of such events in themselves; rather the existing forestructure of labels or methods for socially negotiating reality determine what counts as deviance, suicide, and the like. For sociologists of knowledge such as Barnes (1974) and Latour and Woolgar (1979) this has meant that the scientific laboratory becomes a focus of research interest; what are the social processes at play in the laboratory that produce what we take to be the realities of science?

Poststructuralist thought echoes such work in a different way. Structuralists such as Lévi-Strauss and Chomsky had argued that our means of defining reality are limited by internal dispositions or mental makeup. However, poststructuralist writings have generally externalized these limitations. That is, rather than mental limitations imposed upon language, linguistic limitations are forced upon the mind. These limitations in language are then traced to the social order. For example, Foucault (1966) proposes that our understandings of nature, social life, and knowledge at any point are limited by pervasive, culturally specific *epistemé*—or conditions of knowledge making. These conditions are

294

intimately connected with various forms of social practice—including power relations.

Contemporary literary and hermeneutic theory expands on these themes. Inquiry into what are called *reader effects* in literary study (Suleiman and Crosman 1980) has dominated much recent thinking. As theorists such as Stanley Fish (1980) have argued, what a text says is less the product of its own inherent properties than of the predispositions brought to the text by the reader. Theoretically, then, the same work is open to as many different interpretations as there are articulate readers. For literary thinkers in the deconstructionist mode, this line of thinking is carried to its extreme. As Derrida (1976), de Man (1979), and others propose, writing is not mimetic; it fails to describe a world independent of itself. Rather, critical or expository writing is governed by rules for its own construction; as it is said, writing is self-referring. In this way the supposed object of the writing is deconstructed. A similar theme is amplified by historiographers such as Louis Mink (1968) and Hayden White (1978). As they propose, the writing of history is largely governed by rules of narrative composition. It is thus the literary form that determines our sense of historical reality. Semiotic analysts expand on this perspective by documenting a variety of literary figures or tropes (metaphor, metonomy, etc.) that are employed to construct realistic writing (Brooke-Rose 1981). In effect, the sense of reality conveyed by a text (or research paper) is, in this case, the product not of reality itself but of an array of literary devices.

Constructionist analysts in both psychology and anthropology furnish additional insights as they explore the ways in which understandings of self, others, and world vary across time and culture. As it is proposed, how we think of the child's capacities, the adult's personality, the nature of emotion, the possibility of community, and so on are historically situated constructions with a certain functional value for societies at a given time (Gergen and Davis 1985). Similarly, in communication theory there has been a vital renaissance of interest in the works of Kenneth Burke (1969), Wayne Booth (1983) and others concerned with the use of rhetoric in generating intelligibility. Others have turned their attention increasingly to the ways in which meanings are negotiated or managed over time; reality in this mode is the result of relationship (Pearce and Cronen 1980).

And one must add to this array the works of various independent thinkers such as Nelson Goodman (1978), Norwood Hanson (1958), and Donald Spence (1982). In each of these cases the emphasis shifts from knowledge as representation of objects or events in themselves to knowledge as human artifact.

In large measure we can understand the emergence of the present volume as the result of the progressive realization that across our several disciplines we are participating in a similar dialogue, and sense that this dialogue is at the cutting edge of intellectual and social change. Of special importance, there is the emerging consciousness that we are in the process of performing an intellectual checkmate. In the game of competing ideas this reversal in causal sequence is a form of master stroke. It has been the major preoccupation of most scientific (if not academic) disciplines over the past century to develop, engender, and proclaim knowledge. Yet, from the confluence of arguments just outlined, the warrant for such proclamations of knowledge is fully jeopardized. These bodies of so-called knowledge are not mirrors or maps of an independent reality, as we see, but the result of social negotiation, rules of procedure, literary tropes, rhetorical strategems, and the like. The sciences (and related disciplines) are thus robbed of their capacity to claim truth or knowledge; the world to which they refer is deconstructed, and they are left with only a thin veil of rhetorical justification. Further, as the established institutions come tumbling one upon the other, who steps forward from the debris to proclaim the final victory but the band of literary theorists, sociologists of knowledge, rhetoricians, constructionists, and the like, who have reversed the causal arrow. For it is this assemblage that has seen through the humbug, broken through the ontological sham, and dared to pull the rug from under truth and knowledge. And it is this group that understands the craft of knowledge making—of constructing compelling realities.

Yet, before preparing for the impending celebration of victory, significant pause is required. For if we play out the scenario into the future, what can we anticipate? Are our well-reasoned attacks sufficient grounds for establishing and sustaining a cause—a new brand of intellectual inquiry to guide us into the next century? It is my considered opinion that we are *not* now positioned for such ascendence. We are rapidly developing a powerful arsenal of sophisticated critical skills. However, these skills alone will not suffice for a sustained and significant movement. There are arduous conceptual challenges ahead, and if our present work is to alter significantly the course of intellectual history we must considerably broaden our concerns. We must foster the development of new forms of discourse—new intelligibilities, justifications, and options for practice. My chief concerns are as follows:

296

1. *The Reconstruction of Reference*

At the outset, the rhetorically oriented analyst confronts the age-old attack on relativism. For, when extended, rhetorical analysis does move vigorously in this direction. The sciences do not give us truth, it is announced, so much as artifically contrived constructions. Such constructions could be otherwise, and there is no means of ruling between competing constructions by reference to empirical fact. However, the foundationalist properly responds, in what sense can a relativist account of scientific truth be credited when it purports itself to be furnishing a true account of science? By what standard is it making such judgments? If all is relative, then relativist critiques must also suffer the same fate. There is at least one counter-critique that may be posed by the rhetorical analyst that furnishes a useful prelude to what follows. This counter-critique suggests that the very grounds of the foundationalist defense presume a standard of truth. That is, the attack on relativism is only effective if it is assumed that the relativist is attempting to furnish a true account of science. If this is not the attempt of the relativist quo rhetorician, to tell the truth, then the attack is without consequence. And why should truth be the point of rhetorical analysis? The concept of truth, as commonly employed during the present century (e.g., correspondence with fact), is already saturated with empiricist foundationalism. Thus, it may be ventured, the point of such analysis is not to be truthful (or untruthful), as this very concept presupposes the very structure that is under attack. Rather, the point is to invite readers into linguistic space that, once understood, enables them to transcend the ontology into which they were previously locked.

But let us consider an important variant on the traditional antirelativist rebuttal, one of considerably greater consequence. In this case, rhetorical analysts are vulnerable to the criticism that they have no subject matter. On the rhetorician's account the subject matter of the accepted science has no object. Accounts of object are reduced to the rhetorical forestructure. Yet, if the object of knowledge in the established disciplines is deconstructed, on what grounds is one then to claim that rhetorical analysis itself possesses an object? By the rhetorician's own account, aren't such accounts themselves rhetorical exercises without objects? How is it that traditional disciplines have no object while the rhetorician does? This is no small question, for until an answer can be provided the force of the rhetorical argument is severely blunted. Further, while the established sciences can send rockets to the moon, discover oil, or predict the birth rate, the rhetorician is left with only her inscriptions. And in the long run, the rhetoric of technological advance will surely outweigh the force of words.

One major means of defending against the rebuttal would be to develop a new theory of reference. It is insufficient in this case to demonstrate that words are not mimetic devices; required is a positive statement that would enable us to understand why it has been so captivating to believe that they are. Further, such an explanation should not simultaneously discredit our own enterprise. For example, we must first be able to give an account as to why a rocket engineer's statement that a space shuttle will or will not reach orbit is not merely poetics; such words can be cashed out in ways that make more than an aesthetic difference in human life. The same is true of the doctor's diagnosis of cancer, the directions on one's medicine bottle, and storm warnings issued to small craft. Such verbalizations may not be mirrors or maps, but at the same time, they cannot be reduced entirely to linguistic convention.

I am ill equipped to provide a fully developed alternative to existing theories of reference. I view the essentialist programs of Kripke (1980) and Putnam (1978) as reactionary and regressive in this case, serving as they do to derive the essence of reality from language conventions. However their concern with the utility of language in facilitating action does suggest that linguistic pragmatics may be the most promising avenue for solving the rhetorician's problem. That is, rather then viewing language usage as governed only by the rules of the language games themselves, we may view them as embedded within more extended patterns of action ("life forms" in Wittgenstein's sense). As these broader patterns emerge and are stabilized in a culture (or subculture), linguistic integers become anticipatory signals within the more extended conventions. Thus, words become devices enabling these more elaborated patterns of action to be completed successfully.

To illustrate, in the case of language, if I say, "John hit . . . ," you may justifiably anticipate the appearance of a third term, an object as it were, ("the ball," "the attacker," etc.), to follow subject and verb. Yet, in the more extended case, if I announce that the space shuttle "will fly successfully" this utterance has pragmatic implications for what happens when NASA officials do things that we call "give orders" and engineers engage in what we call "launching the rocket." If we take this pragmatic orientation, we are able to retain the position that theories of the world are not ontological guides or maps; the sciences (and related disciplines) do not give us "true" pictures of reality. The problem is that when the pragmatic integers of language prove useful within what is viewed as successful sequence (e.g., launching a rocket, creating a powerful book, curing disease), they are granted mysterious powers. They are imbued with the sanctity of "truth."

A pragmatic perspective would also enable us to say that the words of scientists, and our own words, can and do have important pragmatic effects. It allows us to perform demonstrations of the pragmatic utility of various rhetorical strategies while at the same time not proclaiming the truth of such theoretical accounts. It is not that our own accounts map reality, then, but that they become a means of altering the use of language and the various practical sequences of which they are a part. To explore the components of narrative form, for example, is to enable historians, developmental psychologists, and diachronic linguists to develop more intelligible and compelling theoretical accounts. With insightful theories of metaphor, the scientist is better equipped to break theoretical traditions and open new vistas of research.

2. A Reconstruction of Knowledge

Embodied in the traditional empiricist account of knowledge is the assumption that knowledge is essentially propositional. Theoretical descriptions and explanations serve to store information about the real world and enable deductions about new situations. Thus one's capacities for prediction and control are increased. Yet, from the standpoint of the "rhetorical revolution," this orientation is seriously misleading. Not only do theories fail to store information, but we must view the process of deduction itself as a form of rhetorical strategy. At the same time, when confronting the vast technological advances of the past century alone, such critiques seem pallid. If the harnessing of electrical energy, the development of innoculations against illness, the emergence of nuclear power, and the like are not derived from propositional networks, then how are we to account for them? In effect, to make good on the rhetorical analysis, a positive account must be furnished of what has heretofore been viewed as knowledge.

There are several directions one might wish to pursue in this case. However, it will prove most useful if we return to the preceding sketch of the pragmatic orientation as a reference point. Here we viewed propositions about the world not as mirrors, but as active constituents of broader patterns of relationships among persons and between people and the world. From this standpoint, such propositions are not expressions of psychological dispositions or reflections of representational systems within the mind. Knowledge cannot properly be viewed as "in the mind." Rather, such propositions are integral to the practical activities of persons attempting to coordinate themselves with each other and with the world in which they live. In some cases propositions may play little role in such coordination. The highly sophisticated skill of the ceramic artist seems to depend very little on the availability of verbal articulation; similarly, complex accomplishments can be achieved by skiers, modern dancers, and basketball teams with little reliance on words. In other cases, however, words may play a vital role in such coordination. Various biographical accounts suggest that shared symbol systems within the scientific community were possibly essential to the development of the atom bomb and the construction of DNA. In neither of these cases, however, need one view the shared system of symbols (the theories) as "holders" or "containers" of knowledge. They are esentially devices for communal coordination.

From this standpoint, knowledge is not a static, decontextualized "knowing that," but the active participation in unfolding patterns of relatedness—of which language is but a part. If I move my hand in a certain way this motion remains nonsense until others respond by treating it as a signal (such as "beckoning," "warning," or "waving"). It is the coordination of our actions that produces the meaningfulness of what I am doing or saying. The same may ultimately be said of what we term advances in the natural sciences. It is the mutual coordination of material, scientific activity, and social assent that yields what we call scientific advance (Gergen 1988 presents a more detailed account of this process). Improved capacities for production are essentially the result not of a theory but of coordinated action. From the point of view of social pragmatics, what we call knowledge derives from forms of relatedness.

3. A Reconstruction of Human Communication

From the traditional standpoint, language is said to be largely a product of our mental representations. It contains the results of our observations and rational deliberations—both assumed to be mental processes. Speaking (or writing) is thus not important in itself (as such activities would only be a collection of assorted sounds or markings); it is the mental state (meanings) of the speaker or writer that is ultimately of interest. In effect, the process of reading or listening is traditionally viewed as one in which we attempt to ascertain the underlying intentions of another. On this account, communication is a form of intersubjectivity. Again, however, we find that from the perspective of the rhetorical revolution this view of communication proves deeply problematic. As we have already seen, deconstructionist analysis suggests that reading and interpreting can adequately proceed without any insight into or comprehension of the author's intentional state. From the deconstructionist standpoint, the act of reading obliterates the author's intentions. The process of decoding a communication is, in effect, an encoding. As we also discussed, the concept of knowledge need not require an assumption of mental representation. Words may be adequately viewed as constituents of relationships, as pragmatic devices, or *illocutionary implements* in Austin's (1962b) terms. They have operational currency without one's inquiring into the actor's state of mind. And we have also seen that from a Wittgensteinian standpoint, all that may be said about the mind is embedded within the existing language conventions of the culture. Observation, then, places no constraints on our use of mental predicates; or, to place the Wittgensteinian formulation in modern context, the construction of the mind is guided principally by rhetorical convention.

Thus, we find that when various strands of argument within the rhetorical revolution are extended, the traditional ontology of mental events is severely threatened. And if the mind is deconstructed, then the traditional view of communication as intersubjective connection ceases to be compelling. This latter position is indeed a challenging one, but until the challenge incites the creative energies of the rhetorical theorist, it also places the movement in a vulnerable position. For, as it may be argued, what the rhetorical revolution succeeds in doing is nothing less than concluding that communication is impossible. And, because it is palpably clear that people do indeed communicate, mustn't the assumptions underlying the rhetorical critique be misleading? If a series of premises leads to a conclusion that is wholly untenable, the premises must be at fault.

The most powerful antidote to such counter-critique is again a positive account of how communication does take place. I do believe that those theorists arguing for the continuous management and negotiation of meaning in relationships are beginning to open the right door (cf. Pearce and Cronen 1980; Mishler 1986). And it seems appropriate to shift the focus to systems of relationship as opposed to the traditional focus on the individual (as communicator or recipient of messages). If such work can be expunged of residual psychologisms, it also proves congenial with many of the preceding suggestions regarding reference and knowledge. Let us consider briefly the contours of a theory of communication as coordinated action. In particular, let us consider the case of emotion. We have traditionally viewed the emotions as mental events, and our emotional predicates (e.g., "I feel happy," "I am depressed," "You make me angry") as vehicles for expressing these internal states. However, as the present analysis suggests, these terms are not maps of an internal region; my knowledge

301

of you cannot be reduced to propositions about your mental condition. And when you state the way you feel, I am not trying to draw inferences from the surface to yet another level of reality inside your head. Rather, emotion terms may be viewed as components in a more elaborated dance of meaning of which at least the two of us are a part.

In our own inquiry on this topic we have asked persons how they would respond to various expressions of emotion (Gergen and Gergen, 1988). In this case we rapidly discern that there are important cultural constraints on one's replies to such expressions. For example, if a friend tells you that he is depressed, there are only a handful of conversational moves that will allow you to "make sense" by contemporary cultural standards. And if we then ask additional research participants (now playing the part of the depressed person) how they would respond to these various reactions, we find again that there are only a small number of meaningful actions possible. If this research procedure is followed out, we find that emotional expressions form parts of elaborate scenarios (or *relational narratives* as we have called them). They are constituent parts of lived stories, as it were, that require at least two participants to complete. As it happens, completion is typically the "happy ending" of the Aristotelian romance. In effect, emotion terms are embedded within relational forms. Love, anger, sadness, and the like are parts of cultural performances coordinated by two or more actors. Emotional expressions do not depend on coordinating one's actions with an internal event, but with cultural patterns of meaningful action. In this sense emotion is a possession of relationships, not individuals.

4. The Restoration of the Concept of Progress

As we have seen, the rhetorical turn acts so as to undermine established authority. The proclaimer of objective knowledge is brought low. Yet, to follow the lines of the preceding analysis, we cannot play the part of spoiler unless others are willing to serve as foils. In effect, the position we now find ourselves in is essentially parasitic. If all those who now lay claim to objectivity were to abandon the pursuit in favor of rhetorical analysis, such activity would be indeed short-lived. As many believe, this is precisely the position that deconstructionist literary theory has reached. Like solipsism, it is a supportable position; however, once you have laid claim to this position, productive dialogue is at an end. Once we have moved to the checkmate of rhetoric, the game is finished. Or to use Carse's (1986) terms, we have succeeded in developing a *finite game* of words that forecloses on the myriad possibilities inhering in an *infinite game*, in which

302

words are secondary to being. How is such an abortive end to be avoided? Two forms of argument seem required in this case.

Most essential for the continued viability of the rhetorical movement is a revitalized conception of progress in inquiry. Such a conception might properly include the process of critique; however, the problem is not solved until the account can include a broader range of activity. Elsewhere (Gergen 1985) I have attempted to sketch a possible theory of paradigm shifts congenial to the rhetorical turn. Within this formulation, the paradigm is viewed as a system of intelligibility serving to justify and coordinate a range of practices—both interpersonal and between person and environment. Thus, for example, in the sciences the system of intelligibility is typically composed of four bodies of interdependent discourse: A *metatheoretical* discourse that furnishes a conception of knowledge and its attainment, a *theoretical* discourse that ostensibly informs one of the nature of the world, a *methodological* discourse that serves to justify a set of practices in keeping with assumptions made at the metatheoretical and theoretical levels, and an *evaluative* discourse that provides normative sanction for the practice as a whole.

To the extent that any given paradigm gains adherents to its discursive procedures and related practices, it may be said to generate enclaves of power. That is, the reigning system of intelligibility promotes certain patterns of organized social action and at the same time forbids or discourages a range of competitors. In effect, each paradigm operates simultaneously as a productive and repressive force. As a result of continued exposure to various paradigmatic pursuits, participants within Western culture have developed a series of discursive maneuvers enabling the blocking or subverting of existing commitments. These *conventions of negation*, as they may be called, take a variety of forms. These include replacing positive statements with their negations (what *is*, by dint of the existing paradigm, is said to be nonexistent), with their opposites (what *is*, in terms of the prevailing paradigm, is said to be its opposite) or with alternatives (what *is*, is actually something other). Thus, to state what is the case in terms of any given paradigm operates much as an invitation to a dance in which other interlocutors may select among various conventions of negation.

We may speak of this initial phase of negation as the *critical phase* of the paradigm shift. It is a phase that is, in fact, manifested in much of the rhetorical critique composing the present volume. That is, a rhetorical analyst who unmasks the devices employed by various scientists to create a "sense of the real" is effectively negating the scientists' invitation to the reader to join them within the folds of a given paradigm. The same argument can be made in the case of deconstructionist renderings, along with analyses of the critical school in the social sciences, and feminists' undermining of andro-centered theory within both the social and natural sciences. All cast severe doubt over the ontologies established by existing orders.

Yet, in the case of paradigm transformation this critical phase must be viewed as an essential preliminary. It is preparatory for a second phase that may be termed *generative*. In this phase the discursive implications of the critique are progressively elaborated. As this elaboration begins to establish an alternative ontology (theoretical, metatheoretical, methodological and evaluative) with associated practices, it may begin to serve as an alternative basis of social power. To illustrate, much of the early feminist writing challenged the male construction of gender differences within the sciences. As it pointed out, these theoretical constructions discredit the female in a variety of ways and thus seem to act as justifications for continued male dominance. Yet, as such critiques expanded, it also became clear not only that the scientific findings were questionable, but the very conception of science (metatheory) along with the experimental procedures (methodology) were saturated with masculine ideology (Keller, 1985). As these criticisms have been expanded and elaborated, it has also become clear that they contain the seeds for alternative conceptualizations. We are now witnessing the results of this elaboration in what are termed "feminist standpoint epistemologies" (Harding 1986) and a variety of explorations into intrinsically feminist methodology (Roberts 1981; Reinharz 1985). These latter pursuits are beginning to establish alternative discourse systems on both the metatheoretical and methodological levels. As these discursive ventures become progressively embedded in new social and scientific practices, it may properly be said that feminists are bringing about a genuine transforation in paradigms.

Yet, it may be asked, in what sense is such a transformation progress? Isn't this process simply one of transferring one set of conceptual blinders and comcomitant power relations to another? The answer would appear negative on two important grounds. First, in the case of traditional scientific pursuits of prediction and control, paradigm shifts of the kind envisioned here should be an asset. If various forms of discourse (particularly theoretical) are embedded within patterns of action (including those of predicting events in nature), then the emergence of new paradigms opens new arenas of prediction. For example, in the case of the feminist shift, researchers now attend to gender differences in rates of mental illness, treatment outcomes, patterns of therapist behavior, and so on. With each new ontology, new "events" are created and rendered subject to predictive excursions. This is not simultaneously to pay homage to the traditional empiricist model of science. The process of developing technologies of prediction is not the sole possession of empirical science. Prediction is a process intrinsic to virtually all human pursuits. Further, the rhetorical revolution succeeds in breaking the semantic link between the discourse employed within the process of prediction and its outcomes. The ability to predict successfully in no way improves on the ontological validity of the discourse employed within the process.

However, there is an additional way in which paradigm shifts of the present sort can enhance the human condition. In particular, if various forms of discourse are viewed as practical devices, in accordance with the preceding discussions of reference and communication, then transformations in paradigms serve to increase the range of practical implements available to the culture. With each new paradigm the symbolic resources available for carrying out daily relations are enhanced. New ways of solving old problems may be generated, new alternatives for action engendered, and new forms of human expression made possible. To illustrate with the feminist case once again, in challenging the traditional sex-role distinctions, feminists have succeeded in challenging the concept of gender and weakening the demands of existing practice. The masculine-feminine distinction is no longer viewed as a dichotomy, and traditional traits collected around the antipodes of the distinction need not be considered dependent on genital construction. Men and women may thus be freed from the regimented expectations of traditional culture, are invited to explore new possibilities for human relatedness, and are offered a discourse for justifying their new forms of expression.

In summary, we have reached a point in the present century in which all that has passed for knowledge in Western culture is rendered suspect. The rhetorical analyst is deeply engaged in fashioning increasingly sophisticated weapons for engendering the downfall of established knowledge. However, if this venture is to be the vanguard of an intellectual revolution of sweeping proportion—and not merely a temporary fashion—positive programs must be forthcoming. Such programs will include an elaborated metatheory, alternative theories of human action, new products of inquiry, and a revivified vocabulary of human understanding. As we have also seen, there is ample reason for optimism in each of these cases. Whether we can succeed in such ventures may depend on our ability to move from the critical phase of rhetorical analysis to a more generative era in which the implications of such analysis are more fully elaborated and examined.

REFERENCES

Austin, J. L. 1962a. *Sense and Sensibilia.* London: Oxford University Press.
———. 1962b. *How To Do Things with Words.* Cambridge: Harvard University Press.
Barnes, B. 1974. *Scientific Knowledge and Sociological Theory.* London: Routledge and Kegan Paul.
Becker, H. S. 1963. *Outsiders.* New York: Free Press.
Booth, W. 1983. *The Rhetoric of Fiction.* 2d ed. Chicago: University of Chicago Press.
Brooke-Rose, C. 1981. *A Rhetoric of the Unreal.* Cambridge: Cambridge University Press.
Burke, K. 1969. *A Grammar of Motives.* Berkeley: University of California Press.
Carse, J. 1986. Finite and Infinite Games. New York: Macmillan.
de Man, P. 1979. "Shelley Disfigured," in *Deconstruction and criticism,* ed. H. Bloom, P. de Man, J. Derrida, G. Hartman, and J. H. Miller. New York: Continuum.
Derrida, J. 1976. *Of Grammatology.* Baltimore: Johns Hopkins University Press.
Feyerabend, P. H. 1976. *Against Method.* New York: Humanities Press.
Fish, S. 1980. *Is There a Text in This Class? The Authority of Interpretive Communities.* Cambridge: Harvard University Press.
Foucault, M. 1966. *Les mots et les choses.* Paris: Gallimard.
Garfinkel, H. 1967. *Studies in Ethnomethodology.* Englewood Cliffs, N.J.: Prentice Hall.
Gergen, K. J. 1985. "Psychological Inquiry in an Age of Social Epistemology." Paper presented at the Boston Symposium in the Philosophy of Science.
Gergen, K. J. 1988. "The Concept of Progress in Psychological Theory," in *Recent Trends in Theoretical Psychology,* ed. W. Baker, L. Mos, H. Rappard, and H. Stam. New York: Springer-Verlag.
Gergen, K. J., and K. E. Davis, eds. 1985. *The Social Construction of the Person.* New York: Springer-Verlag.
Gergen, K. J., and M. M. Gergen. 1988. "Narratives and the Self as Relationship," in *Advances in Experimental Social Psychology,* ed. L. Berkowitz New York: Academic Press.
Goodman, N. 1978. *Ways of Worldmaking.* New York: Hackett.
Hanson, N. 1958. *Patterns of Discovery.* London: Cambridge University Press.
Harding, S. 1986. *The Science Question in Feminism.* Ithaca, N.Y.: Cornell University Press.
Hubbard, R. 1979. "Have Only Men Evolved?" in *Biological Woman: The*

Convergence Myth, ed. R. Hubbard, M. Henifin, and B. Fried. Cambridge, Mass.: Scheniman.

Keller, E. F. 1985. *Reflections in Gender and Science*. New Haven: Yale University Press.

Kripke, S. 1980. *Semantics of Natural Language*. Cambridge: Harvard University Press.

Kuhn, T. 1970. *The Structure of Scientific Revolutions*. 2d revised ed. Chicago: University of Chicago Press.

————. 1977. *The Essential Tension*. Chicago: University of Chicago Press.

Latour, B., and S. Woolgar. 1979. *Laboratory Life, the Social Construction of Scientific Facts*. Beverly Hills: Sage.

Mink, L. D. 1968. "Philosophical Analysis and Historical Understanding." *Review of Metaphysics* 21:667–92.

Mishler, E. G. 1986. *Research Interviewing: Context and Narrative*. Cambridge: Harvard University Press.

Pearce, W. B., and V. E. Cronen. 1980. *Communication, Action, and Meaning*. New York: Praeger.

Putnam, H. 1978. *Meaning and the Moral Sciences*. Boston: Routledge and Kegan Paul.

Reinharz, B. 1985. "Feminist Distrust: Problems of Context and Content in Sociological Work," in *Exploring Clinical Methods for Social Research*, ed. D. Porg and K. Smith. Beverly Hills: Sage.

Roberts, H. 1981. *Doing Feminist Research*. London: Routledge and Kegan Paul.

Rorty, R. 1979. *Philosophy and the Mirror of Nature*. Princeton, N.J.: Princeton University Press.

Ryle, G. 1949. *The Concept of Mind*. London: Hutchinson.

Spence, D. 1982. *Narrative Truth and Historical Truth*. New York: W. W. Norton.

Suleiman, S. R., and I. Crosman. 1980. *The Reader in the Text*. Princeton, N.J.: Princeton University Press.

White, H. 1978. *Tropics of Discourse*. Baltimore: Johns Hopkins University Press.

Wittgenstein, L. 1963. *Philosophical Investigations*. Trans. G. Anscombe. New York: Macmillan.

12

Reconciling Realism and Relativism

Joseph Margolis

When very large questions are posed that have been posed and reposed through the ages, questions that threaten to lose their nagging edge through fatigue and familiarity, questions we cannot entirely set aside without setting ourselves aside, we are inclined to settle for small clues, small suggestions, new ways of entering old disputes. What after all is human science? we ask. What can we legitimately claim to know of reality? What is our cognitive place in the world? How should we live, granting the natural context in which we do live and exercise our powers of survival? These are tired questions at best but also inescapable ones. In posing them one hardly waits for an answer. We want to know, rather, what particularly penetrating instruction may now be offered about how such questions should be taken or addressed, what conditions may have been overlooked (or may have gradually come to focus in our own time) that might orient us compellingly, without yet providing full answers.

A certain convenience declares our questions to be second-order questions, and so they are, except that they and their answers cannot fail to have first-order implications: the quality of human life depends on human theories of the quality of human life, particularly those reflexively concerned with what we are able to know—or able to do in virtue of what we are able to know. And the clues we tend to favor center in quite a subtle way on worrying how to adjust provisionally standard ways of addressing such questions.

The role of rhetoric, we may hazard, will supply the right sort of clue. And so it may, if only we remember that it has its own captive history, and therefore can serve our purpose only if it is forcibly disentangled enough to permit us to redraw the entire network of conceptual and practical relations within which the first- and second-order questions at stake have been effectively stalemated.

The clue, then, is this: distinguish carefully between *argument* and *argument form*. Do that, and you will see that the practice of argument need not be—or is not best construed as being—the application of antecedent argument forms within real-world encounters, and that, therefore, argument and rhetoric are not rightly opposed, as in the usual contrasts with the usual derogatory intent. The charm of our clue lies entirely in watching how it affects our reception of the large questions with which we began, as we move it from uncertain shadow to center stage. Because such a change of clue catches up, here and now—not in another age with its own experience—an incipient but quite particular tolerance for reordering the ingredients of our picture of our world and of our place in it. *Rhetoric* signifies the apt meshing of such an exercise with the saliencies of our own acknowledged world; and *argument* signifies any dialogue within the space thereby marked off or confirmed that yields findings, judgments, commitments, or the like esteemed as reasonable or similarly compelling to rational review. Once our clue is placed within the theoretical setting of our own time—with its strong emphasis on the profoundly historicized nature of human existence, with its repudiation of every form of cognitive transparency and foundational certitude, with its denial of a disjunction between theory and practice, with its drift toward holism, and with its insistence on the impact of the survival of the species (obviously through its cognitive capacities)—then, at once, realism is inescapable, however problematic. Then nonconverging realist interpretations of our science and effective practice cannot fail to proliferate; and with respect to both science and practical life, if all our reliance on at least a moderate relativism cannot be denied out of hand, then if our original clue can show this, we should have accomplished a great deal with very little. Also, in redrawing the world, so to say, we should have redrawn the distinction between argument and rhetoric as well.

This naive beginning is quite convenient: it affords a ready way of penetrating quickly enough to the essential questions without disturbing, more than is really needed for the moment, our conceptual expectations. But how radical the clue's effect may actually be is not a function merely of how we first enter the field but also of what we suppose we find there. Reinscribing, restructuring, revalorizing—to draw some of the fire of the more fashionable and threatening idioms—is hardly arbitrary; it actually implicates the still-intelligible structures of whatever our ongoing tradition has habituated itself to as its own enclosing world. In doing that, we find ourselves forced to acknowledge an essential economy—which is to say, more brusquely, that we are spared at a stroke a number of the more disingenuous incoherencies of the moment.

Distinguish, then, between internalist and externalist questions. By an *internalist* question, understand a first- or second-order question (that is, a question about the world as cognized or about what we theorize is our capacity thus to have knowledge of the world), formulated in accord with a conceptual system or network that we cannot in principle elude, so as to mount a privileged review of how *that* network actually fits an independent world. And by an *externalist* question, understand a question, meant to be more radical than—in fact, meant to be incommensurable with—mere second-order questions, formulated so as to worry the very legitimacy of *any* internalist enterprise as such. Distinguish further between *internal* and *external* questions within an internalist idiom, simply by treating internal questions as first-order questions and external questions as second-order questions of the legitimating kind. Under the conditions given, the distinction between internal and external will itself prove to be a second-order, or external, question, and the distinction between internalist and externalist questions will always be managed by the use of an internalist idiom aporetically applied—that is, reflexively posed to pose a would-be challenge to its own legitimacy by the use of the very idiom under fire.

This of course is the key puzzle of the entire Nietzschean tradition, ranging from Nietzsche himself, through Heidegger, through Foucault, through Derrida at least. It is the key puzzle of what is usually marked as perspectivism (in Nietzsche), *de-struktion* (in Heidegger), genealogy (in Foucault), and deconstruction (in Derrida). Call all such doctrines *externalist* versions of *relativism:* in the sense that, on the thesis—for example, Nietzsche's regarding the essential deception that *is* language, or Foucault's regarding the normalization of the forms of thought—we admit that the most comprehensive conceptual schemes we can imagine are all partial, fragmented, contingent, historically bounded, ultimately blind, and radically ungrounded, *suspected* (from within) of being the chance internalist idiom we possess. Externalism, therefore, is a kind of self-subversive internalism, and internalism is a kind of self-assuring externalism; and the distinctions between the internal and the external, the internalist and the externalist, are invariably and necessarily heuristic and symbiotic—which is to say, benign.

Nevertheless, they are most important distinctions. What they confirm is that there is no coherent way to relate doctrines that are frankly internalist *and* externalist in any dialectically shared debate about the cognitive status, or credentials, or ultimate legitimacy, *of any internalist claims taken distributively.* Wherever admitted, externalist inquiries function only holistically and only allusively, that is, to cast doubt on or to "situate" any would-be totalized idiom. Their message is always and simply that there are no such idioms. They cannot descend to particular quarrels, for in doing that they become expressly internalist in function. This is why the entire Nietzschean tradition, for all its exuberance and remarkable gymnastic skill, rests on the sole force of the single theme that every conceptual scheme floats in an indeterminable way within reality—that no conceptual scheme is, in principle, ever capable of being shown to link up determinately and distributively with the actual structure of the world it pretends to represent (and thereby successfully "deceives" us into accepting). Consequently, *mixing* distributed internalist questions with piecemeal externalist worries is essentially incoherent. Externalist versions of relativism are, therefore, ultimately boring though important (witness Heidegger and Derrida) or, where inappropriately mingled, self-defeating and quite incoherent (witness Foucault and Nelson Goodman, who comes as close to the Foucauldian theme as any American constructivist can).

Broadly speaking, then, an externalist challenge is a challenge made *en bloc*, holistically, globally, without qualification, and in such a way that it makes no sense to consider it distributively, that is, for each and every particular cognitive claim. In this, it *appears* to resemble the pragmatist (or internalist) vindication of science—which is also holistic and incapable of descending to particular claims. But the externalist challenge focuses only on the surd of every ramified inquiry, in the sense that there can be no ultimate *cognitive* entry assuring the match of world and word in *any* way; whereas the internalist challenge focuses only on the critical, the *cognitive*, scruples with which an *admitted* first-order science may have to be disciplined or qualified or restricted (legitimated) in second-order terms. Externalist charges are aporetic if they are taken discursively, since they undermine their own intervention; but they may well be no more than insinuations or doubts implicated in any achieved science. Internalist charges are entirely sanguine about science; but *they* must bridge the difference between a pragmatist (a holist and *non*cognitivist) vindication of the realism of science (the mere viability of the race that depends on science) and a distributed and critical assessment of the particular claims of science (that the history of science makes salient and that cannot be derived from externalist sources). Both may be understood as generating, or constituting, a distinctive rhetoric. One worries the condition (that cannot be specified) on which the very possibility of intelligence depends; the other worries the condition (that may be reflexively posited) on which intelligence actually takes itself to proceed—with, of course, its characteristic success. The first is Nietzschean and the second is pragmatist.

What, suitably ramified, the relevant argument would show is that there are no viable relativisms that are not internalist in orientation. There may be no viable relativisms at all; but there surely are none that are viable in the sense in which an externalist doctrine might pretend to be. The limited use of externalist doubts is very much like the limited use of skepticism: one can't apply skepticism selectively with regard to the detailed inquiries of sciences; one can only challenge science thus *en bloc*. The upshot of a strong Nietzschean theme, then, is to lay the ground for indefinitely many competing conceptual networks—hence, to prepare us at least for an ineliminable relativism. To describe Nietzscheanism itself as a radical relativism is, therefore, to disallow any "linear" comparison with whatever relativisms the practices of science and ordinary life might actually support. Furthermore, any sympathy for a Nietzschean counsel confirms the impossibility of defending a strong disjunction between rhetoric and argument; for whatever may be the argument forms we install as the forms of rational dispute, those forms must be abstracted from within an internalist world and must be made to function effectively only by the use of the linguistic distinctions we spontaneously apply within that internalist world.

This is perhaps a heavyhanded way of stating the obvious. Imagine that we dispute the admirable thrift of some small businessman. You call into doubt my characterization, *citing* other possible interpretations of his behavior: you cannot then be a skeptic about just that particular claim; to contest it is to encumber your own account with *its* eligibility among its alternative fellows. Or suppose you call into question the aptness or fittingness of that and all related characterizations within the set normally admitted to apply, *inventing* supplementary distinctions that change the effective weight of what we would otherwise have first applied, or *citing* or *improvising* alternative conceptual schemata to be preferred in dealing with the apparent case in hand: you cannot then disallow that particular network of distinctions; to formulate the pertinent contrast is just to encumber your own account with the problem of systematic choice between *such* options. And yet, both skepticism and the Nietzschean form of subversion remain permanent, ever-present challenges *interior* to the smooth functioning of every investigative idiom.

Their force lies elsewhere: in debunking every form of conceptual and cognitive fixity, every dream of totalized system, every presumption of universal scope or ultimate correctness of categories. But that is to say they never effectively do subvert, disorganize, disallow, disable, or dismember the *smooth* continuity of our discursive or discursible encounters with the things of the world. On the contrary, they parasitically depend on that very functioning in order to make their message felt. There's the double sense in which the Nietzschean theme—which after all is very nearly the most prominent in all of Western theorizing nowadays—*prepares* us for the onset of relativism, without really being a relativism of its own in any sense pertinent to the assessment of particular truth claims, and *invites* us to consider clues easily collected and focused by the distinction earlier proposed between argument and argument form. The upshot is that, under these constraints, *realism and relativism must be compatible*; also, *favoring a relativist account of realism entails construing argument itself as a (or any) rationally focused use of rhetoric.*

How's that? someone will ask.

On the side of realism, one consideration is decisive. If we abandon every theory that holds the real world to be cognitively transparent to our investigations—distributively transparent—then the following must hold: first, realism itself can only be made plausible in terms of the effective survival of the human species, because that survival, in any viable view, involves man's epistemic capacities, his epistemically pertinent development within, and his involvement with the world, whatever that may be; secondly, concession itself accommodates the Nietzschean theme, since it claims no cognitive privilege for distributed claims; and thirdly, such a realism is entirely and merely holistic. It is also a minimal realism, in the sense that a ramified science could hardly be legitimated solely in its terms, and no effort at such legitimation could, in that regard, fail to admit the continuity between the detailed procedures of an effective science and the practices of a surviving society that practiced such a science. The union of these and similar doctrines is what, contemporaneously, has come to be recognized as *Pragmatism*. So, on the realist side of the question, pragmatism seems ineluctable in general, insufficient (as formulated) for the distributed claims of science, and therefore hospitable once again to a relativist reading of a distributive realism—that is, to a reading, say, that explored whether the entities of high-level physics were real or not, or whether Freudian or Marxist or Weberian or similar interpretive and explanatory schemes within the human sciences had actually captured the real structures of human existence or not.

Minimal realism, therefore, is easy to vindicate, but it is hardly interesting in the context of science; and a ramified distributive realism would simply be one that an external, legitimating inquiry would be capable of making argumentatively compelling, but it is hardly obvious that it could ever yield a unique recommendation. The only question that remains then—it is not itself a simple question—concerns the full compatibility of relativisms (of what we have termed the *internalist* sort) with a minimal or ramified realism.

There are basically three forms of internalist relativisms, either tradi-

313

tionally discussed or reasonably worth pursuing. One is the most ancient form, *protagoreanism*, which is standardly construed as self-contradictory, incoherent, or self-defeating in some profound sense. Presumably it maintains something like this: that the same proposition or claim (for all propositions or claims) may be both true and false at once. On *that* formulation, it is merely self-contradictory. The question remains whether it may be redeemed in an interesting way: the evidence suggests that where it can be, it is either not a recognizable form of relativism or reduces to what we shall (in a moment) identify as the third form of relativism. The most disputed contemporary form of relativism may be termed *incommensurabilism*, which maintains something like this: that an apparent claim may and must be interpreted in accord with one conceptual scheme or another and assigned truth values on (and only on) the basis of such disjunctive interpretation; that alternative conceptual schemes arise within the practices of science and may be incommensurable with one another just as conceptual schemes; and that there is no neutral conceptual scheme within which all such schemes may be suitably reconciled so that truth claims within the diverging systems may be brought within a single more comprehensive system. The thesis is both obscure and incompletely developed by its contemporary protagonists (chiefly, it is said, in the views of Feyerabend and Kuhn—although Kuhn has pretty well disowned it or drastically weakened it if ever he defended it, and Feyerabend has never met objections directly). It may be that it is incoherent—as it would be if it equated mere commensurability with full intelligibility; for a specific form of incommensuration does not entail the impossibility of assigning truth values, and the utter incomparability of truth values seems to signify the mutual unintelligibility of alternative conceptual schemes. It may however be that somewhat diverging conceptual schemes are thus characterized only because of the *contingent but not in-principle* failure to provide mutual paraphrastic facilities from one conceptual scheme to another. (The thesis may, not unreasonably, be said to be Foucauldian.) Under that circumstance, a *moderate* incommensurabilism—that is, a de facto but *not* (yet) de jure failure of commensuration—is indeed a coherent possibility, and judgments and claims may be *relativized* to such schemata. But it is difficult to say—or to deny—that the result would be a form of relativism, in the sense that the judgments and claims in question could not be said not to change their meaning from the one scheme to the other (whatever their truth value); although the result could also reasonably count as a form of relativism, in the sense that one could not insure that truth values assigned to particular judgments and claims would be assigned in accord with fully commensurated conceptual schemes. So, extreme or radical incommensurabilism is incoherent and not worth bothering with; and moderate incommensurabilism is a viable but logically restricted form of relativism insofar as it disputes the assignment of truth values only on the prior grounds of uncommensurated divergences of meaning or conceptual schemes.

A third version remains, however, that may be termed *robust* or *moderate relativism*. It holds the following: (1) that a sector of inquiry behaves relativistically if any pertinent set of judgments, claims, or the like that would be incompatible or contradictory in a bipolar model of truth and falsity are, on an adjustment applied to that sector (admitting logically weaker values than the bipolar values), no longer treated as such; and (2) that, for particular sectors of inquiry but not necessarily for all, reasons substantively bearing on the nature of some domain in question legitimate the fiat noted in (1). Such a doctrine exhibits the following interesting features: it is applied piecemeal and not globally; it is applied on what may be regarded, generously, as empirical grounds; it is compatible with inquiries that are not construed relativistically; it presupposes a theory of truth common to relativistic and nonrelativistic practices; it preserves, where wanted, formal notions of contradiction, incoherence, and the like; it does not invoke any dubious theories of meaning or of conceptual incommensurabilities; it is not itself internally inconsistent in any way; it accommodates natural appraisals of a comparative sort (as of better and worse and of rankings); it is a logical thesis, or a thesis about the logic of truth-value assignments; it raises as an entirely open question whether and where it may and should be applied or not; it is not, as a mere pluralism is, a policy of tolerance formulated from a nonrelativistic base, but is rather a strong claim that, for a given sector, we cannot legitimate truth values logically stronger than relativistic values; it is compatible with a moderate incommensurabilism; and it need not concede that it must give way, in principle, to a stronger bipolar model everywhere. These, then, form a lovely and powerful set of advantages.[1] In effect what the thesis signifies is that, for example, regarding the defensibility of suicide, or the interpretation of the Vietnamese War, or the appraisal of Courbet's paintings, or the like, it is entirely possible for particular judgments to be affirmed in accord with regularized evidentiary practices, without being obliged to reject one or another of incompatible pairs of such judgments, or without being unable to acknowledge pertinently the comparative strength of competing judgments, or without being ignorant of such conflicting claims or of the grounds for their individual support, or without retreating to arbitrary or idiosyncratic reasons, or without being disqualified from affirming, jointly, the cognitive viability of such contending claims.

Without attempting a full-scale defense, we may reasonably suggest that relativism is generally favored wherever evaluation, interpretation, historical perspective, intentionality, ontology, theorizing about unobservable entities, background beliefs, diverging conceptual schemes, ideologies, and less-than-universal regularities are involved. That covers a lot of ground—certainly the human sciences and large parts of the natural sciences at least, history, literary and art criticism and interpretation, moral and legal judgment, political commitment, the characterization of human behavior, the interpretation of speech, and philosophical theorizing. The linkage with realism is elementary: it is simply supplied by (2), that relativism is invoked only on some reasonable theory of the capacity of a given sector of reality to support truth-value assignments no stronger than relativistic ones. On that view the bipolar values (true/false) are found inapt for relevant sectors of inquiry; the admissible values (reasonable, plausible, apt, and the like, and their graded forms) are (on a theory) assigned a *domain*—not merely the fruits of exercising our cognitive powers relative to that domain. Of course, it is always possible to defend a weaker (merely evidentiary) relativism, that is, in terms of limitations of some sort on the mere accessibility to human investigators of evidence relative to issues raised; but we are here favoring the stronger thesis. So realism and relativism are clearly compatible and readily reconciled.

Apart from the relativistic issue itself, several additional themes may be developed that bear in an important way on the relationship between argument and rhetoric—in a way, in fact, that very subtly affects the relativistic thesis and is affected by it. Two themes may be mentioned because of their close bearing on one another. At the present time, human existence is characteristically taken to be very strongly historicized; that is, not only do human societies exhibit histories in some paradigmatically distinctive sense, but human inquiry, human understanding, and human science are functions of changing and limited historical horizons. Secondly, within the terms of reference of a philosophical orientation that rejects all forms of cognitive transparency, all empirically discovered would-be universal regularities are radically subject to revision or restriction, both because of the limitations of any historical horizon and because of the unavailability of a fixed cognitive foundation on which we may suppose we are somehow approximating (and therefore actually capturing in part) regularities that, at some moment in inquiry, could be taken as the formulation of fixed, real, essential, or universal regularities that no later

316

history of science could possibly show to be seriously mistaken *in that regard*. Holism, however, the Nietzschean theme, fallibilism applied to itself, and similar considerations all signify the hopelessness of pretending to more than contingent regularities of however universal a form. One way of pressing the point is to take note of the fact that, within the terms of an historicized existence, it is impossible to make determinate sense of the notion of all possible worlds—considered distributively—not because of any supposed infinitude of such possibilities but rather because historicism sets unsepecifiable but real limits to our conceptual imagination, which historical time invariably confirms piecemeal and after the fact. In short, on the argument, historicism and universalism are incompatible, though the search for candidate universals remains empirically eligible and even eligible for the relativist.

We come now to a few final remarks. In general, there are three lines of strategy for avoiding our third, robust, sort of relativism. The first, now generally treated as illicit or utterly without defense, bases inquiry on some privileged cognitive access to reality: if the whole of reality is cognitively transparent, then of course there is no need for relativism. In giving up such privileges, however, one may yet maintain (as by the second strategy), for instance, as in inductivism or by self-corrective means other than induction, that the world is cognitively accessible even if not transparent, in such a strong sense that in principle the indefinitely extended, self-corrective methods of inquiry yield truth in the limit. Such a view requires an extremely sanguine sense of linear progress, conceptual continuities, the cumulative benefits of critical correction, the strong convergence and commensurability of pertinent theories—all opposed by the Nietzschean tradition and its allies. In the view of many, therefore, the assumptions of the second strategy pretty well require a cryptic commitment to those of the first: as, for instance, in Karl Popper's charge that every would-be approximation to the true universal laws of nature amounts to essentialism. The third strategy concedes the futility of the first two and insists on historicized limits; it simply eschews transparency, essentialism, universalism, and the like. But it pretends, within the very movement of history, to have discovered—one may say, empirically—that the *saliencies* of every age effectively converge toward some moving, variable, diachronic analogue of universalism and that, therefore, every age effectively is part of the thus reuniversalized, reunified, uniquely *indicative* common history of mankind. This is the recent theme of Hans-Georg Gadamer's hermeneutics and of the doctrines of others within the Anglo-American tradition—for instance, Charles Taylor. It is hard to see how it can possibly be anything

317

but a crypto-essentialism of some sort—what may fairly be called traditionalism.

There are no other general strategies for avoiding relativism. What this signifies is that the saliencies of every age—the central puzzles, the persistent beliefs and theories, the sense of phenomena, the description or explanation of which is particularly stubbornly shared within a society— need not be and are often not strongly convergent in particular sectors of inquiry. Nevertheless, every convincing form of argument must come to terms with such saliencies at least. They may well change under the pressure of discoveries motivated by an earlier saliency. For instance, our conception of outer space is first guided by the saliencies of our immediate vicinity, the earth, the moon, the near planets, the sun at a distance; but our later conception even of these may be radically altered under the force of what we learn of black holes, the universe at its limits, cosmic beginnings or the like. Here, one comes to understand the full sense in which argument is inseparable from rhetoric—in the most profound realist spirit we can command.

By *saliencies*, we may understand, therefore, those accepted truths, beliefs, conceptual categories, unsolved problems, entrenched methods and practices of inquiry, notions of effective evidence, characteristic interpretations, shared instances of large discoveries that have deeply affected our consensual views, hopes and fears and superstitions that form the very core of what the apt members of an historical society are convergently inclined to view as requiring a considerable counterforce to upset, replace, or dismantle. Saliency is what remains of the provisional weighting of whatever enters an argument or rational review of a field, once the transparency thesis is rejected and a general historicism installed. Effective argument, therefore, cannot fall back to the timeless forms of rational debate; for those would-be forms and fears and superstitions themselves have been gradually abstracted from the accumulating saliencies of our historical experience, however skillfully (at some late moment of reflection) we may have managed to formulate a seemingly unassailable canon to include them. An effective argument assembles the elements of our history effectively, and in doing that it must address the habits of conviction of a living society—which, on the thesis here favored, are always embedded in the shifting saliencies of our shared experience.

In that sense, argument *is* rhetoric: the attempt to assemble the pieces of a developing heritage in fresh ways that yield would-be findings compelling to those who remember the strong, collected exemplars with which, by analogy at least, to compare and judge the upstart effort, now that new premises are offered. If such saliencies are not sufficiently uniform or universal (as seems to be the case), then even in the practice of argument one cannot hope to escape the invasion of relativism. Merely formal canons are likely to be either largely ineffective for disqualifying relativistic competitors or even under suspicion themselves (like the deductive-nomological method of explanation) wherever an actual sector of inquiry is closely observed. The linkage between argument and rhetoric remains entirely neutral (at first) between robust relativism and the third strategy intended to avoid relativism—traditionalism. But a closer inspection tends to show that traditionalism itself is a faulty and extravagant claim, and that admission returns us once again, wherever needed, to the logically weakened picture of realist disciplines here recommended.

Rhetoric, therefore, may be said to exhibit two entirely different forms: one, internalist, in which *argument is inseparable from rhetoric*, in which the weight of particular disputes cannot be resolved merely by appeal to the formal structure of argument but depends on the practices of reaching consensual conviction within an actual society; the other, externalist, in which *rhetoric signifies the completely gratuitous normalization of societal practices themselves* from one era to another. The first marks the pragmatizing of human argument; the second, its genealogical fortunes. Both confirm the irresistible drift toward relativism: the first, within a conceptual space (otherwise vacant) in which it can never be privileged or even assured a steady state, or grounded. The consensus of human societies, in the second sense, is no more than arbitrary, cognitively meaningless, a form of inertia; consensus in the first sense is best described as Wittgensteinian, the sharing of a historical or natural "form of life" in which doubts do come to an effective end in the spontaneous accommodation of the ongoing practices of an enveloping society—which keeps changing with each improvisory extension of its practices but not in a way that disables further such extensions. Rhetoric, taken seriously, is the adjustment of our sense of argument forever congruent with the changes and variable tolerances of such extensions.

NOTE

1. The full account of this thesis may be found in Joseph Margolis, *Pragmatism without Foundations: Reconciling Realism and Relativism* (Oxford: Basil Blackwell, 1986).

13

Symbolic Realism and the
Dualism of the Human Sciences:
A Rhetorical Reformulation of the Debate between
Positivism and Romanticism

Richard Harvey Brown

My rhetorical strategy in this essay is dialectical. Under the rubrics of *positivism* and *romanticism*, I elaborate the agonistic struggles of various antimonies in order to encourage the emergence of synthetic truths. The primary tension is between the post-Nietzschean, deconstructive relativism of the romantic tradition, as against the foundationalist standards of both absolutist positivism as well as reductivist hermeneutics. From this tension emerge rhetorical criteria for discourse and judgment. These rhetorical criteria are more permissive but more rigorous than those of subjectivists or radical skeptics. Some are criteria for conversation that are presupposed by the very idea that scholars are members of the party of truth. Others concern forms of argumentation, such as the preference for explanations of causal or generative mechanisms over mere descriptions of facts or meanings. Still other criteria are traditional, such as consistency, economy, and the like. Another is political—does a given form of truth-telling support an emancipatory practice?

Since ontologies secrete epistemologies, any criteria of intelligibility or truth-telling must be partly self-referential. We cannot push the bus on which we are riding. Moreover, even such modest criteria are easily relativized to particular contexts, purposes, or interests. This in turn raises the questions of when and on what warrants may different criteria be applied, and of the possibility of agreement of rhetors across different contexts and with different purposes or interests. The search for trans-situational criteria of intelligibility and agreement leads us back to the question of foundationalism . . . and so the dialectic continues.

I am grateful to Robert Brulle and Herbert Simons for their criticisms of this essay, and especially to Herbert Simons for helping me to understand what it was that I had intended to say.

320

The problem is overwhelmingly real, and not simply theoretical. Briefly, it could be summarized as the incompatibility of cognition and identity. . . . The price of genuine, powerful, technically enriching science is that its style of explanation ruthlessly destroys those very notions in terms of which we identify ourselves. . . . The world we live in and the world of [scientific] thought are not the same. The *Labenswelt* loses its status; though we must need go on living in it, for we have no other, it becomes devalued, and we cannot treat it seriously. (Gellner 1975, 101)

Rhetoricians of the human sciences investigate how language is used to gain knowledge of human experience. Why choose language as a key? Partly from despair, partly as an affirmation. The despair is for apodictic truth, revealed as an impossibility through reflection on the relativity of our ways of knowing. The hope, the affirmation, is for a renewed humanism that transcends both positivist nominalism and romantic idealism even as it affirms reason and freedom.

Such a renewed humanism requires a transvaluation of both positivist and romantic theories of language. The positivist sees language as a copy of facts or things; the romantic sees it as an expression of thoughts or feelings. Each is the other's twin, each blind in one eye. One twin opens the door with his right hand, the other closes it with his left. Through this unwitting cooperation a whole movement is formed. Neither twin speaks to his brother nor sees that they pass through an illusory portal. For language is not something one passes through to an other side, whether that other side be the world of facts and things or the world of insights and meanings. Instead these worlds and all others do not exist for us outside of language but within it.

The one-eyed postivist twin, call him Ayer (1946), says that language is nonsense if it does not stand for facts or for logical relations between such facts. And so he is blind to any practical wisdom, aesthetic knowledge, or even his own metaphysics. By contrast, the one-eyed romantic, who could be named Hirsch, sees language as an instrument for expressing a prior intention, thought, or psychic state. And so not only is he distracted from the truth as it manifests itself in language; he also can not find the subjectivity behind language that he seeks. When he does discover a meaning or intention in a text, his claim that this represents an "expression of mind" (Hirsch 1967) or "mentalities" (Q. Skinner 1969) prior to language is at best redundant (Gadamer 1975).

The debate between these twins has grown sterile. Adequate social theory, like effective social policy, must be both objectively valid and subjectively meaningful; it must yield understanding of persons' agency as well as explanations of social forces beyond their control. Yet in terms of the debate between positivists and romantics, such theory would appear to be methodologically impossible, in that each side cherishes different assumptions concerning the nature of social reality and how we can know it. At the same time, however, each position presupposes and completes the other, and each is self-refuting if it stands alone. For example, a behaviorist such as B. F. Skinner (1971, 77–92, 99, 191–92, 195) cannot with consistency defend his position with good reasons since, as such reasons appear in *consciousness*, they are by definition inadmissable in the behaviorist's analysis. The behaviorist presumably has chosen environmental determinism as the superior position, a position which, however, she has refuted in *choosing* it. If the possibility of determinism being false is not a real possibility for Skinner, then he cannot claim for it scientific truth. Yet if falsity is really possible, he is free (March 1983, 482).

The opposite position, of complete indeterminism and freedom, is equally self-refuting. A world with no prior determination comes to appear arbitrary, meaningless, and absurd, a world in which, as Sartre (1964, 418) put it, there are only two alternatives: "Either man is wholly determined . . . or else man is wholly free." Yet Sartre's arguments that people are condemned to freedom contradict his premises, for why should freedom, good faith, or reason be preferred or even believed in a world that is totally absurd? Sartre's freedom turns out to be a freedom that is humane and honest, has positive content, and is delimited by certain structures (March 1983, 485).

Both positivist and romantic absolutisms are thus self-refuting. The assumption of a totally determined world that permits total agreement contradicts itself. The assumption of total personal freedom that engenders total dissimilarity of viewpoints leads to absolute relativism, with no shared criteria for truth or even intelligibility (Wright 1977a, 1977b). The paradox, however, is that although the aspiration for total freedom is logically incoherent, it underlies all our notions of personal responsibility and moral judgement. Both social order and human dignity thus appear to depend on two opposite and self-contradictory assumptions: the positivist commitment to objective causality and the romantic conception of subjective freedom.

The intensification of this polarization would be catastrophic for the prospects of a truly humane culture in a science-oriented society. The polarization—between positivism and romanticism, determinism and freedom, systems efficiency and personal agency or, at the extreme, between survival and dignity—also takes an epistemological form. On one side are the gatekeeper philosophers who name what may enter the kingdom of science and consign all else to the purgatories of superstition, emotive expression, or unfounded opinion. These gatekeepers—the many-headed dogs of positivism—assert that knowledge is science, that science is knowledge, and that there is no other. Their advocacy helped clear space for a critical interpretation of nature in part by establishing from the outset a strict separation of object and subject, body and mind, nature and culture. Positivist epistemologies are not descriptions of what scientists do or how science works. Instead, they are normative; they idealize and justify a certain form of knowing (Gellner 1975). Nonetheless, according to positivists, since scientific thinking is basic to modern civilization, our very survival depends on the preservation of the scientific world view.

On the other side of the crisis are open-admission philosophers of the romantic tradition who seek to dethrone positivism and to provide an epistemological warrant for human self-understanding. Romantic thinkers, as I am using this term, take artistic interpretation rather than scientific explanation as their model. They are sympathetic with Novalis' (1953) dictum that "Poets know nature better than scientists," or Coleridge's (1839) statement that "The true naturalist is a dramatic poet." Such anti-positivists relativize science by arguing that it is a social, historical, political, and linguistic practice. For positivists, the problem has been to keep narrow and straight the gates to knowledge; for romantics it has been to open them wider.

It could well be argued that the opposition I have defined is already outdated, and that few sophisticated thinkers today accept the image held by both positivists and romantics of a solid foundation for knowledge. Yet such an argument would be only partly correct. Most practicing researchers in most disciplines still accept the foundation metaphor, as does the public at large. Moreover, a surprising number of leading philosophers, such as Derrida, Gadamer, Gellner, Habermas, or Winch, presuppose this bifurcation as the bases of their theories of knowledge, and others, like Searle, are highly ambivalent.

As an example of the continuity of this bifurcation we might compare Peter Winch's (1958) subjective idealist position to Durkheim's (1965) supposedly objective conception of social facts. Winch and Durkheim both assume a strict, even an absolute, separation between interpretive and causal ways of knowing. Winch cited Durkheim as stating "that social life should be explained, not by the notions of those who participate in it, but by more profound causes which are unperceived by consciousness." Then Winch proceeded to elaborate an alternative romantic epistemology that is an intaglio of Durkheim's positivism.

Similar antinomies are visible in the debate between Jacques Derrida and John Searle (Derrida 1977; Searle 1977, 1983). According to Derrida, the conventions of intelligibility are "by essence violable and precarious, in themselves and by the fictionality that constitutes them." Yet as Searle pointed out (and as can be argued from Derrida's own earlier writings), Derrida's absolute relativism provides no standpoint from which such conventions could be labeled a fiction. That is, no matter how hard we try to put intelligibility into question, we can only do so from the standpoint of intelligibility. Otherwise we are talking nonsense. Structures of sense-making are inescapable: all interpretations, even those that challenge intelligibility, depend on some assumed framework or grammar from which meanings can be generated.

In remarks to literary scholars Searle moved beyond this sterile dichotomy between determinate meaning and total relativity (Searle 1983, 78–79):

> When I have lectured to audiences of literary critics, I have found two pervasive philosophic presuppositions . . . both oddly enough derived from logical positivism. First there is the assumption that unless a distinction can be made rigorous and precise it isn't a distinction at all. . . . People who hold the assumption that genuine distinctions must be made rigid are ripe for Derrida's attempt to undermine all such distinctions. . . . Second, and equally positivistic, is the insistence that concepts that apply to language and literature, if they are to be truly valid, must admit of some mechanical procedure of verification. . . . The crude positivism of these assumptions . . . is of a piece with Derrida's assumption that without foundations we are left with nothing but the free play of signifiers.

Yet elsewhere Searle committed the same positivist crimes of which he accused the literati: Searle's (1969, 1977) own theory of speech acts is quasi-positivistic in its insistence on univocality of meaning—its recourse to "literal" meanings of verbal expressions. In literal speech, "sentences are precisely the realization of intentions," said Searle (1977, 202). Moreover, Searle atomized speech acts by defining them purely as the verbalization of the speaker's intention without regard to audience reception.

This decontextualization of meaning is a kind of verbal factism. It may

324

tell us how speech acts must be viewed by members, but it begs the question of how intersubjective comprehension of intention actually is realized. "I take it to be an analytic truth about language," Searle wrote, "that whatever can be meant can be said" (1969, 17). But not everything that is said is meant, and not everything that is *meant* is understood. Signs may not relate to an external object world, nor to an intention, nor to other signs, with any determinate meaning (Derrida 1972, 378). If we wish to discover and account for the coming to be of shared meanings, we may assume that *members* must behave as if differences between intention, locution, and interpretation are negligible. But the *researcher* is not required to make such an assumption. Instead, to acknowledge an "as if" quality in the structure of human intersubjectivity is also to recognize that reciprocity is a members' idealization that enables intelligibility, and that the fact of this intelligibility is also a fiction (Schutz 1962, 32; Wright 1983: 394–397).

In sum, Derrida is right to point out that absolute objectivity is a chimera, and Searle is right to note that absolute relativity is self-defeating. But why should we have to choose either? Instead, the task is to find a metaphor and method that can overcome yet include both of these positions. Neither of these absolutisms encourages critical reflection. In the case of positivism, this is explicit. In the case of reductive hermeneutics, no viewpoint is provided from which to critically assess the accounts of agents. Such a hermeneutics can treat understanding and meaning, but it cannot distinguish *mis*understandings, *non*comprehensions, and *false* meanings from correct ones.

The indeterminism of both positivist and romantic paradigms has been attributed to the nature of reality or the lack of fit between theories and evidence. But it is much more useful to construe this indeterminism rhetorically as a feature of language itself, for language is the medium through which we constitute reality as an object of experience and by which we shape both theories and data. The advancement of science itself depends on the imprecision and multivalence of language. Even the willfully denotative language of science must preserve sufficient ambiguity and incompleteness to leave room for stating later what one at the moment does not know. Garfinkel (1952, 28) made this point empirically by showing how an openness to future possible meanings is a precondition of the intelligibility of even the most precise communications:

> No matter how specific the terms of common understanding may be, they attain the status of agreement for persons only insofar as

the stipulated conditions carry along an unspoken but understood
et cetera clause.

It is essential to science, law, and other domains of discourse that one
be able to say *something* without knowing everything (Bondi 1967, 10). If
language were able to precisely exhaust any matter at hand, and therefore
if it were not polysemeous and malleable, we would not be able to speak
at all, since intersubjectivity would not be possible between persons in
different particular settings. To be determinate, language (or theory or
facts, etc.) must also be partly indeterminate. If reality for us were wholly
determinate, sane persons in the "same" situations would never disagree
with others and, hence, would never know that they ever agreed. And if
others did not disagree with us about the way the world is, we could not
know either them or the world to be real (Wright 1977a, 1977b).

Thus neither positivism nor romanticism can become fully determinate
or absolute. To overcome their mutual exclusion and mutual dependence,
both must be reformulated and sublated into an ontology and epistemology
that encompasses both scientific and artistic modes of representation. As
Randall Collins (1975, 28, 34) said, "Positivism needs to be purged. Romanticism needs to be borrowed from. It is the combination of determinism and freedom, after all, that constitutes the greatest art; advances in
scientific sociology can move its aesthetics beyond a tired romanticism,
hopefully into something greater."

A critical rhetoric of reason helps such transformations. It is maeutic, a
midwife between different forms of imagination and belief. Rhetoric eases
us into new conceptual experience by naming the conditions for possible
kinds of knowledge, advocating certain procedures as correct and certain
statements as true, and inviting and legitimating belief in a certain (version
of the) world. What then are the conceptual and preconceptual worlds
legitimated by different rhetorics of reason? What rhetoric, pure and applied, would most support the telos of human emancipation as well as the
mastery of our complex systems?

BEYOND THE POSITIVIST ROMANTIC DEBATE

The critics of positivism are themselves vulnerable to attack, for in some
ways their theories are reverse images of that which they scorn. For example, in place of empiricism's brute facts as a foundational datum for the
human sciences, hermeneutic thought posits brute interpretations. Just as
the epistemology of positivists cannot explain our intellectual practice, so

the conception of self-contained language games renders ordinary language philosophers incapable of explaining the possibility of their own discourse or indeed of any social science. Similarly, social historians of knowledge have linked science to communitarian practices, but they have tended to see this scientific community as abstracted and disconnected from a larger political-economic context, much as positivists view science itself. In place of Descartes' a priori cogito of the individual, pragmatists, ordinary language philosophers, and social phenomenologists posit an a priori collective cogito of the community of investigators.

It thus appears that human works, taken by Vico as *the* content for the human sciences, share the same difficulty as the apodictic cogito posited by Descartes for the study of nature: neither works nor mind can provide their own epistemological guarantees. For the cogito to initiate its axiomatic play, Descartes had to supply some content that was not itself rationally justified by his system. And this prior content, which the cogito cannot demonstrate but must presuppose to do its proofs, of this it must remain uncertain. Similarly, for man to make his works, Vico must supply a preexistent something from which they can be made. And this prior something, which man himself did not make, of this he has no privileged understanding (Bhaskar 1982, 289–90; Gödel 1962; Husserl 1931).

With the revival of Vichian thought in the human sciences, Interpreting Man is replacing Explanatory Man. The categories have been recut to show persons as self-interpreting and self-motivating creatures of language. Thus the would-be explanatory scientist now faces her subject matter as "already preinterpreted, as linguistically and cognitively 'done' as it were, prior to any scientific investigation of it. These preinterpretations are *not* externally related and contigently conjoined to what happens in social life, but internally related and constitutive of it" (Bhaskar 1982, 289; see Taylor 1971).

Given this view of humans as interpreting animals, it was natural to assume that such interpretations, beliefs, or works could provide a foundation for the human studies. This was true whether the hermeneutic foundation was viewed as a finished product, as in early symbolic interactionism or functionalist anthropology, or whether it was conceived dialogically as emerging from cultural practices, as in ethnomethodology or cognitive anthropology. In its weaker form the hermeneutic foundation metaphor assumes that knowledge is rooted in, and therefore must not be inconsistent with, members' self-interpretations. In its stronger form it holds that social knowledge is exhausted by the intentions and meanings of members. But either way that the foundation metaphor sheds its positivist garb, it reappears in hermeneutic drag.

Subjective idealist hermeneutics shows that absolute objectivity in positive social science is a fiction. But it also interprets conduct in terms of motives that are identical with the subjects' own assessments of the situation. In this subjectivist approach, meanings become equivalent to the linguistically articulated meaning; that is, they are assumed to be isomorphic with the verbal statements by which the actors orient themselves. But as ordinary language analysts themselves have acknowledged, explanation in terms of motive is not the same as explanation in terms of cause. Motives or intentions do not cause actions; instead they provide a teleological account for them. Language-interpretive human sciences have demonstrated that intentional action is relatively autonomous of nonintentional "natural" constraints, and that it must be accounted for by rules rather than by laws. Yet the question remains, Whence come these rules? And it is here that a *critical* hermeneutic can show that purely language-interpretive approaches are themselves a kind of myth, in that they posit as their subject matter a hermetic world of language outside of time or space (Wellmer 1971).

A *critical* hermeneutic reveals the factual limits of subjective idealist social science. Society is not only praxis, but also practico-inert. It is, in part, like nature. To the extent that society is the product of conscious human intentions, hermeneutics better encompasses what is salient. But history also is made behind the backs and against the wills of even powerful persons. More importantly, history—especially history of the *longue durée*—is also made before the eyes but below the awareness and intentions of virtually everyone. Language-interpretive social theory does capture what is or can be communicated. But much, perhaps most, of what goes on is not and cannot be stated, and at least part of what is stated misinterprets this unstated and often unmentionable domain. It is a disavowal of critical reflection to deny that a social structural or naturalistic level of reality enables and emerges from a communicative one. To accept all forms of consciousness as, in their ways, true is to eschew analysis of forms of consciousness that are false.

The subjective idealist theory of meaning confuses the transcendence of particular language games with the transcendence of everything (Gellner 1975). The clarification of language games and the subversion of positivism's absolutist pretensions were achievements of ordinary language philosophy. But to show that there is no absolute ultimate ground for knowledge is not to show that there are no relative penultimate ones.

328

Epistemological transcendence of self-endorsing parochial visions of reality need not be a transcendence to some absolute first sensa or principles. Instead it can be a transcendence to a more cogent, embracing, and comprehensive system of significations, that is, toward a more universal audience (Perelman and Olbrechts-Tyteca 1969).

Language idealists such as Winch tend to endorse every circle of ideas as unitary, true, and complete, a kind of self-justifying first foundation. "What has to be accepted, the given, is—so one could say—forms of life" (Wittgenstein 1953, 226). In the view of such thinkers, "Reality is not what gives language sense. What is real and what is unreal shows itself *in* the sense language has" (Winch 1958, 82). But a less absolute idealist look at practical uses and forms of lived speech would reveal them to be anything but self-contained, internally consistent, or simply given. For example, in his essay, "Understanding a Primitive Society," Peter Winch (1970) treated Azande culture and its magic as a fully coherent web of ideas and practices, and thereby ascribed to contingent empirical "forms of life" or "language games" a rationality and intelligibility that logically could be possible only on the plane of wholly nondistorted communication. As Evans-Pritchard (1965, 105, 106, 110) observed, however,

> Azande themselves say that the authority of their leaders was
> strengthened by war and the increase in numbers of their followers
> each new conquest brought them. Another consequence has been
> ethnic intermingling of great complexity. I have listed over twenty
> foreign peoples . . . who have contributed to the Zande
> amalgam. . . . In the Sudan alone, in addition to Zande, there are
> spoken in Zande country seven or eight different languages. . . .
> Zande culture is a thing of shreds and patches.

If cultures or historical epochs really were as self-contained as Winch's absolutism of language games asserts, we would be unable to interpret or translate them into the idiom of another language, except as a complicitous restatements of their official versions of themselves. This would be the reduction ad absurdum of any social-science knowledge, since no social understanding or explanation on Winch's account is possible other than an inward familiarity with concepts used in a society by its members. The practices of comparative anthropology or historical sociology contradict and are contradicted by the conception of a wholly hermetic and internally self-contained cultural language game. The solution, however, is not to seek an extralinguistic, positive Philosophy of Science to provide transcultural rules of interpretation, because in such philosophies the subject matter of language games and cultures ceases to exist or is reduced to a set of behavioristic signals.

A nonpositivist corrective to Winch is provided by Winch himself in an earlier essay on "Nature and Convention." Here the author did not say that standards of truth-telling are culturally variable and self-contained from one language game to another. Instead he adduced truth-telling to be a noncontingent precondition for the operation of any discourse or interaction. Other emergents, such as canons of integrity or fair play, also were presented in this light. In a similar spirit, Garfinkel (1967) and others noted that interactions have properties that do not vary and that are presuppositions of any meaningful discourse, even though the rules of the interactions may be different in different cultures or settings. As Karl-Otto Apel (1967) pointed out, arguments and findings of this type imply an ideal language game that is differently distorted as it is incarnated in different particular language praxes. Such an ideal is not an empirical hypothesis that can be tested. Instead it functions as the transcendental premise in cross-cultural and historical research and also, though less evidently, in interactions between contemporaries (Dallmayr 1981, 151–52).

Critics of positivism have considered science and magic as simply two different language games. This is fruitful if one's purpose is to delegitimate scientific absolutism and reductivism. By the same token, however, the proposition that rival epistemologies are mere language games also implies that any cognitive practice can be evaluated in terms of its telos or existential function. Once this shift is made, it becomes clear that we can establish cognitive hierarchies for various purposes in terms of which certain forms of thought will be distinctly superior to others. Positivist models in social sciences, for example, highlight mechanisms and structural properties and are thus often superior at revealing scarcities and constraints. Conversely, critical hermeneutic models distinguish between depth and surface meanings and so are especially useful at unmasking contradictions, miscommunications, and relations of domination disguised by ordinary language.

The limits of both purely objectivist or purely subjectivist approaches seem to be understood implicitly even by microsociologists who ally themselves with Winch's philosophy; in their actual research practice they pursue a more critical agenda. This research shows how actors' meanings are accomplished interactively in contexts, but it makes little use of the actors' avowed intuitions as a primary resource or first step toward explanation. Some ethnoscientists even proclaim themselves uninterested in actors' intentions, and most give their attention to the routine practices of everyday life that apparently are not specifically motivated. By this tactic such researchers construe individually meaningful intentions to be derivative rather than constitutive of these situated interactions, speech practices, and larger social structures (Knorr-Cetina 1981, 18; Menzel 1978).

The power to constitute is not merely an abstract quality of language itself, but lies in the speech community that authorizes a language and invests certain users and usages with authority. The hierarchically superior authors of regulations, sermons, five-year plans, orations, or vocabularies of lineage and honor often impose what they state and tacitly demarcate what is thinkable and unthinkable, thereby helping to maintain the social symbolic order. "Language is real, practical consciousness," said Marx in *The German Ideology* (1970), but part of the reality and practicality of language is that it masks as much as it reveals, suppresses as much as it expresses, takes as tacit more than it makes explicit. Language distinguishes the universe of what can be said and the universe of what must not be stated or what goes without saying. This is why an emancipatory rhetoric of reason must be critical of both positivism and romanticism, of reifications of both structure and meaning, for only such a critical analysis can elevate the "return of the repressed" to the level of articulate consciousness. In Marxian terms, to draw what cannot be articulated into a previously unavailable discourse is to abolish a linguistically encoded false consciousness (Bourdieu 1977, 21, 170; Gavronsky 1979). Such a process is a beginning of political awareness and self-direction.

To see knowledge and experience as symbolically constructed is to break the spell of the positivist epistemology that is in fact a white man's magic, a metaphysics of society dressed up in the language of logic or natural science. But to see knowledge and experience as exhausted by or necessarily consistent with the speakers' versions of it is to invoke another form of magic—hermeneutics as hermeticism (Festugiere 1950–1954; Yates 1964). Both these magics confer a perfect coherence on inchoate historical practice. They transform the methodological postulates of Explantory Man or Understanding Man into epistemological conclusions. They equate intelligibility with ontology. Social orders do this; critical thinkers must avoid it. Instead of acting like shamans and priests who seek to produce a closed unity of mental structures and social structures, human scientists can assume a critical posture by showing how such unities, whether positivist or hermeneutic, help to make the arbitrariness of any social order appear to be part of nature.

SYMBOLIC REALISM: TOWARD A FUSION OF HORIZONS

Currently we have, on one hand, the rhetoric of old-fashioned positivists who advocate not only explanatory laws to which everyone must agree, but laws that assume a purely material world and deny all subjective reality, including that of the theorist. Opposing this is the rhetoric of subjective romantics who want no laws, but experience and intuitions that, they claim, are a higher kind of science. Sublating both these views would be a critical rhetoric of reason that defended generalized explanations of the natural as well as of the human world, including subjectivity, but without a reductive materialist or mechanist bias. This view finds its justification in a postpositivist, postromantic, dialectical, symbolic realist theory of knowledge. In such a view, causal, law-like explanation is itself an interpretive procedure, and critical interpretation itself can be a rigorous way of knowing.

Ironically, the earlier positivists' program to reduce our vague language to instant-by-instant experience is precisely the problem of setting sociological abstractions on an experiential basis. Only now this empiricism need not be either objective or subjective, but can be intersubjective and mediated by a self-conscious critical rhetorical practice. Informed by continental and pragmatic thought, contemporary empirical research may abandon the idea of a self-subsisting world-out-there, a world the data of which could speak for themselves before any theorizing. Instead, a critical rhetoric of reason recognizes that scientific reality is itself symbolic, that validity always depends on the fit of our ideas and perceptions, and that what makes a theory powerful is its capacity to make things coherent most strikingly and economically.

The subject-object dichotomy of the early positivist-romantic debate also is transformed. For in the symbolic realists' view, one's own subjective states can be analogic instruments for observing the subjective states of others. Such observations differ only in degree, not in kind, from so-called objective observations; both types of observations are linguistically mediated, both are shaped by their instrument of observation, and both are subject in principal to validation by their coherence with a larger body of data and theory.

In contrast to both scientific realism and subjective or symbolic idealism, symbolic realism seeks a warrant for both scientific *and* ethical judgments, and hence for a public discourse that would be adequate both for moral self-understanding of the lifeworld as well as for management of complex systems. In such a perspective, scientific and ethical discourse—

that is, forms of talk presupposing causality or freedom—are both rational in that they presuppose various criteria of economy, congruence and consistency. Such criteria are those by which we organize experience into formal structures of which "knowing" is constituted.

In the symbolic realist view, language is not a reflection either of the world or of the mind. Instead, the human world and mind emerge from the social historical *practice* that is language. Symbols are understood as taking their meanings not from things or intentions, but from socially coordinated actions. Words help constitute and mediate social behaviors, provide legitimating or stigmatizing vocabularies of motive, and mask or reveal structures of domination. Semantic changes express cultural conflicts. As C. Wright Mills put it (1974, 677), "Because . . . words carry meanings by virtue of dominant interpretations placed upon them by social behaviors, . . . we can view language functionally as a system of social control."

The worlds of language are not made from extralinguistic things or ideas—not from Heraclitus's fire nor from Thales's water, not from brute facts nor from brute interpretations. There is no primary stuff out of which worlds can be made because there is no stuff nor worlds for us without communicative action. Human perception requires conception, and conception presupposes a social symbolic world. Thus facts are tiny entrenched theories, and true theories begin as objects held at arm's length (Hanson 1958; Quine 1960). Social facts are things, as Durkheim said, but only to the extent that all things already are social facts. Words are signs for things and facts. Things and facts are socially objectified, pragmatically concretized signs for words.

How then are worlds made? They are made from other worlds. And there are no worlds without words or other symbols. Worlds are shaped linguistically through metaphor, beginning much like dialect or pidgen (Brown 1987). Swahili and biophysics both are new worlds created from old ones. The search for a universal or necessary beginning of human worlds—in facts, innate ideas, or meanings—is thus akin to the search for the beginnings of human language, popular in the nineteenth century. Anthropology, paleontology, or developmental psychology may study social, protohistorical, or individual comings-to-be of worlds, but the search for a first world is as misguided as the search for a first moment in time or the search for the last elephant upon which all elephants stand who hold up the earth (actually they stand on a tortoise). Such "investigations" are futile because they mistake a regulative principle for an empirical one. The concept of first origins, like the concepts of structure or evolution or causality, is much like a Kantian synthetic a priori. It enables us to organize our perceptions into comprehensible experience, but cannot itself be empirically or logically grounded. Symbolic realism is such a regulative principle for dialectical inquiries.

This is not to say that we shouldn't mind mind, or that matter doesn't matter. Original thinkers design as much as they discover what they describe. But most science (or art, etc.) is mainly an elaboration of existing modes of representation, and even highly original thinkers cannot design in any way they choose. Unless they respect the regulative principles shared with their public, they are unlikely to gain credence or even to secure an audience. "While readiness to recognize alternative worlds may be liberating, and suggestive of new avenues of exploration, a willingness to welcome all worlds produces none" (Goodman 1978:97). Which worlds are to be accepted as true is both a normative and practical question, both epistemological and political, aesthetic and moral. Yet epistemology and politics, aesthetics and morals, also are symbolic constructions. They are worlds as well. Both the ingredients and the criteria of worlds are rhetorically constructed from (other) worlds.

The universe is always a universe of discourse in the classic sense given by de Morgan (1847, 41) in his *Formal Logic*, "a range of ideas which is either expressed or understood as containing the whole matter under discussion." Such discursive understanding also includes the tacit and necessarily unnoticed realm that is undiscussed, unnamed, and admitted without argument or scrutiny but that is, nevertheless, contained in language, though it may be unstated or expressed only as irony, blasphemy, or euphemism. Symbolic realism thus takes Plato's remark as literal: "The philosopher is a mythologist." But it adds that the philosopher also can be a demythologizer.

This critical thrust of symbolic realism also is directed against the radical relativism of purely subjectivist language interpretation. It shows how either purely analytical or purely interpretive accounts inevitably miss their target because neither can "bring out the incoherence of a discourse which, springing from underlying mythic or ideological schemes, has the capacity to survive every *reductio ad absurdum*. Systems of classification which reproduce, in their specific logic, the objective classes (i.e., divisions by sex, age, or position in the relations of production)," contribute to the reproduction of power relations by securing the misrecognition of the arbitrariness on which they are based (Bourdieu 1977, 164).

Pierre Bourdieu's criticism of conventional theories of knowledge is in the tradition of great "deconstructive" humanists such as Nietzsche, Marx, or Freud. What they had in common was their decision to take the whole of consciousness as false consciousness. Each was a great doubter in the manner of Descartes. But each took his doubt still further, into the inner fortress of Cartesian thought itself: each doubted that consciousness is as it appears to itself; each questioned whether, in consciousness, meaning and consciousness of meaning coincide (Ricoeur 1965, 32). Such radical doubt has corroded subjective humane values and undermined objective scientific knowledge. Such a humanism and such a science cannot be restored. But they can be transvalued and sublated by new methods and new metaphors—for example, by a deconstructive, critical exegesis of both science and values as rhetorical constructions. Such an exegesis is not merely an explanation of possible meanings as they are constructed in various disciplines, authors, or texts. It also includes, indeed focuses on, the methods by which knowledge, selves, and realities are produced. Rhetorical analysis deconstructs "texts" to reveal how historical forms of consciousness are constructed and, by implication, how such forms misrepresent practical social relations of domination. This is not a matter of correcting symbolic misrepresentations of a material reality. Instead it is a question of identifying and decoding disjunctions and mistranslations between different levels and orders of symbolization. At the same time, a critical rhetoric of reason affirms a more sophisticated humanism and a more sophisticated science in two ways. First, it undertakes a critique of the basic forms, categories, and methods of social and historical be-ing; and second, through such a critique, it seeks to confront men and women with the choices inherent in their actual historical possibilities.

The enemy of the symbolic realist, then, is neither the scientist nor the humanist as such. Instead, her typical adversary is the cognitive monopolist who maintains that his system is preeminent and all-inclusive, and that every other version must eventually be reduced to it or rejected as false or meaningless. Symbolic realism "implies no relaxation of rigor but a recognition that standards different from, yet no less exacting, than those applied in science are appropriate for appraising what is conveyed in perceptual or pictorial or literary" or other "versions of the world" (Goodman 1978, 5).

The rubble of failed attempts to definitively appraise theoretical works attests to the futility of seeking permanent binding canons of judgment for forms of theory. "Theoretic value means value in use, and use-value is tied to occasioned want in situated contexts" (Green 1989, 418). We thus should respect the relative validity of reasoning from different postulational systems, just as different forms of reasoning should respect the general rules of cogency and inference that make such discourse rational.

The assessment of the habitus of positivists or romantics is not a matter of purely rational deduction nor purely emotive choice, so much as it is a matter of prudential judgment. And as Foss (1971, 246, 248–49) pointed out, "Prudence is a practical virtue, an action concept. . . . [Thus] the justification of frameworks is a function of shifting environmental demands and the species survival needs to which these give rise." Symbolic realists' conception of a critical rhetoric of reason provides a metanarrative that facilitates such prudential judgment (Brown 1987). The point of symbolic realism is not to be truthful or untruthful in any ultimate sense, but to create with the reader a new textual space and a new rhetorical practice that, once established, enable both rhetor and reader to transcend the ontological assumptions and cognitive and behavioral norms that have served in part as their prison.

Our analysis finds a space between personal agency as articulated through a hermeneutic interpretation, and structural determinism as articulated through a positivist vocabulary. This space is the field for emancipatory theoretical practice. Deterministic theories deny agency explicitly; subjective hermeneutics vaporizes it by making it impossible to find error in any group's (version of the) world. Explanatory science poses the question of the conditions of the possibility of primary experience, thereby revealing that this experience, as understood in a hermeneutic phenomenology, is fundamentally defined as *not* posing this question. Whereas positive science takes itself too seriously, lifeworlds take themselves for granted. But from a critical perspective, emancipation is neither unrestricted agency nor unlimited determinism, but the *overcoming* of determinism by agency (Bhaskar 1982).

Reformulated this way, the sterile dichotomy between positivism and romanticism becomes a fecund dialectic. A scientific critique of lay and protoscientific ideas gives an emancipatory impulse to the human studies, provided that such a critique respects the existential significance of those ideas and does not itself make absolutist claims. Many social phenomena are emergent and hence require a realist explanation. For such explanations to be critical and transformative, however, they must not become reified, must not lose contact with the lived experience from which they emerged. Stripped by rhetorical analysis of its absolutist and objectivist illusions, social thought rediscovers its in-and-for-itself, its practical and emancipatory will to know.

By investigating our linguistic constraints and capacities, a critical rhetoric of reason sees persons both as carriers of preformed social linguistic structures and as agents who perform culture and speech. A revision of our symbolic representations, of our shared forms of perception and expression, is thus a re-visioning of the world. To be free means to have some mastery of this process.

REFERENCES

Adorno, Theodor, Hans Albert, Ralf Dahrendorf, Jürgen Habermas, Harald Pilot, and Karl Popper. 1976. *The Positivist Dispute in German Sociology.* London: Heinemann. (See this work for general background.)

Apel, Karl-Otto. 1967. *Analytical Philosophy of Language and the Geisteswissenschaften.* Dordrecht, Holland: D. Reidel.

Ayer, Alfred Jules. 1946. *Language, Truth and Logic.* New York: Dover.

Bhaskar, Roy. 1982. "Emergence, Explanation, and Emancipation," in *Explaining Human Behavior, Consciousness, Human Action, and Social Structure,* ed. Paul F. Secord. Beverly Hills: Sage, 275–310.

Bondi, Hermann. 1967. *Assumption and Myth in Physical Theory.* London: Cambridge University Press.

Bourdieu, Pierre. 1977. *Toward a Theory of Practice.* New York: Cambridge University Press.

Brown, Richard Harvey. 1989. *Social Science as Civic Discourse. On the Invention, Legitimation, and Uses of Social Theory.* Chicago: University of Chicago Press.

———. 1987. *Society as Text: Essays on Reason, Rhetoric, and Reality.* Chicago: University of Chicago Press.

Collins, Randall. 1975. *Conflict Sociology.* New York: Academic Press.

Coleridge, Samuel Taylor. 1839. *The Stateman's Manual.* London: W. Pickering.

Dallmayr, Paul. 1981. *Beyond Dogma and Despair. Toward a Critical Phenomenology of Politics.* Notre Dame, Ind.: University of Notre Dame Press.

de Morgan, Alfred. 1847. *Formal Logic: Or the Calculus of Inference, Necessary and Probable.* London: Taylor and Walton.

Derrida, Jacques. 1972. "Structure, Sign, and Play in the Discourse of the Human Sciences," in *The Structuralist Controversy: The Languages of Criticism and the Sciences of Man,* ed. Richard Macksey and Eugenio Donato. Baltimore: Johns Hopkins University Press, 2–18.

———. 1977. "Signature, Event, Context." *Glyph* 1: 172–97. Johns Hopkins Textual Studies. Baltimore: Johns Hopkins University Press.

Durkheim, Emile. 1965. *The Rules of Sociological Method.* Trans. Sarah A.
Solvoay and John H. Mueller. New York: Free Press.

Evans-Pritchard, E. 1965. *The Position of Women in Primitive Society and
Other Essays in Social Anthropology.* London.

Festugiere, A. J. 1950–1954. *La Revelation d'Hermes Trismegiste.* 4 vols. Paris.

Foss, Lawrence. 1971. "Art as Cognitive: Beyond Scientific Realism."
Philosophy of Science 38(June): 234–50.

Gadamer, Hans-Georg. 1975. *Truth and Method.* New York: Seabury Press.

Garfinkel, Harold. 1967. *Studies in Ethnomethodology.* Englewood Cliffs N.J.:
Prentice-Hall.

———. 1952. "The perception of the other: A study in Social Order." Ph.D.
diss., Harvard University.

Gavronsky, Serge. 1979. "Reality and Literary Languages." New York:
Department of French, Barnard College, Columbia University, mimeo.

Gellner, Ernest. 1975. *Legitimation of Belief.* Cambridge: Cambridge
University Press.

Gödel, Kurt. 1962. *On Formally Undecidable Propositions.* New York: Basic
Books.

Goodman, Nelson. 1978. *Ways of Worldmaking.* Indianapolis: Hackett.

Green, Bryan S. 1988. *Literary Methods and Sociological Theory.* Chicago:
University of Chicago Press.

Hansen, Norwood. 1958. *Patterns of Discovery.* New York and London:
Cambridge University Press.

Hirsch, E.D. 1967. *Validity in Interpretation.* New Haven, Conn.: Yale
University Press.

Husserl, Edmond. 1931. *Ideas: General Introduction to Phenomenology.* Trans.
W. R. Royce Gibson. London: Allen & Unwin.

Knorr-Cetina, Karin D. 1981. "The Micro-Sociological Challenge of
Macro-Sociology: Towards a Reconstruction of Social Theory and
Methodology," in *Advances in Social Theory and Methodology,* ed. Karin
D. Knorr-Cetina and Aaron V. Cicourel. London: Routledge & Kegan
Paul.

March, James L. 1983. "The Irony and Ambiguity of Freedom." *Poetry Today*
4, no. 3: 479–92.

Marx, Karl. 1970. *The German Ideology.* New York: International Publishers.

Menzel, Herbert. 1978. "Meaning—Who Needs It?" in *The Social Context of
Method,* ed. M. Brenner. London: Croom Helm.

Mills, C. Wright. 1974. *Power, Politics, and People. The Collected Essays of C.
Wright Mills.* Irving Louis Horowitz, ed. New York: Oxford University
Press.

Novalis (F.L.F. von Hardenberg). 1953–1957. *Fragmente, Werke,* 5 vols. E. Wasmuth, ed. Heidelberg.

Perelman, Chaim and Lucy Olbrechts-Tyteca. 1969. *The New Rhetoric. A Treatise on Argumentation.* Notre Dame Ind.: Notre Dame University Press.

Quine, Willard van O. 1960. *Word and Object.* Cambridge: MIT Press.

Ricoeur, Paul. 1965. *History and Truth.* Trans. Charles A. Kelbley. Evanston, Ill.: Northwestern University Press.

———. 1973. "Hermeneutique et Critique des Ideologies," in *Ideologie et Demythisation,* ed. Enrico Castelli. Paris: Aubier.

Rommetveit, R., and Joachim Israel. 1954. "Notes on the Standardization of Experimental Manipulations and Measurements in Cross-National Research." *Journal of Social Issues* 10, no. 4: 61–68.

Sartre, Jean-Paul. 1964. *Nausea.* Trans. Lloyd Alexander. New York: New Directions.

Schutz, Alfred. 1962. *Collected Papers.* Vol. 1. *The Problems of Social Reality.* Ed. Maurice Natanson. The Hague: Martinus Nijhoff.

Searle, John. 1969. *Speech Acts.* London: Cambridge University Press.

———. 1977. "Reiterating the Differences: A Reply to Derrida." *Glyph* 1: 198–208. (Johns Hopkins Textual Studies. Baltimore: Johns Hopkins University Press.)

———. 1983. "The Word Turned Upside Down." *New York Review of Books,* 27 October, 74–79.

Skinner, B. F. 1971. *Beyond Freedom and Dignity.* New York: Knopf.

Skinner, Quentin. 1969. "Meaning and Understanding in the History of Ideas." *History and Theory* 8, no. 4: 3–53.

Stanley, Manfred. 1978. *The Technological Conscience. Survival and Dignity in an Age of Expertise.* New York: Free Press.

Taylor, Charles. 1971. "Interpretation and the Science of Man." *Review of Metaphysics* 25, no. 3, 1–45.

Weinsheimer, Joel C. 1985. *Gadamer's Hermeneutics: A Reading of "Truth and Method".* New Haven: Yale University Press.

Wellmer, Albrecht. 1971. *Critical Theory of Society.* New York: Herder and Herder.

Winch, Peter. 1958. *The Idea of a Social Science and Its Relation to Philosophy.* New York: Humanities Press.

———. 1970. "Understanding a Primitive Society," in *Rationality,* ed. Brian R. Wilson, ed. Oxford University Press.

Wittgenstein, Ludwig. 1953. *Philosophical Investigations.* Trans. G. E. M. Anscombe. Oxford: Blackwell.

Wright, Edmond. 1977a. "Perception: A New Theory." *American Philosophical Quarterly* 14, no. 4: 273–86.

———. 1977b. "Words and Intentions." *Philosophy* 52, no. 199: 45–62.

———. 1983. Introduction to "The Ironic Discourse." *Poetics Today* 4, no. 3: 391–98.

Yates, Frances A. 1964. *Giordano Bruno and the Hermetic Tradition*. Chicago: Regnery.

14

Rhetoric and Its Double:
Reflections on the Rhetorical Turn
in the Human Sciences

Dilip Parameshwar Gaonkar

THE FLIGHT FROM "MERE" RHETORIC

Rhetoric cannot escape itself. Rhetoric cannot escape its "mereness," or to use the fashionable vocabulary of our time (here I am alluding to Derridean deconstruction), it cannot escape its status as a "supplement." Yet this simple fact that there is no exit for rhetoric, nor an exit from rhetoric, escapes many friends of rhetoric. Rhetoric cannot efface itself to become its traditional counterpart, dialectic, as Perelman and Valesio would have it.[1] Nor can it recast itself, as Grassi proposes, as the seat of primordial poetic utterance, which apprehends and articulates "the first principles" on which the rational speech of philosophy, in turn, depends.[2] Nor can rhetoric be equated with a hermeneutics of suspicion, as the linguistically inclined followers of Marx, Nietzsche, and Freud would suggest.

To be sure, rhetoric stands in a historically fluctuating relationship with other disciplines, especially those formal disciples which are its neighbors. To a certain measure, its identity and its fortunes are linked to those fluctuating affiliations. For that reason, Roland Barthes tells us that "rhetoric must always be read in the structural interplay with its neighbors (Grammar, Logic, Poetics, Philosophy): it is the play of the system, not each of its parts in itself, which is historically significant."[3] Sometimes its systemic proximity to one of the neighbors is so great and compelling that one is prone to overlook its distinctive character and its essential difference. If such a misreading of rhetoric happened but occasionally, it would be understandable.

However, when scholars repeatedly fail to distinguish rhetoric from its neighbors, and do so even in a period marked by a renewed and self-conscious interest in rhetoric, it is reasonable to suspect that something more than an accident is involved. The tenacity of this error, if error it is, should give us pause and prompt us to review this impulse (this habit of the mind) which urges us to make rhetoric into something other than itself.

341

What is involved in these misreadings, in my opinion, is simply a "flight from rhetoric," or to be more precise, a flight from "mere" rhetoric—that is, rhetoric conceived as a "supplement." What is so frightening, you may ask, that one should seek to flee from "mere" rhetoric in so deliberate a manner?

Once rhetoric is conceived as a "supplement," it becomes a formal, hence an empty discipline. It is without substance, without a secure set of referents, or to put it mundanely, it has no subject matter of its own. To be sure, one can take the general and recurrent lines of arguments (topics) and certain structural/functional resources of language (tropes and figures) as the special province or the subject matter of rhetoric. But this does not resolve the difficulty. Such a view, it seems to me, while recognizing rhetoric as a mode of practical reasoning and discourse production does so precisely in terms of its formal character as a language art. Thus deprived of substance, rhetoric stands in a parasitic relationship vis-a-vis substantive disciplines such as ethics and politics. Sometimes this "parasite" becomes so deeply entangled with the affairs of an alien body, especially the "body politic," it forgets its own nature and purpose and pretends to be a substantive entity. Perhaps this is what Aristotle had in mind when he said, "It thus appears that rhetoric is an offshoot of dialectic and also of ethical studies. Ethical studies may fairly be called political: and for this reason rhetoric masquerades as political science, and the professors of it as political experts."[4] For much the same reason, Plato reached a more severe judgment and dismissed rhetoric as a counterfeit art (*Gorgias*, 464–65).

Brian Vickers, a distinguished contemporary champion of rhetoric, notes that rhetoric, having no subject matter of its own, functions a bit like a "service industry," and thereby gets into territorial disputes with other disciplines.[5] The very fact that rhetoric is without a domicile is seen as profoundly threatening to the integrity of substantive disciplines. The territorial disputes between two substantive disciplines, say, law and sociology, are far less acrimonious than when rhetoric enters the picture and attempts to transform and use the materials characteristic of either of those two disciplines. Here I am reminded of Cicero's characterization of Marc Antony as a "homeless" transgressor in the *Fourth Philippic*. According to Cicero, one could negotiate with an enemy on some "settled principle" so long as he has "a republic, a senate house, a treasury, harmonious and united citizens" which he hopes to protect and promote. But Antony, says Cicero, "is attacking your republic, but has none himself; is eager to destroy the Senate, . . . but has no public council himself; he has exhausted your treasury, and has none of his own. For how can a man be supported by the unanimity of the citizens, who has no city at all?"[6] If we substitute rhetoric for Antony, we have an apt image for the kind of danger rhetoric represents to the established disciplines. Rhetoric can spring up any time, from within or without, to pollute and possess what is not its own for the sake of temporary advantage and gratification. Thus, rhetoric is seen as a nomadic discipline that threatens the integrity of the republic of knowledge itself. Why would anyone want to admit such a discipline to the council of learning when it refuses to abide by the academic rules of property and propriety?

Such is the impulse of an empty discipline to become substantive, to become something other than itself. It is as if rhetoric were in search of its other, the substantive other, who, when found, would fill out its formal emptiness. But this other which is to provide rhetoric with a grounding, relieve it from that epistemic anxiety with which it has been burdened since Plato, will always elude us. Perhaps this is the fatal game which animates rhetoric and keeps it going.

The flight from "mere" rhetoric consists of a double movement which, in my view, regulates, shapes, and determines the self-image of rhetoric. This double movement simultaneously propels rhetoric on a vertical axis downward into its past to find itself a suitable history and on a horizontal axis sideways to situate itself within the discursive practices of special "substantive" sciences, especially the human sciences. Rhetoric moves diachronically to discover for itself an alternative historical tradition that will free it from its supplementary status, and it moves synchronically to find itself in the discursive body (textuality) of other disciplines that will confirm its "presence."

These two movements motivated by their distaste for "mere rhetoric" direct us to flee from it, especially if we are serious about this business of rehabilitating rhetoric as "the once and future queen of the human sciences."[7] They play on our disciplinary "lures" and anxieties (which are predictably many), and urge us to make rhetoric into something other than itself.

This double movement in the contemporary self-understanding of rhetoric is not necessarily fully "articulated." Nor is it an entirely "implicit" and subterranean movement which I am somehow magically bringing to light. If this movement is partially "invisible," its invisibility is not due to its obscure presence but to what Alfred Schutz calls its "taken-for-granted" character.[8]

As you may have inferred from my characterization of this double movement as a "lure," I regard it as fundamentally problematic and pos-

343

sibly destructive of rhetoric as a vocation. However, I am not here to reject it but to contest it. In fact, this double movement is not something which can be either accepted or rejected, for it is one of the "essentially contested" features of our discipline.[9]

THE FIRST MOVEMENT: THE SUPPLEMENTARY TRADITION

The idea that rhetoric is no more than a "supplement" makes its initial appearance in the fabled encounter between the Older Sophists and the Platonic Socrates, the first site of the so-called quarrel between rhetoric and philosophy. Naturally, there are several strands to this quarrel between rhetoric and philosophy, but both historically and in our own time much of the dispute concerns the epistemic status of rhetoric.[10] The idea that rhetoric is no more than a "supplement" has its origin in the articulation of this question.

The question in its simplest form is this: Does rhetoric, the art of discovering available means of persuasion in a given case (Aristotle), have anything to do with the generation of knowledge? If not, as Socrates, Plato, and Aristotle appear to have assumed, then we may ask, as Heidegger asked of poets: *What are rhetoricians for?*

The Aristotelian compromise on this question, which sets into motion the "supplementary" tradition in rhetoric, is well known. For Aristotle, among other things, rhetoric makes knowledge more readily comprehensible and acceptable in the domain of civic discourse. That is, rhetoric cannot generate knowledge but is useful, possibly indispensable, for the transmission of knowledge discovered by philosophy and the special substantive sciences. Rhetoric, to use a term popularized by Jacques Derrida, is a supplement to knowledge, much as writing is a supplement to speech.[11]

The placing of Aristotle within the supplementary tradition is somewhat problematic. In the Aristotelian scheme, while demonstrative (apodictic) reasoning belongs to the domain of the necessary, rhetoric and dialectic operate within the domain of the contingent and the probable. Further, neither rhetoric nor dialectic "is a science that deals with the nature of any definite subject, but they are merely faculties of furnishing arguments."[12] Rhetoric, in other words, is a general art consisting not of knowledge about substantive fields but a flexible system of formal and prudential devices— topics, tropes and figures, inferential schemes, probabilities, prudential rules, and so on.[13] At the same time, however, this general art is functionally implicated in managing and transforming common opinion for

344

persuasive ends. This functional link to common opinion, according to Leff, prevents rhetoric from becoming a purely formal discipline, and its practical applications extend to the whole field of human affairs.[14] Moreover, the functional aspect of rhetoric is particularly decisive in the civic arena when citizens have to make judgments on issues without recourse to the special sciences to guide their deliberation.[15] This unresolved tension between the formal and the functional dimensions of rhetoric threatens its identity in two distinct but contradictory ways. On the one hand, rhetoric cannot posit a substantive identity because it has no subject matter of its own; on the other hand, its functional involvement with *doxa* threatens its formal identity by what Ricoeur calls an "overburdening of content."[16] Thus, rhetoric is simultaneously empty of subject matter and overburdened with content.

It is against this background one has to negotiate the question as to whether rhetoric has an epistemic function. The centrality of "invention" in the rhetorical tradition as a whole hints at a generative rather than a purely managerial and transmissive function for rhetoric. Yet a closer examination reveals that the aim of rhetorical inquiry is quite different from that of dialectical inquiry. A distinction introduced by Kenneth Burke is particularly useful in this context. Burke, following Aristotle, recognizes that both dialectic and rhetoric begin their inquiry with a critique of common opinion in the realm of the contingent and the probable. But the two critiques have different ends. Although the dialectical critique occurs in the scenic order of truth with a view toward transcending the conflict intrinsic to opinion, the rhetorical critique occurs in the moral order of action with a view toward managing and transforming conflicting opinions in accordance with the exigencies of a given situation. Hence rhetoric, unlike dialectic, is not constitutive of general truths and propositions but of specific beliefs, attitudes, and actions.[17]

Roland Barthes arrives at a similar conclusion regarding Aristotle's treatment of the passions. What Aristotle offers in his *Rhetoric*, according to Barthes, is a "projected" psychology: a psychology as everyone imagines it—not "what is in the mind" of the public, but what the public believes others "have in mind." In Barthes' view, Aristotle's innovative treatment of the passions (in contrast to the technographers who preceded him) lies precisely in his decision to view them "*in their banality*" and to classify "the passions not according to what they are, but according to what they are believed to be: he does not describe them scientifically, but seeks out arguments which can be used with respect to the public's ideas about passion."[18] Rhetorical psychology is therefore quite the opposite of a reductive psychology that would try to see what is *behind* what people say and attempt to reduce anger, for instance, to *something else*, something hidden. For Aristotle, public opinion is the first and last datum; he has no hermeneutic notion (of decipherment): anger is what every one thinks about anger, passion is never anything but what people say it is.[19]

Rhetoric thus puts together a disparate set of materials and insights originating in common opinion and popular understanding by recourse to a flexible system of formal devices on an ad hoc basis. Despite its generality as a formal system, rhetoric is marked by a radical particularity in its practices and products. Thus, unless one is prepared to collapse the distinction between knowledge and belief, understanding and action, it seems unreasonable to invoke the authority of Aristotle to claim that rhetoric has an epistemic function.

At any rate, according to the "supplementary" tradition, the quarrel between sophistic rhetoric and Platonic philosophy, as mediated by Aristotle, was decided in favor of the latter. Rhetoric was pushed into the margins of philosophy and the special sciences, and there it was forced to function as *a supplement to knowledge.* The subsequent history of rhetoric is the history of a supplement, living in the margins of philosophy, periodically attempting to widen that margin, as in the case of Cicero and the Renaissance Humanists, or to deepen the dignity of supplementary function, as in the case of St. Augustine.[20] On the whole, however, it is not a history of violent opposition and rebellion against philosophy, but one of accommodation, adjustment, and redefinition.

This tradition of the *supplement* has led many students of rhetoric into a conceptual impasse, as illustrated by John Quincy Adams, the first holder of the Boylston Professorship of Rhetoric at Harvard. In a lecture given in 1806, he declares that rhetoric "which has exhausted the genius of Aristotle, Cicero, and Quintilian, can neither require nor admit much additional illustration. To select, combine, and apply their precepts, is the only duty left for their followers of all succeeding times, and to obtain a perfect familiarity with their instructions is to arrive at the mastery of the art."[21] The same frame of mind prompted the English scholar J. E. C. Welldon in 1886 to praise Aristotle's *Rhetoric* "as being perhaps a solitary instance of a book which not only begins a science, but completes it."[22] Such is the praise heaped on a text (an incomplete set of lecture notes to be precise) that, whatever its genius, stands profoundly divided against itself. This is the extent to which rhetoric had been emasculated within the rubric of a "supplementary" tradition by the end of the nineteenth century.

Understandably, the revived interest in rhetoric in this century is marked by a desire to break free from such a conceptual impasse. The tale of twentieth-century rhetoric, at least in its theoretical speculations, if not in its critical practice, can be read as a revolt against the "supplementary" tradition.

THE SOPHISTIC TRADITION

This escape from "mere" rhetoric takes many forms and employs many strategies. One way to escape from the conceptual impasse brought about by the "supplementary tradition" is to revive its historical opponent, the sophistic tradition. The rehabilitation of the older sophists that began in the early part of the nineteenth century under the sponsorship of Hegel in Germany and Grote in England has gained considerable momentum in this century. Their name, if not their work, is prominent in the current revival of rhetoric.[23] A return to their skeptical outlook on the "language-ridden" world of human culture is regarded as central to any serious attempt at reviving rhetoric. This revival of the sophistic tradition consists of two related sets of moves, the philosophical and the historical.

The philosophical move in restoring the sophistic tradition to its former glory requires one to de-center the epistemic question. Instead of asking whether rhetoric can generate knowledge, a more fundamental (ontological) question is pushed to the center: How is rhetoric possible?[24] This Kantian type of question refers to the ultimate grounds of rhetoric. In response to this question, two unavoidable human characteristics are offered as the ultimate grounds of rhetoric. First, to use a phrase of Kenneth Burke, humans are symbol-using (misusing) creatures. Second, to use a pharse of Hannah Arendt, life is given to humans under "the condition of plurality."[25] From these two ultimate grounds, one can derive, in turn (as de Man and Todorov do), two distinct but related concepts of rhetoric.[26] They are rhetoric as persuasion and rhetoric as trope. Although the dimension of plurality, marked by "unity in division" (Burke), imposes on humans the necessity of persuasion, the tropological dimension of language makes them susceptible to persuasion. The basic strategy here is to derive in a global fashion the inevitability of rhetoric from our social relations as they are mediated by language. This strategy clearly favors certain theories of language and social relations over others. For instance, while the theory that views language as a transparent medium for the communication of things and ideas is clearly unacceptable, the thesis that social reality, among other things, is linguistically constructed and legitimated is enthusiastically endorsed.[27] The main difficulty with this strategy, with rare exceptions, is that it operates at an extremely high level of generality and almost equates rhetoric with language use and sociability. As a result, this philosophical strategy is disconnected from the sense of rhetoric as a local phenomenon which is so central to the human experience of rhetoric as a material force.[28]

The historical move is far more intriguing. The return to the sophists requires a reconstitution of the history of rhetoric. One cannot traverse 2500 years back to the origins of rhetoric without acknowledging the intervening steps. According to this reconstituted history, there are not one but two histories of rhetoric—a manifest history and a hidden history. And they are dominated by two different traditions—the manifest history by the "supplementary" tradition, and the hidden history by the sophistic tradition.

The manifest history begins predictably enough with the older sophists and their celebrated quarrel with the Platonic Socrates; it moves through Aristotle, Isocrates, Cicero, Quintilian, and St. Augustine in the classical world, and then through the Middle Ages and the Renaissance and the eighteenth century neoclassical rhetoric and the Scottish School. This is the official history of Boethius, Alcuin, George of Trebizond, Agricola, Ramus, Bacon, Fenelon, Lawson, Campbell, and Blair, which finally culminates in Bishop Whately's *Elements of Rhetoric*. This is the history of rhetoric conceived as a "supplement," a history of obscure places, unfamiliar names, and forgotten texts.

The other history of rhetoric, its hidden history, also begins with the celebrated quarrel between the sophists and the Platonic Socrates, and moves indecisively alongside the manifest history until the end of the classical world; then, suddenly, it disappears, until it is *rediscovered* by Kenneth Burke. The "hidden" history places a somewhat different interpretation on the quarrel between sophistic rhetoric and Platonic philosophy. According to this version, the fabulous quarrel that held the Greek mind captive during the declining years of Periclean Enlightenment involved more than the competing claims of two skirmishing disciplines. Rather, it was a contest between two competing ways of life, *the vita activa* and *the vita contemplativa*. Their competing claims to civic attention is described vividly, but with a decided bias, in the Platonic dialogues, especially in the *Theaetetus* (172c–175e). Such a contest could not be settled in a single generation, even if that generation could produce so rare a phenomenon as Socrates. So it continues to engage our attention to this day in varying degrees of intensity. At any rate, for a variety of reasons, both political and intellectual, this competition for cultural hegemony ended in a defeat for the sophists, and they were promptly driven out of the cultural milieu by their philosophical detractors. Thereafter sophistry, insofar as it is a permanent opening for man, had to live an underground, subterranean existence. Later when Aristotle made the compensatory move towards rhetoric and granted it the status of a supplement, rhetoric and sophistic became divorced. While rhetoric, in its attenuated form as a "supplement," was allowed to live in the margins of philosophy, sophistic was "repressed." Thus, rhetoric continued to function as a supplement to philosophical knowledge, where it regulated certain discursive practices and products, but it could not function as a supplement to a sophistic *Weltanschauung* marked by ethical relativity and epistemic skepticism. In this managerial placement, style retained a legitimate interest for the art, but rhetoric seems incapable of generating its own grounding as a mode of persuasion. This partly explains why the theory of invention in rhetoric became moribund, but the theory of *lexis* (*eloqutio*) was endlessly refined and elaborated.

But what is "repressed" is not erased. It must resurface in various symptomatic forms. Besides, the natural affinity between rhetoric and sophistic would continually draw the two together. Hence, there follows a series of illicit relations and subterranean connections, which constitute the "hidden" history of rhetoric. In some sense, this is the "return of the repressed." And the most distinguished chronicler of this return is none other than Kenneth Burke.

In Burke's A *Rhetoric of Motives*, this proposed reconstruction of the "hidden" history of rhetoric was brilliantly outlined, if not filled out in detail. His initial project in this book was to extend the range of rhetoric, but that extension, as he quickly realized, required an historical grounding, which forced him to depart from the manifest history. He began "by showing how a rhetorical motive is often present where it is not usually recognized, or thought to belong":

> In part, we would but *rediscover* rhetorical elements that had
> become obscured when rhetoric as a term fell into disuse, and
> other specialized disciplines such as esthetics, anthropology,
> psychoanalysis, and sociology came to the fore (so that esthetics
> sought to outlaw rhetoric, while the other sciences we have
> mentioned took over, each in its own terms, the rich rhetorical
> elements that esthetics would ban).[29]

He continues:

> But besides this job of *reclamation*, we also seek to develop our
> subject beyond the traditional bounds of rhetoric. There is an
> intermediate area of expression that is not wholly deliberate, yet
> not wholly unconscious. It lies midway between aimless utterance
> and speech deliberately purposive.[30]

In order to analyze this rhetorical area, Burke has to shift from reliance on "persuasion" to "identification" as the key term of rhetoric:

> Particularly when we come upon such aspects of persuasion as are
> found in "mystification," courtship, and the "magic" of class
> relationships, the reader will see why the classical notion of clear
> persuasive intent is not an accurate fit for describing the ways in
> which the members of a group promote social cohesion by acting
> rhetorically upon themselves and one another.[31]

At this point, I am not interested in examining Burke's concept of identification, which has already received ample critical attention. What interests me is the implications of this shift from "persuasion" to "identification" for a history of rhetoric. Consider, for instance, the second part of the book, which bears the title: "Traditional Principles of Rhetoric." In the first few pages (49–84), Burke examines some classical texts by Aristotle, Cicero, Quintilian, and St. Augustine where "persuasion" is the key term. Then, on page 90, there occurs a "break," a "rupture," in the text, as Burke begins to move with "identification" as the key concept into what I would call the "hidden" history of rhetoric. Here the task of "reclamation" proper begins: Bentham's theory of fictions, Marx on "Mystification" (*The German Ideology*), Carlyle on "Mystery" (*Sartor Resartus*), Diderot on "Pantomime" (*Neveu de Rameau*), De Gourmont on "Dissociation" (*La Dissociation des Idées*), Pascal on "Directing the Intention," Administrative Rhetoric in Machiavelli, Dante's *De Vulgari Eloquentia*, and so on. After a long underground existence, the sophistic tradition in rhetoric has been rediscovered, reclaimed, and reconstituted.

Here Burke, the "reclaimer," is in his "true form." While tracking down the implications of "persuasion" in classical texts, Burke is impatient, restrained, like a tiger in a cage, summarizing the formal/tropological principles laboriously catalogued by Cicero in a mere page or two, and then quickly moving on to something else, say, Longinus' *On the Sublime*. But once we come to Bentham's *Book of Fallacies*, a dazzling intellectual journey begins, a veritable *tour de force* through the corridors of the history of ideas, interweaving text upon text, in the same breath speaking of Pascal and Joyce. It is a consummate performance.

It is almost impossible not to be seduced by this other "hidden" history of rhetoric, as "reconstituted" by Burke, especially when he invites "other analysts" to join him in "the task of tracking down the ways in which the realm of sheerly worldly powers become endowed with attributes of 'secular divinity.' "[32]

Who can refuse such an invitation, especially someone about to embark on rhetoric as a vocation. If accepted, this invitation calls at one level for extending the range of rhetoric, which I find perfectly legitimate. But that extension, in turn, requires a "reinterpretation" of the history of rhetoric that is problematic, if not ill-conceived.

Such is the seductive tale of the two histories of rhetoric. There are, to be sure, many other tales about the birth, the rise, the decline, the fall and even the "death" of rhetoric. These tales have been constructed frequently by those who are not themselves, as I am not, full-fledged historians of rhetoric. They are clearly political tales, meant to account for the troubled relationship between rhetoric and other disciplines and culture in general. They are designed so as to legitimate its claim to renewed intellectual and cultural attention. Each putative revivalist of rhetoric has to tell a tale of its glorious origins, its civilizing effects, its unjustified suppression, and its eventual demise and dispersion. So the tale I have told above on behalf of Kenneth Burke (unauthorized, to be sure) is only one among many tales circulating among the current revivalists of rhetoric. As a revivalist tale it is only partly true. And this tale, like so many of the recent tales about the history of rhetoric, is epistemologically driven. It speaks as though the quarrel between Plato and the older sophists over the epistemic status of rhetoric continually and exclusively shaped its complex history. It fails to acknowledge that from late antiquity to the high Middle Ages, Latin rhetorical instruction was largely dominated by two manuals of what George Kennedy calls "technical rhetoric": *De Inventione* and *Rhetorica ad Herrennium*.[33] It completely overlooks the third tradition in rhetoric, the tradition of civic humanism that stretches from Protagoras through Isocrates and Cicero to the Renaissance humanists, and continues to manifest itself in the activities of great orators like Edmund Burke. But these errors, repeatedly corrected by the orthodox historians like Kennedy and Vickers, continue to remain occluded from a disciplinary consciousness obsessed with abstract epistemological questions.

My reservations are quite simple. The "lure" of the hidden history has led to a denigration of the manifest history of rhetoric. One simple fact attests to this. Despite all the talk about the "Revival of Rhetoric" and the coming of the "New Rhetoric" in this century, we have yet to produce a definitive history of rhetoric. As an intellectual enterprise, rhetoric cannot continue to be viable without an adequate understanding of its own history, even if that history is an uninspiring one, which I don't think it is. If there is one thing we can learn from Jacques Derrida, it is that the history of a supplement may be more interesting than the history of that which is in need of a supplement.

THE SECOND MOVEMENT: THE RHETORIC OF INQUIRY

The second horizontal movement that propels rhetoric to constantly reconfirm its "presence" in the discourse of other disciplines is fashionably characterized these days as the "rhetorical turn" in the human sciences, or as the Iowa School prefers to call it the "rhetoric of inquiry."

In this paper I am not primarily concerned, as the Iowa School avowedly is, with the discovery of rhetoric by the practitioners of human sciences and the consequences of that discovery for the discursive practices of their disciplines. What interests me at this moment is the impact of that discovery on the self-understanding of rhetoric itself. To be sure, I recognize that rhetoric and the human sciences interpenetrate one another in innumerable ways, and the evolving dialectic between the two has a long history. What I seek to problematize here is but a single aspect of that dialectic.

The "rhetorical turn" refers to the growing recognition of rhetoric in contemporary thought, especially among the special substantive sciences. It means that the special sciences are becoming increasingly rhetorically self-conscious. They are beginning to recognize that their discursive practices, both internal and external, contain an unavoidable rhetorical component. *Internal* here refers to those discursive practices that are internal to a specific scientific language community; *external* refers to the discursive practices of that scientific language community in respect to its dealings with other scientific (or nonscientific) language communities and the society in general. While the external dimension is sometimes noted, the work of the Iowa School clearly emphasizes the internal dimension.

The existing body of literature pertaining to the internal dimension of the rhetorical turn in contemporary thought can be further divided into two groups: the explicit rhetorical turn and the implicit rhetorical turn. By *explicit* rhetorical turn, I refer to those works that explicitly recognize the relevance of rhetoric for contemporary thought and where rhetoric is used

352

as a critical and interpretive method. The works of the following scholars, including those generally identified as the new rhetoricians (Chaim Perelman, Kenneth Burke, Richard McKeon, I.A. Richards, and Richard Weaver), may be placed in this category: Wayne Booth, Paul de Man, Walter J. Ong, Ernesto Grassi, Paolo Valesio, Northrop Frye, Tzvetan Todorov, Harold Bloom, Hugh Dalziel Duncan.

Clearly, however, those authors are not equally enthusiastic about rhetoric. While some of them have written several books on rhetoric, others confine their observations on rhetoric to a mere essay or two. While some of them view rhetoric as a general theory of discourse (hence a metadiscipline), others simply admit the importance of rhetoric for the human sciences and employ it as a critical instrument in their analyses of literary and social texts; and there are those who simply scatter the word *rhetoric* carelessly through their texts. For instance, there is a renewed interest in rhetoric among the literary critics. But the nature and intensity of interest varies significantly. Thus, while Wayne Booth, operating from a distinctly humanistic perspective, concentrates on the argumentative dimension of literature, especially novels, Paul de Man, operating from a deconstructionist perspective, stresses the figural dimension of literary language.[34] Other critics, like Frye, Todorov, Mailoux, and Bloom, have paid varying degrees of attention to rhetoric, but as opposed to Booth and de Man, we could not properly entitle them "rhetorical critics."

Finally and perhaps most important, there are also texts that evince signs of an *implicit* rhetorical turn. These are texts whose authors, while relatively unaware of the rhetorical lexicon, seem to be groping for a vocabulary that could adequately characterize the tropological and suasory aspects of the discursive practices that remain occluded from disciplinary consciousness.

The list of authors and their texts that evince signs of such an implicit rhetorical turn is truly formidable: Thomas Kuhn's *The Structure of Scientific Revolutions*, Paul Feyerabend's *Against Method*, Steven Toulmin's *The Uses of Argument*, Lacan's *Ecrits*, Gadamer's *Truth and Method*, Foucault's *Archeology of Knowledge*, and Habermas's *Legitimation Crisis*, to name a few. These are the master texts of our time, and they are, we are told, bristling with rhetorical insights, even though they often are not consciously recognized.

Furthermore, on some accounts, whole "schools of thought" reveal a decisively rhetorical orientation. Here one might list the sociology of knowledge tradition (from Scheler to Berger and Luckmann), the symbolic interactionists, the dramatistic movement in anthropology and sociology

(Geertz, Turner, and Goffman), and various philosophical positions that stress the role of language and language action (e.g., the "later" Wittgenstein and the "early" Heidegger, Austin, Searle, and other speech-act theorists). The contemporary intellectual landscape is, thus, replete with signs of an implicit rhetorical turn. With a bit of diligence and, of course, with requisite faith, anyone could read those signs and celebrate what they portend.

The *locus classicus* of this implicit rhetorical turn in contemporary thought is Kuhn's *The Structure of Scientific Revolutions.*[35] The reasons for the choice of this text are quite obvious. *First,* it examines the discursive practices of the hard sciences, such as physics and chemistry. *Second,* it brings to light the rhetorical aspect of discursive practices internal to the scientific language community. *Third,* Kuhn makes these profound observations without the slightest awareness of the rhetorical lexicon. *Fourth,* though unconscious of rhetoric, he makes a fairly radical claim for the primacy of rhetoric when he asserts that "paradigm shifts" in any scientific community are more like religious conversions than carefully considered and well-reasoned shifts in scientific practices. *Fifth,* he calls for a reexamination of the history of science from a sociological perspective. He rejects the textbook version of the history of science as an idealization which assumes that the growth of knowledge is a purely logical-rational enterprise. These aspects of Kuhn's work have made him into the very embodiment of the rhetorical turn. If the discourse of the physicists cannot detach itself from rhetoric, how can the chatter of lesser mortals, such as historians and sociologists, hope to emancipate itself from rhetoric?

In short, it appears that there is more to the "rhetorical turn" than the mundane explicit turn. Just as there are two histories of rhetoric, the manifest and the hidden, there are two rhetorical turns, the explicit and the implicit. The lure of the implicit rhetorical turn is infinitely greater than the reality of the explicit rhetorical turn. Although the explicit rhetorical turn is a result of practical necessity—a literary critic like Booth, for example, is unable to make sense of novelistic prose without recourse to a rhetorical vocabulary and rhetorical sensibilities—the implicit rhetorical turn is a largely theoretical and epistemological enterprise. If the explicit rhetorical turn is only a decade or two old, the implicit rhetorical turn is of more ancient vintage. Its roots can be traced all the way back to that celebrated quarrel between Platonic Socrates and the older sophists. If Kenneth Burke is the chronicler of the hidden history of rhetoric, Professors Nelson and Megill have undertaken to chronicle the story of the implicit rhetorical turn. Nelson and Megill, along with Donald

McCloskey, are the leading figures in the Iowa School, which has done much to place claims of the rhetorical turn before the scholarly community.

THE NELSON AND MEGILL MYTH

In a recent essay, Nelson and Megill set out to furnish the "rhetoric of inquiry" with what they call an "animating myth."[36] They write:

> Rather, we sketch the development of the field so far, focusing on how early contributors have regarded rhetoric and inquiry. This is not the history of rhetoric, science, or philosophy widely familiar to scholars of communication. It is instead an animating myth of the new field.[37]

They are, however, certain that "what begins as myth ends as history." A myth of this sort requires a set of precursors who were but dimly aware of what they were doing, that is, preparing the way for the progressive dismantling of a logic of inquiry which is to be replaced by a rhetoric of inquiry.

Nelson and Megill do, indeed, give us a myth, a good one at that. It is reminiscent of Protagoras's reply in Plato's dialogue of that name when Socrates asks him to identify what he does. Protagoras admits to being "a sophist and an educator" (317b). But he claims to practice an ancient art and not something new and fashionable as people assume. According to Protagoras, since sophistry seems to arouse, however unjustifiably, suspicion among people, those who practiced it before did not admit to being sophists. They adopted suitable disguises and worked under the cover of some other profession. Homer, Hesiod, and Simonides claimed to be poets, Orpheus and Musaeus claimed to be musicians, and Herodicus of Selymbria claimed to be a physician. In fact, however, they were all sophists (316d–e). But that strategy of concealment did not work. They were discovered for what they were, and their attempt to disguise their art excited even greater mistrust. So Protagoras freely admits to being a sophist and welcomes any opportunity to explain and defend his art, for only through constant public exposure can sophistry hope to overcome the undeserved fear and suspicion with which it is presently regarded.

However, the myth which Nelson and Megill want to weave for us cannot be a simple Protagorean tale of exposing one's timorous and somewhat inept precursors. For them, rhetoric, and by implication the rhetoric of inquiry, is a ubiquitous and unavoidable component in human belief

355

and behavior. Since rhetoric always already exists, it cannot be simply discovered and enunciated. It has to be rediscovered and reconstituted. For that reason, it must be first repressed and made to disappear. If someone is going to be credited with recovering and recuperating rhetoric, then someone must be charged with its prior repression and dispersion.

The story of the progressive repression of the rhetoric of inquiry begins, predictably enough, in the seventeenth century with the birth of modern philosophy—with Descartes' quest for "clear and distinct ideas." In the quest for certainty, the "empiricist" Locke and the "idealist" Kant follow the "rationalist" Descartes. They embrace mathematics as the ideal model of conviction and "dream of dispelling disagreement through demonstration." Thus, rhetoric comes to be repressed. The repression is carried out through a series of dichotomies: truth vs. opinion, object vs. subject, conviction vs. persuasion, all of which valorize the logic of inquiry over rhetoric.

This repression also had political implications. According to Nelson and Megill,

> Plato denigrated opinion and rhetoric so as to celebrate truth and order at a time of Greek conflict and Athenian decline. Similarly, Aristotle subordinated mythos to logos and rhetoric to dialectic. In an era when radical disagreements racked the peace of Europe, Descartes wrote off rhetoric in favor of mathematical reason and Hobbes enslaved language to the sovereign. Later, Kant sought perpetual peace through pure and practical reason.[38]

The sole voice of dissent on behalf of rhetoric in the late seventeenth and early eighteenth century was Vico, who opposed Cartesianism with the same sort of vigor with which Isocrates had once opposed Platonism. According to Nelson and Megill, effective opposition to the hegemonic rule of modern philosophy over scholarly inquiry did not occur until the late nineteenth century, and it is Nietzsche who emerges as the leading *persona:* "One *implicitly* rhetorical challenge to the sovereignty that modern philosophy claims over scholarship actually begins with Nietzsche's assault on the subject/object dichotomy."[39] As the opposition gathered speed and momentum in the twentieth century the privileged set of dichotomies was challenged, undermined, and dissolved. The quest for certainty was questioned. The fear of disagreement abated. The mathematic model of conviction began to yield to the discursive model of persuasion. Modern epistemology came to be seen as a source of, rather than a shield against, the philosophical anxiety about "skepticism, solipsism, and nihilism." This challenge to "the Cartesian foundations and Kantian principles of modern philosophy" followed from a series of internal discursive crises and tensions in philosophy and science. Nelson and Megill identify three such crises (but do not discuss them): the philosophical attack on foundationalism, the philosophical reconstruction of science, and, the rhetorical conception of epistemology. And they enumerate a list of twentieth-century thinkers (a now familiar litany from Dewey and Heidegger through McIntyre and Rorty) who recognize and grapple with these crises and thus, unwittingly, open the way to a rhetoric of inquiry.

All this intellectual ferment, Nelson and Megill conclude, leads to Iowa City in the 1980s where the logic of inquiry is officially transformed into a rhetoric. This transformation yields a good many benefits: We will escape from the clutches of "Western rationalism and its paradox of authoritarian liberation." As we begin to pay more attention to the actual reasoning that goes on in scholarly inquiry, we will learn to "recognize that rhetoric is reasonable and reason is rhetorical." As we begin to notice that scholarship is also a mode of communication addressed to an audience, we will learn to "insist that rhetoric is contextual and context is rhetorical."

Such, then, is the history of the implicit rhetorical turn. (Note that, of the writers cited in this history, only Perelman, Burke, Booth, and White make systematic use of a rhetorical lexicon in their studies.) Nelson and Megill are, indeed, worthy successors to Kenneth Burke. They do for the implicit rhetorical turn what Burke has done for the hidden history of rhetoric.

THE LURE OF THE IMPLICIT RHETORICAL TURN

Once again, in my opinion, the lure of the implicit rhetorical turn will gradually overwhelm, if it has not done so already, the promise of the explicit rhetorical turn. The implicit rhetorical turn will have the same sort of psychological hold over our disciplinary imagination as the hidden history of rhetoric has had since the publication of Burke's A *Rhetoric of Motives*.

The reason for this is quite simple. The study of the explicit rhetorical turn is, in the long run, a tedious affair, which is only occasionally redeemed by critical excellence and achievement, while the pursuit of the implicit rhetorical turn is a boldly constitutive, well-nigh archeological, venture, which "lures" us to discover "traces" of rhetoric virtually everywhere. The explicit rhetorical turn suffers from sheer obviousness. Once it is recognized, as it ought to be, that the discourse of the human sciences contains an unavoidable rhetorical component, the task of analysis consists in making explicit the functioning of that component in the production and the reception of discourses. There are some brilliant instances of such critical analysis. In an excellent essay, Hexter unpacks the rhetoric of history in terms of the historian's habitual and distinctive use of quotations, footnotes, and statistics in writing history, and he shows how the rhetoric of history differs from the rhetoric of natural sciences.[40] The type of rhetorical analysis of historiography that Hexter offers is unlikely to un- settle the self-understanding of rhetoric. For Hexter has merely shown how the discourse of history cannot productively emulate the rhetoric of natural sciences; and, his explication of rhetorical elements in historiography is analogous to the explication of "manifest" rhetoric in any discursive prac- tice. The model for unpacking the argumentative strategies and the play of stylistic devices is much the same in history as in oratory.

In contrast, the implicit rhetorical turn is engaged in a far more gran- diose project. It is, in essence, a philosophical enterprise, or to be more precise, it is a critique of Western metaphysics that begins with Nietzsche and continues in the work of Heidegger and his deconstructive followers. It is preoccupied with the theme of the end of philosophy (modernism, or the end of modernism), and sees in rhetoric an alternative to the founda- tionalist epistemology. The implicit rhetorical turn is thus largely a prod- uct of an internal crisis in philosophy. Here rhetoric becomes entangled in the schemes of those who are attempting to articulate a counter-tradition in philosophy. And the story of rhetoric's initial suppression and the sub- sequent recuperation is read, in the Nelson and Megill version, in terms of an objectivist/subjectivist dichotomy that has fractured Western conscious- ness since the beginning of philosophical reflection. Nelson and Megill are quite correct in asserting that an objectivist epistemology is generally damaging to the fortunes of rhetoric, while a subjectivist/relativist episte- mology is more encouraging to its growth. But this observation is so broad as to be banal and not easily translatable into concepts for use. Moreover, such an enlarged epistemological perspective makes the idea of rhetoric so thoroughly elastic as to incorporate anyone averse to objectivism and foun- dationalism. In short, while the explicit rhetorical turn is local in its application, the implicit rhetorical turn is global in its aspirations.

Thus, it is hardly surprising that Nelson and Megill's prospectus for the "rhetoric of inquiry" should end, not with a whimper but with a bang:

Our world is a creature and a texture of rhetorics: of founding
stories and sales talks, anecdotes and statistics, images and rhythms;
of tales told in nursery, pledges of allegiance or revenge, symbols of

358

success and failure, archetypes of action and character. Ours is a
world of persuasive definitions, expressive explanations, and
institutional narratives. It is replete with figures of truth, models of
reality, tropes of argument, and metaphors of experience. In our
world, scholarship is rhetorical.[41]

This is, alas, the fate of rhetoric. Like Blanche DuBois in Tennessee
Williams's A *Streetcar Named Desire*, we, the rhetoricians, have always
relied on "the kindness of strangers," but too much kindness could kill us.
We are either dismissed out of hand, excommunicated, cast out from the
realm of light and truth, or we are given the whole world all to ourselves
and asked to preside over "the conversation of mankind."[42]

Such is Nelson and Megill's myth for the new field. But the myth calls
for some finer interpretation. How important is this story of repression and
the subsequent regeneration of rhetoric of inquiry in the development of
modern philosophy from Descartes to Derrida? Even Nelson and Megill
will not venture to place it on the center stage. There are, to be sure, some
negative comments about rhetoric in Descartes, Locke, and Kant. On the
whole, however, they and their philosophical followers simply ignored
rhetoric. If their work had the effect of repressing a rhetoric of inquiry,
which I admit that it did, it was a latent outcome rather than a manifest
intent. It would be preposterous to imagine that Kant set out to write the
three critiques in order to repress rhetoric or to obviate a rhetoric of inquiry. The motivation for his labor came from different sources. Similarly,
the dismantling of the modernist dogma in this century by Heidegger,
Dewey, Wittgenstein, and others was not motivated by a manifest desire to
make space for a rhetoric of inquiry. (I am not trying to suggest here that
the suffocation of the rhetoric of inquiry under the modernist dogma was
not genuine and severe simply because it was latent. Perhaps, it was more
insidious because of its latency.)

Neslon and Megill will probably disagree with me on this point. For
them the repression and the subsequent regeneration of the rhetoric of
inquiry in modern philosophy is a critical thread. For me, it is a sideshow.
The fact that it is a sideshow does not make me apologetic about the place
of rhetoric in the life of the mind. The fact that it is a sideshow is in
keeping with the nature and function of rhetoric.[43]

In the long and enduring quarrel between rhetoric and philosophy, the
latter has not always set out to undermine the former.[44] Rhetoric has
often been trampled on accidentally in philosophy's quest for certainty
or whatever else it is bent on pursuing at any given time. Historically,

philosophers have not evinced a profound concern with rhetoric. There is a sort of narcissistic streak in philosophy, an overdetermination of its own self-sufficiency and autonomy, which keeps it from seriously entertaining the competing claims of rhetoric.

There was only one philosopher, in my opinion, who set out earnestly to repress rhetoric; and when he couldn't, he sought to and pretty much succeeded in emasculating it. That was Plato. There was only one orator/rhetorician who seriously attempted to reconcile the competing claims of rhetoric and philosophy and pretty much succeeded in uniting the competing claims of eloquence and wisdom in his own person. That was Cicero. We might add other names to either column in this list, but, even by a liberal standard, the list would not be long.

This brings me to the main point. Academically rhetoric has never been able to determine its own fortune. It lies embedded in the cultural practices of the time. It is always already there as a supplement, as an insert. Extract it from that to which it is a supplement or from that within which it is embedded, and it evaporates. It is present, to borrow a phrase from Lacan, only in "the discourse of the other." Ironically, the art of eloquence has no voice of its own within the academy. Pure persuasion is possible, as Kenneth Burke tells us, only in the furthest regions of religion and poetry where one hesitates, as in *Finnegans Wake*, between sound and sense.

The fortunes of rhetoric, more than any other discipline, turn on the roll of cultural dice. Rhetoric has good days and bad days, mostly bad days. This is one of the good days. If there is a myth about rhetoric, it is that of an outsider whose day of reckoning is deferred, time and again.

This is my counter-myth for an old discipline which constantly seeks to escape itself. If you had to choose between the two myths, I suspect Nelson and Megill would carry the day, despite my carping . . . At least, that is what my myth requires me to believe. After all, this is one of the good days for rhetoric.

CONCLUSION

Finally, what is the significance of the rhetorical turn in the self-understanding of rhetoric? At the sociological level, the rhetorical turn implies a renewed disciplinary legitimacy for rhetoric as an intellectual enterprise. If rhetoric is an unavoidable component in discourses as diverse as theoretical physics, economics, literary criticism, and psychoanalysis, then, the story of rhetoric is a tale well worth telling. However, this would also suggest that the "legitimacy" of a formal discipline, such as rhetoric, is relative to its measurable "presence" in the substantive disciplines. This could be problematic, because, if rhetoric requires a constant "reconfir-mation" of its "presence" in the discourse of other disciplines, it would suggest that rhetoric is a supplement to those discourses rather than con-stitutive of them. To put it differently, one could argue that rhetoric is parasitic vis-a-vis the special discourses rather than productive of them in the way that a "rule" is productive of a series of rule-governed actions, or that the "deep structure" of a natural language is said to be productive of its "surface structure." I believe (and this is a provisional statement) that an adequate understanding of the rhetoric of the human sciences is possible only when we have an adequate grasp of the logic of supplementarity within which rhetoric is habitually caught.

At another level, the rhetorical turn sets up an expectation that there would be a renaissance in rhetoric in the near future—that rhetoric would regain its lost glory as "the queen of the human sciences" in our time, and that it would preside over other disciplines as the metascience of culture in the Isocratean sense. The anticipation of a rhetorical turn could, thus, revive and set in motion the dormant foundational aspirations character-istic of formal, hence empty, disciplines like rhetoric, dialectic, and her-meneutics. That is, one has to travel but a short psychological distance to make that fatal move from anticipating a rhetorical turn in contemporary thought to proclaiming rhetoric as the foundational discipline (obviously, in its capacity as the general theory of discourse) for the human sciences.

Before we become intoxicated with such visions of grandeur, we have to ascertain exactly what role, if any, rhetoric as an academic discipline has played in bringing about this rhetorical turn, other than recognizing and celebrating its alleged arrival. As I indicated earlier, Kuhn's *The Structure of Scientific Revolutions*, which is treated as the *locus classicus* of the rhetorical turn, is entirely innocent of rhetoric as a discipline. This inno-cence or ignorance of rhetoric is not uncommon among the writers and the texts cited earlier as participating in the implicit rhetorical turn.

Even among those who write self-consciously about rhetoric and its presence, and whose texts were cited earlier as constituting the explicit rhetorical turn, few are conscious of rhetoric as an academic discipline. As for the majority, if they acknowledge their debt to rhetoric, it is usually to some classical texts, especially to Aristotle's *Rhetoric*; among the moderns, it is invariably Kenneth Burke and occasionally Perelman, and rarely I. A. Richards. For these writers, contemporary rhetoric simply means the idiosyncratic works of Kenneth Burke. This is best exemplified in the work of sociologist Hugh Dalziel Duncan, who has systematically, albeit mechanically, sought to reinterpret social theory from a decidedly rhetorical perspective, but the rhetorical perspective here simply means a Burkian perspective.[45] For other American writers like Geertz, Goffman, and Hayden White, who are clearly conscious of rhetoric, Burke provides the only link between classical rhetoric and its contemporary possibilities. The continental writers like Lacan, Derrida, Ricoeur, Gennette, and Gadamer, whose texts bristle with rhetorical concepts and terms, are either entirely unaware of Burke's work or only marginally aware of it.

But on the whole, it is clear that rhetoricians have played but a limited role in bringing about this rhetorical turn. What concerns me here is not the sociological embarrassment resulting from the fact that we who celebrate this "rhetorical turn" in contemporary thought have contributed so little to its making. What does concern me is the fact that people like Kuhn and Toulmin were driven to make certain observations, which we characterize as marking a rhetorical turn in their respective thinking, by the internal logic (both synchronic and diachronic) of their own special discourses. They became, as it were, infected with a "rhetorical consciousness" by immersing themselves in their own special discourses and by tracing the discursive implications of their own distinctive theory and practice. It was not as if they were struggling for a vocabulary, absent in the ordinary language, that could articulate their "break" from the traditional discourse. The "break," or the "rupture," in the traditional discursive practices with which their names are associated neither occurred nor came to be articulated as a result of their sudden acquaintance with the rhetorical lexicon. Kuhn was not awakened from his dogmatic slumber after reading Aristotle or Burke, as Kant allegedly was after reading Hume.

To be sure, one could argue that it would have been easier for Kuhn to articulate his rhetorical insights had he been acquainted with the rhetorical tradition. This could serve as an argument for a greater dissemination of rhetorical lore in our culture, especially in the academy. But one could just as easily argue that in some situations a familiarity with the rhetorical lexicon could be a hindrance. Perhaps people like Kuhn do not really need a stylized rhetorical lexicon to recognize rhetoric; and their rhetorical insights are possibly richer, less labored, and more firmly grounded precisely because they are the insights of someone driven by the compulsions of a special discourse in search of a special knowledge, the knowledge of the world so to speak. The ordinary language which, as Cicero reminds us, is the language of rhetoric, is sufficiently versatile to meet the needs of a Kuhn or a Toulmin. If we follow this logic, then, it would appear that an institutionalized presence of rhetoric is neither necessary nor sufficient for the rhetorical turn.

Furthermore, it may be interesting to note that these fabled rhetorical turns occur in times of crisis. Clearly, Kuhn's theory about paradigm shifts, Habermas's thesis regarding the legitimation crisis in the modern welfare state, and Derrida's method of reading as a textual "deconstruction" refer to and have their origin in specific crisis situations, be they in scientific theory, social theory or literary theory. Perhaps it is during the discursive crises that a scientific language community becomes "rhetorically conscious." Further, we could argue that every special discourse and every scientific language community periodically goes through "rhetorical stages." And sometimes the general culture itself, passing through a general crisis, becomes rhetorically self-conscious. But with the passing of that crisis, the rhetorical consciousness once again erodes. That is, the emergence of a rhetorical consciousness is directly related to a crisis within a special discourse. That relation can be formulated as follows: A crisis, discursive or otherwise, makes rhetoric visible; that is, a crisis brings to the fore the incipient rhetorical consciousness. The sheer possibility of a rhetorical consciousness, the possibility that rhetoric is a permanent though unrealized opening for man, does not by itself induce a crisis, but it is something always waiting to be exploited when the crisis comes. In short, rhetoric is the medium and not the ground of discursive and cultural crises.

N O T E S

1. Chaim Perelman and L. Olbrechts-Tyteca, *The New Rhetoric: A Treatise on Argumentation*, trans. John Wilkinson and Purcell Weaver (Notre Dame, Ind.: University of Notre Dame Press, 1969); Paolo Valesio, *Novantiqua: Rhetoric as Contemporary Theory* (Bloomington, Ind.: Indiana University Press, 1980). For a tendency to subordinate rhetoric to dialectic, see Maurice Natanson, "The Limits of Rhetoric," *Quarterly Journal of Speech* 41 (1955): 133–39; Richard Weaver, "The *Phaedrus* and the Nature of Rhetoric," in his *The Ethics of Rhetoric* (Chicago: Henry Regnery Co., 1953), 3–26.

2. Ernesto Grassi, *Rhetoric as Philosophy: The Humanistic Tradition* (University Park, Pa.: The Pennsylvania University Press, 1980).

3. Roland Barthes, "The Old Rhetoric: An Aide-Memoire," in his *The Semiotic Challenge*, trans. Richard Howard (New York: Hill and Wang, 1988), 46.

4. Aristotle, *The Art of Rhetoric*, ed. and trans. Lane Cooper (New York: Appleton-Century-Croft, 1932), 9.

5. Brian Vickers, "Territorial Disputes: Philosophy versus Rhetoric," in *Rhetoric Revalued*, ed. Brian Vickers (Binghamton, N.Y.: Medieval and Renaissance Texts and Studies, 1982), 248.

6. Cicero, "Fourth Philippic," in *The World's Great Speeches*, 3d ed., ed. Lewis Copeland and Lawrence W. Lamm (New York: Dover Publications, 1973), 48.

7. This phrase—*alte und neue Konigin der Wissenschaften*—comes from Walter Jens, *Von Deutscher Rede* (Munich: Piper, 1969), and is cited by Chaim Perelman in *The Realm of Rhetoric*, trans. William Kluback (Notre Dame, Ind.: University of Notre Dame Press, 1982), 162.

8. Alfred Schutz, *The Phenomenology of the Social World*, trans. George Walsh and Frederick Lehnert (Evanston, Ill.: Northwestern University Press, 1967). Also see his *Collected Papers*, vol. 1, subtitled *The Problems of Social Reality*, ed. Maurice Natanson (The Hague: Martinus Nijhoff, 1971).

9. For a discussion of "essentially contested concepts," see W. B. Gallie, *Philosophy and the Historical Understanding* (New York: Schocken, 1964), 157–91.

10. For an excellent critical survey of the literature on this question in the speech communication journals, see Michael Leff, "In Search of Ariadne's Thread: A Review of the Recent Literature on Rhetorical Theory," *Central State Speech Journal* 29 (1978), 65–91.

11. Jacques Derrida, *Of Grammatology*, trans. Gayatri Chakravorty Spivak (Baltimore: Johns Hopkins University Press, 1976). Also see "Plato's Pharmacy," in his *Dissemination*, trans. Barbara Johnson (Chicago: University of Chicago Press, 1981), 61–171.

12. Aristotle, *The "Art" of Rhetoric*, trans. John Henry Freese (Cambridge, Mass.: Harvard University Press [Loeb ed.], 1926), 19 (1356a).

13. Llyod Bitzer, "Political Rhetoric," in *Handbook of Political Communication*, ed. Dan Nimmo and Keith Sanders (Beverly Hills: Sage Publications, 1981), 225–48.

14. Michael Leff, "The Habitation of Rhetoric," in *Argument and Critical Practices: Proceedings of the Fifth SCA/AFA Conference on Argumentation*, ed. Joseph Wenzel et al. (Annandale, Va: SCA Publications, 1987), 5.

15. Bitzer, "Political Rhetoric," 231.

16. Paul Ricoeur, *The Rule of Metaphor: Multidisciplinary Studies in the Creation of Meaning in Language*, trans. Robert Czerny with Kathleen McLaughlin and John Costello (Toronto: University of Toronto Press, 1976), 30.

17. Kenneth Burke, *A Rhetoric of Motives* (Berkeley: University of California Press, 1969, 1950), 54–55.

18. Barthes, "The Old Rhetoric," 73.

19. Ibid., 75.

20. Cicero, *De Oratore*, 2 vols., trans. E.W. Sutton (Cambridge, Mass.: Harvard University Press [Loeb ed.], 1942); Saint Augustine, *On Christian Doctrine*, trans. D. W. Robertson, Jr. (New York: Bobbs-Merrill, 1958). In Cicero's *De Oratore*, there are a number of references to rhetoric (the art or theory of oratory) as a supplement to inborn talent and correct practice based on imitation of suitable models. Cicero, while exalting the powers of the orator in a variety of ways, repeatedly observes that the art of oratory cannot produce the orator by itself without assistance from nature, which supplies talent, and practice, which deepens and perfects talent. The art itself, according to Cicero, plays but a minor role, and what is there to understand of the art can be obtained easily and quickly. Augustine is more explicit about the status of rhetoric as a supplement. In the fourth book of *De Doctrina Christiana*, rhetoric is clearly drawn into the orbit of hermeneutics as a supplement to elucidate what interpretation has uncovered of the sacred texts.

21. Cited in George A. Kennedy, *Classical Rhetoric and Its Christian and Secular Tradition from Ancient to Modern Times* (Chapel Hill: University of North Carolina Press, 1980), 240.

22. Cited by Lane Cooper, trans. and ed., in *The Rhetoric of Aristotle* (New York: Appleton-Century-Croft, 1932), xii.

23. For a general overview on the sophists in the light of the current revival of scholarly interest in them, see W. K. C. Guthrie, *The Sophists* (New York: Cambridge University Press, 1971), and G. B. Kerferd, *The Sophistic Movement* (New York: Cambridge University Press, 1981).

24. For an early attempt to articulate the ontological basis of rhetoric, see Karlyn K. Campbell "The Ontological Foundation of Rhetorical Theory," *Philosophy and Rhetoric* 3 (1970), 97–108.

25. Hannah Arendt, *The Human Condition* (New York: Anchor, 1958), 10.

26. Paul de Man, *Allegories of Reading* (New Haven, Conn.: Yale University Press, 1979), 103–31; Tzvetan Todorov, *Theories of the Symbol*, trans. Catherine Porter (Ithaca, N.Y.: Cornell University Press, 1982), 60–110.

27. For the most influential account of the "reality construction" thesis, see Peter L. Berger and Thomas Luckmann, *The Social Construction of Reality: A Treatise in the Sociology of Knowledge* (New York: Anchor Books, 1967, 1966).

28. For an account of rhetoric as a "material force," see Michael Calvin McGee, "A Materialist's Conception of Rhetoric," in *Explorations in Rhetoric: Studies in honor of Douglas Ehninger*, ed. R. E. McKerrow (Glenville, Ill.: Scott, Foresman, 1982), 23–49.

29. Burke, A *Rhetoric of Motives*, xiii.

30. Ibid.

31. Ibid., xiv.

32. Kenneth Burke, A *Grammar of Motives and* A *Rhetoric of Motives* (New York: Meridian Books, 1962), 523.

33. Kennedy, *Classical Rhetoric*, 86–107.

34. Wayne C. Booth, *The Rhetoric of Fiction* (Chicago: University of Chicago Press, 1961, 1983); Paul de Man, *The Rhetoric of Romanticism* (New York: Columbia University Press, 1984).

35. Thomas S. Kuhn, *The Structure of Scientific Revolutions* (Chicago: University of Chicago Press, 1962, 1970).

36. John S. Nelson and Allan Megill, "Rhetoric of Inquiry: Projects and Prospects," *Quarterly Journal of Speech* 72 (1986), 20–37. McCloskey appears to share the views of Nelson and Megill on the prospects of a rhetoric of inquiry. This same essay, with minor modifications, appears as the introductory essay in the volume of papers from the Iowa conference held on 28–31 March 1984. See John S. Nelson, Allan Megill, and Donald N. McCloskey, eds., *The Rhetoric of the Human Sciences: Language and Argument in Scholarship and Public Affairs* (Madison: The University of Wisconsin Press, 1987), 3–18.

37. Nelson and Megill, "Rhetoric of Inquiry," 20.

38. Ibid., 22–23.

39. Ibid., 24.

40. J. H. Hexter, "The Rhetoric of History," *History and Theory* 6 (1967), 1–14. For an expanded version of the same essay, see the chapter by the same title in his *Doing History* (Bloomington, Ind.: Indiana University Press, 1971), 15–76.

41. Nelson and Megill, "Rhetoric of Inquiry," 36.

42. This popular phrase among the proponents of the rhetorical turn was originally coined by Michael Oakeshott in "Poetry as a Voice in the Conversation of Mankind," in his *Experience and Its Modes* (1933), and reprinted in his *Rationalism in Politics* (New York: Methuen, 1962), 197–247.

43. On the "marginality" of rhetoric in the disciplinary contest for "status," see Robert Hariman, "Status, Marginality, and Rhetorical Theory," *Quarterly Journal of Speech* 72 (1986), 38–52.

44. The literature on the quarrel between philosophy and rhetoric is quite extensive. For both an historically and conceptually informed general view of the quarrel, see, Brian Vickers, *In Defense of Rhetoric* (Oxford: Clarendon Press, 1988), especially chs. 2 & 3, 83–213.

45. Hugh Dalziel Duncan, *Communication and Social Order* (New York: Oxford University Press, 1968, 1962).

366

CONTRIBUTORS

Herbert W. Simons, Department of Rhetoric and Communication, Temple University

John Lyne, Department of Communication, University of Iowa

John Angus Campbell, Department of Speech Communication, University of Washington

Alan G. Gross, Department of English, Purdue University (Calumet)

Tullio Maranhão, Department of Anthropology, Rice University

Robert E. Sanders, Department of Communication, State University of New York, Albany

Carolyn R. Miller, Department of English, North Carolina State University

Eugene Garver, Chair of Critical Thinking, St. Johns University (Minnesota)

Susan Wells, Department of English, Temple University

Manfred Stanley, Maxwell School of Citizenship and Public Affairs, Syracuse University

John S. Nelson, Department of Political Science, University of Iowa

Kenneth Gergen, Department of Psychology, Swarthmore College

Joseph Margolis, Department of Philosophy, Temple University

Richard Harvey Brown, Department of Sociology, University of Maryland

Dilip Parameshwar Gaonkar, Department of Speech Communication, University of Illinois

367

AUTHOR INDEX

Fisher, S., 118, 134
Fisher, W., 26
Fiske, D., 282
Fitzpatrick, J. W., 94, 95, 96
Flower, L. S., 179
Forster, E. M., 215
Foss, K. A., 28
Foss, L., 336
Foss, S. K., 28
Foucault, M., 7, 24, 294
Frankfurt Institute, 225–26
Franklin, A., 111
Freud, S., 116–41

G

Gadamer, H. G., 21, 91, 92, 99,
   103, 140, 263, 321
Gallie, W. B., 364
Garfinkel, H., 146, 154, 294, 325,
   330
Garver, E., 28, 161, 187
Gautry, P. J., 87
Gavronsky, S., 331
Gallner, E., 321, 323, 328
Genette, G., 216, 217
Gergen, K., 19, 24, 27, 295, 302,
   303
Gergen, M., 19, 302
Geertz, C., 3, 9, 27, 29, 30
Gieryn, T. S., 3, 47
Gill, M., 132
Glodek, G. S., 102
Glymour, C., 118
Gödel, K., 327
Goedecke, R., 202
Goffman, E., 154
Goitein, B., 172
Goodman, N., 295, 334, 335
Goodnight, G. T., 177

Gould, S. J., 37
Gouldner, A., 239
Grassi, E., 25, 341
Green, B. S., 335
Greenberg, R. P., 118, 134
Greenfield, D. W., 102
Greenstone, J. D., 240
Greer, S., 248
Gregg, R., 26
Grice, H. D., 156, 157
Grünbaum, A., 118, 120–21
Gunnell, J. G., 286
Gusfield, J., 3, 10, 106
Guthrie, W. K. C., 365

H

Habermas, J., 5, 53, 90, 107, 108,
   109, 226, 228, 239, 241, 263
Halbwacks, M., 246
Halloran, M. S., 24
Hanson, N. R., 284, 295, 333
Harding, S., 304
Hariman, R., 366
Harpham, E., 288
Harré, R., 44
Hartsborne, C., 40
Hayes, J. R., 179
Heilbroner, R. L., 287
Held, D., 230
Hellriegel, D., 168
Helm, C. J., 288
Herbert, S., 87, 89
Heritage, J., 153
Hexter, J. H., 358
Higgins, J. C., 169, 173, 175
Hikins, J., 286
Hill, B. J., 287
Hirsch, E. D., 321
Hitt, M. A., 168

SUBJECT INDEX

A

Academic: professions, rhetoric of, 6;
world, 35; discourse, 47;
relationship among fields, 52;
theory, 171
Action: 35, 176, 178, 198–99, 261;
possibility of, 116; insufficiency
of, 137–38; sublimation of,
138; practical, 196
Adapted structure, 80–81
Adjudication on scientific grounds,
43
Advocacy: as distinct from inquiry,
4; in criticism, 124;
institutionalized methods of,
148
Aesthetic: goodness-of-fit, 2;
preoccupations, 15; insight, 60;
wisdom of the age, 62, 68, 78;
criteria, 102–3, 173
Aesthetics, as a discipline, 191
Agency: of rhetorician, 15; talk, 39;
external, 75
Altruism, as a problem for
sociobiology, 40
Analogy: 45, 59; in Darwin, 65, 70,
74, 78, 79, 80; in Freud, 129;
experiential, 242; immigration,
252–53; to politics, 26
Anarchy, 266, 280

Anthropology, symbolic, 7, 13
Anthropomorphic: overlay, 40;
baggage, 45
Arendt, Hannah, 7, 260, 270–80
Argument: 4, 18, 67, 105, 141, 145,
149, 152, 223, 225, 238, 259,
264; forms of, 6, 148, 303;
formulation of new, 13, 62;
lines of, 17, 70, 148;
enthymematic, 17; strategies,
59; sequential, 59; from
analogy, 65; conventional,
scientific, and theological, 66,
79; a fortiori, 66, 72, 80;
evolutionary, 68–69; resources
of, 71; double-hierarchy, 73;
aesthetic, 76, 79; in science,
100, 148; as strategic
communication, 149; over
incommensurable values,
187–95; Machievelli's theory of,
188–90, 194–95; in politics,
197; dual regime, 239
Aristotle, 107, 110, 117–18, 141,
148–49, 162–63
Audience: adaptation, 5, 19, 66–67,
81, 84; constitution, 19; user-,
45; role of, 51; variety of, 51; of
academics, 51, 100; of
sociobiology, 51; and expertise,

376

SUBJECT INDEX